VOLUME 2

Foundations of
FUTURES
STUDIES

Human Science for a New Era

VOLUME 2
Values, Objectivity, and the Good Society

Foundations of
FUTURES
STUDIES

Human Science for a New Era

WENDELL BELL

TRANSACTION PUBLISHERS
New Brunswick (U.S.A.) and London (U.K.)

Copyright © 1997 by Transaction Publishers, New Brunswick, New Jersey 08903. This is the second part of *Foundations of Futures Studies* ["History, Purposes, and Knowledge"], published by Transaction Publishers © 1997.

This book is printed on acid-free paper that meets the American National Standard for Permanence of Paper for Printed Library Materials.

Library of Congress Catalog Number: 96-22496
ISBN: 1-56000-281-6
Printed in the United States of America

Library of Congress Cataloging-in-Publication Data

Bell, Wendell.
    Foundations of futures studies : human science for a new era / Wendell Bell.
        p. cm.
    Includes bibliographical references and index.
    ISBN 1-56000-281-6 (v. 2 : acid-free paper)
    1. Forecasting. I. Title.
CB158.B45   1996
303.49'09'04—dc20   96-22496
                                                               CIP

For my wife Lora-Lee,
whose art enriches me,
whose friendship I cherish, and
whose love I will return, always.

Contents

List of Figures

List of Tables

Acknowledgements

I wish to thank the following publishers for permission to reprint in this Volume (usually in revised form) some short pieces that I had published earlier:

The World Future Society for:

"Professional ethics for futurists: Preliminaries and proposals," *Futures Research Quarterly* 9, No. 1 (Spring 1993): 5–18.

"Why should we care about future generations?" Pp. 25–41 in Howard F. Didsbury, Jr. (ed.), *The Years Ahead: Perils, Progress, and Promises.* Bethesda, MD: World Future Society, 1993.

"Using religion to judge preferable futures: An assessment," *Futures Research Quarterly* 10, No. 3 (Fall 1994): 5–17.

Butterworth-Heinemann journals, Elsevier Science Ltd. for:

"Values and the future in Marx and Marxism." *Futures* 23, No. 2 (March 1991): 146–62.

Blackwell Publishers for:

"Bringing the good back in: Values, objectivity, and the future," *International Social Science Journal*, XLV, No. 137 (August 1993): 333–47.

The Institute for the Integrated Study of Future Generations for:

"The liberation of women and the well-being of future generations." Pp. 203–18 in Tae-Chang Kim and James A. Dator (eds.), *Creating a New History for Future Generations.* Future Generations Studies Series II. Kyoto, Japan: Institute for the Integrated Study of Future Generations, 1994.

* * *

Also, I have used some figures and quotes from other authors and I wish to thank the publishers for their kind permission to reprint them here (figure numbers are from my chapters):

Population Reference Bureau, Inc. for:

Figure 5.1 and Figure 5.2 from p. 32 and p. 33 in Joseph A. McFalls, Jr., "Population: A lively introduction." *Population Bulletin* 46, No. 2 (October 1991): 2–41 (Washington, DC: Population Reference Bureau).

Butterworth-Heinemann journals, Elsevier Science Ltd. for:

Allen Tough, "Making a pledge to future generations," *Futures* 25, No. 1 (January/February 1993), p. 91 (with additional thanks to Allen Tough).

Also, the reader can find additional acknowledgements in volume 1.

Introduction

We saw in chapter 2 of volume 1 that a concern with ethics, morality, and human values follows directly from the futurist purposes of discovering or inventing, examining and evaluating, and proposing *preferable* futures. As Mika Mannermaa (1986: 659) says, "Futures research is basically a normative activity, and the role of values in futures research is more emphasized than in social sciences generally." Thus, I devote volume 2 of this work to a discussion of the ethical foundations of futures studies.

Futurists are concerned about the nature of the good society and the standards of evaluation by which it is defined and judged. A major goal of futurists is to contribute to human betterment. But what is human betterment? If we give an answer, how do we know that it is the right answer? How can we convince other people that it is the right answer? How can we resolve conflicts of opinion about what human betterment is? How can we make value judgments objectively?

In chapter 6 we learned that futurist methods often include an attempt to establish and assess the preferable. The study of the preferable is partly based on empirical studies of leaders', experts', and ordinary people's hopes and fears, their goals and value judgments, and their preferences. It is partly based on the exploration of people's images of the good society. And it is partly based on other things, including the observation of the choices, decisions, and actions that people take and the norms of entire societies.

Knowing what the good society is, however, requires more. What is needed—and what futurists have not yet done much to create—are some procedures and standards of moral judgments by which norms and values themselves can be evaluated. Futurists, activists, and decision makers want and need to know not only what people *think* is right. They also want and need to know what *is* right. They want and need to be able to demonstrate objectively that it is reasonable to believe that certain propositions about what is morally right are justified.

1

Not only futurists, of course, but all applied or policy scientists face the question of the validity of value judgments. For they too are concerned with social action and must, therefore, deal with the human goals and values that are served or affected by action. Decisions, policy-making, program evaluation, and choosing objectives all involve making value judgments. For that matter, a great deal of scientific research is directed at creating knowledge not as an end in itself but as a means for solving practical problems or achieving other valued ends, such as finding a cure for a disease or finding more productive ways of growing food crops.

Often, futurists and other researchers have simply taken for granted that it is good to direct research at such things as reducing pollution, the wasteful use of scarce resources, unemployment, crime, racial discrimination, poverty, mental illness, and inequality of educational opportunity. They have simply assumed that research aimed at promoting peace, global communication, the survival of threatened species, political democracy, a sense of personal worth, social justice, and sustainability is morally justified.

Probably it is true that these *are* good things. Most people seem to think so. But how do we really know? What of other research aims, such as creating an atomic bomb, a poisonous gas, nuclear energy plants, storage facilities for nuclear wastes, ways of making people hate each other, or new techniques of abortion? Can the reasons put forward to justify such ends withstand critical moral examination?

Even though such phenomena themselves have been studied endlessly, the preferences or values underlying some of these judgments remain largely unexamined and the grounds for belief in them have been insufficiently justified by any explicit reasoning. Even the otherwise highly detailed and objective work of researchers such as the authors of *Beyond the Limits* relies on underlying values that, although stated, remain unjustified—little more than the authors' personal opinions.

Thus, the task that I undertake in volume 2 of this work is an attempt to provide ethical foundations for futures studies. I discuss human values, their role in futures studies and in defining the good society, and how our belief in them can be objectively justified.

Contemporary futurists, with a few notable exceptions such as Rushworth M. Kidder (1994, 1995), have contributed relatively little to the explicit examination of human values. But there exists a rich tradition exploring the nature of the good society in the works of the precursors to contemporary futurists, the utopian writers. Thus, in chapter 1, I begin with an analysis of a few major utopian works, starting with those of Thomas More and concluding with those of Karl Marx, that have helped shape both past and present images of the good society. I ask, what values did these utopian writers choose to serve in their works and what justifications of them did they give?

In chapter 2, I show that, although it has dominated both philosophical and scientific thinking for the last several generations, the dogma that value judgments cannot be objectively assessed is questionable. As examples of available methodologies, I give three models for the objective assessment of value judgments. One of them, Keekok Lee's (1985) epistemic implication, is an especially promising tool for futurists in their attempts to judge preferable futures and deserves to become a widely used method not only in futures studies but in all fields in which social policies are formulated, recommended, or criticized.

In chapter 3, I evaluate several strategies for judging the preferable—including religion, law, and the collective judgments of group members themselves—that are commonly used by futurists and others. I show how each is related to the three models of moral analysis described in chapter 2 and how each may contribute to an objective assessment of values. Yet each ultimately fails—with the possible exception of some aspects of the law—in comparison with the power of epistemic implication. I conclude chapter 3 with a provisional discussion of the norms of professional conduct that ought to guide the behavior of futurists themselves.

In chapter 4, I show that another aspect of cultural relativism that has dominated scholarly thinking for several generations, the belief in great cultural diversity and incomparable cultural differences, rests on shaky empirical ground. The fact is that many universal or near-universal cultural values and practices do exist. Contrary to the dominant view in most academic and intellectual circles as I write, the principles of morality—including a set of core values—are largely the same in all societies and cultures. This is so because the origins of human values are to be found in the similar nature of all humans as biopsychological beings, in the preconditions of social life that are the same everywhere, and in universal features of this earthly physical world.

In chapter 5, I discuss the most important of all human values, human life itself. I show how human life expectancies have changed over time and how unequally distributed they are, both among and within societies.

I show how the quantity and quality of individual human lives may change in the future and how they relate to the effort to control future population growth, economic development, social justice, the debate about abortion, and the value of nonhuman forms of life.

Finally, in chapter 6, I consider the possibility of a coming global society of the future and how some human values ought to be changed in order for human society to thrive under the new conditions it may bring. I discuss changes in the value of human life, reproductive values, the value of sufficiency, the value of women's lives, the value of peace, the value of a world moral community, and the value of caring about future generations. A major conclusion of chapter 6 is that people ought to be concerned about the freedom and welfare of all presently living human beings on Earth and of future generations of people as yet unborn.

I call the task of volume 2 "ethical" because it deals with human values, goals, and preferences. Values include "orientations toward what is considered desirable or preferable by social actors" (Zavalloni 1980: 74). They are standards of desirability and include judgments such as good or bad, beautiful or ugly, pleasant or unpleasant, right or wrong. They are used "as *criteria* for preference or choice or as *justifications* for proposed or actual behavior" (Williams 1970:27; 442). Values are beliefs both about how we ought or ought not to behave and "about some end-state of existence worth or not worth attaining" (Rokeach 1968: 124).

Such values may be socially organized and invested with strong feelings of identification and emotional commitment. They may be basic to collective understandings of the good and involve social sanctions, that is, rewards and punishments, administered by agents of the community, and they may appear as moral statements regarding the proper behavior of individuals. As such, they are more than mere individual preferences. Rather, they include underlying ethical principles, normative properties, moral responsibilities toward other people, and the practices of right conduct that are often perceived as beneficial, if not necessary, for the freedom and well-being of individuals, groups, and entire societies.

I call the task of volume 2 "foundations" because critical appraisals of value judgments and moral principles are fundamental to futures studies. They are the base or bedrock on which assertions about preferable futures and the good society rest. As action scientists, futurists cannot rightly avoid the responsibility of critically evaluating the desirability of the ends, means, and future consequences of human action and inaction just as they cannot rightly avoid seeking relevant knowledge of the past, present possibilities, cause and effect, and surrogate knowledge of future consequences.

In the last four chapters of volume 1, we dealt with the foundations of *knowledge* in futures studies. We considered the assumptions, postulates, and premises underlying the theory of knowledge known as critical realism. Such knowledge is relevant to designing the future and making action more effective and competent.

Here, in volume 2, we deal with the *ethical* foundations of futures studies, that is, the grounds underlying the core values that define desirable futures and make the purposes of human action morally responsible and right. Knowledge about past and present facts and posits about future possibilities and probabilities alone cannot direct decision, choice, and action. Ethical judgments are also essential, and they, too, like knowledge claims, may be valid or invalid, right or wrong. Hence futurists examine values, objectively assess them, and explore the meaning of the good society.

By "ethical foundations," however, I do not mean some absolute set of everlasting standards that permit no argument or disagreement. Rather, I propose some methods for deciding what things, events, arrangements, actions, and consequences are better than others. The ones I propose involve giving reasons to support—or negate—contentions of desirability, reasons that competent people can evaluate as being warranted within a critical realist theory of knowledge. Thus, the methods of moral analysis discussed here are not to be learned and applied uncritically. They are intended to encourage and to structure rational thinking about the "good society" and about the validity of reasons that can be offered to defend or question judgments of the "good."

1

Values in Utopian Thought

Let's begin the discussion of the ethical foundations of futures studies by examining the values that a few key utopian writers throughout history used to define the good society and how they tried to justify their belief in them. Of course, given the immense literature on utopian and social thought, this account is merely an illustrative sample of utopian writers. A comprehensive account has been written by Frank E. Manuel and Fritzie P. Manuel (1979) and I gratefully acknowledge that I rely on it heavily.

Thomas More and Utopia

The Utopian Scenario

Thomas More first published his *Utopia* in 1516, coining his title from two Greek words to mean "no place." Raphael Hythloday, More's fictional protagonist, travels to "no place" after sailing with Amerigo Vespucci on three of his four alleged voyages of exploration. At the farthest place away from Europe, during the third voyage, Hythloday leaves Vespucci and travels on to more distant lands, finally arriving in the kingdom of Utopia. More tells his readers that he meets Hythloday in Antwerp and learns of Utopia from him in a conversation that takes place in a garden of a friend's house. Book I gives Hythloday's opinions on the "sorry state of the realm of England" at the time and Book II gives his description of life in Utopia as he experienced it during his stay there.

Before the end of the sixteenth century, More's book had been imitated so much that a new genre of literature was born. Typically, such utopian writing included a hero setting off on travels to geographical places far from Europe. Often a shipwreck resulted in the traveler's chance arrival in an ideal society, where he lived for some length of time. Eventually, the traveler returned to Europe where he reported his adventures and the wonders of the ideal society he had come to know. By contrasting the customs of the ideal society with those of existing society, the traveler produced a critical analysis of the real social world.

At first, "utopia" referred to works imitating More. Today, of course, two major meanings have come down to us. One is of a visionary, impractical scheme for social improvement and another is the depiction of some nonexistent society representing ideal perfection. It is the second meaning that concerns us here, a place—and, as we shall see later, a time—if not of ideal perfection, at least of substantial improvement in social life compared with the known, everyday world of the author.

Thus, when I refer to "utopian" or "utopia," (or the opposite, "dystopia") I mean a vision of some other place or time that is: (1) judged as more (or less) desirable than existing society; (2) critical of existing society; (3) not currently actually existent; and (4) usually, implicitly or explicitly, a call for some human action to bring a society better than the present one into existence, to work to create the utopia (or to prevent the dystopia) depicted.

This definition is similar to one proposed by Zygmunt Bauman (1976: 17), but Bauman neglects to include a place as well as a time, and he adds to his definition some "measure of hazard." This latter element seems unnecessary as part of the definition, although it is true that utopian writers sometimes have been put in jeopardy by the reactions of others to some perceived threat to the powers that be in their utopian writings.

Bauman fails to include dystopias in his definition. This must be corrected, because in the general "utopian" literature, we need to include those other fictional societies that are less, as well as more, desirable. For they, too, are critical of existing society, not currently actually existent, and usually call for some human action to bring a better society into the world. They do so, however, by depicting some terrible "Other" that humans must avoid. Often, this is some projection of trends of existing society that require some human intervention if the trends are to be prevented from continuing, the familiar doomsaying strategy. Thus, in the general utopian literature there are utopias (strictly speaking, "eutopias") that depict desirable societies and there are dystopias that depict undesirable societies.

For this discussion, I'll leave aside the question of a utopia's impracticality. It is, ultimately, a matter of empirical fact, although the question may remain in doubt until after some sort of social experimentation. Even then, it may remain in doubt because few experiments may be deemed fair tests by proponents of some utopian vision. Some envisioned social improvements may be realizable and practical and some may not be, and which is which is the subject of—sometimes hot—debate. Arguments about the feasibility of any given utopia are not my purpose here. Rather, I wish to examine the values underlying the various good societies portrayed and how belief in those values is justified as being reasonable.

More as Proto-Social Scientist

Sociologists credit the nineteenth-century French writer, Auguste Comte, with being "a," if not "the," father of sociology, because of his monumental work systematizing the social science of his day in his positivist philosophy. Additionally, some writers claim, more controversially, that the origins of Comte's sociology are largely to be understood as a conservative reaction to the turmoil and social chaos of the French Revolution (Nisbet 1966). Hence, the focus of sociology is on the social order, one of Comte's major concepts (although this view slights another of Comte's major concepts, progress).

Yet, more than three hundred years before Comte's sociology, a prototypical model of contemporary social analysis can be found in More's *Utopia*. For example, in *Utopia* More describes and analyzes social structures both of then existing European societies, primarily England, and of his fictional Utopian society. *Utopia* contains a basic framework of social categories for the study of social life. It became the model for descriptions of fictional societies, but its framework could also be used to describe real places. Indeed, it became a familiar checklist of topics for later descriptions of existing societies by real travelers. Hythloday's report of Utopia, for example, can be thought of as an imaginary account of anthropological or sociological field work based on participant observation. Moreover, because the results of Hythloday's fictional field observations are placed in a comparative framework with real existing societies, *Utopia* can be thought of as a model for comparative social research as well.

Hythloday systematically describes the Utopian economy, the production, exchange, and distributional systems; the occupational structure

and the system of social stratification; the family and household structure, the organization of sexual relations, the system of household authority, age and sex roles, and the socialization of the young; the form of
government and some of the laws; religious beliefs and practices; patterns of recreation; forms of deviant behavior and social control; and the
conditions and routines of warfare. Thus, Utopia is described in terms
that are recognizable as standard categories of social analysis today.

Although More makes no claim to be doing science, he clearly "offers
an example of a social organization that is conceivable under empirical
conditions" (Habermas 1973: 56). Moreover, he uses a major technique
of futurist methdodology, the scenario. He claims credibility by keeping
his descriptions within the realm of the possible as defined by commonly
understood previous experience and, thus, in a way he "tested" his hypotheses against the everyday observations of his readers.

Yet More did not limit himself to previous experience. Like futurists
today, he went beyond it by conceiving the possible and not yet existent
social forms consistent with his understanding of the *potentialities* contained in then-current knowledge. He was doing protosocial science, to
be sure, but he was doing more than most contemporary social scientists
do, both in creating a possible alternative society and in clearly incorporating value judgments into his analysis.

More as Judge

Facts and values. One difference between *Utopia* and much modern
social science, of course, is that More is writing about an imaginary
society while modern social scientists write about real societies. Another
difference is that More, unlike most modern social scientists, does not
hesitate to judge the "facts" of Utopian society as good or bad. Nor does
he hesitate to judge as good or bad the social facts of England of his day.
Although he in no way confuses facts and values in his analysis of Utopia, he includes both.

For More, making moral judgments is the whole point of his effort.
Evaluation is an essential part of the entire work. He has not relegated
values to a secondary role in his work, nor has he banned them from
consideration. Rather, More uses value standards to reveal Utopian society as an improvement over the actual societies of his day. He is severely
critical of the then-present society and aims to suggest beneficial social

changes, even radical reform. More (n.d.: 232) concludes by saying that "there are many things in the Commonwealth of Utopia that I rather wish, than hope, to see followed in our governments."

More's justification of values. More uses the values of Christian humanism to justify his value judgments. In Utopia, God is the ultimate source of evaluation. True, He is aided both by nature and reason, but they are largely thin veils covering the face of God. Although virtue, for More, is "living according to Nature," people are made by God for that end. Moreover, one lives according to nature by following the direction of reason which is itself also linked to God.

More confronted the realities of life as he knew them, both the low life that he had observed as deputy sheriff in London and the high life that he knew as a member of the English court, with his understanding of the ideals of biblical Christianity.

What is valued? The most fundamental value in Utopia is life itself. Hythloday says that "nothing in the world can be of equal value with a man's life," by which he means, of course, all human life, both man's and woman's (More n.d.: 142). Another major value, which also will appear in countless utopian works to follow, is happiness. Obviously, both human life and happiness are still with us today as major human values.

Other values in Utopia include "good and honest" pleasures (as long as no pain results afterwards), health, the fairness of equality that reinforces an essentially classless society and that includes sharing material things, the satisfaction of natural desires and authentic human needs, learning and education, the tranquil life, physical labor (but only enough to provide little more than the basic necessities of life, not labor for its own sake), moderation, freedom from fear and anxiety, religious tolerance (within some broad limits), cheerfulness and goodnaturedness, concern for the happiness of other persons, and good works. Utopians believe, More (n.d.: 221) says, "that by the good things that a man does he secures to himself that happiness that comes after death."

Devalued in Utopia are the accumulation of individual wealth, the lust for possessions (there is no private property or money), personal adornment (gold and silver are used to make chamber pots and chains for slaves), pride (because it often creates happiness based only on the misery of others), proselytizing zeal even—or especially—on the part of the righteous, and inequality (Manuel and Manuel 1979: 117–49). Utopians condemn premarital sex, adultery, and suicide. They detest war as brutal (although they are militarily prepared and are willing to defend themselves and even to engage in "just" wars).

In his critique of England and France, Hythloday condemns the idleness of the rich and their retainers, cruelty, overly severe punishment, living off other people's work, cheating, love of luxury, poverty, taverns and alehouses, houses of prostitution, gambling, corrupted manners, lying, entering into agreements and then not honoring them, conquering other lands, corrupt rulers who are more concerned with their own interests than the people's, private property, injustice, money as the standard of all things, incompetent rulers, and the many other things in the real social world that are at odds with Christ's teachings.

Equality and inequality. Some explanation must be added about a society put forward as the good society that values equality as fair, but that also contains slaves. The slaves consist largely of criminals (primarily adulterers), prisoners of war, volunteers from surrounding societies who would rather live in Utopia as slaves than in their own societies as free persons, and persons condemned to death in a foreign country who had been redeemed by Utopian merchants and brought to Utopia.

If there are "volunteers," then we can conclude that the life of a slave in Utopia was not as bad as we might believe with the history of African slavery in the Americas as our model. Slaves in Utopia are relatively few in number and their labor is not significant for the economy. Yet slaves are kept at perpetual labor and are chained. They do the killing and butchering of animals and the dirty work in the dining halls, among other labors. If they rebel, eventually they are put to death. But if they behave and show repentance, they may be released from slavery (More n.d.: 198–202).

Other forms of inequality are patriarchy within the family and a meritocratic system in education and learning. In the case of the latter, some particularly talented people are selected to devote themselves entirely to study. They become learned persons who teach others and who occupy a variety of roles in the governance of the society. If such persons do not fulfill their promise, however, they can be returned to ordinary labor (More n.d.: 171).

In other ways, Utopia is an egalitarian society in which people share food, live in houses of equal quality and amenities, give equal respect to all occupations, work no more than six hours a day for the most part, and devote themselves equally to their self-fulfillment. More (n.d.: 228) says that among Utopians "there is no unequal distribution, so that no man is poor, none in necessity; and though no man has anything, yet they are all rich; for what can make a man so rich as to lead a serene and cheerful life, free from anxieties."

The true and the good. Utopia, then, combines both the true and the good. It includes the true in the sense of providing a truthful account of the existing society at the time, although this is given only unsystematically out of More's own considerable experience. It includes the true, too, in describing Utopian society in the sense that the description, as we have seen, is in accord with then current experience and the real possibilities of the time. Utopia really could have been created with early sixteenth-century technology.

It includes the good because it involves evaluation. First, existing social practices in European societies are judged by a clear set of values and found to be wanting. Second, the nature of Utopia itself is shaped by those same values. In fact, Utopia embodies them. Although Utopia was an improvement on existing societies, it was not perfect. More did not presume that much. It was, after all, the work of man, not God, and only God, so More believed, could create perfection in this world (Manuel and Manuel 1979: 117–49).

More's repudiation of Utopia. More later repudiated his utopian vision, spurning the idea of basic equality in his subsequent writings. In his own behavior, he violated his principles of pleasure and tolerance. He sometimes wore a painful hair shirt and whipped himself with knotted ropes, and, as chancellor in Britain, he had Protestants whipped and burned (Manuel and Manuel 1979). Perhaps, we should not be surprised, because, lurking just below the surface of the pleasures and tolerance typical of Utopia, is another view that More occasionally lets creep in, as when he says that people should not stray from "that religious dread of the Supreme Being, which is the greatest and almost the only incitement to virtue" (More n.d.: 226). *Dread* is out of keeping with the general goodwill of Utopian society.

The Legacy of Utopia

But, despite More's renunciation, *Utopia* had a life and an influence of its own. It was part of the social transition from the feudal to the modern world. *Utopia* is antifeudal. There are no great baronial estates or manors. It is largely an urban society where individual freedom and participatory democracy flourish, though they are limited compared with our standards today (Manuel and Manuel 1979: 124).

It both exemplified and promoted an increase in the scope of human consciousness. As such, it was an aspect of the European discovery of worlds new to Europeans and their exploration of the Earth. It was no accident that 1516 was the date of *Utopia*'s publication. The Age of Discovery had begun in 1492 and was well underway when More wrote *Utopia*, using as his ideal Other a distant and unknown land beyond the edge of European travels. By 1504, Vespucci's *Mundus Novus* describing his real voyages, although itself partly imaginary we now believe, was available and offered a first-hand model.

The real voyages added fuel to the flames of curiosity and speculation already burning in Europe, but More went beyond simply using a fashionable interest as his model. He added more coal to the fires by inviting a further leap of the imagination. Who knew what strange and alien peoples and social customs would be encountered next as Europeans traveled beyond the edges of the known world? *Utopia* made the possibilities appear unlimited. It was the *Star Trek* of its day.

Utopia was also part of the information revolution, which had begun with the invention and spread of movable type in Europe in the mid-fifteenth century. The Gutenberg bible was printed about 1456 and was followed by the publication and distribution of major pieces of classical learning. The latter encouraged the confrontation between then-modern beliefs, especially theological doctrine, and earlier Greek and Roman social thought, a clash that was to produce a tidal wave of creative activity. *Utopia*, for example, was influenced by Plato's *Republic* (which is mentioned at one point by Hythloday in his narration). It was, thus, also no accident that 1,200 years before Hythloday arrived in Utopia some Romans and Egyptians had been shipwrecked there and from them the Utopians gained "all the useful arts that were then among the Romans" (More n.d.: 160).

In sum, *Utopia* became a model for a vast literature exploring the ideal society in which scenarios of desirable or undesirable societies were constructed. Utopian authors, following Thomas More, examined the possible, the probable, and the preferable and, by invidious distinction, criticized the imperfections of existing societies and pointed the way for social change by reform or revolution.

Precursors

The Greek Background

Thomas More's *Utopia*, as inventive and character-defining for the genre as it was, had been preceded by a long line of precursors. In Western thought, one important source was Greek writing, especially the myth of an ideal city on Earth (Manuel and Manuel 1979: 15). Some Greek utopias—which we now can call them after More coined the term—look back to a golden age of the past, while others deal with concrete problems of earthly cities contrasting ideal forms of urban life with the existing forms of real cities.

From about 800 to 500 B.C., the works of the poet Hesiod provided both religious authority and a manual of moral instruction. Hesiod gave us a pessimistic view of human history. It began with a most desirable Age of Gold, then declined to the Age of Silver, then to Brass, next to Heroic Metal, and, finally, to the undesirable pits of the then-contemporary Age of Iron. Although the values served may not have been greatly different, Xenophanes and other philosophers of the Athenian period (500–300 B.C.), such as Anaxagoras, Protagoras, and Democritus, rejected Hesiod's pessimistic account and, to the contrary, viewed prehistory as a period of human progress (Wescott 1978: 287–88).

Among the most influential of these pagan, disagreeing—and sometimes disagreeable—Greek writers, of course, was Plato. His *Republic* is still read today. In it, Plato expresses many values and they have a familiar ring to us even today: commitment to truth and knowledge, education and wisdom, courage, patriotism, temperance, endurance, freedom, soberness, industriousness, happiness for all people equally, social harmony and unity, and usefulness (Plato n.d.). Of central importance is justice. In fact, the entire series of dialogues largely focus on the meaning of justice. Mumford (1922: 41) says that for Plato justice meant "the due apportionment of work or function under the rule of 'a place for every man and every man in his place.'"

Plato uses a variety of arguments to justify his values, from divine power to nature. His primary means of persuasion, as every schoolchild knows, is a form of rational argument. By continued questioning, he logically eliminates one after another of the rival answers until we are left with the one that we conclude is correct. His major reasoning in support of justice comes close to the view that it makes social life possible—hence it makes possible the payoffs from living in society rather than living as an isolated individual against all others. The "unjust are incapable of common action" (Plato n.d.: 40). What is at stake is "nothing less than the rule of human life" (p. 41). Exchanging the products of their labor, people are better able to create the necessities of life, such as food, housing, and clothing, as well as the comforts of life (p. 60).

Viewed from a contemporary perspective, such reasoning seems essentially sound. Sociologists, for example, take it as axiomatic that living in social groups and societies, athough there are costs, has enormous net advantages for most individual members of society.

Beyond that, some writers have hypothesized that justice, not only in Plato's sense but in the modern sense of fairness, is a factor that contributes to the legitimacy and, hence, to the survival and effectiveness of social forms. Justice, then, may be viewed in part as an instrumental value that importantly contributes to the maintenance of the social order, to the unity of social life. Such unity was for Plato the "supreme, overriding need" of the city-state (Manuel and Manuel 1979: 112).

Plato's "city of perfect justice" was not one that people today would fully accept—especially if we consider the serfs or slaves who were to be part of it, even though it was possible for a slave to grow rich and a citizen to become impoverished. The rigid classes into which it was divided were set for life, the rulers (guardians) were an aristocracy, and selective breeding helped maintain the class structure. Yet every person's "authentic human needs" were accepted as deserving of being met, while luxury and excess were viewed as corruption and as signs of degeneration.

Plato promoted "the seeds of universal communist and egalitarian conceptions" in utopian thought, "though he, himself, had limited such proposals to relationships within the small ruling class of his *Republic*." Additionally, Plato contributed to utopian thought the notion that it might be possible to achieve the ideal society, at least to some degree, in this earthly world (Manuel and Manuel 1979: 111–12).

Before departing the Greeks, we should acknowledge the delightfully irreverent approach to utopia of the comic dramatist Aristophanes. He heaped wit and ridicule upon Socrates, Euripides, and many others. Although he may not have been regarded at the time as having profound insights, Aristophanes clearly reveals both his values and his serious intentions. In *The Wasps*, he shows that the ordinary individual cares for little else other than his own advantage, certainly, he does not care much for justice (Ehrenberg 1951: 54; Wescott 1978).

In *Lysistrata*, women organize to stop making love to men until the men stop making war with each other. Aristophanes showed both courage and humanity in writing it, because Athens was then at war. It was a time when even to speak of peace was disapproved, and *Lysistrata* must have been viewed as traitorous. For Aristophanes, the most important good was to end the war (Ehrenberg 1951: 61–62). The idea of "make love, not war," obviously, did not originate in the protest against the American war in Vietnam in the 1960s.

In *Ecclesiazusae*, Aristophanes shows a communist system in action and a government run by women, justified by their attempted reformation of the worst existing faults of the state. In *Plutus*, he tells a fairy tale of a system of inequality in which wealth comes to good men. And in his political utopia, *The Birds*, two Athenians try to escape the malignant corruption of the Athenian law courts and Athenian politics. They escape to the sky, to *Nephelococcygia* (Cloudcuckooland), where they hope to be free of vile politics and unfair law courts, and where they make eating and loving their paramount aims (Ehrenberg 1951: 58, 57).

Aristophanes was basically engaged in social criticism and, by implication, he generally encouraged hope for reform. He showed what he thought was right in society, such as the ideals of the autonomy of the law courts and fair verdicts, and ridiculed what he judged to be wrong about current practices, such as cheating jurymen and demagogues. He poked fun at puffed-up pomposity, grand schemes of self-denial, abstract ideology, and even "spiritual excellence" and "supreme virtue" to the extent to which they interfered with the enjoyment of good food, good drink, and good sex. He was earthy in his appreciation of the basic things of life. He valued peace, decent plenty, pleasure after work, healthy appetites, neighborliness, and home cooking. His was a commonsensical utopia of ordinary people (Manuel and Manuel 1979: 101). Even today, we could do a lot worse.

Judeo-Christian Theology

Ancient Greek writers provided one legacy, contradictory though it was within itself, from which later utopian writers, including More, drew both inspiration and models. Another major source on which later utopian writers drew was, as we saw in our discussion of More, Judeo-Christian theology.

Playing a central role, of course, is the paradise myth. On Earth somewhere, it was believed, a Garden of Eden existed—or had once existed. Also, some heavenly world was assumed to exist parallel to the earthly world, a heavenly world that contained all that was considered good. The ultimate good offered was immortality or the after-life continuation of some aspect of a person's existence or consciousness, the human soul surviving in a state of eternal happiness. This reward was held out in return for an earthly life spent following prescribed moral standards. Punishment for transgression meant a ticket to hell.

The prophecies of the apocalypse played a role, too, with their images of terrible destruction followed by rebirth, resurrection, and salvation. Both the Jewish and Christian eschatological traditions, including the specifically apocalyptic tradition, involve not merely individual transcendence, but the creation of a new social order. Although the new world was to be brought about by divine intervention, there was always an explicit or implicit hortatory element urging appropriate human action. For example, members of the elect community who are privileged to receive the revelation must behave in a way that will prepare them to receive and enjoy the coming city of God (Meeks 1989).

Although Judeo-Christian traditions influenced later utopian writings, they also served as limiting influences on the scope of ideological discourse throughout the Middle Ages. The Catholic Church, for example, insisted that the Kingdom of Heaven was the only possible model for a Christian utopia.

Biblical notions of the paradisiacal state are related to a variety of Near Eastern myths and, before that, to the oldest cultures of Mesopotamia (Manuel and Manuel 1979: 35). Thus, such ideas reach back into paganism and the distant beginnings of human consciousness.

As we'll see in the discussion of religion in chapter 3, religious beliefs are still with us and affect the lives of billions of the world's people. Moreover, even though the discoveries and inventions of physical, natural, and social sciences have subverted the Edenic myth and many people no longer believe in a heavenly paradise, overtly religious or religion-like elements can be noted in many subsequent utopias and vestiges can be found in the work of some contemporary futurists.

Robinson Crusoe

Worldwide Recognition

After More's *Utopia* and before the year 1719, hundreds—perhaps thousands—of utopias were written. They included the imaginary descriptions of ideal cities of the Italian Renaissance; the millenarian utopias of Germany and Central Europe, such as that of Thomas Müntzer; the work of the Pansophists, including Giordano Bruno, Francis Bacon, Tommaso Campanella, Johann Valentin Andreae, and Johann Comenius; the so-called Levellers, Diggers, and Ranters, utopian groups that were active during the English Civil War; Denis Vairasses's *History of the Sevarambians*, an imaginary society supposed to exist in then-unexplored Australia; François Fénelon's *The Adventures of Telemachus* which mixed dreams with real possibilities to help educate a future king, the duke of Burgundy; and Gottfried Wilhelm Leibniz's utopian plans for the creation of a Christian Republic throughout the world (Manuel and Manuel 1979).

But why 1719? Because that was when Daniel Defoe's *The Life and Strange Surprizing Adventures of Robinson Crusoe, of York, Mariner* (1972) was published. It was to become one of the most widely read and influential books ever, perhaps second only to the Bible in English. Since it was first published in 1719, over 700 editions have appeared (Crowley 1972: vii) and nearly everyone in the Western world, if not the entire globe, knows about it, thanks also to several Hollywood motion pictures more or less based on the book. Despite widespread disagreement about its meaning, it has become, with some isolated exceptions, part of the collective consciousness of all humankind, a myth of global scale. Thus, it is worth considering at some length.

Importance for Utopian Thought

A deserted island. *Robinson Crusoe* is important to the story of utopian literature for several reasons. First, there is a significant change in the typical situation. To be sure, Defoe follows convention and has Crusoe shipwrecked on an island, Crusoe being the sole survivor. But he breaks with the utopian literary tradition in that Crusoe finds no perfect society there. There are no people, no society, no culture—nothing to observe and report on. Instead, it is deserted. Crusoe is totally alone with nature.

Man builds utopia. Second, Defoe shows the perfect society being created by a human being out of the raw material of nature. Moreover, it is created in a real earthly place. This is a striking change from More and others who believed that only God could create perfection and that there was no real hope for it on Earth.

Yet, on one level, *Robinson Crusoe* does fit the older pattern because it is a spiritual journey, in this case reflecting Defoe's Puritanism. Crusoe argues with his father, disobeys him, and leaves against his father's wishes. He disdains God, experiences a Fall (the shipwreck and his lonely life at the beginning of his stay on the deserted island). But then he repents, finds God and accepts His will, and is redeemed in a series of seemingly providential events contributing to his thriving and happy life on the island, the addition of a servant and companion, Friday, and others to his domain, and his eventual return to England (Crowley 1972: xvi; Defoe, 1972).

On another level, however, the break with an older utopian tradition is complete. Crusoe is a self-made man. Despite his prayers and, presumably, the indirect influence of God, Crusoe, not God, creates his island world. Also, unlike most utopian writing before *Robinson Crusoe*, Dante's *De Monarchia* being a notable exception (Lasky 1976), he builds the ideal society in the here and now. Defoe (1972: 215) locates his utopia in a real place off the north coast of South America near the mouth of the Orinoco River and within sight of the island of Trinidad. Crusoe is a human and earthly Prometheus unchained, and he is concerned about the common realities of ordinary, daily life.

Capitalist values. Third, *Robinson Crusoe* exemplifies a distinctive set of values then rising to dominance in the world, the behavioral codes of a capitalist economy. It is virtually an instruction book in the values of the capitalist class (Watt 1969). Crusoe creates his own world, bringing the civilization of his day to the island in his head. But what he brings is not the totality of culture from the existing societies that he knows. Rather, he brings cultural elements to the island selectively and what he selects primarily is the culture of the emergent, industrial middle classes of England.

For example, "the preferable" in *Robinson Crusoe* includes individualism; industriousness; orderliness; temperance and moderation; quietness (Woolf 1969); materialism; profit-making; contractual relationships; the dignity of labor; economic, social, and intellectual freedom (Watt 1969); prudence; capital accumulation; diligence (Novak 1969); the ability to control the environment (Crowley 1972); practicality (e.g., "That all the good Things of this World are no farther good to us, than they are for our Use..." [Defoe 1972: 129]); and serenity.

The chief value is found in the fact that Crusoe is a hard-working, independent individual. His commitment to entrepreneurship, despite periods of doubts and reverses that turn out to be fortunate, remains as high at the end of his adventures as it was after his first trading trip when he made a profit of 650 percent (Defoe 1972: 17).

Sex and family life are downplayed and subordinated to business. When Crusoe prays for company, unlike Adam in the Garden of Eden, what he desires isn't a wife, but a labor force. His wish is granted; he is given a male slave.

Although capitalism was the immediate form of values as portrayed by Defoe, many of the values are also typical of a larger phenomenon, modernization. Rationality, orderliness, planning, bookkeeping and cost accounting, and international trade transcend capitalism and were to become, we now know, equally characteristic of modern, large-scale socialist economies. Although Crusoe can be viewed as a prototypical capitalist, perhaps especially in his individualism and profit motive, he can be viewed, more widely, as a generic modern, rational man as well. Yet the major features of Crusoe's underlying ethics are most fully captured by the emerging individualistic capitalist spirit.

The value of equality. Fourth, did Robinson Crusoe value equality? Both before and since Defoe, a major theme in utopian writings has been the value of the fairness of equality. In *Robinson Crusoe*, equality of opportunity is valued, to be sure, an equal chance for the individual, hardworking man to get ahead by his own labor. But equality of condition? No, it is not valued.

Early in the book, before he is stranded on a desert island, Crusoe sells into slavery the boy who helps him escape from a Moorish pirate, although with the proviso that the boy will be set free in ten years. Also, although not remarkable for the time, he buys a black slave and a European servant in Brazil. In fact, when his shipwreck occurs, Crusoe is on his way from Brazil to the Guinea Coast of Africa to buy slaves for himself and other plantation owners.

When Friday appears, Crusoe acknowledges that God made all humans the same, that Friday has the same faculties that he has, and that Friday can do some things, such as constructing and sailing a boat, better than he can. Yet he teaches Friday to call him "Master." Crusoe thinks how like a king he is, the whole island being his property and all the people (Friday and, by this time, other European mariners who have arrived) his subjects.

The name "Friday" came from the day of the week when Crusoe rescued him. It may itself be an indication of the servant's lowly status. Friday the person is clearly described by Defoe as an Amer-Indian from the north coast of South America whose people sometimes visited the island. But "Friday" was a typical name, "Cuffee" in the West African language Akan-Ashanti, for an African boy born on Friday. It—along with the other names plantation blacks used to call their children, following their African traditions of naming children for the day of the week they were born—came to be used also by slave owners. Thus, it was associated in the mind of someone such as Crusoe—and as Defoe—with a slave. Also, it meant several things, all uncomplimentary: a stupid person, one who "don't have much speech," one who is easily fooled, or a shrimp (Cassidy 1961: 158). (Of course, Cuffee—or Friday—in the plantation system often had his revenge by pretending to be more stupid than he was.)

Sexism is clearly evident in Crusoe's world. Women are mostly ignored or treated as things. There is talk, for example, of "stocking" the island with some women, as would take place in the less well-known sequels to the first book. Defoe briefly mentions near the end of the first book that Crusoe marries, but only after "his financial position has been fully secured" (Watt 1969: 44). The name of his wife is not given, nor are the names of his three children.

With the exception of the status of women and possibly of nonwhites, however, the inegalitarian system of stratification, unlike the one in Plato's *Republic*, was primarily contingent on what one did. Robinson Crusoe worked for what he had. Throughout the book, in a transformation of spiritual into material values, the rich and the poor, the worthy and the unworthy, are known by the results of their labor, foreshadowing Max Weber's analysis in *The Protestant Ethic and the Spirit of Capitalism* that would not appear until 185 years later.

Self-reinforcing values. Fifth, Crusoe's—that is, Defoe's—values as exemplified in the book are self-validating and self-reinforcing. They are not simply good things that it would be proper to have in an ideal world. Rather, they are values and behavior codes whose effective acting out creates feedback systems of positive reinforcement. Let's discount the praying, reading the scriptures (up to three times a day), and the possibility of God's intervention. Although Crusoe prayed as if everything depended on God, he worked as if everything depended on himself.

Even without supernatural help but with a little bit of luck, controlling the environment, industriousness, diligence, saving, and working, for example, can result in material success. Such success in turn rewards and further stimulates the very behaviors—and the values that prescribe them—that led to success in the first place.

Thus, a system of reciprocal causation is established that enhances human survival and well-being on the one hand and that further validates the underlying values that support them on the other. In *Robinson Crusoe*, achieving "the preferable" is not only its own reward, but it is also instrumental for future achievement as the work ethic and related values become reinforced by material gains. It is the opposite of a vicious circle; rather, it is a synergetic circle. Moreover, it is reasonable to assume, other things being equal, that groups organized by such values have a competitive advantage over other groups that have contrary values in the long-term evolutionary struggle for survival.

A dynamic utopia. Sixth, unlike most other utopias, Crusoe's island paradise is dynamic and changing. Most utopias, understandably, are static, because their authors, having constructed the best possible or perfect society with their words, can imagine no change for the better. Since the best already exists in their depictions of their utopias, what change could improve it? Perfection, once reached, means that further improvement is impossible. Crusoe's constructed world, by contrast, is incessantly being transformed (Watt 1969: 41).

The social nature of humans. Seventh, and finally, *Robinson Crusoe* set the stage for one of the major concerns of eighteenth-century philosophers and of modern social scientists. As Watt (1969: 53) says, "As a reaction to the consciousness of man's aloneness, which *Robinson Crusoe* depicted, a detailed analysis of Man's essentially social nature began." Thus, *Robinson Crusoe* not only can lay claim to being one of the first novels ever written, it also gave a push to the development of social analysis, to the investigation of the relationships between the individual and society, of the consequences of social isolation, and, for that matter, of the nature of both self and society.

The Noble Savage: Rousseau

The Individual and Society

The relationship between the individual and society became a major focus of Jean-Jacques Rousseau, French philosopher of the eighteenth century. He valued both individual freedom and social unity and explored their interrelationships. Dealing with these interrelationships, he has appeared to critics to be contradictory. But his apparent contradictions do not stem so much from ambiguity and confused thinking on Rousseau's part, as some writers have suggested, as they do from a basic paradox of human life. Humans are social beings. Their power and liberation come in part from their ability to create society, that is, from the advantages of cooperating with others in collective action. Freedom from the constraints of nature and from the limited power and abilities of one person acting alone come from communal life and the division of labor. Social life is not a zero-sum game with fixed resources for which people compete. Rather, social life is a resource. It creates power and increases the total assets and goods so that each of its members can benefit.

The paradox is that the very social relationships that empower people also necessarily restrict their liberty. Authority systems limit liberty and place shackles on some individual behavior. Yet such authority systems and the constraints they impose on individual behavior are precisely what may make coordinated human efforts possible. They encourage or discourage, prescribe and proscribe particular individual behaviors. In serving the "general will," powers of authority serve many aspects of the wills of many different people, somehow merging them into a whole that is larger than its parts. At the same time, however, they submerge, shape, dominate, and frustrate particular individual wills for the sake of the general will, for the good of the community. The welfare of the collectivity is, thus, both necessary to and limiting for individual welfare and freedom. The benefits of social life have their costs.

Rousseau may seem inconsistent in his discussion of the individual and society, because, going beyond Plato, he explores this paradox more fully. As is well known, he denounces the artificialities and injustices of civilization while trying to correct them (Huizinga 1976: 160). For him, ancient, as contrasted with then contemporary, peoples are "virtuous, by reason of their ignorance, their simplicity, and even their coarseness of manner, whereas the latter are too subtly refined not to be corrupt" (Derathé 1968: 564). He, thus, glorifies the "noble savage" and "primitive life."

But who was the model for the noble savage? Was it really some "savage" member of a nonliterate society? Or even an ape? Rousseau had never seen a real orangutan but he had read descriptions of them and believed them to be similar to our "savage ancestors" (Wockler 1978). Also, Rousseau was aware of the few members of distant nonliterate peoples who had been brought to England and the continent by this time. Yet neither savages nor apes were primarily whom Rousseau had in mind. Instead, it may have been none other than Defoe's Robinson Crusoe.

In his influential novel, *Émile*, published in 1762, Rousseau gives Defoe's *Robinson Crusoe* a special place in the education of his main character (Crowley 1972: ix). Rousseau uses Crusoe as an exemplar for Émile. Certainly, the model was not Crusoe's man Friday, as at least one author has claimed, because of Friday's late appearance in the novel and his small or nonexistent role in its major conflicts and resolutions. It is Crusoe who designs and builds his own world, mostly before Friday arrives on the scene.

Although he was no "primitive man" untouched by sophistication, Crusoe did experience a solitary existence and a simple, down-to-earth, rustic life on his island which removed him from civilization. Thus, Crusoe on his island was a Rousseauistic ideal of a "natural man" living in nature, unrestrained by "civilized society." But he was a romanticized natural man and his fictional island contained a nature a lot less brutish than in reality it was.

The feeling of belonging was a major value for Rousseau. He understood the feelings of loss and alienation, the new aloneness. Such feelings, of course, were endured by Robinson Crusoe on his deserted island, but Rousseau claimed that they existed in civilized, urban society as well, even when a person was surrounded by the physical, face-to-face presence of other people. He struggled for a reconciliation between the individual and the community, for the simultaneous achievement of individual freedom *and* group belonging (Miller 1984). He conceived of a natural harmony between the individual and society, an organic unity that washed away the contradictions between an autonomous "I" and a communal "I" (Manuel and Manuel 1979: 436–52). He enunciated the modern idea of democracy—the incorporation and direct participation of the people. He emphasized that the sovereignty of the people is the only legitimate form of government, and, hence, the belief that it is the only acceptable justification for restricting individual freedom (Miller 1984).

But Rousseau so merged the individual into the community in *The Social Contract*, for example, that he has been read as having recommended a kind of totalitarian unity "infused with the spirit—though not, of course, equipped with the machinery—of the nightmare world of Big Brother" (Huizinga 1976: 230). In France, he was accused of glorifying the state while sacrificing the rights of the individual (Derathé 1968: 567). One writer or another has accused him of justifying despotism, dictatorship, tyranny, or totalitarian democracy. Such views derive from Rousseau's contention that the state can do anything since it acts in the name of the people (Derathé 1968: 567). In the hands of Robespierre, and of countless demagogues since, the sovereignty of the people became a justification for dictatorships that label its opponents "enemies of the people" (Darnton 1984).

But such developments corrupt Rousseau's meaning. What he was trying to do, drawing in part on the earlier ideas of Thomas Hobbes and others on the notion of the state as a compact among people, was to recreate the freedoms typical of precivilized life within modern social structures while maintaining the advantages, but not the drawbacks, of civilization. He believed that, although it was impossible to return to the simple life of nature, with the social contract individuals in modern societies could enjoy the rights they had had in nature. He substituted civic for natural freedom.

Equality

Although Rousseau valued both individual liberty and social integration, and struggled with their contradictions, he valued most of all equality. For him, "inequality is the original evil, the one that engenders all others" (Derathé 1968: 564). As he explained at length in his *Discourse on the Origin of Inequality* published in 1755, a social order founded on inequality is unjust. Yet there are apparent contradictions in his writings on inequality, as on other subjects, and in this case they are not easy to explain away as the result of the inherent paradoxes of social realities.

On the one hand, in Rousseau's ideal world people were content with their lives as they were and did not seek to rise above their social status.

They cared little for social appearances and the opinions of others, while their own inner feelings meant everything (Manuel and Manuel 1979: 445). On the other hand, Rousseau gave to the coming revolutionaries of France—and later to the world—some of the "seismic slogans" of social protest, such as, "The fruits of the earth belong to us all, the earth itself to no one." "Man is born free, yet everywhere he is in chains." In such terms, Rousseau "sounded the trumpet of the class-war shrilly enough to please a Trotsky" yet often in the same essay he "warned against it in a manner that should have delighted the unfortunate Czar" (Huizinga 1976: 123).

Yet in the name of the fairness of equality, Rousseau proposed not only equality of political rights for all citizens, but also the public education of all children, public property, and taxes on inheritances and luxuries. Going even further, other writers—such as Dom Deschamps and Babeuf—believed that the *moi commun*, the natural harmony between the individual and the community that Rousseau emphasized, could not be achieved without absolute equality (Manuel and Manuel 1979: 448).

The sexes, however, were not to be equal in Rousseau's ideal world. While his hero Émile, for example, receives one type of education, Sophie, his wife-to-be, receives quite another (Nussbaum 1986). Little Émile is taught to think independently and fearlessly, to be self-sufficient, an isolated being who needs nothing from anyone, except, apparently, from Sophie. Sophie, to the contrary, is prepared for "the moment when she will be her own doll." She learns to please and to help her husband-to-be, to manage his household, to love and care for his children, and to anticipate his every want. She is to be confined to the home to create a "bastion of gentleness," to have limited freedom, and to be a complementary unit that, when combined with Émile, will create a single harmonious moral person.

Yet, in the main, Rousseau's writings gave moral justifications for egalitarian and antimonarchist proposals for reform, if not for revolution. Thus, they were seen as being a threat to the monarchist establishment. He was placed under police surveillance, for example, as early as 1753 and the circulation of his *The Social Contract*, when published in 1762, was forbidden in France (Derathé 1968: 568). In the summer of 1762, the Sorbonne and the *parlement* of Paris condemned Rousseau and his *Émile* for being subversive of religion, morality, and decency. Facing immediate arrest, he left France and sought asylum in Switzerland.

Rousseau's Justification of Values

Although Rousseau does not ignore religion, he makes a shift in the justification of the good. Nature plays a large and independent role in his scheme of legitimation. Equality, for example, is natural; inequality is man-made. Hence, equality is good; inequality is evil. One is in tune with nature, the other is not. Hence, the moral advantage of primitive man derives from his life in nature.

But knowing this, humans can act to restore some of the advantages of the simple, natural life, such as individual freedom, within modern society. One way is to create an identity between the individual and the larger society by means of a social contract. An agreement or pact is constructed that establishes the supremacy of the state over its members to which each member voluntarily agrees. In Rousseau's work, the contract is a justification not only on this grand, abstract level of the state, but also on the level of the individual relationships of everyday life. In *Émile*, for example, a contract between student and teacher is reached. On the most mundane level, if you freely agree to something, then you are morally obligated to live up to the agreement. Beyond this, however, is something more profound, and it is what makes Rousseau vital to this story of the development of justifications of values. Underlying the social contract, and laws that may derive from it, is the idea, already mentioned, of the sovereignty of the people, the general will. The "general will," of course, is an abstraction that, though based on individuals, transcends them to mean a collective interest that is more than the sum of individual interests. The collectivity, that is, society, is its own source of justifying its values.

Such a view would be elaborated, refined, and elevated to a sophisticated, quasi-religious secularism by the end of the nineteenth century by French sociologist Émile Durkheim. Recognizing that the spread of secularism and individualism was undermining religious faith and the belief in God, Durkheim sought another source for the justification of right and wrong. He viewed the real object of morality as society and this led him to substitute society for divinity as the authority for morality (Hall 1987: 187).

But it was Rousseau who led the way. In his social analysis, he had already shifted the foundations of morality, first, from God to nature and, then, beyond nature, to society itself.

The Savage Noble: The Marquis de Sade

Social Chaos and the Inconceivable

Utopian fantasies on the eve of the French Revolution reached an extreme in quantity, intensity, and diversity. They also reached an extreme of perversity. An intellectual and emotional revolution was in full swing prior to the violent political outburst itself. Nearly everything in existing society was called into question by one writer or another: the family, sexual normality, the definition of pain and pleasure, the Christian religion, the aristocracy, the monarchy, self-interest, and reason itself (Manuel and Manuel 1979: 431–32). The latter part of the eighteenth century must have been a disturbing time as it churned with intellectual, political, and social upheavals. But out of the chaos came a vast array of utopian and dystopian writing. Perhaps, no eighteenth-century writer represents the turmoil better than the Marquis de Sade, who certainly is a prime candidate for the title, "the savage noble."

Obviously, I am skipping over many important writers, such as the political revolutionaries François Noël Babeuf and Saint-Just. Also, Restif de la Bretonne, Sade's rival on the sexual revolutionary front, should not be forgotten. Yet, of these and others, it is Sade who stretches our minds and moral limits the most and engages us diabolically in "conceiving the inconceivable."

It is farfetched to suggest any continuity between Sade's eighteenth-century fulfillment of obscene sexual fantasies through violence and Herman Kahn's twentieth-century fulfillment of obscene fantasies of violence through future images of the megadeaths of thermonuclear wars, but it is tempting. How much of a difference is there between Sade's "conceiving the inconceivable" and Kahn's "thinking the unthinkable"? One wonders which era—and which violence—should shock us more?

Sadian Utopia or Dystopia?

It may be difficult for the reader to think of Sade as a utopian, rather than a dystopian, writer. Certainly, he portrays behavior and activities that most people, both then and now, would regard as evil and reprehensible; his work is filled with "dreams of absolute, destructive power, manifesting itself through rape, mutilation, and murder" (Weightman

1993: 8). From that point of view, Sade is dystopian in his visions, even though we can still refer to his works, as we can to other dystopias, as being part of the general utopian literature.

Yet from another perspective, as Manuel and Manuel (1979: 535) point out, Sade might be considered utopian in the narrower sense of creating a desirable world, because he did express the positive and not merely the negative side of some values. For example, he called not only for "endless sexual excitment," but also for "freedom from all repression" and can be read as "the most formidable of utopias" (Barthes 1976: 170). Can we find in Sadian writings any support for this claim?

Sade's earliest utopian writings to appear in print followed the tradition of a traveler going to distant places, including Africa and the Indian Ocean (Manuel and Manuel 1979: 543). The bulk of his writings, though, typically locates the action at a château which was as isolated as any distant island. One such Sadian site is Silling, a château in the Black Forest, where Sade's *The 120 Days of Sodom* is set. Four libertines with their harem isolate themselves there for four months. The château is remote from the world. It is protected from intrusion by nearby villagers who allow no one to pass. There is a steep mountain and a high precipice whose only bridge is destroyed once the libertines have crossed over. Also, there is a wall and a moat. The door to the château is walled up from the inside. Finally, an impassable snowfall comes and completes the physical separation from the real social world (Barthes 1976: 15–16).

In this Sadian Other place, there is a perfe t society of sorts, a society of evil where people devote themselves to carnal pleasures. Even though it is pure evil, the Sadian society is just. For it is not hypocritical and its consequences are in tune with nature. By contrast, the unnatural society of Europe was cruel, imposed terrible punishments on people, and produced injustice behind a mask of virtue. In this Sadian utopia, people escape the self-righteous power of the state (Manuel and Manuel 1979: 542–43).

Education and Social Class

Although there are lesser classes, such as major assistants, aides, overseers of debauchery, and jokers, Sadian society is composed of two major classes, or, perhaps, "castes" would be more accurate. They are the upper caste of masters or libertines and the lower caste of subjects or victims. Members of both castes are engaged in "education." In fact, Sadian society is an "educative society, or more exactly a school society." But members of the two major castes do not take the same set of courses. The subjects take technical courses consisting of punishments, injustices, and harangues, but not hypocritical harangues. The educational track of the masters, to the contrary, focuses on refinement, on becoming a master of libertinage. It was school tracking and no crossing over from one track to another was permitted (Barthes 1976: 24).

When social class relations in the larger society are discussed, there is a reversal of the ordinary. Stealing from the rich or forcing the poor into prostitution are commonplace and banal. In a Sadian world, they can hardly be considered to be transgressions. Rather, genuine transgression is created by the perverse reversal of violations, by paradox. Thus, to truly transgress "we must steal from the poor and prostitute the rich" (Barthes 1976: 168).

Yet, in Sade's writing, the class relations of the existing society also have largely been reproduced with all their "banal" injustices. Except for some aristocratic women victims, the libertines usually are drawn from the wealthy classes while the victims are drawn from the industrial and urban proletariat or from the serfs of still feudal lands. Most of the indignities are heaped upon members of the lower classes.

Sadian Values

What values were served by Sade's writings? Even though Sade may have been mentally ill, at least part of the time he was writing, and even though he was confined in a "madhouse" at Charenton for a number of years, we can, nonetheless, analyze the values expressed in his views. Most obviously, Sade valued sexual freedom. No one should deny "a citizen the satisfaction of any of his erotic desires." Although it was usually a freedom that was limited to elites, in at least one work Sade extended the principle "to all members of society equally." Another important value was genuineness, a true congruity between words and deeds, a form of truth. In his utopias, Sade eliminated the hypocrisy that he believed corrupted existing society (Manuel and Manuel 1979: 544).

Less obviously, Sade valued social order, perhaps no less than More and many other utopians. He rigidly organized daily life, creating "timetables, dietary programs, plans for clothing, the installation of furnishings, precepts of conversation or communication" (Barthes 1976: 17). Even sexual activity is rigorously structured. Some people give directions; others follow them. A hierarchical authority system of giving and taking orders worthy of the U.S Marines is necessary, for example, for the intricate positioning and precise timing of the simultaneous orgasms of five people in a group, male and female (Manuel and Manuel 1979: 544). Thus, Sade exemplified the late eighteenth-century concern with the social order that, without the sexual fixation, would become a central topic of the work of Auguste Comte.

Sade leaves little, if any, trace of religion in his justification of the good. Rather, God is banished. Nature is the dominating basis of his justification. Nature, aided by human needs and "the purity of the pleasure principle," justifies the Sadian utopia. He was as nature had made him and nature, Sade believed, has no regard for human morality. It is in accordance with the laws of nature that the only duty of an individual is toward himself and that the strong persecute the weak. Happiness comes from honestly reflecting the ways of nature (Manuel and Manuel 1979: 545, 547).

The First Futurist: The Marquis de Condorcet

An Enlightened Noble

An equally intense rejection of religion can be found in the work of the "enlightened noble," Marie Jean Antoine Nicholas Caritat, marquis de Condorcet. Religion, for Condorcet, was based on ignorance and superstition, both of which in his view interfered with the discovery of truth and the spread of reason. But, aside from an antipathy to religion, Condorcet's image of the good society bears little resemblence to Sade's.

Despite his aristocratic birth, Condorcet joined the French Revolutionary forces, served as a deputy to the Legislative Assembly, and was elected to the National Convention. A member of the Girondists, a more moderate Revolutionary group than the Jacobins, he wrote a version of the constitution, drafted legislation, and designed reforms for the French educational system. Although opposed to the monarchy, he voted against the death penalty for the king, and he objected to the arrest of the Girondists. His own arrest was ordered in July 1793, but until March of the following year he managed to stay in hiding and to avoid detection by the police.

During this time, with little opportunity to consult a library and with his past learning as his major source, he wrote *A Sketch for a Historical Picture of the Progress of the Human Mind*. It was published posthumously in 1795, Condorcet having died in prison shortly after being apprehended (Granger 1968). The *Sketch* signficantly influenced utopian writers who were to follow, including Saint-Simon, Comte, and, especially, Marx.

Progress and the Future

In his *Sketch*, which was basically an outline for a larger work Condorcet did not live to write, he recounted the progressive development of humankind from the beginning of tribal life, through nine stages, up to the founding of the French Republic. He depicted developments of pastoral peoples and agricultural societies, Greece and Rome, the Crusades, through the American and French Revolutions. He focused on the creation and spread of knowledge and on the political, economic, and social conditions that underlay them. Although he reported periods of decline and decadence, the long-term trends were progressive.

After reviewing the past, he turned to the future and described things to come in the tenth stage. He made remarkably accurate forecasts of scientific and technical developments in many fields for more than a century into the future. Also, he both foresaw and advocated the application of statistical methods to the study of social problems and the scientific study of society, as the basis of social legislation and reform (Hampshire 1955: xi).

Additionally, he made forecasts of coming social changes, such as liberal democracy; equal and public education; popular journalism; social security for the elderly, widows, and orphans; equality before the law; freedom of speech; the redistribution of wealth; equal rights for women; the end of slavery and colonialism; the creation of an international peacekeeping organization similar to today's United Nations; and the increase in human life expectancy (Hampshire 1955; Condorcet 1955). These predictions of social changes, too, are quite accurate. He was not on the mark, of course, on every subject. With respect to war, for example, he anticipated its disappearance.

Methods of Forecasting

Condorcet did not pull these and other forecasts out of thin air. Rather, they were based, first, upon his knowledge of long-term social trends and, second, upon the causal factors underlying them. In the first case, he viewed history, despite periods of reversal, as progressively bringing more freedom and knowledge, and the increasing spread of that knowledge equally to all people, women as well as men. Thus, simple projections of past trends into the future led him to some predictions.

In the second case, he had a crude explanatory theory. In a nutshell, it dealt with the mutually reinforcing interplay between freedom and knowledge. Freedom was an essential condition for the creation and spread of knowledge. The greater the amount and spread of knowledge, the more individuals would choose to end "the reign of error" and seek the effective path for greater happiness, perfectibility, and the political and social conditions to preserve freedom. Preserving freedom would result in the continued dynamism of science and technology, since they thrive under conditions of free and open inquiry. Thus, freedom results in the growth of knowledge, and greater knowledge is a condition for continuing freedom, which, in turn, produces the continuing growth of knowledge. Change toward greater perfectibility, in this way, could continue indefinitely.

There is a similarity between Condorcet's theory of the mutual reinforcement of the growth of knowledge and freedom and part of John Stuart Mill's mid-nineteenth-century justification of freedom of expression and discussion. Mill had read Condorcet. In fact, he headed Book V (VI in the eighth edition), "On the Logic of the Moral Sciences," in his *A System of Logic* with a quote from Condorcet's *Sketch*. Since Mill's influence on modern philosophy and methodology of science, including social science, has been considerable, we have here another link between utopian ideas and contemporary social science, from Condorcet, to Mill, to contemporary social scientists.

Additionally, Condorcet used other methods to a lesser extent. He studied the opinions of enlightened men, believing that, as everyone became educated equally, others would come to share enlightened views. Therefore, such opinions were a clue to the future. He assumed that backward countries would follow the path of the advanced countries. Thus, he took the present of the latter as a guide to the future of the former, a technique later used by Marx and Engels.

Also, he postulated common basic needs of all humankind and the existence of a limited number of utilitarian solutions to their satisfaction. Thus, similar technologies would be independently invented or would spread, people tending to select and retain the same most effective technologies when they were free to do so. Given common human needs, rational free will, and the laws of nature, then, Condorcet postulated a kind of technological determinism. It was a determinism, however, that depended on human choice, will, and action in a cycle of reciprocal causation (Condorcet 1955).

Reason, Freedom, and Equality

Condorcet valued many things, such as the pursuit of happiness, justice, tolerance, the welfare of the "whole of humanity without distinction of country, race, or creed," and human life (Condorcet 1955: 141). But there are three sets or clusters of interrelated things that he valued most highly. The first cluster includes reason, knowledge, science, truth, sharing knowledge, and education.

The second involves freedom, including free inquiry, political liberty, and the ability to follow the dictates of one's own reason.

And the third cluster involves various equalities.

By equality he meant not absolute leveling in the distribution of material things, but the elimination of the extremes of both poverty and wealth. He meant, too, equality of all people in having the opportunity to acquire knowledge. Colonialism, racism, and slavery, for example, would not be allowed to stand in the way. They would be eliminated. He predicted the reduction of inequality among nations as well as the reduction of inequality among people within nations. The only kind of inequality that would persist in the future, he believed, would be "that which is in the interests of all and which favours the progress of civilization, of education, and of industry, without entailing either poverty, humiliation, or dependence" (Condorcet 1955: 174), a view somewhat similar to John Rawls's more recent argument that some inequalities are acceptable as long as they redound to the benefit of the disadvantaged, as we'll see in chapter 3.

He was totally opposed to the inequalities between men and women. He believed that the evidence would show that "the differences in the moral and intellectual aptitudes of the two sexes had been grossly exaggerated." He favored social equality between the sexes, because women have the same natural rights as men and also because educated mothers would make an important contribution to the spread of knowledge as they helped teach their children. Another benefit, he believed, was that it would result in happier family life (Manuel and Manuel 1979: 512, 516). He predicted that such equality between the sexes would become reality.

Justification and Explanation

Condorcet's justifications of his values are somewhat muddled, mostly because they are interwoven with the explanations of his assertions about the past and the future. That is, the reasons that he uses to explain what *has* happened and what *will* happen overlap a good deal with the reasons that he gives to support what he believes *ought* to happen.

Appeals to God, of course, are out. No eternal divine laws, as in the writings of Thomas Aquinas or Thomas More, appear in Condorcet's justification. He looked not to God nor to the Church, but elsewhere for moral authority.

He does appeal to nature in the sense of accepting much of the natural law argument of his day. He had read Thomas Hobbes, John Locke, and Montesquieu; moreover, the rights of man (and for him, don't forget, that meant woman, too) and the examples of the American and French Revolutions were salient in his mind. Natural rights were "inalienable and indefeasible" (Condorcet 1955: 140). Although the values of freedom, equality, knowledge, and learning were deduced from natural rights, they also depended on auxiliary assumptions about human nature (Hampshire 1955: x–xi). The latter included the view of humankind as seeking pleasure, avoiding pain, and having the capability of making reasoned calculations. Under conditions of free choice and knowledge, rational people would not only choose the most effective paths to happiness and social progress, they would also choose the most correct, that is, the morally right, paths. In fact, they would be the same paths.

Condorcet struggled to invent modern social science and to give it a role in discovering the good. He aimed to apply the ideas of science, of cause and effect, to society and to construct social laws of change. Building on his earlier work in mathematics, he applied probability theory to human behavior. He proposed both a mathematical sociology for the analysis of large numbers and a methodology for the analysis of intensive case studies (Manuel and Manuel 1979: 511). His educational reorganization included not only an emphasis on teaching natural science, but also social science (Granger 1968). He assumed that some questions of preference could be answered by rational or factual analysis, similar to some of the strategies of moral decision to be discussed in the following chapters.

A Revolutionary Change in Perspective: From Space to Time

There are many other eighteenth-century philosophers who could have been considered at this point, including Diderot, Claude-Adrien Helvétius, Hume, Kant, Adam Smith, Turgot, and Voltaire. But Condorcet captured the eighteenth-century ideology of progress as brilliantly as any other writer and better than most. So doing, he revolutionized utopian writing.

Condorcet set the ideal, more perfect society not in some other "place," but fully and deliberately at some other "time." He moved utopian writing into the future. Moreover, unlike some other early writers who embraced the future, such as Louis-Sébastien Mercier who wrote *The Year 2440* in 1783, he insisted on a scientific approach to it.

Of course, Thomas More, too, must have had the future in mind, when he wished that reforms might be possible in England along the lines of Utopian society. Even Greek writers had used time, but most often the past, not the future, as the time of the Other. But Condorcet produced a cataclysmic mind change. For him, the future became everything. Moreover, he depicted a future that was becoming reality, because of the existence of fundamental laws of social change, a belief, as we shall see, similar to that of Karl Marx, although the laws of change in each case are different.

Change was not mainly circular nor cyclical, it was directional, moving on toward perfection. Progress had occurred in the past and it would occur in the future. Images of future progress were real possibilities and they could be hastened into reality, not by the will of God, but by the actions of ordinary human beings. From Condorcet on, the future would capture the imaginations of most utopian writers. Utopian dreams of a better life as well as utopian plans to make them reality would be about the future. If Thomas More was the first utopian, then Condorcet, the last of the *philosophes* of the *ancien régime*, was the first futurist.

Although Condorcet fused the good and the true in his analysis, he did so in a way that often made it unclear as to which was which. Value judgments and facts were often integrated in a seamless fabric of social theory. As a result, sometimes his justification of the good is lost or taken for granted in his analysis of why or how a given social development has occurred or will occur.

Both values and facts, I have argued, must be taken into account in the futures field, but there should be no confusion about which is which. That is, analytically they should be kept clearly and distinctly separate as far as is humanly possible. As we shall see, Marx carries this unity of value and fact to a breathtaking theoretical level, but ultimately his logic fails. Before encountering Marx, however, we first must consider Marx's more immediate predecessors, Saint-Simon and other utopian socialists.

The Utopian Socialists

Reactions to Revolution and Capitalism

Condorcet did not live long enough to write about his disillusionment with the revolutionary furies that engulfed France, but the so-called utopian socialists, including Charles Fourier, William Godwin, Robert Owen, and Henri Saint-Simon, did. In part, they were reacting to the social chaos and murderous violence of the French Revolution, which discredited its own ideological underpinnings. Fourier and Saint-Simon experienced it first hand, while Godwin and Owen viewed it from England.

These writers were reacting, also, to something else: the growing ills of the early capitalist system. The capitalism so celebrated in *Robinson Crusoe* was showing some ugly sides—from the exploitation of women and children and a disregard of the health and safety of workers in the workplace to hunger and poverty of the underclasses. It now invited criticism and speculation about what alternative social forms might be better.

These writers were "utopian" in condemning the present and constructing desirable alternatives for the future, alternatives that they believed would become reality. They were "socialist" in that they believed the better society of the future could be achieved through social engineering, though by private initiative rather than government action. Each made important contributions to socialist thought, including ideas about authority and governance, inequality and social justice, marriage and the family, and communal organization. The works of Saint-Simon, for example, directly influenced the later programs of European socialists, and each of the utopian socialists influenced Marx and Engels. Although I have followed tradition in labeling them "utopian socialists," by their own lights they were social scientists.

Values and Goals

By lumping these four writers together, I do injustice to some of the differences among them, and, because they wrote over many years and some of their views changed, I gloss over the contradictions within each one's own work. Yet their major values are clear. Their brightest guiding lights were harmony and happiness (Goodwin 1978: 143). Harmony referred to the society while happiness referred to the individual. The utopian socialists constructed word pictures of perfectly functioning future societies, aiming to eliminate social conflict, repression, crime, poverty, and misery and to create happy lives for individuals.

A long list of additional values can be compiled from their writings, but such values are largely instrumental and derivative. The list includes the rejection of private property (except for Fourier); cooperation and goodwill among people; self-development and self-realization; work (except for Godwin who valued leisure and the minimization of labor); love, friendship, and pleasure; knowledge, rationality, and education; the reduction or elimination of government and the state; and compassion, humaneness, and benevolence toward humankind (Goodwin 1978; Riasanovsky 1969: 185).

They devalued violence and revolutionary action, liberal and democratic ideology, political rights, the state and political authority, unbridled egoism and selfishness, established religion and the church, *laissez-faire* ideology, the existing industrial system, domination, individual choice because it was seen as a threat to social harmony, exploitation as the basis of society, and, in the case of Fourier, even the achievement ethic (Manuel and Manuel 1979). The utopian socialists comprehended the "reinforcing connections between, for example, the government, the law and the Church, and intended to abolish these mutually supportive institutions simultaneously" (Goodwin 1978: 155). They aimed to transform the world and to save humankind. They charged ahead, believing that nearly anything was possible.

Reasons for devaluing democracy. Why did they devalue democratic institutions? Partly because such institutions were associated with the chaos of the French Revolution. But there was another reason that they did so. Democratic institutions are a way of negotiating the future, compromising values, and reaching only temporary, unstable, and imperfect resolutions of conflict and selection of collective goals. Some contemporary writers, such as Herbert Simon or Charles E. Lindblom, might argue that that is exactly the point of democratic decision-making. Such "imperfections" are in fact the strong points of democracy. "Satisficing" is a desirable compromise. But the utopian socialists would not agree. Rather, the utopias they offered were final solutions. They created blueprints for perfect societies that needed no further improvements (Goodwin 1978). In their view, democracy could not create perfection.

Differences on equality. With respect to equality, each of these writers wished to abolish poverty and the extremes of inequality between the rich and the poor. Each wanted the satisfaction of at least minimum needs for everyone. Also, each supported the idea of equality of treatment. Yet their views differed on the extent and nature of equality, especially of equality of condition. Godwin and Owen were the most thoroughgoing in their egalitarianism, Owen, for example, advocating absolute equality and communal sharing of township fields. But even in Owen's utopia there would be some inequality, because the equal development of different inherent individual capacities would result in differences.

Fourier's system, which was based on the notion of equal opportunity for self-realization, contained a diversity based on a variety of individual capacities each of which should be allowed to be perfected in its own way. Thus, in his image of the perfect society there were inequalities, in material rewards for example, commensurate with investment in the community, yet all people would share equally in basic emotional and sexual satisfaction and fulfillment of one's distinctive self.

Despite the existence of some inequalities in his utopia, Fourier has been called "the first feminist" because of his denunciation of the unequal conditions of women and men in existing society and his emphasis on women's emancipation and total equality with men (Riasanovsky 1969: 208–9). In his writings, feminism was consistent with his appreciation of Sade's works, because all passions could be turned into "wholesome expressions" once free of repressive and corrupt institutions (Manuel and Manuel 1979: 664). He anticipated some aspects of the pre-AIDS sexual revolution that was to begin in the 1960s when some of his ideas concerning sex, having been suppressed earlier by his own followers as too shocking, were finally published for the first time.

Saint-Simon, rejecting Jacobin equality and believing inequality to be natural, envisioned a meritocracy based on equal social opportunities. He invented an early, if not the first, "version of socialism's most famous distributive principle: from each according to his capacity, to each according to his achievements" (Goodwin 1978: 37). Note the important difference between this meritocratic creed and the famous proclamation attributed to Marx which, while keeping the first part of the statement basically the same, importantly changes the second: "From each according to his ability, to each according to his needs!" (Manuel and Manuel 1979: 699). Actually, followers of Saint-Simon proposed this version, too, before Marx did.

Marx, of course, would abolish the class system. Saint-Simon retains the class system, but a fair one according to his view, based upon a hierarchy of talent, superabundance, and, contrary to the other three writers being considered, a measure of state ownership (Goodwin 1978: 21). Yet Saint-Simon would abolish hereditary wealth in his perfect society, so inequalities would be restricted to one's own efforts and talents.

Justifying Their Values

Although He was not banned from the vocabulary or thinking of the utopian socialists as from Condorcet's, God was mostly a secondary element in the justification of the utopian socialists' values. The existing clergy and the church, certainly, did not enter into the new societies they proposed.

Saint-Simon emphasized the religious aspect of his theories in his last years. Yet even in his "new Christianity," it is not the old church or clergy that will lead the way down the moral path. Rather it will be "artists, poets, moralists, scientists, [and] new theologians." Moreover, despite the fact that some of his followers adopted mysticism, Saint-Simon himself stressed the scientific basis of his thought (Manuel and Manuel 1979: 611; 613–14). His was not a theological religion. It was not supernatural, but contained purely moral ideals (Hall 1987: 131).

For Fourier, who claimed from the start to be constructing God's own system, God tended to dissolve into nature (Riasanovsky 1969: 34). Godwin, too, did not renounce God. But Owen made an issue of his anticleric and antireligious views.

Yet underlying all their views, even Owen's, were emergent religion-like elements, a development that would reach much fuller expression with the coming political religion of Marxism.

The most important justification of values put forward by the utopian socialists was something quite different. They claimed to deduce both their proposed forms of social organization and the values that were to be served by them from a scientific analysis of human nature (Manuel and Manuel 1979: 600). They tried to show that humans had specific needs, passions, and pleasures and that these could be satisfied by the social arrangements they proposed. For example, Saint-Simon devised a social classification based on the human physiology of his day, while Fourier constructed a scheme of 810 characters based on combinations of twelve passions and an overarching synthesizing drive toward unity.

Not only an analysis of human nature, but of nature, too, entered into their justification. For example, since, according to their view, harmony exists in the physical world, they argued that it is an organizational principle and "non-evaluative goal for the social world, which is also part of nature" (Goodwin 1978: 191). This is, of course, a key point in the justification of what they regarded as objective fact.

Thus, these writers were naturalists, but they were also environmental determinists. They believed that external forces cause human behavior and shape individuals. Human beings were to be made the subjects of scientific investigation just as natural objects were; and human action could be explained by environmental forces, especially by the social environment. It followed in their thinking that knowledge of the social forces shaping human behavior, that is, social scientific knowledge, could be used to alter such behavior. Owen, for example, advocated the method that today we call "positive reinforcement," rewarding "proper" behavior to create "good" habits.

There is a contradiction here. Human nature must be viewed as malleable to some extent if people are to be changed as needed to fit the constructed utopian societies. But if human nature is too malleable, then how can values and related detailed organizational forms be justified by deduction from human nature? That is, "the more flexible, environmentally determined or perfectible human nature is considered to be, the less possible it is to *derive* social standards directly from the concept," as Goodwin (1978: 79) says. Even under Fourier's scheme in which the most accomodation appears to be made to accept people as they are, there is social regulation beyond what voluntarism could probably sustain and there are assumptions about individuals changing in response to new conditions, the praise of others, and the success of past efforts. That is, there are assumptions about how people will learn and, presumably, change.

Social Experimentation

The utopian socialists firmly exploited the idea of social experimentation. They not only constructed word pictures of their utopias, they also attempted to make them living realities. Of course, they were not the first to do so. There were, for example, Pythagorean communities in southern Italy about 500 B.C. (Manuel and Manuel 1979: 94). But the social experiments of the nineteenth century have influenced modern thinking about social change and helped shape the modern world as well as conceptions of alternatives to it, partly because they were conceived as what we would now call "demonstration projects."

At the beginning of the nineteenth century, Owen was an innovative and visionary factory manager who created a model mill town at New Lanark in England. In 1824, he undertook a more ambitious project: creating a whole new community at New Harmony, Indiana, in the United States. Even though he invested a fortune, it ended in disaster. In the 1830s, Saint-Simonians created a community in Menilmontant, near Paris, although Saint-Simon's focus was not so much on the small community as on the reorganization of the entire society. There were many Fourierist communities started and they were scattered from Rumania and Russia and throughout several countries, including Brook Farm in the United States, to modern Israel (Manuel and Manuel 1979: 587; 647–49). The utopian socialists influenced efforts to create planned communities, garden cities, and even some communes of the 1960s.

The ideas of the utopian socialists were not intended to describe a fictitious utopia such as More's, or to establish an isolated community to exist totally apart from the larger society. Rather, the aim of their efforts at social experimentation was to prove to the world the truth of their ideas and the superiority of their proposals for social reorganization compared to existing social realities. For instance Fourier and Owen each wanted a real example so "compelling that, better than any arguments, it would persuade the rest of Mankind to adopt their system" (Manuel and Manuel 1979: 587).

In sum, these unlikely bedfellows—Fourier, a son of a prosperous French cloth merchant who lost his inheritance and for a time was a traveling salesman; Godwin, the son of a nonconformist English minister and father of Mary Shelley who wrote *Frankenstein*; Saint-Simon, a French nobleman who fought against the British in the American War of Independence and renounced his titles; and Owen, a successful business-man who made a fortune managing a cotton-spinning factory in England—wrote detailed plans for realistic utopias and expanded arguments for them similar to those that Condorcet had merely outlined in his *Sketch*. They created a kind of utopian social science, claiming "to have pro-duced social theory with practical implications which pointed the way to a better society." It was, however, a flawed social science, partly be-cause the effort to deduce ideal social structures from human nature was not successful (Goodwin 1978: 174, 79) and partly because of the lack of openness to democratic participation and new ideas.

Their aim was a future world of social harmony and individual happi-ness. Their justifications were based on explorations of human nature and of nature, explorations that they attempted to make scientific as they understood the term. Reason—that is, rational thinking—would then persuade people to see the correctness of their views and convince them to take the actions necessary to transform the world. They contributed to the development of the social scientific ideas of environmental and his-torical determinism (Goodwin 1978: 84), as well as to other aspects of social science. Auguste Comte, for example, was for six years a friend and disciple of Saint-Simon and incorporated some Simonian ideas into his own influential positivist works of sociology. They proposed and carried out what they considered to be real social experiments, putting their proposals for the future into practice by creating their ideal com-munities in the reality of the present.

Marxism

The utopian socialists were to be eclipsed by Karl Marx and Friedrich Engels and their followers. But many of their key ideas lived on, because Marxism swallowed them up. Marxism, too, was a call to action, and its call was answered not by a handful of followers, or even thousands, but by a massive worldwide response of hundreds of millions of people. Let us remember that, by the mid-twentieth century, bloody revolutions had been fought, the map of the world had been redrawn, and about half of human-kind was being governed in the name of some version of Marxism.

With the events of 1989 and 1990 in the former Soviet Union, Germany, Eastern Europe, and elsewhere, we saw the decline of Marxism. People were stunned by the rapidity and extent of political changes, from the fall of the Berlin Wall to the breakup of the Soviet Union. We have heard that the West has won the cold war, that communism has failed, that the free market has conquered, that democracy will be the wave of the future, that transition will be difficult and economies might collapse, and, even, that history has ended. Throughout the turmoil, we have heard that the ghost of Marx, finally, has been put to rest and that Marxism is dead.

Perhaps. But, as I write, more than a fifth of the Earth's people still live in countries that consider themselves to be Marxist to some degree and 1.2 billion Chinese are included among them. Moreover, many of the values and images of the future contained in Marxist thought remain with us, whatever the failures of the regimes that ruled in its name, and their appeal may be far from dead even among some of the peoples whose fellow countrymen and women have spearheaded the recent changes. Whatever the disappointments with command economies and the rejections of political repression, concerns for things that communist regimes promised remain, such as social justice, full employment, adequate health care for all, educational opportunities, housing, and the elimination of poverty.

It seems appropriate, thus, to reexamine the values and images of the future in Marxist thought, not only as part of the story of values in utopian thought, but also as an assessment of their validity and viability over the decades to come. Doing so may shed some light on whether Marxist theory was simply betrayed by incompetent, vile, or power-mad leaders or whether the theory is inherently flawed as a vision of a desirable future society and as a means of attaining it.

"Marx" and "Marxism"

Be cautioned. For Marx and Engels sometimes wrote jointly and sometimes separately and what appears under Marx's name may sometimes have been written by Engels without acknowledgement; volumes 2 and 3 of *Capital* were written by Engels and volume 4 by Karl Kautsky from Marx's notes. Also, of course, there have been many interpreters of Marx since. Thus, when I refer to "Marx" or "Marxism," I refer to a system of thought to which Marx, Engels, and others have contributed. It is not always a simple matter to separate, as some writers do, the *classical Marxism* of Marx, Engels, Lenin, Luxemburg, Trotsky, and Gramsci, the *vulgar Marxism* of Kautsky, Stalin, or Mao, and the *Western Marxism* that evolved in the universities of Western Europe since the 1930s and that emphasized philosophy and idealism (Callinicos 1982: 3–4).

Additionally, it is not always possible to describe what Marx thought at one time without fear of contradicting something he or Engels themselves may have written at some other time. What Marx wrote early in his life, for example, does not always agree with what he wrote later. Moreover, few writers have been written about at such great length by so many different people with more disagreement than have Marx and Engels. Thus, there may not exist any uncontroversial formulation of Marxist theory.

Three Marxist Images of the Future

Marx condemned utopians and denied his own utopian intentions vigorously and explicitly. In *The Communist Manifesto*, Marx and Engels (1962), for example, speak of the socialist and communist systems of Henri Saint-Simon, Charles Fourier, Robert Owen, and others. Although they see these utopian socialists as precursors to themselves and take many ideas from them, some of which they acknowledge, Marx and Engels thoroughly criticize their views. They state that the utopian socialists are not scientific, fail to appreciate the historical role of the working class, are opposed to political and revolutionary action, foster reactionary sects pandering to the bourgeoisie for support, propose only small experiments doomed to failure because they do nothing to change the social conditions of the larger society, and paint pictures of a future society that are mere fantasy.

Yet Marx himself created one of the most influential utopian visions in human history. The opening line of the *The Communist Manifesto* gave the thesis of the detailed historical analysis to come, "The history of all hitherto existing society is the history of class struggles" (Marx and Engels 1962: 9). Thus, the past was described. But the end of the struggle was in sight. Every school child now ought to know it's concluding call to arms, "The proletarians have nothing to lose but their chains. They have a world to win. Working men of all countries, unite!" If the call was heeded, they believed, then the future would be hastened into birth by the actions of the working class.

Thus, for all of Marx's denials that he was utopian, his work is prophetic as well as analytical, filled with images of the coming demise of capitalism and the subsequent rise of communist society. It is filled, that is, with a vision of an ultimate Other, future society more desirable than the capitalist society Marx knew and without which the past itself could not be understood. Leszek Kolakowski (1978: 525) says that Marxism "would not be Marxism without its claim to 'scientific knowledge' of the future."

I'm not referring merely to the few lapses into fantasy that Marx made when he wrote of people fishing in the morning, doing factory work in the afternoon, and (since he had no foreknowledge of the hypnotic effect of prime time television) reading Plato at home in the evening. Rather, I'm referring to the main body of his work: to his general theory of evolution that includes the "laws of capitalist development" from which a network of hundreds of interconnected predictions apparently are deduced. For example, Fred M. Gottheil (1966), culling the major works of Marx, finds 153 prophecies. They range from specific predictions, such as "The proletarian revolutions in England, America, and Holland may be attained by peaceful means" and "A Russo-German war will act as the midwife to the inevitable social revolution in Russia" (p. 189) to primary predictions such as "Production under communism will be planned" and "Distribution under communism will be according to needs" (p. 187).

The predictions can be divided into three major periods of the future:

1. Those that describe the development of capitalism from the present (when Marx was writing) up until the time of its collapse;
2. those that describe the transition from capitalism to communism, under the first phase of communism; and
3. those that describe the future communist society during its second and final phase.

The images of the future for each of these periods are quite distinct. For example, the period of capitalist development contains images of the increasing misery of the proletariat as unemployment increases, wages decline to subsistence levels, and the rate of profit falls. Marx depicts it as a period of increasing economic instability, polarization into two conflicting classes, the development of working-class consciousness, and, eventually, a final economic crisis and a working-class revolution overthrowing the inhuman, unjust, wasteful, and inefficient capitalist system

(Gottheil 1966). At the same time, though, the productive forces of society are developed under capitalism so that communism will be viable.

Although Marx analyzes as if everything depends on impersonal economic and social forces, he urges workers to act as if everything depends on them. Marx may have been what I called in chapter 3, volume 1 a "compatibilist determinist." If so, then he could believe that socialism was determined (not fated) at least partly because of people's predictable reactions to capitalism. That is, the workers' miserable conditions under capitalism would motivate them to struggle for a different economic system and this struggle would eventually be successful (Mills 1989). Capitalism, of course, though evolving continually into different social forms, has not collapsed in the sense or way envisioned by Marx.

By contrast to the image of the future of capitalism, the final stage of communism contains Marx's image of the good society after the "evils" of capitalism have been removed and the transition to communism has been completed. In this final stage, we can deduce from his theory, that there would be:

1. the end of antagonistic society (i.e., the end of warring social classes);
2. the disappearance ("withering away") of the state;
3. no private ownership (i.e., only one owner, the people);
4. no exploitation of some people by others;
5. no false consciousness;
6. a reduction of work hours;
7. the opportunity for each person to realize his or her own individual potential;
8. the end of alienation;
9. the end of inequality; and
10. the end of scarcity.

The values underlying these interrelated future developments are clearly similar to social harmony (e.g., the end of antagonistic society and warring social classes) and individual happiness (e.g., no exploitation, reduction of work hours, self-realization, the end of alienation) and a variety of derivative values not unlike those of the utopian socialists. Particularly, social unity, freedom in the sense of self-determination, equality, and self-realization are key values. Equality, in the final stage of communism, is defined by the aforementioned motto, "From each according to his abilities, to each according to his needs." Also, society would be organized coherently and rationally.

Perhaps because he is unwilling to admit that he is engaged in utopian construction, Marx fails to confront the threats to the validity of his assertions about the future. He confidently predicts on and on: "The rate of interest will continuously decline." Free education for all cannot occur under capitalism (Gottheil 1966: 190, 192). Marx seldom considers one of the futurist's major tenets: the uncertainty of the future. Recognizing such uncertainty should result in caution, in "a preference for reversible choices and a greater reluctance to impose certain [present] suffering for the sake of uncertain [future] benefits" (Elster 1985: 117).

Marx often writes so as to encourage the belief in unconditional future facts, a belief which, as we have seen, contemporary futurists judge to be fallacious. This may partly explain why Marx's ideas have sometimes been appropriated by fanatics and terrorists. What is to restrain them from taking the most heinous and dreadful present acts imaginable against others if they view such a certain future as justifying them? As Steven B. Smith (1987: 289) reminds us, for Marx, as for Hegel, "history is a 'slaughter bench,' and...until its end is reached there are no absolute constraints on the kinds of sacrifices the present generation can be expected to bear for the sake of the future."

Equality in the Transition Stage of Communism

The transition stage between capitalism and full communism was characterized by Marx in both political and economic terms. Politically, it would contain the "dictatorship of the proletariat." Marx did not mean, however, the antidemocratic image that these terms conjure up for us today. Rather, he meant majority rule operating outside the legal system of the old society (how could it be otherwise if the society was undergoing fundamental change?) and the dismantling of the state apparatus. Economically, it would be a form of state capitalism (Elster 1985: 448–49).

Although, Marx condemned the inequalities of capitalism and valued a more egalitarian system ultimately, he said that the first phase of communism, the transition stage from capitalism, had to be inegalitarian. In his *Critique of the Gotha Program* which he wrote in 1875 as a response to a draft program of the German Workers' Party, Marx (1962) attacked egalitarianism. What concerned Marx when he wrote the *Critique* was the immediate future after the revolution and the early days of establishing the communist system on the legacies of capitalism.

He criticized the idea of "instant equality" and the proposition that equality means social justice. For the transition period, his motto was a meritocratic one like Saint-Simon's: "From each according to his abilities, to each according to his work," allowing, of course, for certain deductions for administration, costs of production, and social welfare payments. Marx dismissed those who favored equality as a goal in the early stages of communism as failing to recognize the need for technological developments that would be the foundations on which full, mature communism would be constructed. Without such development, equality would mean merely sharing poverty, an equality of paltriness. The productive capacities of society had to be increased before the second stage of communism with its egalitarianism could begin.

Thus, Marx valued an equality of plenty, but not an equality of destitution and privation. Presumably, people would have to be motivated to work by unequal rewards until productive capacities and levels of living were high, abundance sufficient to satisfy everyone's needs was achieved, and automated machines took over much of the production (Whitney 1962).

A Static Image of the Future

It is ironic that Marx, whose theory of the transitions from feudal to capitalist to socialist society and whose analysis of capitalism are thoroughly dynamic and change oriented, brings history—or, as he sometimes wrote "prehistory"—to an end in the second stage of communism. It is doubly ironic, given his explicit critique of the utopian socialists, that he appears to succumb to the pitfall of perfection. Marx, too, gives a "perfect" end of history in the implications of his theory for the second stage of communism, despite his explicit denial of giving any picture of utopia at all.

Implicit in the logic of Marx's theory is the conclusion that he shuts off the engine of social change in the second stage of communism. There will be no more class struggle. Hence, the engine of change-producing conflict is turned off.

Some Marxist scholars have denied this conclusion. Callinicos (1982: 158), for example, says that the class struggle is not the motor of history but a resultant of the "competitive struggle between capitals—which provide the objective framework within which the struggle between capital and labour unfolds." But, presumably, such competitive struggle will end, too, so the future appears to remain static.

Cohen (1978) devotes much of his book to denying the theoretical centrality of the class struggle to Marx's vision of historical development. Rather, referring to Marx's preface to *A Contribution to the Critique of Political Economy*, he emphasizes, as the engine of change, the contradiction between the forces of production and the relations of production. But once again, in the final stage of communist society, presumably, this contradiction, too, would be eliminated.

Perhaps we can reinterpret Marx's theory as being based upon still another engine of change, technological innovation. To adopt this view, indeed, does permit a picture of a communist (utopian) society that remains dynamic. But it distorts some of Marxist thought and creates other problems of inconsistency and logic, such as not explaining how conflicts of interest will be prevented. Also, some writers, such as Callinicos (1982: 142–48), vigorously deny that Marx was a technological determinist.

Finally, another possibility for an engine of change in communist society may be found in Marx's discussion of the development of human capacities and needs (and hence the continued invention of new wants and ideals), but at least some of these are collectively self-defeating as far as the *equality* of self-realization is concerned, for example, "the need for relative excellence" which cannot be achieved by everyone (Elster 1985: 69).

Obviously, neither perfection (however attractive an idea) nor an end to social change is credible, as long as there are living people around to create and tinker with human societies. There remain the challenges of hereditary and nutritional changes that may produce individual differences and the possibility of innovative behavior; incomplete socialization from one generation to the next during which some old patterns of behavior may fade from view; variations in population size, in birth and death rates, and age distributions through time that invite or demand structural changes; the problems of the human-environmental relationships (e.g., air, water, food, the disposal of waste) and newly invented ways of solving them; nonconformity, including both below and above average role performances that can lead to new behaviors; and the indefinite possibilities of the invention of new wants and ideals and improved ways of achieving them (Moore 1963). All these things can lead to continuing innovations and social change and only the last appears to be fully included in Marx's thought.

The main conclusion, however, remains: compared with his analysis of capitalism, Marx gives no clear-cut and powerful engine of change once the second stage of communism is reached. This may simply mean that once the class struggle no longer existed, then some other engine of change would develop about which Marx felt it would be pointless to speculate. Prehistory would end with the second stage of communism, but "real" human history would then begin, free from the barbarities of class society (Mills 1989). But Marx's readers are left largely in the dark about what forces of social change will remain.

An Attempt to Justify Values Scientifically

There are several different arguments given by Marx, mostly implicitly, to justify the values that for him define the good society. One is the familiar recourse to human nature, although in Marx it is complicated by both needs and capacities, the latter, when developed, giving rise to new needs. For Marx, it is desirable that "true" or "genuine" needs be fulfilled. Such needs flow from Marx's conception of the "true nature" of humans which differs both from nature in the sense of environment and human nature in the sense of biological needs, by transcending present facts into possibilities for the future. Thus, there is a dialectic at work.

Additionally, for Marx, man's social being was an important part of human nature. This opened the door to the possibility of justifying values by requirements of social life itself, some of which may be universal. Indeed, there are preconditions for social life, conditions that must be met to make social life possible, as we'll see in chapter 4.

There is another kind of justification that Marx offers, one that seemingly validates a moral judgment by a scientific theory and fact. It is found throughout Marx in his efforts to show by his scientific analysis the inevitability of future developments and, hence, of the values that such developments served. It can be illustrated by the concept of "exploitation."

Exploitation provides a major moral justification for class-hatred on the part of the proletariat for the bourgeoisie. Moreover, it also provides outside observers with an objective basis to make normative judgments. "Exploitation is wrong; exploiters are morally condemnable; a society that tolerates or generates exploitation ought to be abolished" (Elster 1985: 166). It justifies righteous indignation.

But exploitation is also a scientific concept within Marxist theory. Marx defines the rate of exploitation by the relation between surplus value and the wages actually paid the worker. The labor necessary for the production of those things indispensable to the life of the worker and his family is, according to Marx, less than the labor given by the worker to his/her employer within a working day. The difference, allowing for deductions of the cost of materials, distribution, and administration, is surplus value, and it is appropriated by the capitalist.

Here is a concrete, quantitative number to measure exploitation. Exploitation is objectified. A scientific analysis is linked directly to and supports a moral judgment. What an extraordinary, dual-purpose word "exploitation" is in Marxist thought, since it is both a key concept in a scientific theory with empirical grounding *and* accusatory, value-laden, and morally judgmental.

Thus, even though he dismissed writings "about justice and fairness as bourgeois ideology," Marx was engaged in a deeply moral enterprise. It is true that Marx, and especially Engels, were contradictory and ambiguous on this point, condemning moralizing while also visualizing the truly moral. As a result, "dogmatic Marxists," as Eugene Kamenka (1972:2) says, "have vacillated helplessly between the belief that Marxism is a 'value-free' science which destroys the very basis of moralism and exposes moral demands as no more than economic interests in disguise and the belief that Marxism is the most progressive, the most humane and the most ethical of all world-views."

But what is undebatable is that Marx condemned capitalism as unjust both on the grounds that labor was wrongly separated from the means of production and also "on the grounds of distributive injustice"; moreover, he laced his analysis of capitalism with condemnatory labels, such as "robbery," "theft," "embezzlement," and "fraud" (Elster 1985: 216, 222). His scientific theory purportedly explains why exploitation amounts to cheating the workers and why it should be judged as morally wrong.

But is it valid as a moral theory? Elster (1985: 228–29) gives three reasons why it is not. All three have to do with the fact that people differ and, therefore, might justly end up in employee-employer relationships. These differences are inborn skills (which lead to inevitable inequalities because some people can do some things better than others), leisure-income preferences (which, if some people prefer leisure to income, allow an interpretation in some cases that the poor exploit the rich), and time preferences (which allow some people who are willing to defer gratification to save and accumulate wealth, rather than to consume, and, which, thus, allow them to hire others "to the benefit of all parties").

Also, every modern economy, if it is going to continue to exist and possibly grow, requires that part of the annual production must be accumulated to maintain, replace, improve upon, or create machinery or other tools of production. Moreover, in addition to the costs of materials, distribution, and administration are the incentives and costs of entrepreneurial risk taking. "Marx never really catches on to something that Adam Smith knew—that what makes things is not labor but know-how, and that part of this know-how lies in the administration of decision-making processes in relation to property and exchange" (Boulding 1985: 198). Without capitalists, for example, would workers have had anything that capitalists could rob them of? (Elster 1985: 225). Thus, we are back where we started. The judgment of how much workers should receive in the form of wages and how much capitalists should receive in the form of profits cannot be so easily objectified and determined. It remains debatable.

Finally, after reviewing the arguments for and against the view that Marx made critical normative judgments, Norman Geras (1989: 266–67) concludes that indeed he did and that his ethical commitments not only included the values of freedom, self-development, human well-being and happiness, but also "the ideal of a just society in which these things are decently distributed."

The fact that Marx publicly denied and repressed his own ethical commitments represents an inconsistency on Marx's part. When they followed this obfuscation, socialist authorities not only confused themselves and others, but they also encouraged a moral cynicism that disgraced socialism by condoning tragic crimes against humanity.

Is Self-Realization Feasible?

In addition to justice, another attractive Marxist value is self-realization. Marx condemned capitalism because it prevented human development and self-actualization (Elster 1985: 83). In contrast, under communism, the free development of each person will become the condition for the free development of all, an equality of self-realization through creative work and a unity of individual self-realization and the community. Obviously, the repression typical of those regimes calling themselves Marxist actually suppressed self-realization. But, putting that aside, let's look at the goal of self-realization simply from a theoretical standpoint.

There are several difficulties with self-realization that have led some writers to conclude that it is not feasible as a master, underlying human value on which we can base our efforts to construct the good future society. For example, some needs are more expensive than others, and as a result, some people put far more demands than others on what are inevitably limited resources (Dworkin 1981). The goal of creativity, often emphasized by Marx as an important aspect of self-realization, may demand some kind of consumers, such as audiences, viewers, readers, listeners, and so on who may not be available, especially if they are out pursuing their own goals of creative fulfillment (Elster 1985: 232). Also, as Elster (1985: 51, 54) says, it may be unrealistic to assume, as Marx appeared to do, that anyone and everyone wants to, can, and will do everything.

Other difficulties include the overly demanding nature of self-realization (would some people prefer passive consumption?); raising self-realization to the central value of society might result in narcissism or self-indulgence; much essential work in modern society does not allow great latitudes of self-realization; some activities needed by some people to realize themselves might be by their very nature abhorrent to most other people (witness the uproar and charges of pornography that greeted the photography exhibit of Robert Mapplethorpe in the United States); and there is no guarantee that self-realization will produce the technical efficiency in society as a whole that is its precondition (Elster 1985: 522–26).

Despite these criticisms, I believe that the value of self-realization through creative work, within limits, can be used as one justifiable criterion of the good society. Just as freedom is limited for any one individual if it results in the encroachment on the freedom of others, so, too, any one individual's self-realization must be restrained by the impact it may have on narrowing the self-realization of others, and, of course, on the material conditions that make it possible.

Clearly, this is related to Rousseau's struggle with understanding the relationship between the individual and the community. Except for a Robinson Crusoe on his deserted island before the appearance of Friday, self-realization must be considered in a social context. It can be facilitated and retarded, widened and constricted by the self-realization of others because of the existence of interdependent social relationships with other people and because some forms of self-realization depend directly upon others. Furthermore, it can be evaluated not only as to its benefits to the individual, but also as to its benefits to the community. For some forms of self-realization may enrich the entire community as well as the individual.

Thus, self-realization, no less than freedom, is a serviceable criterion for making value judgments about the good society, especially if the focus of judgment is on the equality of opportunity for its achievement and if it is used along with other criteria, such as doing no harm to others.

In sum, Marx was engaged in a moral purpose and had an implicit theory of morality contained within a science of society. That theory of morality, however, was flawed and, ultimately, unconvincing. Moreover, the fact that Marx explicitly denied the independent causal influence of ethics and attacked mere moralizing led to a tragic unintended consquence. He and his followers never consciously came to grips with the moral dilemmas involved in the relationship of means to ends. Nor did they address ethical questions directly, armed as they were with what appeared to be scientific proof of the inevitability of their ends. Thus, they saw no moral conflict as human freedom was extinguished, justice denied, and people murdered in the name of the good communist society to come (Lukes 1985).

An Overtly Futurist Variant of Marxism

Ernst Bloch (1954–59), who claimed to be working in the Marxist tradition, is worth noting because of his overtly futurist orientation. Bloch, a German philosopher, who was born in 1885 and who died in 1977, emphasized the existence of possibilities and the importance of human will and hope in their realization. Hope, for him, was something more than mere idle dreaming. It involved a kind of knowledge, revealing what the real possibilities are. He showed the existence of "anticipatory consciousness" throughout history, focused on the "Not Yet," and emphasized the propensities, tendencies, and latencies of things. He understood that the future, even though it does not yet exist, has some reality in the possibilities latent in the present. With the guiding hand of humans, the ultimate future will be either perfection or destruction. Bloch believed, according to Kolakowski (1978: 421), that the "significance of being is revealed only in acts directed towards the future."

Some of the things that Bloch said about possibilities makes good sense if placed within a more limited framework of giving reasons for speculations about the future. Many possibilities for the future, as we have seen, indeed *do* exist in the present and their realization sometimes certainly *does* depend, contingently, on human choice and action.

Although modern futurists would agree that the future should not be condemned to the limitations of the present, most seek more solid foundations for their beliefs about alternative futures than Bloch gave. Bloch, even though he made scientific claims for his own views, was basically antiscience and gave little of convincing substance in its place for the validity of his views. Kolakowski (1978: 421–49) argues that Bloch scorned mere facts, empiricism, and logic. He condemned positivism. He gave no empirical explanations or logical reasons for his views and denounced people who asked for them. He confused the distinction between foreseeing the future and creating the future, and wrapped his views of the future in mysticism and obscurantism. Perfection was clearly a major value, but it is not clear what he meant by it in concrete terms.

Some other self-identified followers of Marx were also antiscience, antipositivist, and antiempiricist. Take Herbert Marcuse, for example. A darling of the New Left in the 1960s, he is best known for his book, *One-Dimensional Man* (1970), in which he proposed a future of sexual liberation, among other things. His attack on positivism (the "worship of facts") was unrelenting and at the center of his critique of technological civilization (Kolakowski 1978: 396–420).

Were Bloch, Marcuse, and others simply distorting Marx or was there some basis in Marx for their antiscientific views?

A Developmental, Reflexive Science

Certainly, much of Marx's work can be viewed as scientific, because Marx gathers evidence, formulates theories consistent with the evidence, and gives worldly reasons for his projections into the future. "Scientific socialism" gets its science label mostly from Marx's labors with theory and data. At the same time, there are romantic elements in Marx that stray from the scientific path. More important, Marx was, after all, struggling to make assertions about the future and we have seen how many logical pitfalls there are in that effort.

Despite his scientific claims, Marx upon occasion did attack facts and science if they described only the surface of present realities without taking into account how realities were changing or how they could change. Also, he did not abide a factual description of the present that implied, often through scientific explanation, why or how social realities *had* to be as they were. It may be true, as Marcuse said, that sometimes science is conservative and "affords no ground for social protest" because it encourages acceptance, as well as understanding, of present conditions (Kolakowski 1978: 409). But it is not true of science that it necessarily ignores possibilities for change.

Marx often merged the "what is" and the "what will be" in the idea of "becomingness," for example in some "inevitable" future development. One analogy is that of a tiny seed that has within it the capacity to become a great tree. Marx was constantly looking for the tree in the seed and not simply describing the seed in its present condition, not as an immanent development but as a path-dependent social development in which each step or stage puts additional constraints on later developments. Capitalism, to repeat the cliché, contains the seeds of its own destruction, that is, the seeds can become the giant trees of socialism.

Modern science, of course, is filled with examples of developmental thinking such as this—human fetuses to adult men and women, tadpoles to frogs, caterpillars to butterflies. The idea is commonplace. With elimination of the immanent, fatalistic element, the analogy can be brought over to social science, as Lasswell did with his developmental analysis. Obviously, there is seldom the rigid developmental necessities in social life between present and future states as in biology. Few of us today would be willing to accept Marx's implications that "what is coming to be" is somehow more truly real or necessarily more moral than "what is."

The wholesale condemnation of science such as made by Bloch, Marcuse, and others is misplaced. True, some scientists may not observe the tree in the seed and describe, measure, and explain only the seed as it is. But other scientists will see the potential for the tree. The failure to see one or the other is not inherent in science, but in the limitations of particular scientists or in the particular perspectives with which they may be working at the time.

Somewhat in Marx and overwhelmingly in Bloch, beliefs about "what will be" were shaped by their judgments of "what ought to be." There is an obvious danger in this, because wishful thinking can become so contrary to the facts and real possibilities for the future as to be dangerously misleading. Marx worked mightily to support his assertions with empirical evidence and scientific theorizing. Bloch did not.

Yet when "what ought to be" is asserted and communicated to others, it itself becomes a fact in the situation and a possible factor in shaping the future through influencing human action—whether it be a communist manifesto or a Pope's encyclical letter. Thus, if enough people judge some alternative, as yet nonexistent future as morally right and more desirable than what now exists, their judgment and its expression can manifest itself in social action and become a force for social change. Thus, Marxist theory is not only developmental, but also reflexive.

Of course, all of these processes—identifying present possibilities for the future, judging the good, the effects of the judging on people's subsequent actions, and the social consequences of such actions—can be studied scientifically. It may be difficult and complex and may challenge a researcher's ingenuity in given cases, but it is in principle possible. But this does not mean, obviously, that anything is possible, no matter what, even if it is judged as good and even if people work mightily to bring it about. Their efforts may fail.

Marxism Today

Regarding the role of values in utopian thought, Marx illustrates a strategy of justifying values that links science and morality. True, just as some other utopians did, he appeals to human nature, emphasizing the unfolding of the social being of human beings, as the justification of his values. There is already some blurring of the line between fact and value in this view. For example, the "facts" of human nature imply certain human needs that "ought" to be fulfilled and reveal capacities for potential development that are inevitable (if nature is allowed to run its course).

But Marx goes further. He can be read as trying to derive a moral judgment from a social scientific theory in his analysis of surplus value. On the one hand, he formulates a theory that explains certain facts of economic and social relations (e.g., the theory of surplus value). On the other hand, the same theory gives a basis for a moral judgment that existing society is unjust. It is a brilliant fusion of facts and values. It is a fusion, moreover, that may explain much of Marxism's mass political appeal. For Marxism as a system of thought is not only a social scientific theory based on facts and logic, but also an image of a just future that contains both its own justification of its morality and a plan of action to help historical forces bring it into being.

Today, we know that most of the political regimes that have come into being claiming to be Marxist have soiled the name by their political tyrannies, economic failures, and social inadequacies. "The worker in Communist countries," as Eugene Kamenka (1986: 20) points out, "is [or was] as alienated as the worker in Western countries and much poorer and more regimented." As early as 1976–77, a group of young Parisian intellectuals, the *nouveaux philosophes*, "produced a series of books and articles in which they proclaimed marxism a machine for the construction of concentration camps" (Callinicos 1982: 5). Certainly, the Soviet Union under Stalin, Kampuchea under Pol Pot, or Romania under Ceausescu were not what Marx envisioned.

At the same time, developed capitalist countries have changed in ways that Marx did not foresee, improving the conditions of major sections of the working classes and reaching unprecedentedly comfortable average levels of living. Capitalism today is not the same system that Marx attacked. Moreover, it is constantly changing (Boulding 1985: 198).

Marxist thought, just as Marxist regimes, also has been discredited. Its theoretical and logical inconsistencies have been revealed, the failure of many of its predictions demonstrated, and its shortcomings in understanding modern social developments pointed out. Some scholars, thus, have concluded that Marxism is dead as a serious intellectual system. Kolakowski (1978: 530) says that today what passes under the name of Marxism "changes content from one situation to another and is crossbred with other ideological traditions. At present Marxism neither interprets the world nor changes it."

But such a view is too simple and too negative. First, Marx demonstrated the utility of the concept of modes of production (or social formations) in the comparative study of societies, the concept of class as a fruitful way of looking at social cleavages, and the idea that ideologies are conditioned by social circumstances, among other things.

Second, classical Marxist theory has some continued relevance in today's world. Certainly neither monetarism nor Keynesianism offer acceptable explanations of the periodic economic crises of modern capitalism. Marx's theory of state capitalism does. In particular, it helps explain how "competition on a world scale has come to be dominated by multinational firms closely integrated in the national state" (Callinicos 1982: 223).

Tony Cliff (1974) contends that so-called socialist regimes, including the former Soviet Union, were largely examples of bureaucratic collectivism or state bureaucratic capitalism and, as such, their development into politically repressive and economically stagnant regimes can be explained by classical Marxism. We have yet to see, to continue this line of reasoning, a true workers' socialist regime.

Yet there remain inherently tragic consequences of social action that flow from reasonable interpretations of Marxist theory, even classical Marxist theory. That theory fails to recognize adequately the uncertainty of the future, while encouraging the belief in unconditional future facts; it allows an unrestrained willingness to compel present generations to make huge and intolerable sacrifices for the sake of uncertain benefits to future generations; it commits its followers to irreversible choices; it fosters moral indignation and class hatred based on a false explanation of exploitation; and it explicitly banishes a direct, conscious consideration of ethical concerns and, hence, implicitly endorses a willingness to adopt immoral means to achieve the "good" communist society to come. The result, as we all know too well, was to extinguish human freedom within existing regimes claiming to be Marxist.

What, then, explains Marxism's appeal for the dispossessed, downtrodden, and oppressed people of the world as well as for some intellectuals? For some, no doubt, its very flaws are—and will remain—its attractions: the certainty, the apparent scientific explanation of exploitation as theft, and the promise of guaranteed success in the irreversible rise of the working class.

But there is more to it than that. The image of the good society underlying Marxist theory includes valid universal appeals to all humankind. It includes, as we have seen, the end of alienation, the end of warring classes, and the end of unfair inequalities. It includes the promise of high levels of productivity and high levels of living, social justice, and freedom in the sense of self-determination, the development of human capacities, and self-realization. It includes an image of a future in which all authentic needs would be met and a plan of action to help historical forces bring it into being. It includes the promise of a coherent and rational organization of society. It includes the major values contained in most utopian writings throughout the ages: social harmony and individual happiness.

The smugness we felt in the West in the early and mid-1990s with the failures of many communist regimes fresh in our minds can be tempered with the fact that such values are not uniquely Marxist. Rather, they are worthy goals for humankind. No doubt, people will keep striving for them in the future. If they cannot be achieved under democratic, capitalist systems, then some other systems will be invented, perhaps some further modified form of Marxism.

Can we in the West afford to be smug with homeless men and women sleeping in our streets? With millions of people living below the poverty line? With children dropping out of school or graduating from secondary school without adequate skills of reading and writing? With our urban cores being battlegrounds for warring gangs, drug dealings and conflict, and sometimes unsafe for ordinary citizens? With health care costs soaring beyond the means of many working- and middle-class people? With garbage and toxic wastes creeping into our air, water, and food? With some of our business and political leaders corrupted by greed? And with our willingness to hate members of other races and ethnic groups both in and out of our own countries? Has capitalism succeeded or has it, too, failed?

Additionally, our smugness in the West can be tempered by the fact that, although the collapse of the Soviet system may have been a victory for human freedom, it was also a defeat for human aspirations. The idea that government intervention in society can produce human betterment was dealt a crushing blow. Capitalism may remain the dominant economic system for generations to come, but considerable public spending—or, more accurately, investment—in education, basic research, health, and infrastructure, such as transporation and communication, financed both by taxes and public borrowing probably is essential for success (Heilbroner 1993).

Finally, for futurists and nonfuturists alike, Marx provides important lessons. He underscored the importance of looking for possibilities, things as they could or might be as well as things as they were or are. He showed the usefulness of images of the future in understanding the past and the present. He demonstrated the power to change the world contained in an image of the future, showing that a prophecy once made becomes not only a fact in the world but a catalyst for change. He incorporated and gave life to the idea that humans can, through action, change their own circumstances and, thus, can change themselves as well as society.

Also, his followers have, quite unintentionally, given us a cautionary tale: they have illustrated the dangers of believing in the certainty of the future, revealing how true believers can become oppressors in the present in the name of what they believe to be a coming future without oppression.

Conclusion

In this chapter, we barely scratched the surface of the immense utopian literature. Since Marx, for example, there have been thousands of utopias written. Some of them—from Edward Bellamy and H. G. Wells to Aldous Huxley and George Orwell—have been significant factors in shaping human thought and development. Bellamy is of particular note, since his work was seen as an alternative to Marxism. In 1888, he published *Looking Backward, 2000–1887*. More than a million copies were sold. In fact, in the nineteenth century only *Uncle Tom's Cabin* sold more copies in the United States. It became the most influential utopian work every written by an American. Among other things, Bellamy predicted a peacful transition from capitalism to a kind of socialism in which order, efficiency, and equality were valued. Bellamy's ideas were widely followed in the United States and Europe and served to fuel a variety of social reform efforts through Bellamy Clubs.

But this illustrative summary must stop somewhere and, by now, the reader ought to be prepared for a few major conclusions about the history of utopian thought. Briefly summarized, they are: First, utopian writers base their better or perfect society on some identifiable values, such as social harmony and individual happiness, or equality, justice, freedom, or self-realization. There is, to be sure, a diversity of values comparing one utopian writer with another, yet, despite this diversity, the same basic values tend to recur over and over again.

Second, utopian writers differ, within a somewhat limited range, in the type of justification they give—or take for granted—to support their basic values. Each writer, however, has such a justification, usually more than a single type. In the *Republic*, for example, although Plato appeals to both divine power and to nature, it is primarily reason that drives his argument, a rational, hypothetico-deductive system of thinking, a kind of thought experiment. For Thomas More, it is God, although both nature and reason sometimes reveal His will. For Rousseau, it is nature and society. For the utopian socialists, it is nature and human nature. For

Marx, it is the potential in the social nature of man himself, and it is scientific lawful, and therefore inevitable, social development. God, Nature, Reason, Human Nature, and, to a lesser extent, Society and Science in one form or another, separately or together, recur in utopians' attempts to justify their values.

Also, with the notable exception of those writers reacting to the chaos of the French Revolution such as the utopian socialists, there is a shift through time toward justifying values by appealing to the People, toward democratic theory, and toward social inclusivism, that is, toward taking into account the well-being of everyone in a given territory as a member of society on an equal basis with everyone else.

Third, much of the utopian literature rightfully belongs to the history of social science. Even though the earliest works generally are fiction, especially when dealing with the construction of perfect societies, they include, in varying degrees of explicitness, analyses and critiques of actual, existing societies.

In the descriptive and analytic concepts they used to portray individuals and societies, both real and fictitious, utopian writers anticipated many modern social science concepts. In those cases where utopians moved from thought to action and attempted to create real models of their perfect societies, as did followers of the utopian socialists, they also pointed the way to social experimentation and applied social science, to a concern about social cause and effect and human engineering.

Also, some utopian writers, such as Condorcet, the utopian socialists, and Marx, added a self-conscious attempt to construct social science in order both to know and to shape the future. It was a social science, however, that combined both the true and the good. Today, disavowing or being ignorant of most of their utopian history, many contemporary social scientists have lost both a part of their heritage and a part of their mission. In their efforts to split values off from their concern with social facts as beyond scientific inquiry, contemporary scientists *qua* scientists have abdicated their moral responsibilities and left important moral judgments about the proper uses of knowledge to others.

Fourth, the well-recognized trends toward secularization, rationality, human mastery, and other aspects of modernization can be observed in the utopian literature as well as in the larger society. There is a long-term trend toward the perspective that human beings, not God or nature, create their own social worlds, and they do so in some real place here on

Earth in this life, not in heaven or some otherworldly place. They do so using reason and analyzing nature, human nature, and society. Most important, they do so by creating images of the desired future and taking individual and collective actions to bring them into reality.

But there remains in the contemporary world a great diversity of views, almost as if every dominant world view of the past remains with us today, expounded by some group or other, no matter how small or large, somewhere in the world. Refuting some utopian beliefs in ways convincing to everyone appears to be more difficult than creating them. Moreover, in the general society, religion, as we'll see in chapter 3, can be expected to remain an important source of belief for the indefinite future.

Fifth, utopian writing is a reaction to social existence, to what is going on in the world. Utopian writing does not occur in a vacuum. For example, Aristophanes reacted to widespread judicial corruption and to war, Defoe's Robinson Crusoe to the promises of capitalism and modernization, Sade to the turmoil of the French Revolution, and Marx to both the evils and potential benefits of capitalism. Utopians provide warnings about and alternatives to the social world as it is and where it appears to be heading. They provide an Other as a creative response, by picturing how the social world might be or ought to be, or, contrariwise in the case of dystopias, how it should never be allowed to become. Thus, utopian writing aims to change the social world.

Sixth, utopian writing reached a watershed in the late eighteenth century when a dramatic shift in the location of utopian society occurred, from a different place in space to a different location in time, the future. Before Condorcet, most utopias were located in the present but at another place, separated from existing societies by geographical space. After Condorcet, most utopias were located in the future, separated from existing societies by time. Although I have not discussed it here, it is worth noting that, with the rise of modern science fiction, utopias elsewhere in the universe became separated from earthly societies by both space *and* time.

In the next chapter, I continue the discussion of human values and the moral judgments that underlie preferable futures. I try to show that, although Marx failed to do so adequately, it is possible to be scientific when making moral judgments. Thus, we continue the discussion of how society *ought* to be.

2

Making Value Judgments Objectively:
How do We Decide What is Preferable?

Introduction

Whether they intended to do so or not, many utopian writers were doing human or social science. They were describing and analyzing both the existing societies of their day and some other, more desirable society that they had imaginatively created. For example, Condorcet, the utopian socialists, Marx—even More and Rousseau—were doing human science in this sense. Much of the history of utopian thought, thus, deserves a place in the history of human and social science.

As carried out by utopians, human science, as we have seen, included more than ostensibly true descriptions and analyses of then-current social realities and their possibilities for improvement. It also included moral evaluations of them, an ethical dimension. According to utopian writers (and I include Marx), some social arrangements were good, decent, beneficial, fair, or compatible with human nature and others were not. Some deserved praise, others condemnation.

As the social sciences continued to develop, particularly in Britain and the United States, they directly and explicitly incorporated this ethical dimension. That is, pioneer social scientists continued to combine ethical prescription with scientific analysis. But beginning about the time of the First World War, values began to be banned from social science by social scientists who came to view ethics as inappropriate to the study of society based on natural science models. In the United States, for example, these views came to dominate the social sciences in the decades after the Second World War. By that time, "moral concerns were regarded as an intrusion more characteristic of muckrakers, do-gooders, and reformers than appropriate to new disciplines striving for professional status" (Bulmer 1983: 163). By then, science—including social science—was supposed to be "value-free."

In the case of the social sciences, there are, of course, some obvious exceptions to the view that values have been banned and that science is value-neutral. Economics, for example, has Paretian optimality, efficiency, real growth in GNP per capita, and other measures that describe a desirable end state, although not without challenge (from some environmentalists, for example, who question whether continued economic growth is always a good thing). Additionally, the applied, policy, or action-oriented wings of each of the social sciences, from clinical psychology to evaluation research in sociology, necessarily have reference to some valued end or condition (Kimmel 1988). In these cases, however, the underlying values being served, usually of some client or sponsor, are seldom questioned or critically examined. Generally, they are accepted on some extra-scientific basis.

There are, as well, codes of professional ethics for various social scientific groups, although they are more often collections of current right practices than a reasoned justification of the principles underlying them. Also, with the rise of postmodern thought, the belief in the possibility of value neutrality has declined. Today, even research done for the sake of theory has come to be seen as serving the values and interests of some groups as opposed to others. Many people have come to believe that there is and can be no value-free science.

Despite these examples, most contemporary social scientists, unlike their utopian predecessors, believe that the task of making value judgments objectively is impossible. The current orthodoxy among scientists is that moral propositions or value judgments, unlike factual statements, cannot be shown to be true or false by scientific methods. This has been the standard view for many decades, often supported in the social sciences by references to the early twentieth-century arguments of Max Weber (1949). Derek L. Phillips (1986: 5), whose own views are to the contrary, documents the continuity in this view and its continued hold over the thinking of contemporary scientists and social scientists.

This dogma has such a grip on contemporary social scientists that they seem impervious to any arguments to the contrary. For example, in recent years several efforts have been made to give methods of objectively justifying values and of incorporating them into the discourse of social science (Foss 1977; Haan 1983; and Phillips 1986). But they have been largely ignored.

In this chapter, I reexamine the belief that value judgments cannot be shown to be true or false and invite the reader to view it with an open mind. For there are some reasonable grounds to question it.

Most persuasive, however, may be to demonstrate how values can be objectively tested. Then, abstract arguments about whether we can do so or not seem irrelevant. We simply do it and show how. Toward that end, in this chapter I describe three models—commitment-deducibility, means-ends, and epistemic implication—by which to bring a moral dimension back to the center of the critical discourse of human science. The last model is by far the most powerful. Using epistemic implication, we can make objective tests of the grounds on which value assertions rest and, thereby, show that some warrant our reasonble belief because they survive serious attempts to falsify them and others do not.

Thus, in evaluating preferable futures, I propose to go beyond studying the preferences of respondents, either ordinary citizens or experts or individual informants, as described in some of the methods discussed in chapter 6, volume 1. I propose to go beyond, too, merely stating the values underlying an image of a desirable future, justified by no more than opinion, expertise, or authority. I propose, additionally, to go beyond the justifications of the utopians given in the last chapter, although I have built upon them.

I demonstrate that moral assertions and value judgments can be as logically and empirically sound as scientific predictions. Objective methods, that is to say, can be used to justify assertions about what *ought to be* and about what we *ought to do* in about the same way as they are used to justify assertions about what can be, what might be, and what will be.

Moreover, given the increasing recognition of the uncertainty and corrigibility of scientific knowledge itself, moral assertions and value judgments may be as open to valid grounding as are truth statements about what was and what is. The critical realist theory of knowledge can incorporate the testing of value propositions just as it tests truth claims about the past and present.

Futurists, of course, have no choice but to incorporate human values and goals and their evaluation into their discourse. By the very nature of futures studies, they, and policy scientists more generally, necessarily deal with moral evaluation since they aim their work toward social betterment. Thus, futurists bring the utopian program into their work. As a result, futures studies today may point the way to the human sciences of the twenty-first century by restoring the "good" to scientific inquiry into the human condition.

Two final introductory comments are necessary. First, to attempt to be rational and objective about value judgments, about morality, about what is good and evil is not in the slightest to be without emotion. Thinking is absolutely essential for emotion. No emotion ever occurs without it. Thinking about people and events, interpreting our experiences, giving meaning to things are what produce emotions. "Without meaning," for example, "emotion would be reduced to pleasant or unpleasant sensations of bodily arousal." The meanings that we give to things are what cause our emotions (Baumeister 1991: 19).

Interpreting another person's acts toward you as unjust, for example, is what guides your emotions toward, say, righteous indignation or anger. Judging your own behavior in some situation as being morally right may give you joy. Judging it as morally wrong and imagining counterfactually what you rightly might have done may give you feelings of regret. The emotion itself is dependent on what you think. Being objective about what you think helps make your interpretations accurate and your emotions appropriate to a given situation.

Second, I am not proposing that social science ought to be displaced by ideology. Irving Louis Horowitz (1993, 1994) has eloquently described the dangers of such a development. My aim is the exact opposite. I want to examine ideology, morality, ethics, and human values critically in open and civil discourse. I want to question them and subject the grounds on which they stand to objective test, especially to serious efforts to falsify them. Where possible, I want to displace the blind faith, ignorance, and fanaticism that may now support some value assertions by conjectural knowledge. Where not possible, that is, when currently held value assertions are refuted, then I want to begin a search for justified belief in alternatives. That is, if I hold a moral judgment and it is wrong, I want to know that it is wrong so that I can change it.

In this chapter, I begin with a discussion of the role of values in positivism and in postpositivism, showing how each has erred. Next, I describe three models or methods of evaluating moral assertions objectively, highlighting Keekok Lee's method of epistemic implication as being the most powerful. Then, I show that making ethical judgments is inherently future-oriented and rests on posits about the future. If this is so, then we can make some additions to epistemic implication to enhance its utility for futures studies. I conclude with some final comments about the nature of moral judgments and the future.

The Parallelism Betweeen Is/Will and Is/Ought

Remember David Hume's argument against induction. Take a premise: "I observed the sun rise today and yesterday." Draw a conclusion: "Therefore, the sun will rise tomorrow." The premise in an example such as this, Hume said, refers to some set of observed events that have occurred while the conclusion refers to another event that has not been observed and has not yet occurred, that is, to a future event. This, Hume argued, is logically defective because of the gap between the premise and the conclusion. A standard way to put the matter is to say that the premise contains "is" or "was," while the conclusion contains a new term "will" for which there is no strict logical connection. Although the sun may indeed rise tomorrow, the facts that it rose today and yesterday don't prove that it will.

As we all know, Hume has had a parallel argument attributed to him against deducing "ought" statements from "is" or "was" statements. The premise contains "is" or "was," while the conclusion contains a new term "ought" for which there is no strict logical connection. "I observe that fire burns my hand." From that premise, if Hume is correct, we cannot logically deduce, "Therefore, I ought not to stick my hand in the fire."

To reach such a conclusion would be to commit the "naturalistic fallacy," which has come to mean deducing "an evaluative conclusion from premises that are entirely nonevaluative" (Williams 1985: 122). The phenomenon of fire burning my hand, the argument goes, is a fact; the conclusion that I ought not to stick my hand in the fire is a prescriptive statement, a matter of preference, choice, decision, or judgment, but not a fact (Lee 1985).

Now here is a strange thing: the members of the scientific community, including both philosophers of science and social scientists, responded to these parallel arguments in contradictory ways. On the one hand, many shrugged off Hume's argument about not going from "is" to "will," while, on the other hand, they accepted the argument about not going from "is" to "ought." Skepticism among scientists regarding induction and prediction was largely suppressed. Thus, prediction, as we saw in chapter 2, volume 1, is widely accepted as a legitimate task and hallmark of science. At the same time, skepticism regarding the justification of value judgments has become orthodoxy. "Ought" statements, which were such an important part of the utopian enterprise, were banned from scientific discourse.

Of course, efforts to define the "good," to logically derive or empirically prove the "good," or to show the opposite, that no such derivation is logically valid or that no empirical proof is possible have preoccupied some thinkers from the beginnings of recorded history. One watershed in the search for a rational way of justifying moral judgments can be found in Immanuel Kant's *Foundations of the Metaphysics of Morals*, which appeared near the end of the eighteenth century. Another was G. E. Moore's *Principia Ethica*, which was published at the beginning of the twentieth century. Moore argues that the search for any critical basis for moral beliefs is fruitless, except for the principle of consistency (Lee 1985: 8).

Although the history of ethics and metaethics is well beyond the scope of this book, we must reconsider briefly the positivist program, especially that of the logical positivists of the Vienna Circle and Berlin Association. They were certainly not the first nor the only philosophers who have ever asserted the irreducibility of value judgments to existential statements, but they played an important role in defining the terms of current thinking about the possible objective justifications of values, morality, and ethical systems.

Values and Positivism

Deducibility

As we saw in chapter 5, volume 1, the positivists took as one of their major aims the systemization of knowledge. Taking mathematics as their model, they tried to show that empirical findings could be cast into a system of interrelated propositions, theorems, and subtheorems, that there was an underlying deductive structure to factual knowledge. Scientific knowledge, for them, in addition to having empirical reality as a referent, involved a hierarchical structure, subsumption of some statements by others, lawlike propositions, and the possibility of elaborating the interrelated system of statements according to rules of logic. Carl G. Hempel's

Deductive-Nomological approach is a good example. From antecedent conditions and laws, Hempel (1965) argues, empirical pheonomena can be explained through logical deduction.

The influence of the logical positivists on philosophical thinking, in the extreme, led to the dominance of the view that the only rational, unproblematic, and certain propositions were those that could be logically deduced in some strict sense. Thus, the logical positivists, by adopting strict logical derivability as the only legitimate relationship allowed between any two or more propositions, supported the belief that "ought" statements cannot be logically deduced from "is" statements, and that, thus, "ought" statements must be irrationally held (Lee 1985: 3).

Why didn't they reach the same conclusion in the case of predictive statements? Probably because, as we saw in chapter 5, volume 1 with the case of the older empiricists, they wrongly believed that knowledge of the future was basically the same type as observational knowledge because it can be confirmed or denied at a later time. "Ought" statements appeared to be different, because these same empiricists believed that they could not be confirmed at all, either now or later.

Empirical Import and Meaningfulness

Another aspect of logical positivism led to this same conclusion. For a proposition to be meaningful, the positivists claimed, at some point it must be amenable, directly or indirectly, to empirical test. They were not rationalists, deriving reality from a set of propositions, but positivists who demanded that theorizing be based on observations. Science, from this perspective, is a set of hierarchical statements about some aspect of reality that are true, or, that are at least partly empirically testable. To verify a proposition is to say that observations of some aspects of reality support the proposition. Or, in Popper's terms, the support may be through some hypothesis failing to be refuted. "Ought" propositions, the positivist argument goes, even though they may refer to concrete empirical instances, cannot be accepted or rejected by empirical test.

For example, categorical judgments of value, Hempel (1965: 85–86) says, such as "Killing is evil" do "not express an assertion that can be directly tested by observation." Can they be indirectly tested, then? "Again, the answer is clearly in the negative... 'Killing is evil' does not have the function of expressing an assertion that can be qualified as true or false;

rather, it serves to express a standard for moral appraisal or a norm of conduct.... Descriptive empirical import...is absent; in this respect a sentence such as 'Killing is evil' differs strongly from, say, 'Killing is condemned as evil by many religions', which expresses a factual assertion capable of empirical test."

Hempel appears to be inconsistent. We saw in chapter 2, volume 1 that he believes that the "is-to-will" problem is only a "minor inconvenience" about which he recommends wariness in factually grounding scientific discourse. He argues persuasively, demolishing arguments to the contrary, that "the claim that every adequate explanation is also a potential prediction...is sound" (p. 374). Yet, at the same time, he believes without doubt that the "is-to-ought" problem cannot be overcome and that it defeats the purpose of factually grounding moral discourse.

The Role of Values in Science

This is not to say that Hempel and other philosophers of science see no role at all for values in science. Quite to the contrary, following the sociologist Max Weber (1949), Hempel (1965: 81–96) enumerates multiple roles of values in science. They include the following:

1. The consequences of science are judged by some system of values outside of science. For example, science has solved some problems that people have valued, such as raising material levels of living, and science has created some other problems, such as the threats of nuclear wastes to human health. (He might have added that scientific work is judged by some system of values *within* science, too, for example, by theoretical relevance, amenability to empirical testing, congruence with the facts, efficiency and effectiveness of research design, technical competence, intellectual honesty and integrity, originality, theoretical importance of the results, and so on, although these are instrumental judgments related to the goal of science to create knowledge.)

2. A related point is that moral valuations external to science are required to make use of the "technical control" that science makes possible, that is, "instrumental judgments of value" can be made. For example, if you have decided upon a goal, then scientific investigation may help you (a) to decide whether or not it is, in fact, attainable; (b) to know which means may be more efficient or effective in achieving it compared with other means; (c) to specify what side effects the means might pro-

duce; and (d) to ascertain whether several proposed ends can be simultaneously achieved. But science, according to this view, cannot tell you whether or not you ought to want to attain your goal.

3. Hempel would agree with Weber's (1958a: 151) claim that the scientist can state whether a given act or specific goal is logically consistent or inconsistent with a fundamental value position. Thus, the scientist can contribute to making value judgments explicit and clear. For example, is trying to do z or to attain y really an instance of the fundamental value x? Although such clarification and logical analysis in no way validates the fundamental value position itself, they may validate a given act or specific goal as being consistent with it.

4. Picking a scientific career rather than some other career involves the extrascientific preferences and value judgments of the chooser; how highly is such a career valued compared with others?

5. When scientists select a particular topic on which to work, they often take into account the values that they place on different topics and on the possible social consequences of their work. Ought they to work on psychological, economic, social, biological, or physical problems? Ought they to work on cures for cancer, heart disease, or AIDS? Such decisions involve valuation.

6. Values themselves can be the subject of scientific inquiry. Hempel recognizes this when he points out that the assertion, "Killing is condemned as evil by many religions," is a factual statement and can be tested objectively. Systematically studying different cultures, anthropologists have attempted to describe and analyze societal value systems. Sociologists study changing values in various societies through time or, say, the values of adolescents compared with those of adults at one point in time. Such studies do not validate the values, but simply document and measure their existence, their distribution among different populations, their function in social interaction, their causes, consequences, and forms of transmission. That is, such studies do not make moral judgments themselves. Rather, they factually report on the moral judgments other people make.

7. In applied research, extrascientific values may enter into the decision to accept or reject a hypothesis. For example, if action is going to be based on the decision, then the consequences of accepting as true a hypothesis that is in fact false or of rejecting a hypothesis as false that is in fact true must be evaluated. Which error would cause the greater harm or benefit? For example, take a possible treatment for a dread disease,

where the cure would lead to saving thousands of lives if administered. A decision might be made to go ahead and treat people before all the tests on it were completed on the chance that it might work and save lives that otherwise would be lost. Such a value judgment, of course, is not itself, according to Hempel, scientifically justifiable.

8. Finally, and more problematically for Hempel, the goal of science itself, quite apart from any instrumental utility, is supported by a value judgment. That goal is "the attainment of an increasingly reliable, extensive, and theoretically systematized body of information about the world" (Hempel 1965: 93). Is such a goal good? Perhaps, yes, but in the positivist view, it cannot be proved. Not everyone may believe in the value of scientific truth. As Weber (1958a: 152) said unequivocally in his classic statement in 1919, whether or not science is worthwhile is a value judgment.

Despite Hempel's undogmatic and reasonable statement of the positivist view, despite his pulling back, as we saw in volume 1, chapter 2, from the doctrine of empirical certainty (though not from logical certainty) as a hallmark of science, and despite his enumeration of the many ways in which science and values interact, he concludes, as have so many philosophers and scientists before and since, that it is logically impossible to validate "ought" assertions objectively. Valuation questions cannot be answered by means of the methods of empirical science.

This conclusion is debatable. At least two of the above-stated relationships between science and values as recognized by Hempel and others suggest possibilities for the rational and objective assessment of value judgments. For example, in item 2, instrumental judgments of value are accepted, what I have called the "means-end model" below; and in item 3, the possibility of judging the logical consistency between a fundamental value and an act, what Lee (1985) calls the "commitment-deducibility model" which is also given below, is acknowledged. These are not trivial possibilities. Through them and other methods—especially Lee's epistemic implication—moral discourse can be brought back into human science (and human science brought into moral discourse). Values can be judged objectively.

Values and Postpositivism

Those who wish to argue for objective methods of appraising values must contend not only with the positivist view that trying to ground value judgments is meaningless metaphysical nonsense, but also with postpositivist views that have encouraged subjectivism and relativism.

Although they directed their criticisms at justifications of scientific knowledge, at truth or fact rather than at the good or value, the postpositivist and postmodern writers discussed in chapter 5 of volume 1 also undermined attempts to find evidential grounds for value judgments as well by encouraging cognitive relativism.

Postpositivist claims that encourage cognitive relativism include the beliefs that scientific truth is merely what some community of scientists happen at the time to believe, that facts don't overturn theories, that theories cannot be tested against each other, that scientific results necessarily are biased both by the personal life histories of scientists and different cultural and social settings, and that, in the extreme statement, there really are different realities.

Cognitive relativism postulates that every form of life contains "its own standards to 'truth', 'validity', 'objectivity' and 'rationality'" (Lee 1985: 13–14). Obviously, it implies ethical relativism in that there are no crosscultural or universal standards by which moral codes and practices in different societies can be judged (Lee 1985: 12). If there is no objectivity, knowledge, or truth outside of the parochial beliefs of particular groups, then there is no way to test value propositions other than to accept whatever is common practice and belief in particular times and places. In other words, the culture makes anything right that it defines as right no matter what it is.

Regarding subjectivism, the Australian philosopher J. J. C. Smart (1984: 38) says that it has "fallen foul of the objection that the theory implies that if one person says 'This is good' and another says 'This is not good'..., they would not be contradicting one another. Yet they certainly seem to be contradicting one another: there is a disagreement between them."

We have already seen in chapter 5, volume 1 some of the monstrous possibilities of the distortion of the truth that can follow from accepting the tenets of cognitive relativism. Ethical subjectivism and relativism are equally subject to criticism, as we shall see below.

In sum, although they disagree about the objectivity vs. the subjectivity and relativity of *facts*, positivists and postpositivists basically agree with each other that *values* and moral assertions are necessarily subjective and relative. Both agree that moral assertions cannot be objectively assessed. Moreover, the general principle of cultural relativism has been vociferously advocated by thoroughgoing positivists, especially in anthropology and sociology, as well as being reinforced, more recently, by the nihilism of postmodern antipositivists.

From Cultural Relativism to Critical Evaluation

As I write, cultural relativism is widespread, endorsed both by distinguished professors and eager students. It is understood by its adherents to be an enlightened position, suitably understanding and tolerant of the actual diversity of cultures, values, and lifestyles in the world. Observational knowledge of other cultures, it is thought, leads to understanding, then understanding leads to appreciation, and, finally, appreciation leads to tolerance.

But relativism confuses understanding and appreciation. Description may lead to understanding, but neither description nor understanding is the same as critical evaluation. Such evaluation might well lead to the rejection of some cultural values and practices rather than their appreciation or acceptance.

Moreover, it is one thing to tolerate any and all *beliefs* in the course of exploratory discussion and critical discourse. It is quite another thing to tolerate *action* that actually damages or destroys real people. The honor code at the U.S. Military Academy at West Point, for example, acknowledges the limits of tolerance. It reads: "A cadet does not lie, cheat, or steal, *or tolerate those who do*" (emphasis added).

Some relativists are guilty of making the same mistake that positivists contend many people make who endeavor to justify values objectively. They make an illogical jump from the "is" of the factual observations of cultural diversity in the world to the conclusion that there "ought" to be such diversity. Obviously, because there exists a diversity of values and practices does not in and of itself prove that there *ought* to be such diversity, nor does it prove that the various values and practices themselves are equally valid or acceptable.

Perhaps there *ought* to be some cultural diversity in the world, but we must search for other reasons. For example, some diversity may maximize the chances of human survival through evolutionary processes, which, if true, appears to support maintaining some cultural diversity. That is not to say, though, that every cultural trait is as good as any other, nor that every cultural trait that exists ought to exist, nor, for that matter, that imagined cultural traits that do not now exist ought not to exist.

What I try to show below is (1) that cultural relativism may be a false doctrine, especially when held in the extreme, and (2) that the grounds on which value judgments and moral assertions, and therefore cultural practices, rest can be objectively assessed. Rather than accepting all cultural beliefs and practices as equally good in their own terms, we can question and judge cultures on an objective criterion of morally good and bad.

Robert B. Edgerton (1992) has surveyed the accumulated anthropological data on known cultures and has demonstrated the poverty of cultural relativism. He asks whether or not a culture positively contributes to the survival and flourishing of its population, to the physical and mental health of its members by satisfying their needs, and to the life satisfaction and happiness of its members.

He undermines the long-standing assumption among anthropologists that traditional beliefs and practices would not have persisted unless they played some positive role in the lives of members of a given culture. What he demonstrates is that not every group has been able to invent the most efficient and effective ways of doing things, that many less than optimal solutions to social problems exist, and, indeed, that some societies are sick. Some cultures have been so maladapted that they have become extinct—from the Yahi, Hohokam, and Chaco Canyon peoples of North America and the aborginal culture of Tasmania to the great civilizations in Central America, Crete, Anatolia, Greece, Egypt, Mesopotamia, and the Indus Valley. Others continue to exist, but with merely tolerable cultural practices (Edgerton 1992).

Some examples of maladaptive practices include the failure of the Jalé of Irian Jaya to create effective means of conflict management to prevent widespread killing; the belief in witches among many peoples, including the Navaho, that leads to fear, violence, suffering, and sometimes the death of innocent people; endless feuding, vicious circles of violence, retaliation and more violence, as among the Nuer of Sudan; many examples of undernourishment because of inefficient horticulture practices or of refusing to eat certain foods even when they are available; lack of caring about one another's welfare, as among the Sirionó of eastern Bolivia; and apathy and fatalism, as the case of the Polynesian peoples on Ontong Java before World War II (Edgerton 1992).

Other examples include the gratuitous torturing of domestic animals, as the way the Inuit sometimes treat their sled dogs or the Machiguenga Indians of the Peruvian Amazon their hunting dogs; gender inequality in many societies from India and West Africa to Morocco and South America, where adult men eat their fill while women and children are deprived of animal protein and fat; traditional health practices that are not only ineffective cures, but also downright dangerous, such as the mixture of green tobacco leaves marinated in urine that the Yoruba of Nigeria force on children with convulsions—often leaving the patient nearly unconscious; and false reproductive beliefs and practices based on them such as those of the Marind-anim people on the southwest coast of New Guinea who periodically throughout a woman's reproductive life force ritual sexual intercourse on her with as many as ten men a night "to fill her with semen" so as to enhance her fertility, with the probable result that severe pelvic inflammation produces the opposite consequence of infertility and a decline in population that threatens the survival of the group (Edgerton 1992).

To take a different example, in the name of carrying on cultural tradition, 85 to 115 million women now living in Africa have had their genitals mutilated by having had all or part of their clitoris and minor labia cut off with crude tools and without anesthesia resulting in excruciating pain and sometimes death. Often, the child's vagina is sewn closed as well. We can question the validity of such cultural beliefs and practices only by rejecting ethical relativism and the moral rightness of particular social conventions. We can question them in the name of medical science, because these clitoridectomies violate humans as biological beings.

We can question them, too, in the name of transcultural social values that they violate, such as freedom, justice, and caring. They are mutilations whether or not they are carried out in the name of tradition, and, since they are done to children, they also are child abuse (Konner 1990). The final report of the United Nations Conference on Population and Development that met in Cairo in 1994 advocates abolishing female genital mutilation.

Another example is the foot-binding of women in China. Hundreds of millions of Chinese women over a period of nearly a thousand years had their feet ritually deformed. The toes of their feet were bent under their arches and the arches broken, bent back and tightly strapped, producing agonizing pain. As a result, many could not walk at all. Others could only limp about. Apparently, Chinese scholars, including Western writers, largely ignored this "nightmare practice, reputedly performed for the sensual delectation of men." They did so, or so speculates China scholar John King Fairbank, so as to avoid confronting the whole problem of Chinese women's subjugation and not to give offense to the Chinese (Spence 1992: 2). Foot-binding, like clitoridectomy, was well established in local traditions and custom, yet it, too, can be judged by objective standards that transcend particular cultural traditions.

Another problem with relativism is its unstated assumption that to judge a culture is necessarily to be ethnocentrically biased, rigid, or absolutist. Objectivity and its possibility are here confused with absolutism and dogmatism (Lee 1985: 13). Quite the opposite is the case. First, the attempt to test values is to question them, which is opposed to the idea of blind acceptance of "absolute" values.

Second, objectivity in testing attitudes and values does not mean that such attitudes and values, even if they survive efforts to falsify them, are accepted as valid for all times and places. Rather, they are held, just as all scientific conclusions are in the critical realist perspective, as contingent and corrigible. They are conjectures, preliminary assertions that are capable of being revised or disconfirmed by some future evidence.

Underlying some relativist views is the assumption that for morality to be objective, it is necessary that there be only one correct answer to moral problems. This is faulty reasoning. Different situations may call for different applications of the same value. For example, different societies may share the value of life and an injunction not to kill. Yet one society, leading a precarious existence may face a number of situations in which it is necessary to kill, engage say in infanticide, so that others might live and the society survive.

Also, some situations may invoke competing values in such a close balance that good moral arguments may be available to support different answers (Lombardi 1988: 35–37). For example, abortion, as I say in chapter 5 of this volume, may be such a case with a clash between the right of freedom of the pregnant woman and the right to life of the fetus. Such situations in no way negate the possibility of carrying out rational and objective analyses of the issues involved in the moral choices.

In sum, no society is perfect. Everywhere, even in those societies where people are healthiest, happiest, and longest-lived, there is imperfection. Everywhere, there are some people who live in misery, who are fearful, lonely, or sick. All societies, including small-scale, nonliterate societies as well as large-scale, industrial societies, contain some senseless cruelty, needless suffering, and social disharmony. Every society contains some beliefs, values, and practices that are false. Sometimes such false beliefs and values are neutral, having no damaging effects. Sometimes they are harmful, but tolerable. Yet sometimes they are deadly, imperiling the very survival of a society itself (Edgerton 1992).

Some societies contain many more harmful customs, values and social institutions, beliefs and practices than other societies. And some societies do a better job than others of meeting their own survival needs and flourishing as collectivities. Some do a better job, too, of satisfying the needs of their members, creating healthy, happy, harmonious, and long-lived people.

Recognizing this, we can discard cultural relativism and move, as Edgerton (1992) recommends, to critical evaluation. We can search for objective and legitimate ways of identifying what on the one hand is good and beneficial and on the other what is bad and harmful in cultural traditions. We can carefully assess all cultural values as being beneficial or harmful, neutral, or merely tolerable.

We can begin by considering ways of evaluating specific moral propositions or value judgments, recognizing that they are the foundations both for evaluating various aspects of entire cultures and for helping people in specific situations to decide what they ought to do. Thus, let's turn to three methods by which value judgments can be assessed objectively.

A Commitment-Deducibility Model

The first method is the commitment-deducibility model. It is widely used in everyday life and is well understood. It is clearly recognized, for example, in item 3 in the earlier discussion of the roles of values in science in which logical consistency can be determined between a fundamental value position and a given act or specific goal. It is, however, limited in that it provides no test of the fundamental value position itself.

As positivism became dominant, some moral philosophers, such as R. M. Hare (1952), came to accept one of its distinctive features: strict logical implication. This model imitates the logical hierarchical structure of science as conceived by the positivists, except that the propositions involved are value judgments, not statements of fact. Logical

relationships exist among the propositions. A lower-order moral assertion can be justified by a higher-order assertion, and it by others, and
so on. Thus, there is deducibility through logical consistency.

But—and here's the catch—ultimately the highest-order assertion, and
thus the entire system of justification itself, rests on an act of faith or
will, on "sincere commitment" to the highest-order principle. Thus, there
is no rational or objective justification for the commitment to the highest-
order principle itself. Such a commitment is both subjective and relative,
possibly totally arbitrary, if it is based merely on personal decision and
choice. Because of this, the commitment-deducibility method of justifying values has been attacked as untenable (Lee 1985).

Yet the commitment-deducibility model does have some utility in
judging preferable futures. The deducibility part of the model is valid
when done correctly, as both Hempel and Weber would agree. It en-
ables people to exercise rational, objective, and critical judgment *up to
a point*. When people agree on some general principle as morally right,
then that principle can be used as a yardstick to judge other values and
actions and can aid in dispute settlement. For example, if we can agree
that satisfaction with the quality of one's life is a good thing, then
logically we can concur that anything that is an instance of it, such as
satsfactions with one's health, marriage, family life, friendships, housing, and so on (Campbell et al. 1976) are also good. It becomes a matter of logical subsumption.

The commitment-deducibility model emphasizes whether a given act,
event, process, etc. is an instance of or consistent with the value to which
a commitment has been made. For example, if a sincere commitment is
made to the value of showing respect for other human beings, then in
culture x, we can ask, is bowing to another person an instance of it? If so
and if we want to show respect, then we ought to bow to others in culture
x. Such a commitment might be made to a particular value or to a collection of prescriptive or proscriptive statements, such as the traditions of
some group, the laws of some country, the tenets of some religion, or the
doctrines of some political ideology. If such a commitment is shared,
then disputes about what is right may be settled by rationally appealing
to the value or the statements to which common commitment has been
made.

An example from the futurist literature is the "stakeholder audit," a
tool that is a part of what has been called "ethical strategic planning"

(Murphy 1992). It is simply a method in which the ethical accountability of an organization is assessed by judging present management decisions in terms of their compatibility with the organization's long-range ethical commitments as expressed in its mission statement. That is, the "commitment" is to the general ethical vision of an organization. Then, current management decisions are evaluated as being—or failing to be—deducible from them. Such an analysis provides benchmarks for the reformation of future management practice, the idea being to bring the practice into line with the underlying ethics of the organization.

The commitment-deducibility model, like the means-ends model to be discussed next, is a practical method of deciding value questions commonly used in everyday life, but, ultimately, it fails as a fully adequate method of moral reasoning because the commitment itself remains a matter of faith. Only the deducibility part of the model is open to objective and rational determination within the model itself.

A Means-Ends Model

Cause and Effect

The second model is a means-ends model that many philosophers have long agreed can be used to test what has been called an instrumental or a "practical-ought" statement. This is a statement that says "If you desire x, then you ought to do y," the grounds being that y is a means of attaining x. Or, to state it somewhat more complexly, "Y is better than z for attaining the goal of x." After a goal x has been selected, then it becomes a matter of fact whether or not y is a means, or a better means than z, of reaching it. The goal or end itself in the means-ends model remains unjustifiable within the model, the goal being a matter of the preferences, desires, or values of some individual or collective agent.

The means-ends model puts an emphasis on causal knowledge and empirical fact. What one ought to do to achieve some particular goal is partly a factual question of cause-and-effect relationships and the empirical conditions under which they apply. If we accept equality of educational opportunity as our goal, for example, then it is an empirical question whether or not racial integration of schools helps to achieve it. Also, it is another empirical question whether or not busing students is an efficient and effective means for achieving racial integration. If so, then we can rationally and objectively conclude as a first approximation that we ought to favor both racial integration and busing (if we have reason to assume that the causal relationships will continue to hold long enough into the future so that equality of educational opportunity will be achieved and won't be prevented by unintended consequences).

In the example above, I say "as a first approximation," because there may be other grounds for not busing children that must be considered, such as the time-cost factors involved in the busing itself. Thus, the means must also be evaluated as an end. Values often conflict in real life situations and, thus, produce extenuating circumstances.

Harman (1977: 120) reminds us of a useful distinction made by the philosopher W. D. Ross between a "prima facie ought" and an "all-things-considered ought." Standing alone, all value statements are prima facie and all have exceptions under certain circumstances. For example, you have promised to attend your daughter's performance in a school play, but your best friend asks you to be his best man at his wedding at the same time. You have an obligation to do both things, but they appear to conflict. You ought to go to the performance *and* you ought to attend the wedding. But they do not really contradict each other, because they are prima facie "ought" statements. They do not say what you ought to do "all things considered." Only by weighing your reasons and deciding which is of higher priority can you determine that.

For example, we are told not to lie to one another by the Bible (Colossians 3:9) and that a false witness will not go unpunished (Proverbs 19:5). Yet Christians who concealed Jewish refugees or members of the resistance from the Nazis during World War II, lied to protect such people from torture and murder. All-things-considered, lying can be justified if it is done to prevent unjust suffering and to protect human life.

In sum, the coherence of your selection of means to an end necessarily contains an explanation, at least an implicit cause-and-effect proposition. For to plan how to do things in a certain way presupposes some explanatory knowledge (Harman 1977: 128). For many practical purposes, then, testing beliefs about cause and effect and constructing warranted posits about the consequences of action are all that is necessary to resolve disagreements and to make choices. If it can be shown that x is not a means to y, then we can agree not to do x in order to get y.

Means Also Have Consequences

One criticism of the ethical theory known as "consequentialism" is that in determining the good the focus is on the consequences or end states while the means are simply taken as instrumental. This opens the possibility of blindly using means without regard to their possibly harmful side effects (Charnov 1987: 7).

Futurists can guard against this by realizing that means may have many consequences, other than the end in view. Such consequences, too, can be posited and ethically evaluated before decisions are made and actions taken. Ethical deliberation remains incomplete if it is limited to seeking the means, any effective means, of some particular end. Such a limitation is useful only as a temporary oversimplification. Deliberation can include whether or not we *ought* to use a particular means to achieve a specified end given the way in which it will affect our other desires or the well-being of other people (Stevenson 1963: 108). Such deliberation can lead us to revise the end to which the means were selected.

The means-ends relationship, of course, may not be a simple one. For example, something may be pursued both as a means *and* as an end (as when a person walks to the office both as a means of reaching the office and as a pleasurable activity in its own right). There is, additionally, always the danger that a means may come to be regarded as "good-in-itself" rather than simply as a means, as in the case of the miser who hoards money for its own sake (Monro 1967: 33). Finally, real people in everyday life situations may be at a loss to say whether they wanted something mainly as a means or as an end, because they often do things for a variety of different reasons, like having a new car for transportation and for status in the eyes of their friends, for the satisfaction of ownership, and for the love of a beautiful object.

Despite these complexities, the means-ends model, if applied with sophistication, can be a useful tool in evaluating the rightness of many "ought" assertions. The causal relationships on which it rests are subject to test and possible refutation against current scientific theory and data. It has, additionally, the advantage of being familiar to people, because it is consistent with everyday ideas of practical rationality.

Like the commitment-deducibility model, however, the means-ends model leaves the ultimate preferences, attitudes, desires, and values of people or norms of society largely unexamined and untested. It fails to deal, for example, with the possibility of evil wants, desires, and ends. Thus, ultimately, it, too, fails as a fully adequate method of moral reasoning.

Keekok Lee's Epistemic Implication Model

Both in philosophy and social science, there have been recent efforts to bring value judgments into objective critical discourse and to go beyond the limitations of the commitment-deducibility and the means-ends models (Gert 1988; Gewirth 1978; Habermas 1973; Midgley 1993; Phillips 1986). One such effort is that of Keekok Lee (1985) who has proposed what she calls "epistemic implication."

Although Lee does not claim strict logical deducibility for epistemic implication and casts it within "ordinary knowledge" (i.e., naturalistic knowledge obtained under empirical conditions), she shows that it is similar to a scientific model of verification/falsification. In fact, she places it squarely within Popper's fallibilism, which she applies to the grounds supporting value assertions and which she enriches by requiring criteria of relevance. Hence, it can be considered to be a part of the critical realist theory of knowledge.

Using Lee's epistemic implication, we can subject the descriptive elements of value assertions to a series of criteria, including empirical testing, and, by implication can reach a tentative judgment about the validity of value assertions. We can develop a consistent, coherent, rational, and objective morality. She gives five criteria to be met in making such a test:

1. Serious Evidence

The evidence required to support or falsify an assertion "must not merely refer to the attitude of the speakers towards their assertion or their psychological state of mind regarding it" (Lee 1985: 87). That is, the evidence must be "serious," something more than a personal commitment or decision alone. Thus, mere individual preferences, desires, or wants are not admitted as serious evidence. Rather, serious evidence requires that there be some public external features of the situation referred to in the assertion. It includes only assertions that can be denied or confirmed by independent observers, by some kind of objective or intersubjective process.

For example, take the *assertion*: People ought not to smoke tobacco.

Supported by the *evidence*: Because to do so increases their chances of dying of lung cancer.

This is serious evidence because it refers to objective characteristics that can be tested, that is, confirmed or falsified by independent observers. What does current scientific evidence and theory have to say about the relationship between smoking and lung cancer (not to mention additional possible effects of smoking such as throat cancers, chronic bronchitis, emphysema, and heart disease)? These are matters of fact that are independent of the subjective state or judgment of individual smokers.

What is an example of nonserious evidence? It is something that cannot be confirmed or falsified by independent observers. A man may hear inner voices and conclude that God told him that smoking is a sin. Although independent observers might agree after interviews with the man that he sincerely believed that he heard such voices, there is no way we now know of that they could deny nor confirm that he really did. Even more difficult would be to deny or confirm that a voice he thought he heard was God's. Thus, it fails as serious evidence. This is not to claim that God does not exist, nor that God did not speak to him, nor that smoking is not a sin. Rather, it is to say that there is no naturalistic way that such assertions, if false, can be falsified by independent observers.

2. Referentially Relevant Evidence

Evidence, in addition to being serious, must be "referentially relevant." By this is meant that the assertion and the reasons for it must be about the same thing. They must "share a common term, that is, the subject term" (Lee 1985: 87). To say that "this young woman fainted" as evidence for "this young woman is ill" is referentially relevant. Both the evidence and the conclusion concern the young woman. To conclude, further, that "this young woman ought to be taken to a doctor for examination and possible treatment" continues the relevant reference to "this young woman."

Take the *assertion*: Criminals released from prison ought to receive severance pay plus a bonus for getting a job.

And the *evidence*: Because criminals released from prison who are so treated are less likely to commit new crimes than criminals released from prison who are not so treated (Rossi 1987).

The evidence is clearly relevant, dealing with "criminals" and with "severance pay plus a bonus" as does the assertion. (We are not now concerned with whether or not the evidence is true, only with its *relevance*).

If we offer in evidence of the assertion "because 2 + 2 = 4," then we have failed to meet Lee's criterion of referential relevance. Even though the statement used as evidence or grounds, "2 + 2 = 4," is true according to the arithmetic of real numbers, none of its terms is relevant to the assertion prescribing severance pay and a bonus for released prisoners who get a job. Thus, it cannot serve as evidence.

Referential relevance is a matter of classification. The grounds purporting to provide evidence for a moral assertion (or any other kind of assertion for that matter) are inadequate if they do not deal, at the very least, with the same class of objects, people, or events. The "*justificandum* and the *justificans*" must be "talking about one and the same object" (Lee 1985: 115).

3. Causally Relevant Evidence

Additionally, the evidence cited to test a moral assertion must be "causally relevant." It must bear on the assertion in some causal way. Thus, like the means-ends model, epistemic implication also depends upon a basic assumption of cause-and-effect. In the example of smoking and lung cancer, we assume the testable proposition that there is a causal link between the two, smoking somehow causally contributes to lung cancer. To say that "people ought not to smoke, because to do so results in their going blind" would not be causally relevant (unless someone can show a causal connection between smoking and becoming sightless).

Thus, Lee's method is based on the assumption of causality in the world and our ability to discern and confirm—or refute—causal relationships. This opens the door, of course, to all causal knowledge, especially scientific theory and research. It also is a limitation, obviously, since human understanding of causal relationships in the world is incomplete.

Evidence might be referentially relevant, but could still fail the test of causal relevance. For example, to say "'oxygen is colourless' as evidence for 'oxygen is necessary for combustion'" fails because there is no causal connection between the color of oxygen and its combustibility (Lee 1985: 88). Even though the assertion about combustibility and the evidence offered both concern oxygen, the evidence is not acceptable as causally relevant.

To take another example, to argue that the living room ought to be redecorated on the evidence that it is on the ground floor fails because the evidence is causally irrelevant. Being on the ground floor, as far as we can imagine, has nothing to do with the decision to redecorate. This is not causally relevant evidence (unless some causal link can be provided that is not apparent). Thus the premise is not supported. Relying on this evidence produces a non sequitur.

4. Causal Independence

Lee's (1985:99) fourth requirement is that the referentially and causally relevant serious evidence must be "causally independent" of the conclusion. The evidence is not acceptable if it is produced by the conclusion itself, as in a self-fulfilling prophecy. The evidence, in other words, must have occurred earlier in time than the conclusion and it must not have been a result of the conclusion.

For example, causal independence is established in our example of smoking and cancer by time priority (smoking comes before cancer), by manipulative priority (you can't give a person the smoking habit by giving him or her cancer), and by explanatory theory. Causal order—the direction of cause and effect—is clearly established. The fact of having cancer does not cause smoking.

Let's take a contrary case where the time priority conceivably is reversed and where causal order may run in the opposite direction. For example, take a white supremacist assertion in the period of plantation slavery in the Americas that "Africans ought to be treated as socially inferior," the evidence being that "Africans in fact *are* socially inferior" (adapted from Lee 1985: 135). The evidence is serious evidence because it refers not to subjective states but to an external characteristic that can be checked by others. Are Africans socially inferior or not? We could specify some objective indicators and collect evidence about them.

The evidence is referentially relevant, dealing with "Africans" and "social inferiority" as does the original assertion.

Let's grant that it is causally relevant, that being socially inferior might be a cause of being treated as socially inferior, although this is shaky and can be challenged. Even so, the fact is that, historically, doctrines of racial inferiority were often used by defenders of the plantation system in the Americas to justify the slavery of Africans (Goveia 1956).

But the evidence fails because it is not causally independent of the original assertion. That is, the value judgment contained in the original assertion may have caused the evidence. If the whites' attitudes are that Africans ought to be treated as socially inferior and, therefore, do treat them as socially inferior, then it is not surprising that on any number of objective criteria from respect, authority, occupation, education, wealth, and income to housing, clothes, medical treatment, and freedom to travel they empirically might be shown to be "socially inferior," that is, to be relatively less well off than whites on each criterion. But such evidence is inadmissible in support of the assertion because it is not causally independent of it. If African slaves were socially inferior because of being treated as social inferiors, then it is circular reasoning to justify treating them as social inferiors because they are socially inferior.

A moral assertion, imperative, or any "ought" statement that causes the evidence offered in its support is not supported by that evidence.

5. Empirical Test

Finally, there is the requirement to put the evidence to "an empirical test," to assess whether it is true or false. If the evidence meets the above four criteria, then the evidence, if true, would serve to support the assertion, while if false, would serve to refute it (Lee 1985: 99). This is a matter of using standard scientific and scholarly methods to test the propositions offered as evidence within a critical realist theory of knowledge.

Let's take an assertion of a male chauvinist: "Women ought to obey men's will." He gives as evidence his belief that "women are less intelligent than men." This evidence is serious and referentially relevant. It may not be causally relevant, however, because more intelligent people may not advise people to do the morally right thing any more than less intelligent people. Thus, the evidence may fail by not being causally relevant. But let's grant that it is for the sake of continuing the example.

The proffered evidence fails on other grounds. It is empirically false. On average, men and women have about the same level of overall intelligence. They do not significantly differ (Lee 1985: 133). Thus, even though it might meet the first four criteria of serious, referentially relevant, causally relevant, and causally independent evidence, it is not acceptable on the fifth. It is refuted by the facts. If the male chauvinist wants to argue, objectively and rationally, for the morality of women's subjection to men, he will have to find other grounds to do so.

The ought-assertion in the earlier example about the negative effects of smoking, however, is overwhelmingly supported by many different empirical studies, including the epidemiological evidence compiled in the U.S. Surgeon General's Report of 1989. That is, the hypothesis that smoking causes lung cancer has survived many efforts to falsify it.

Academics, even those who reject the possibility of supporting "ought" statements by "is" statements, of course, engage in such behavior themselves all the time. In the activities, for example, of grading students, writing letters of recommendation, deciding whom to hire or to promote, reviewing books, evaluating papers for publication and research proposals for funding, evaluating applications for fellowships, agreeing on the content of professional ethics, and so on, university scholars attempt to make value judgments and support them with empirical evidence.

For example, take the *assertion*: This person ought to be promoted.

Evidence:

1. Because she is one of the most highly competent and most knowledgeable scholars in her field;
2. because she has carried out and published considerable research of high quality that has contributed significantly to knowledge;
3. because she has been a superior teacher of both undergraduate and graduate students, articluate, well-informed, and inspirational;
4. because she has been widely recognized in her profession as a leader in the field;
5. because she has made important contributions to the public welfare through her years of service as a consultant and adviser to government and business; and
6. because she has been a witty and congenial colleague who willingly shoulders her share of departmental and university administrative burdens.

No respectable university appointments committee, of course, would allow these generalities to stand as they are. Each must be supported by specific examples, so that, in the end, quite detailed factual evidence constitutes the grounds for an "ought" assertion. Such evidence contains the implicit claim to be serious, referentially and causally relevant, causally independent, and empirically true, that is, to be objective, intersubjectively verifiable knowledge.

Moreover, each of the value criteria used themselves can be subjected to the same critical analysis using Lee's method: Ought promotion of faculty members in a university to be based on their competence and expertise, published research, contributions to knowledge, teaching ability, contributions to public welfare, collegial congeniality, and sharing administrative burdens? We can ask what evidence can be specified in each case? Does the evidence meet Lee's five criteria? Thus, are the criteria of promotion supported or not?

The Underlying Logic

The logic underlying Lee's epistemic-implication model is straightforward. Although it does not argue that one can go from "is" to "ought," it assumes that prescriptive statements contain or rest upon some descriptive contents that can be tested; that is, either falsified or confirmed by surviving serious efforts to falsify them. If the prescriptive statements depend on their descriptive components, then they are brought into question if their descriptive components are falsified. For example, if prescriptive statement A rests on descriptive statement B, then, if B is false, therefore, A is false. Put in the terms we have used, if the grounds or reasons are false, then the premise, imperative, or original "ought" assertion is false also. If the grounds or reasons are not falsified, then the premise is not falsified.

By such a process, rival value judgments, conflicting "ought" assertions, can be eliminated. That is, it is reasonable to believe value assertions for which supporting evidence and grounds are unrefuted after serious efforts have been made to refute them. To the contrary, it is unreasonable to believe value assertions whose supporting evidence and grounds have been refuted. Scientific reasoning aimed at falsifying or verifying factual assertions, as we saw previously in chapter 5 of volume 1, are similar.

As Lee (1985: 105) points out, such logic has been around for some time in moral philosophy. For example, she shows that the Kantian dictum, "'ought' implies 'can,'" is similar. You are not morally obligated to do what you cannot do. Lee's epistemic implication includes this logic, that is, the logic of *modus tollens*. But it is broader because it makes the descriptive elements or grounds of any prescriptive statements subject to test. For example, the grounds that women are less intelligent than men offered to support the assertion that women ought to obey men's will is not of the "ought-implies-can" type.

Following Lee's five criteria or requirements, a researcher can provide warranted assertibility, by finding objective support or refutation for the grounds on which value assertions rest and, by implication, for the value assertions themselves. Her method includes making explicit and intelligible arguments, testing for logical coherence, looking for congruence or conflict with generally accepted scientific assumptions and theories, and searching for relevant empirical data.

Epistemic implication, however, cannot stand totally alone. Like any method of reasoning, *including the scientific method*, it rests on numerous auxiliary assumptions that may range in any given case from the laws of physics to the nature of human biology. It rests, for example, in part on other well-known principles of rationality, such as consistency and avoiding known fallacies of reasoning (e.g., non sequiturs, *petitio principii*, etc.). It rests, too, on assumptions about the kind of natural being we humans are (beast, psyche, social actor, etc.) and the kind of environments, both natural and social, we inhabit (Lee 1989). Thus, the facts of biology, psychology, anthropology, sociology, and the other sciences and social sciences are relevant.

The avoidance of pain, for example, is not mere preference. Pain is, rather, "a biological signal to us that our bodies are being subjected to damage and harm and hence a signal to us to take avoiding action to retreat from the harmful situation" (Lee, personal communication, 2 April 1990). To take another example, the preconditions of social life are not arbitrary and require behaviors such as trust and cooperation (see chapters 3 and 4, this volume). These matters are factual, although, of course, not all—or perhaps even most—of the facts are in.

In the example of smoking and cancer, an unconvinced reader may have to be pushed to test the assumption that life, health, and well-being are preferable to death, sickness, and pain. Not just a single ground for an assertion but many may be necessary, and the grounds may progress to a fundamental assertion about the nature of human beings and society, in this case to the ultimate statement that humans ought to choose life over death (as a prima facie choice). What are the grounds?

There are too many to enumerate here, but in summary: it is human nature to want to live. The occasional martyr who sacrifices his or her life so that others might live (as an all-things-considered choice) affirms that truth. If you need grounds, you might start with your desires for good food, good drink, and good sex, à la Aristophanes. Then, you might move on, if those reasons are not enough, to the consequences of your living or dying for the future of your loved ones, for the work you are doing, and for the contributions you might make to create a better world. If you remain unconvinced, then consider that, when your life ends, there are no more possibilities for you in this world and no guarantee that there will be any other (see chapter 5).

Thus, although the content of moral discourse is not solely determined by it, epistemic implication is a rational, objective, and coherent method of testing moral propositions. Raz (1977: 210) goes so far as to say that a statement such as "X ought to do y" is logically equivalent to a statement such as "There is a reason for x to do y." Using epistemic implication, sometimes we can show that the reason survives serious efforts to refute it. When we are able to do so, then such a reason provides warranted assertability on which we can decide how to act rightly.

I emphasize the "discourse," "communicative," or "deliberative" aspect of moral judgment using Lee's method. When carried out by a single individual who may be in a quandary about the rightness of alternative acts, using Lee's method encourages a conversation with oneself. When carried out by several individuals who may have a disagreement, Lee's method provides a framework for communication and discussion. Issues can be clarified, points of agreement and overlap discovered, evidence and predictive grounds organized and critically examined, reasons for alternative judgments understood from several perspectives, the consequences of compromises spelled out, and, with a little luck and good will, conflict reduced as the parties mutually agree on some acceptable actions (Perry 1978: 20).

As we all know, there are countless human acts in the world that violate ethical principles, even when people know what those principles are. Because some people behave and act immorally, however, does "not threaten the objectivity of morality any more than the fact that some people add incorrectly threatens the existence of objective principles in mathematics" (Lombardi 1988: 39).

Values and the Future

Although it is not widely recognized, all ethical thinking necessarily contains some futures thinking. This is most obvious when judging consequences, because, as we have seen, consequences always occur in the future from the time some action is being contemplated. Thus, we easily see that for "a consequentialist the future must matter" (Sumner 1987: 207). Judgments of the good on which people base their decisions to act rest upon anticipations (Charnov 1987: 5).

Also, contractarianist, utilitarianist, deontological, and other theories of ethics contain an inherent futures orientation. Ethics implies standards of conduct, not just for the past and the present, but for the future (Charnov 1987: 4). In the case of contractarianism, for example, the chief import of a contract is to bind the parties to it to future relationships and obligations to each other that are defined in the contract. Contracts are largely agreements to fulfill certain stated reciprocal behaviors in the future.

The theory of ethics known as utilitarianism says to act so as to create the greatest good or happiness for the greatest number of people. Clearly, utilitarians judge their possible alternative acts according to their future results. Harman (1977: 153), for example, says that utilitarianism is forward, not backward, looking. What is important, he says, "is not what has happened in the past, but what might happen in the future as a consequence of the various things you might do." This is obvious in the case of so-called act-utilitarians, who attempt to follow the injunction and evaluate anticipated consequences in every case as they decide what actions to take. But it is also true of rule-utilitarians who may follow rules, such as "Be honest," "Treat other people with respect," and "Don't cheat," under the assumption that in the long run following an ethical rule *will* result in the greatest benefit to the greatest number of people.

Although it is less easy to see, deontological ethical theories, too, deal with the future. These are theories that emphasize doing one's duty and giving respect to individuals. They are thought of as nonconsequentialist theories because they focus on the reasons for taking an action (i.e., one's intentions) rather than the results of the action. If you are honest only because you want a good reputation in the community, then, according to this view, your action is not moral. To be moral an act must flow from duty (Tong 1986: 84). Take, for example, a formulation of Kant's (1958) categorical imperative: act only according to the maxim that you want to become a universal law.

Kant is not a consequentialist in the philosophical sense, because his categorical imperative must be followed, even if acting otherwise would result in good consequences (Tong 1986). But the categorical imperative deals with the future not only because an intention itself is future oriented, but also because it does deal with a particular consequence that takes precedence over all other consequences that might flow from an action: that is, that the moral principle underlying your behavior will become a universal law.

When will a universal law that is willed become influenced by your act? It can only be *after* your act. In this sense, it becomes a consequence of your act. Thus, by your acts that follow the categorical imperative, you are creating the moral laws of the future. The categorical imperative is asking you to think about the kind of future moral world you wish to create before you act and, then, to act accordingly.

Moreover, all ethical theories contain motivations for acting in particular ways. For example, Sprigge (1988: 150) says, "There is no real recognition that something is good or bad unless it embodies some degree of motivation to pursue or shun it, do or refrain from it." Motivation involves goals desired but not yet achieved, whether those goals are happiness for the greatest number or universal moral laws. "Morality gives people reasons to do things" (Harman 1977: 91) and the goals for which things are done are always in the future.

Additionally, the motivation to behave in a moral way, for example to help another person when you have no reason not to, comes partly from the belief that it may help you to satisfy your own desires in the future. Some kind of reciprocity might occur. Perhaps, your help will return to you later as a direct result of your moral act through the agency of the person you helped or his or her friends. Perhaps, it will return indirectly through your contribution to creating a world in which it is normal for people to help each other: "What goes around comes around" and, eventually, it "*will* come around" to you or your loved ones. Perhaps, doing the right thing will just make you feel good about yourself, which, as we have come to learn, may itself literally benefit your future health.

As Boulding (1985: 173) sums it up, "One of the most secure propositions of normative analysis is that benevolence is desirable as leading into positive-sum processes [everybody wins], whereas malevolence is undesirable as leading into negative-sum processes [everybody loses]."

Imperatives, of course, are a form in which ethical principles are often given. Not only the categorical imperative but all imperatives are future oriented. Smart (1984: 56) says that "Do X" is short for "You ought to do X" which itself is short for "Doing X *will* bring about what you want to happen" (my emphasis). To achieve brevity, then, we often speak in imperatives or "ought" statements, but they substitute for longer, more accurate statements framed in the future tense.

The philosopher John Dewey shared the view that all ethical deliberation is futures oriented. He saw ethical problems typically arising out of the need to resolve a conflict in attitudes. To solve the problem rationally, we make an appeal to consequences. We do this, he argued, by an imaginative dramatic rehearsal of the different consequences that would flow from alternative choices and actions. This dramatic rehearsal is ethical deliberation and our choice of a course of action is an ethical conclusion. Viewed in this way, ethical deliberation, however much retrospection may be involved, in its aim and conclusion *is* a form of futures thinking (Stevenson 1963: 95).

Applied to historical actions, a futures orientation remains relevant to value judgments since the consequences of any choice and action, past or present, always occur at a time after a choice is made and an action taken (using the B-series conception of time as described in volume 1). Also, intentions always refer to the future, even when we are analyzing past behavior. What, for example, did the accused intend when he bought a gun and went to the home of the victim he shot last August 13th? That is, within any historical period, just as in the present, consequences and intentions always refer to a time that is in the future relative to the time they are being considered as factors in decisions to act.

There is the additional fact that a latent, if not always manifest, purpose of communicating ethical judgments, including those about past actions, is to influence people's future behavior. For example, when correcting the behavior of a child, we "usually add to our ethical judgment the remark, 'see that you don't do it again.'" Even when ethical judgments refer to past or imaginary acts, they still serve a dynamic purpose—that of discouraging (or encouraging) similar acts at some future time (Stevenson 1963: 143).

Predictive Grounds: An Extension of Lee's Method

Thus, value judgments necessarily rest partly upon posits about the future, including intentions as well as predicted consequences of alternative actions. Because of that, Lee's statements of serious and causally relevant "evidence" as well as the definition of "empirical test" require expansion to include predictions. Assertions about the future, when they are warranted by specific grounds, constitute "evidence" to support or negate value premises, the same as do facts about the past and present.

For the sake of clarity, that is, to maintain the distinction between evidence in the strict sense (which is based on observation of the past and present) and predictions (which refer to the future and, thus, are not evidential in the same sense), I recommend not calling them "evidence," but rather "predictive grounds." Thus, surrogate knowledge or presumptively true predictions, that is, warranted assertions about the future, can be used as predictive grounds.

One example of the futures aspect of Lee's "evidence" can be found in the case of President Reagan's decision to invade Grenada which I discussed in chapter 5, volume 1. If you recall, I concluded that the prediction that American students in Grenada would be taken hostage or harmed in some other way was presumptively false. Thus, the invasion ought not to have taken place, at least not on that "predictive ground."

To give another illustration let's reformulate an example given earlier:

Assertion: People ought not to smoke tobacco.

Predictive grounds: Because smoking tobacco probably *will* increase their chances of dying of lung cancer *at some future time*.

Obviously, for living smokers who currently show no signs of cancer, that prediction, since it is based on past observation about other people, can only be "presumptively true." The best we can do is "warranted assertability," not because of errors in our methods of observation or the limitations of our senses, but because the prediction refers to events that have not yet occurred and, thus, cannot yet be observed. Yet if the smokers wait to stop smoking until the prediction is confirmed by observation of their particular cases (i.e., until it is "terminally true"), then, clearly, the utility of the prediction for increasing the length of their lives would be lost.

Another example of the use of predictive grounds can be found in the difficult case of the morality of revolutions or riots. This example also illustrates the use of evidence in the strict sense along with the use of predictive grounds. Let's assume that the time is the late 1950s and we are among the local people of a Caribbean country that is under the political rule of a European power. We are trying to decide whether or not to start a revolution whose purpose would be to gain our people's political freedom, remove the imperial power from authority, and transform our colonial territory into a new democratic nation-state. The revolutionary-nationalists might argue as follows:

Assertion: We ought to begin an armed rebellion in order to overthrow foreign political rule and establish a new nation-state that is politically independent, autonomous, and self-governing.

Evidence:

1. Clear-cut and gross inequalities (civil, political, economic, social, and cultural) exist in our land that place us (the local, indigenous inhabitants) at a disadvantage compared with the representatives or agents of the foreign power that rules us.
2. These inequalities are institutionalized, legitimated, and enforced by imperial political rule against our will.
3. We local people, both leaders and ordinary people, are acutely aware of these inequalities.
4. We local people judge these inequalities to be unfair, as would any people in our situation who value liberty, equality, and fraternity.
5. There exists a set of leaders from among the local people who are committed to the values of liberty, equality, and fraternity.

Predictive Grounds:

1. Such local leaders *will* be able to mobilize sufficient human, material and organizational resources to sustain a revolutionary movement against the foreign political rulers.
2. Changes toward a more just (i.e., egalitarian, fair, free, and open) society under continued foreign colonial rule *will* be impossible or very slow in coming.
3. A revolution *will* be successful in overthrowing foreign rule and attaining political separation from the imperial power.
4. After the revolution, we local leaders and ordinary people *will* be successful in establishing viable political, economic, and social orders after becoming a politically independent nation-state.
5. After the revolution, we local leaders and ordinary people *will* be successful in creating a fair society based on equality of civil and political rights and equal opportunity for everyone in the economic, social, and cultural spheres, where public liberties and a competitive political system based on universal adult political participation *will* be maintained.

Obviously, every item of evidence and of predictive grounds might be challenged. In the case of the evidence, the debate becomes a matter of fact. For example, data about the existence of various kinds of inequalities, how conscious people are of them, whether or not people judge them to be unfair, and so on are more or less reliably available.

In the case of the predictive grounds, we have the additional problem of the limitations of presumptive truth. Here we must rely on present indicators that may only indirectly bear on the future. Will we, indeed, have the revolutionary support in human and material terms actually needed to carry out an armed struggle and a successful revolutionary transfer of power? Do we, indeed, have the expertise needed to establish and run an economy and a fair and democratic society? Moreover, have we considered all the consequences? How many of our own people will be killed in the revolution? How much destruction will be heaped upon our land? What factual evidence is there to support these predictive grounds as being warranted or not?

Human action, or course, does not—in fact, cannot—wait on fully informed and documented answers. People do the best they can to get some plausible answers.

Change the time and place of our hypothetical revolutionary-nationalists to the British colonies in America in the 1770s. The situation was somewhat similar. In retrospect, ought the American Revolution to have taken place? Would you have decided for revolution at the time? The founders of the United States did so, before the fact, and to do so they had to decide based on factors very similar to the ones given above from whatever evidence and logical and empirical support for "predictive grounds" they could muster.

In sum, predictions are often a necessary part of the "evidence" that is needed to support or discredit an "ought" statement. I suggest that Lee's "evidence" be expanded to include predictions, but, since predictions deal with the as yet nonevidential future, I have called them "predictive grounds."

Value Conflict or Disagreement About Predictions?

Some of what appears to be disagreement about moral issues actually may be disagreement about the future consequences of an action, that is about predictive grounds, rather than a conflict of values. For example, in recent times there have been various proposals made about legalizing or decriminalizing recreational drugs in the United States. Although often cast in moral terms, the major disagreements among the disputants are really not basically moral conflicts, since the adherents propound values that are largely shared. They disagree, however, on what would happen in the future *if* drugs were legalized.

One view is that marijuana, heroin, cocaine, and other such drugs ought to be legalized (or decriminalized) and regulated much as alcohol and tobacco are now. The grounds given to support that assertion include, among other things, the predictions that the streets would be safer because the drug wars would cease, that there would be fewer drug-related injuries and deaths (the main cause now being the violence connected with the illegal drug trade), that less money would have to be spent on law enforcement, that there would be greater opportunity and success treating and curing current addicts, and that total abuse of such drugs would be reduced (especially if educational campaigns were launched similar to those about the damaging effects of tobacco use). Also, they argue that some banned drugs may have important medicinal uses, as in the case of marijuana that provides relief from nausea, pain, and muscle spasms, and alleviates symptoms of glaucoma, multiple sclerosis, AIDS, migraine, and other debilitating ailments. Additionally, they believe that current law enforcement efforts have failed and will continue to fail to reduce the use of the drugs and the violence connected with it.

The opposing view generally contests these predictions about future results and instead posits, if drugs were legalized, that there will be future increases in drug use, in injuries and deaths due to the use of the drugs, in the births of damaged babies from drug-using mothers, and other negative consequences—all of which are challenged by the pro-legalization advocates. The people against legalization also often believe that current law enforcement efforts or some improvement in them will work in controlling the problem or, at least, that injuries and deaths, and other negative consequences will be fewer under continuation of the legal ban compared to what would occur under legalization.

Each group contends that moral purposes would be achieved better by following its policy rather than the opposing one. Both groups agree that to reduce human suffering and save lives are moral things to do. Thus, much of the debate rests not on a value conflict but on a disagreement about future outcomes of particular policies. Since we cannot know what the outcomes really will be until after the fact, we must decide which set of predictive grounds is more plausible. That is not a question of a clash of values, but of the validity of the facts, theories, and logical deductions given to support the different predictions. What is needed is a critical evaluation of the presumptive truth or presumptive falsity of the conflicting predictions of future consequences.

It is Moral to Acquire Knowledge

For futurists, morality is not merely a matter of intentions. It is much more a matter of actual results or consequences. Because this is so, it follows that it is moral to acquire knowledge and to act on accurate and true beliefs about the world. Let me explain why.

Actions can have consequences other than those intended or anticipated. To be fully responsible and accountable, a person, when deciding how to act, must take into account unintended consequences and appraise their effects. Thus, it is not enough to intend to do what is right. "It is also necessary to make sound judgments about reality. A man gathering mushrooms as a treat for his family can kill everybody by collecting the wrong sort" (Grisez and Shaw 1988: 229). We may act wrongly, in other words, even if we have good intentions, because we are ignorant of the relevant facts. "Thus physicians used to kill off their patients instead of curing them not because they did not wish to do as they would be done by, but because they falsely thought that bleedings, purges and other horrifying treatments did in fact have the effect of curing diseased people" (Smart 1984: 130).

On this issue, I part company with Etzioni (1988:43) who emphasizes the role of intentions at the expense of consequences in making moral judgments. This leads him to say, "In purely moral situations, the means-end scheme does not apply." Not so. Although, of course, intentions matter, it is moral to *do* right rather than merely to *intend* to do right. For example, in the 1970s the Pol Pot regime of Democratic Kampuchea was responsible for the deaths of a million Cambodians, an incredible one out of every eight Cambodians then alive. "They died from warfare, starvation, overwork, misdiagnosed diseases, and executions." The regime did not intend for most of these people to die and they did not intend to create "the killing fields." But their "lack of evil intent does not 'alleviate the horror' nor relieve the leadership of responsibility (Kamm 1992: 7; Chandler 1991).

Acquiring accurate relevant knowledge about the way the world works, including the social world, and making presumptively accurate predictions about the future consequences of one's actions are aspects of being a morally responsible and accountable person. You are as responsible for the unintended and unanticipated consequences of your actions as you are for the intended and anticipated consequences. Moreover, if it were within your power and capacity to predict the unintended and otherwise unanctipated consequences of your acts, you certainly ought to be held accountable for them. So you are cautioned to investigate to the best of your ability and available knowledge all of the consequences of your proposed action in order to minimize unpleasant surprises and to avoid doing harm out of ignorance and stupidity.

Thus, we have discovered a justification for believing in the value of scientific knowledge itself:

Assertion: Acquiring accurate, relevant knowledge about the way the world works, including the social world, and making presumptively accurate predictions about the future consequences of your actions are aspects of being morally responsible and accountable.

Predictive grounds:

1. Because to do so will increase the chances of your being competently responsible for yourself and successful as you make your way in the world, and because it will decrease the chances of your becoming a dependent burden to others;
2. because to do so will decrease the chances of your doing harm to yourself or to others unintentionally; and
3. because to do so will increase the chances of your good intentions being achieved.

Note that we have found, also, another justification of the role of prediction in futures studies. Both knowledge *and* predictions are necessary for adequate moral reasoning. It is moral to know what you are doing—and that includes "knowing" in advance of your acts the probable future that you will create by your acts.

Finally, a paradox must be noted. On the one hand, the human race today has extraordinary power. For example, for the first time in history, we have the power to destroy the human race, the Earth's plants and animals, and the life-sustaining capacities of the Earth. On the other hand, our powers of foresight generally lag behind our technical knowledge and capacity to act.

Thus, although we have a moral obligation to know what we are doing and to choose benevolent actions, we also have a moral obligation to recognize our massive ignorance and, therefore, to behave cautiously and prudently because our actions may have unknown effects despite our efforts to know them. It is moral to know what is relevant to our actions *and* it is moral to know that there is much that we do not know—and to act accordingly (Jonas 1981: 29).

Follow Rules, But Allow Exceptions

Some ethical theories emphasize following behavioral rules, as we have seen, while others emphasize choosing appropriate behavior, not by such rules, but by the desirability of its consequences in particular situations. There is wisdom in each of these views and they can be used in tandem to increase the moral sophistication of decisions and actions.

Actual decision situations, as we all know, are often complicated. Thus, having behavioral rules of thumb are useful, as any routine habitual behavior may be, such as tying our shoelaces or walking without having to think about each small step. If we had to stop and rethink each move, our efforts would be laborious—as people have learned when they must relearn their motor skills after an accident or a stroke. Similarly, if we had to review every situation to figure out what action would benefit the most people or to use epistemic implication to analyze all the relevant factors, we would have precious little time left in a day. Thus, for ordinary people in their everyday lives, it is quick and easy to follow rules, such as "Tell the truth," "Don't steal," "Treat other people with respect." "Be responsible for yourself." "Do no harm." "Help others when you can." "Honor thy father and thy mother." They allow us to act without rethinking all our reasons and applying them to a new situation. They are easy for us to learn and teach to others and to invest with emotive force, including the guilt we may feel when we violate them.

Also, trying to figure out the best action to take in each situation not only takes time, it may result in error. Unless one has a great deal of information about the consequences, not only the primary consequences but also the secondary, tertiary, and on down the line, we can make serious mistakes.

Ethical rules, in contrast, have been tested over long periods of human history and represent the accumulated wisdom of past experiences of how behaving this way or that turned out, both in the short and long run. Thus, it saves time and may reduce error to have rules of thumb (Harman 1977: 155).

Clearly, rules are useful, even necessary, in making value judgments, but exceptions are too, because values often appear to conflict in real life situations and, thus, produce extenuating circumstances. Thus, the distinction made earlier between prima facie and all-things-considered "ought" statements is relevant here too. No rule says, "Do this all things considered." Moral law is conditional and flexible (Stevenson 1963: 100–1). Each case invites us to decide it on its own merits, to choose which rules are relevant and which have priority over others, to decide what to do "all things considered." All major religions, for example, include respect for truth, but acknowledge exceptions (Snell 1988: 225).

Finally, the futurist qua futurist clearly has an obligation to go beyond ethical rules of thumb in his or her work and undertake the task of trying to specify clearly the grounds for his or her judgments of futures as preferable or not. The first step is to make an explicit statement of the values that he or she is using as standards of judgment. The second, more difficult, step is to follow some objective methodology such as one of those proposed here—the means-ends, commitment-deducibility, or, especially, epistemic-implication model—to test the validity of the values so used. And the third step is to deal with all-things-considered "ought" statements in particular cases, taking into account side effects as well as intended consequences.

Beliefs Can Change Attitudes

A link between fact and value that is often overlooked is that our beliefs about the way the world really is can change our judgments about what is good and bad. Hume's arguments to the contrary, beliefs *can* change attitudes "just as a child ceases to *want* to touch a live coal when he comes to *believe* that it will burn him" (Stevenson 1963: 4). To take another example, a growing child learns both that a sharp knife can cut his hand (a description) *and* that he ought to be careful not to cut his hand with it (a prescription).

Another example can be found in the case of smoking. During the last several decades people have come to know the facts about the devastating health effects of cigarette smoking. This knowledge has resulted in a series of individual and organizational behavioral changes. Many individuals have given up smoking themselves, and various organizations, including various levels of government, have made collective decisions that prohibit smoking by anyone in public places. It has also resulted in a growing judgment that smoking is not only bad for your health, but also a morally bad act as well. Smokers are being redefined as people who are doing a bad thing, perhaps even becoming perceived as bad persons. This is most evident when they "inconsiderately" smoke where other people may be harmed "second-hand" by breathing the smoke they produce, but it also appears to be occurring because of what they are doing to themselves and their inability to control their own behavior. They are, after all, drug addicts, even though the drug is legal.

Take a hypothetical example of a person who believes, first, that "ought entails can." As described earlier, this belief involves the idea that you can't be expected to do that which you cannot do. Let's assume that the person also holds the value assertion, second, that some form of socialist, command economy is the only fair system. To that belief-value structure let's add, third, a new belief for this person that recent experience has clearly demonstrated that socialist, command economies in any form do not and cannot work.

What is the result? The person might conclude that his value commitment to socialist, command economies must be abandoned on the empirical grounds that they cannot work. Some underlying value this person has to "fairness" may remain, but the way he or she expresses that value in specific action via a means/end model has totally changed. Moreover, the definition of the value of "fairness" might itself change in the person's mind, if it appears that it cannot be achieved in reality. For example, it may be that fairness defined as complete equality of rewards for economic work would fail to motivate some people to work and make people in the whole society on average somewhat poorer.

One of the early interpretations of the well-known social experiments on income maintenance, briefly described previously in chapter 6, volume 1, gives another example. One result appeared to negatively affect the stability of the family, a societal value. That is, couples with guaranteed incomes divorced more frequently than couples not receiving such incomes. Probing more deeply, researchers discovered that guaranteed incomes enabled some people, usually women, to get out of rotten marriages in which they had been trapped. This fact helped to shift the value referent of the researchers and relevant policymakers from that of stable families to that of the pursuit of happiness and self-actualization: A guaranteed income may increase divorce (and, thus, increase family instability), but it also freed women from unhappy marriages. Is family stability a good thing when it is achieved at the cost of unhappy people? Researchers moved in their judgments toward giving priority to individual happiness.

Relevant facts clearly can influence what people think they "ought" to do, possibly shift their value priorities, and perhaps even reverse their value judgments.

Conclusion

If the investigation of preferable futures is to take its equal place with the exploration of probable and possible futures on the futurist agenda, then futurists—or at least some futurists—must go beyond merely observing attitudes and preferences of various respondents and become as expert in moral reasoning as they now are in the various methods of forecasting and scenario-writing. Moreover, futures studies would benefit if at least some moral philosophers would break through the confining walls of their discipline and turn their attention to the analysis of the preferable within the specific contexts of contemporary social science and futurists' constructions and assessments of images of the future.

Futurists—and, for that matter, ordinary people making their daily life decisions—need some explicit and systematic methods of making moral judgments to ground the normative assumptions and statements that they make about preferable futures. They need some ways of knowing what makes an act moral and good and knowing what futures are better than others. In an age in which some people have embraced various and conflicting fundamentalisms and in which others have grown totally skeptical of religious and other traditional foundations of morality, there is a common need to find some objective and universal procedures for settling disputes about what we ought to do that go beyond appeals to religious faith, political ideology, community conventions, cultural traditions, authority, bribes, threats, and brute force.

Thus, I have given three methods that can be used by futurists and others to examine value judgments concerning preferable futures objectively: (1) commitment-deducibility; (2) means-ends; and (3) epistemic-implication. The first two have been long recognized, while the last appears to be unknown to futurists and most social scientists.

All three methods frame communicative acts among people about the good, and they encourage coherent, critical, and reasoned discourse. They invite intersubjective agreement through verification and falsification by independent observers. Thus, conclusions reached about the good are not arbitrary results or personal idiosyncrasies. They become matters publicly open to review by any competent person.

The commitment-deducibility model is especially suited to testing whether secondary conclusions follow from the basic assumptions. The means-ends model is especially suited to test the relevant matters of fact concerning causal relationships. The epistemic-implication model, clearly the most powerful method, can do both and, in addition, it can test by implication even fundamental moral assumptions themselves.

Thus, epistemic implication suggests a most promising path by which to progress beyond the ultimately subjective judgment in the first two methods. It fits within Popper's fallibilism, what I have elaborated in this book as the critical realist theory of knowledge. Applying Lee's five criteria of serious, referentially and causally relevant, causally independent, and empirically true evidence results in the implied confirmation or falsification of the value assertion that rests upon it.

Adding predictive grounds to serve as permissible evidence in the method of epistemic implication, as I have proposed, increases the utility of the method by explicitly putting the assessment of value judgments in the context of foresight. Thus, I place the process of critical evaluation within the future-oriented processes of decision making, choice, and social action.

This is necessary because intelligent and effective action requires that people "know" both the future consequences of alternative possible actions (a prediction problem) *and* whether such future consequences will be desirable or undesirable (a value-judgmental problem). Strictly speaking, Hume may have been correct about the logical difficulties of going both from "is" to "will" and from "is" to "ought." In real life, however, people have no choice but to do both. This is so even when people don't appear to act, since not to act is itself a decision, a choice, and an act of sorts.

By urging the adoption of these methods of assessing moral judgments, I am not suggesting that the solution to deciding what futures are preferable is thereby totally given. They are a beginning to investigation and deliberation, not an end. When used with skill, understanding and knowledge—just as with the methods described in volume 1—they can produce sound and useful results. In this case, they allow the critical assessment of value judgments.

Such critical assessment can be grounded with as much objectivity as can scientific predictions, especially if they are stated appropriately and if the criteria of epistemic implication are applied systematically. Although we may not be able to achieve absolute certainty either in predicting the consequences of our actions or in judging which of them are most desirable or undesirable, we can often achieve some degree of warranted assertability in both instances.

Moreover, given the post-postpositivist recognition that scientific knowledge itself is corrigible and conjectural, the grounded conclusions of value testing using epistemic implication are not fundamentally different from the grounding of truth claims. Conclusions are not rigid, dogmatic, nor absolute. Rather, they are provisional, conditional, and open to change with the introduction of new information. They are conjectural knowledge.

I am not proposing here that futurists and other social scientists and scientists drop their scholarly and scientific methodologies for the sake of gratuitous and undisciplined moralizing. There is too much of that in the world already. Also, I have no desire to return to the situation that Weber faced, that is, the *privatdozents* in the lecture hall professing their political or religious biases.

To the contrary, what I am proposing is the exact opposite: that the scope of applicability of scholarly and scientific methodologies be expanded to include the objective assessment of value judgments. Weber, ironically contradicting his own belief by his behavior, did so; for, as Kohlberg (1981:113) points out, "when Weber takes a value stand (including the stand of value neutrality) he attempts to support it by a very careful rational argument."

By giving "a very careful rational argument," futurists can bring moral judgments into the critical discourse of futures studies with rigor. In this way, images of preferable futures, that is, images of the good society that ought to be human goals for the future, can be objectively and systematically grounded, critically examined, refuted if wrong, and opened up to the possibility of free and mutual understanding in communication (Habermas 1984).

In any event, today there is precious little value-free science and few, if any, science-free values. All ethical arguments directly or indirectly relate to some more or less accurate common knowledge of the day—and today that knowledge is infused with science. Thus, the task is to make such knowledge explicit, open to critical social deliberation, and as sound as possible. For no one's value judgments are better than another's except insofar as the reasons for them are better grounded in logic, scientific theory, or empirical fact.

In the following four chapters, I continue to discuss objective ways of making value judgments that define the good society, moving from the abstract and philosophical models given in this chapter to some concrete examples. In the next chapter, I review some practical strategies that have been used to evaluate preferable futures.

3

Some Practical Strategies for Judging Preferable Futures

Introduction

In this chapter, I describe some practical strategies—from religion to professional ethics—that have been used as guides or aids in reaching judgments about how people ought to behave and how to define preferable futures. They are drawn not so much from the work of futurists as from ordinary life and from the work of other professionals and social thinkers who have analyzed values and ethical rules of conduct. They are samples of what is culturally available to deal with value questions. They involve appeals to some legitimating source that some people use in their everyday lives to justify their judgments of the good and bad.

None of the strategies given here is a fully adequate substitute for a detailed analysis of a specific ethical issue in a given case using epistemic implication. But most of us, as I said in the last chapter, have neither the time nor the information needed to carry out such an analysis every time we face a decision to act. Thus, we tend to follow a mish-mash of sometimes contradictory rules of thumb based on fragments of religious and moral codes we have been taught, the laws of our country, the lessons we think we have learned from our own experiences, our personal preferences, the conventions and traditions of the groups to which we belong, our ineffable and intuitive gut feelings, and, of course, myths and superstitions of many kinds.

All of these things are heuristic devices that help us in particular times, places, and social situations to decide what is dutiful, right, good, and preferable. They are useful because they allow us to make speedy decisions about how to act as opportunities and problems present themselves. They are useful, thus, partly because they tend to be habitual and basically thoughtless. They prevent the paralysis of indecision and allow us to act.

But thoughtless they often are, and, if consciously examined, some of these strategies or appeals would more or less fail the tests of rationality and objectivity. They would more or less fail, that is, to lead to moral and good acts and they would more or less fail to lead to desirable futures. What I propose here is their reexamination, keeping in mind the methods of evaluating moral judgments discussed in the last chapter, so that they can be used more responsibly, where possible, and replaced or supplemented by sounder, more objective reasoning, where necessary. We may be able to shape our own habitual actions more consciously so as to achieve the moral ends we desire, because we have examined and reflected upon the consequences and ethical justifications of our actions.

Appeals to Religion

Importance of Religion

Most humans, as far as we can tell from the archeological evidence, always have recognized some superhuman power or powers, a god or gods of some kind (supreme being, the creator, Allah, Brahma, Yahweh, the Messiah, the Holy Spirit, or whatever), that presided over their universe. They have always believed in stories that told of how such deities dealt with humans and they have always used such stories to interpret and direct their lives (Greeley 1989: 1). Religion has proclaimed values, norms of conduct, guides of what is right and wrong, and given to the human community a justification of them. It has given people both the love or fear of God and the promise of Heaven and the threat of Hell to motivate them to act rightly. It has given them, too, the ultimate meaning of life and the reassurence "that there is some purpose in life beyond life itself" (Greeley 1989: 1).

Religions are sets of beliefs that "involve some conception of a supernatural being, world, or force, and the notion that the supernatural is active, that events and conditions here on earth are influenced by the supernatural" (Stark and Bainbridge 1985: 5). Religions provide satisfactions to human desires and, distinctively, to those desires that go beyond the available material satisfactions of this world. They involve some meaning and purpose to life beyond the natural world of our senses.

Religious beliefs compensate for scarce rewards and suffering in this worldly life by promising otherworldly rewards in the future afterlife (Stark and Bainbridge 1985: 6, 431).

One attraction of using religious values to justify preferable futures is that they are widely held. Most people today have religious beliefs, although not everyone who does is strongly devout. About 80 percent of the world's people at least belong to or identify with one of the world's religions. In mid-1992, there were more than 1.8 billion Christians, nearly one billion Muslims, about 733 million Hindus, and about 315 million Buddhists, and, of course, hundreds—perhaps thousands—of other smaller religious groups from Jews and Sikhs to Confucians and Baha'is.

Even in the world's economically advanced countries, religious believers and practitioners constitute significant percentages of the population. For example, according to national sample surveys in the United States in the 1980s, 95 percent of the respondents believed in God, 71 percent believed in heaven and 53 percent in hell, about 40 percent say they have strong religious convictions, about 68 percent belong to a church or a synagogue, and 40 percent attended church in the past seven days (Greeley 1989).

These are relatively high percentages compared with some European countries, an exception being Ireland whose population also ranks highly on such indicators. For example, a revealing comparison can be made using belief in "life after death." In the United States, 74 percent believed in a life after death and it is about the same in Ireland. In Spain, Finland, and Italy, though, only 50 percent so believed; about 40 percent did in Great Britain, Norway, and the Netherlands; about 33 percent did in what was then West Germany, Belgium, and France; and only about 25 percent did in Denmark (Greeley 1989: 15). Although the percentage of people in Europe who are religious is a significant proportion of the population there, religiosity is comparatively low in many European countries. But it is the European countries that are deviant, not the United States and Ireland. Most of the rest of the world's population profess religious beliefs to a greater degree than in Europe.

Secularization and Sacralization

Societies are constantly changing and religious beliefs have been seriously challenged. Secularization is the process by which a culture changes from one in which the sacred, the supernatural, and the mysteries of superhuman powers permeate the entire life of society and dominate the explanations of events in it to one in which naturalistic viewpoints and explanations come to dominate more and more aspects of life. Science, human control and agency, utilitarian and rational this-world views, demystification, innovation and change define more and more of the daily experiences of people in societies becoming more secular.

The shift toward secularization includes a progressive expansion of worldly, rather than otherworldly, ideas and understandings, especially as a percentage of all views held by individuals. It includes the facts of religious beliefs becoming more subjective and private, more partial and compartmentalized as they face the rise of alternative interpretations of life, more nonrational as they conflict directly with expanding scientific knowledge, more fragmented socially as such institutions as the state and the university become independent of them, and increasingly confined to shrinking spheres of human activity (Schluchter 1989).

Despite temporary fluctuations and initial slow change, the long-term trend over the last 10,000 years has certainly been toward increasing secularization in most aspects of human experience, most of the change probably having occurred during the last 300 years. For example, an increasing number of scientific, engineering, technological, and scholarly advances have created an explosion of knowledge. Many things need no sacred explanation any longer, because their natural causes are known. From viruses and atomic particles to the origin of the universe and the nature of far reaches of the solar system, we have increased human knowledge.

When first created, religions tend to be in accord with the scientific beliefs of the day in many of their assumptions and details. As given religious beliefs continue to exist through time, especially written beliefs, discrepancies begin to appear between new scientific beliefs and continuing religious assumptions. Auxiliary religious beliefs about the nature of the everyday world tend to be static compared with scientific beliefs which continue to change, sometimes very rapidly. For example, literal interpretations of the Bible concerning creation and the flood have been challenged, as have underlying astronomical and geological assumptions, such as the sun revolving around the Earth or the sun being stationary in the sky (Stark and Bainbridge 1985: 435).

In 1633, the Inquisitors forced Galileo to recant his findings that the Earth moved. They did so because they worried that, if his ideas were taught, they would undermine the Catholic tradition. Three-hundred-fifty-nine years later, on October 31, 1992, the Catholic Church finally admitted its error, finding that Galileo's Inquisitors had been incapable of dissociating faith from an age-old cosmology, the biblical vision of the Earth as the center of the universe. The Church and its members, of course, had long since accommodated Galileo's cosmology and much more in addition.

Despite the knowledge explosion, however, science has only scratched the surface of what there is in the universe to know and understand. There remain mysteries beyond the science of our day, and we can safely predict that some mysteries also will remain beyond the science of many tomorrows, even if we assume optimistically that modern civilization will not come crashing down, as have so many civilizations before it, as a result of some catastrophe.

Thus, Galileo's Inquisitors need not have worried. Questions such as "What are the purposes of human existence?" and "What is the meaning of life?" continue to tease the human imagination. Also, science "is completely helpless in the face of claims made of a being, world, or force beyond the natural world" (Stark and Bainbridge 1985: 14).

Thus, it is not surprising that many people throughout the world, despite the use of modern science and technology as meaning systems for an ever increasing percentage of their total life's experiences (e.g., when their car does not start, they call a mechanic not a priest or a rabbi), nonetheless continue to identify with a religion, attend religious services, and believe in a supernatural power and a life after death. For the United States, except for a onetime decline among younger and better-educated Catholics in acceptance of the literal truth of the Bible, Greeley (1989) finds that over the past half century there has been relatively little change in levels of religious commitment, conviction, and practice.

It is wrong, however, to conclude that secularization has not taken place. It is always taking place, even within religious organizations themselves, such as the Catholic Church. In fact, the church itself and the bureaucratic structure it has evolved into are classic examples of aspects of secularization processes, such as professionalization, intellectualization, and rationalization. Additionally, the dominant and established institutions of society tend to become progressively more worldly not only in the structures of their organizations and styles of operation, but also in their views (Stark and Bainbridge 1985). For some modern people, as Weber (1958a: 155) said, the world becomes disenchanted.

When it comes to the basic questions of the meaning of life, those things that remain unknown and perhaps unknowable, secularization has fostered two countervailing religious reactions. One is the emergence of revival groups, or *sects*, that aim to return to less worldly and more fundamental religious views abandoned by other meaning systems and by secularized religions. As established religions become more and more worldly, for example, sects break off from them and challenge them by reaffirming supernatural beliefs, by reasserting otherworldly doctrines. Hence, sects constitute not only fragmentation but also a move toward fundamentalism.

Another is the creation of new religious groups and traditions. Such new religions, or *cults*, constantly appear in society, and they, too, may reassert fundamentalism. The vast majority of cults, perhaps, have only a short life, but, partly depending on the vigor—or lack thereof—of the established religious organizations and partly on their own access to resources, they sometimes catch on and thrive.

Thus, the history of religious traditions is not only one of decline in some parts of society and in some aspects of life's experiences, but is also one of constant revitalization, birth, and growth in others. Although the sources of religion may shift constantly, the relative amount of religion in any society stays about the same (Stark and Bainbridge 1985: 3). Processes of secularization and sacralization both may go on all the time. If for some people God is dead or dying, for others He or She is alive and well or constantly being reborn.

Thus, the future of religion seems secure, even though religion may not always be a significant force in the great collective decisions of increasingly technological, knowledge-based, and large-scale societies.

The "Good" as Defined by Religion

We are all familiar with the saintly behavior of devoutly religious people, their kindness and compassion, their affection and love for others, their benevolence, their efforts to reduce human suffering and misery, and, sometimes, their austerity and self-sacrifices. We are familiar, too, with the ability of religious faith to console individuals with the promise of salvation, to renew human hope, and to lessen violence and to promote cooperation in society (Boulding 1985: 51).

The "thou shalt nots" and the "thou shalts" of nearly every religion have within them codes of behavior that include a generosity of spirit toward other human beings. All five of the world's major religious traditions—the Buddhist, Christian, Hindu, Jewish, and Muslim—teach a morality of generous goodwill, love, and compassion toward others as a central ethical principle (Hick 1989: 316). Biblical values include the sanctity of life, justice, freedom, equality, brotherhood, mercy, simplicity, innocence, love of truth, purity, and peace. The virtues of Confucianism include benevolence and trustworthiness. In the down-to-earth contemporary world, followers of the liberation theology of the Roman Catholic Church in Latin America have opposed dictatorships, defended human rights, organized trade unions, and fought for land reform.

In the case of monotheism an important value can be found in the fact that the boundaries dividing people were abolished, at least theoretically. Social inclusivism of all human beings as basically equal members in a single collective entity was an implication. To believe in only one god is to believe that all humankind "must be a single community in the eyes of that god. And if that god is the source of morality, then all men [and women] are bound into a single fellowship of duty" (Naroll 1983: 49).

In the past, the Christian churches, as Wuthnow (1993) shows, helped to create a sense of community among people, provided identity, and motivated trust and compassion. Even in modern, secular societies, religious people are more likely than nonreligious people to do good deeds, volunteering their time and money to benefit others. Methodists, for example, are fond of repeating a rule of their church's founder, John Wesley, "Do all the good you can, by all the means you can, in all the ways you can, at all the times you can, to all the people you can, as long as you ever can."

Yet we must recognize that the "good" as defined by most religions usually is two-faced. First is the view that God is beyond good and evil and that one ought to do what God commands whether right or wrong, such a principle, for example, as "*fiat justia, pereat mundus*" ("Act justly though the world perish."). The evils that have been done in His (or Her) name under such a doctrine are legion. No human atrocity is necessarily incompatible with it. Humans obey and leave the results to the Lord rather than accepting responsibility and giving an account of the foreseeable results of one's action (Weber 1958b: 120). Such a view is incompatible with modern futurists' belief systems that include a concern with the consequences of social action and human responsibility for the future.

Second, throughout much of history in both the Middle East and the West, tolerance of contrary beliefs was not defined as a virtue nor intolerance as a vice by religious doctrines. Nonbelievers were often simply defined out of the population of the select and dehumanized. They became the alien and subhuman "Other." There was—and is—little room for reasoned discussion of religious differences where hostility and hatred exist toward members of religious outgroups and where zealous convictions will not tolerate doubt or dissent.

Third, all kinds of ghastly behaviors have been sanctified by some sacred text or priestly caste, not only in the historical past but also today as I write. Human sacrifice, for example, was commonplace among the Toltec and the Maya and must have reached a peak among the Aztecs. The Aztec gods ate people and were provided fresh human hearts and human blood by the priests (Harris 1977: 99).

Human sacrifice may have been an anomaly, but animal sacrifice was worldwide. The Old Testament, for example, not only recommends it, but in the Book of Leviticus describes in detail how it ought to be done. As far as the killing of human beings is concerned, members of all the major religions have gone "to war to please their gods or carry out god's will." (Harris 1977: 107, 117).

I could continue by describing the persecutions of heretics and witch hunts, the tortures on the rack, the burnings at the stake, many forced denunciations of the truth, the Inquisition, the Crusades, etc.—the outrageous, base, and miserable things, the absolute horrors and terrors, that some people have done to debase, enslave, and murder other people in carrying out what they believed to be the word of one god or another. They would make a long and shocking list of ruthless and vicious acts. Moreover, their justifications in sacred documents are legend, for example, extreme violence in Old Testament texts, including genocide in Deuteronomy and murdering enemies in Ezekiel, and slavery and the subordination of women in New Testament texts.

Enough has been said, I trust, to convince the reader that the "good" as defined by various religious leaders and teachings has included not only benevolence toward others but also a multitude of abominations. Such abominations in the name of religion continue as I write, for example, in Northern Ireland, Iraq, Israel, Armenia, Bosnia, Kashmir, Sri Lanka, Tibet, New Guinea, among many other places. It is difficult to exaggerate the harm that has been and is being done in the world by true religious believers. On the one hand, most religions teach mutual love and respect toward others. "On the other hand, they teach (implicitly if not openly) that only *certain* people can be saved—those who believe as they do; that only *certain* people are chosen people; that there is only one real truth—theirs" (Rokeach 1968: 189).

Religious Justification of the Good: An Assessment

There are two reasons why religion cannot stand alone as a justification of preferable futures. The first is, as we have seen above, the fact that there is no guarantee that what some religion or another justifies as "good" would indeed be good by some other criteria. Who knows what evils may be masquerading as religious "goods," such as, for example, murdering all nonbelievers—or attempting to assassinate one accused of blasphemy, as in the case of the price put on the head of novelist Salman Rushdie by the Shiite Muslim leader, the Ayatollah Ruhollah Khomeini. Thus, even though most of the world's people are believers, uncritical faith in religious doctrines cannot be accepted *in toto* as justification for believing in particular values or ethical prescriptions.

Second, on the theological level, religious justifications (e.g., "the word of God," "the Bible says," "This is God's will") transcend naturalistic reality as we understand it and rely on supernatural justifications. If religious ethics are ultimately a set of God's—or of some gods'—commands, then they rest on theological beliefs that ultimately defy negation, even if they are false. God's "infallible revelations," "eternal truths," and "absolute certainties" rely on faith, mysticism, and mystification. Moreover, when supernatural authority cannot be questioned nor human consequences of "righteous" actions evaluated without fear of reprisals, then, earthly responsibility is abdicated. Again, we must conclude that something other than religion is needed. Religious beliefs in and of themselves do not—and cannot—constitute conjectural knowledge.

Yet there are at least four ways that religious beliefs and values can constructively enter into critical discourse about preferable futures and the values underlying them. The first is settling disputes about the good among people who share the same faith. A commitment-deducibility model can be applied. For example, make a sincere commitment to some holy word (as when people of the same religion share a belief in the Koran or some other sacred document) and, then, deduce from it what behavior is, therefore, right or wrong. This is not to say that such deduction is easy or undebatable, given the perplexing ambiguities, errors, and contradictions of most sacred texts, not to mention the varying degrees of literality that might be applied to the same text. Yet for people who are willing to agree on the rightness of a given text, the commitment-deducibility model has some utility for objectively agreeing on the good. The deducibility part of the model can be carried out according to the rules of logic.

Thus, if it is proposed that we ought to behave in a particular way because the Bible says so, we can, at least, argue objectively whether or not the Bible does indeed say so. The exegesis of sacred texts, therefore, may have a role to play in resolving disputes about the preferable among people who share a belief in the same religious texts.

For example, the National Council of Churches finds justification to condemn racism in a "Pastoral Letter on Contemporary Racism and the Role of the Church." And Catholics find justification for their reproductive behavior in Pope Paul VI's encyclical letter on birth control (*Humanae Vitae*) reaffirming the Catholic Church's prohibitions against the use of any "artifical means" of contraception.

Believers of different religions, however, who could not agree on a sacred text as the ultimate authority would not be helped in their dispute resolution by the commitment-deducibility model. Israelis who believe that God promised the West Bank and the Gaza Strip to Jews and that they ought to remain Israel's forever and ever cannot convince skeptical Palestinians that God so promised. Also, no religious text would have much influence over those people who believe, as the Greek Xenophanes was, perhaps, the first to point out, that it was not God who created man, but man who created God (Macquarrie 1985).

Thus, although it can be used to frame and resolve disputes among relevant believers, the commitment-deducibility model, as it always does, ultimately fails. In the particular case of religion, it fails both because the transcendental commitment is not grounded within the religion in naturalistic terms and because nonbelievers may be unwilling to make the original commitment.

Second, the means-ends model is of some utility in choosing specific courses of action. If people of the same—or even different—religions can agree that it is morally right to treat other people with generous goodwill, love, and compassion, how can we go about doing so? How can we teach people to behave toward others in these ways? What social structural changes can we make that will encourage people to do so? What kinds of community supports do we need? Clearly, the answers to such questions are to be found largely in the social sciences. They are means to ends and, as such, they can be answered objectively, even though some of the answers may be elusive.

As in the case of the commitment-deducibility model, the means-ends model ultimately fails because the ends remain unjustified by objective analysis.

Third, religion nonetheless remains useful as a storehouse of values to be objectively tested within a naturalistic framework. Sacred writings give rules of behavior. There are, for example, rules and imperative sentences in all parts of scripture that tell us what we ought to do (Meeks 1993: 89). Additionally, religions contain general principles, examples of personal behavior, and cautionary tales from which rules can be derived (Meeks 1993: 89). Such rules define ethics, values, and norms. Although they derive from the teachings of particular religions, as prescriptions or proscriptions they are not necessarily uniquely religious. After all, they purport to guide human behavior in *this* world. They may be—or could be—shared by many ethical systems, including different religions, and we can use human reason to find out if there is any objective evidence to support them in the naturalistic world.

For example, let's take a version of the Golden Rule, not as a command from God, but simply as a down-to-earth assertion about how we ought to behave: "Do unto others as you would have others do unto you." If this is interpreted not only as treating others well, but when abused to "turn the other cheek," then there is some evidence to suggest that you ought not. Rather, you ought to behave in a somewhat different way. For example, take the *assertion*:

> You ought to reciprocate other's benevolence toward you, but, when treated malevolently by a person, you ought to withdraw your cooperation from that person and defend yourself as necessary.

And support it with these *predictive grounds*:

> Because to reciprocate benevolence will enhance future cooperation and the possibility of a win-win result for everyone in a relationship; and because to withdraw your cooperation and to defend yourself when treated malevolently will reduce the chances of your future exploitation and will teach the exploiter that he or she ought not to exploit people and, thus, will encourage reformation of his or her future behavior.

The predictive grounds meet Keekok Lee's (1985) criteria of serious, referentially relevant, causally relevant, and causally independent grounds. But is there any empirical evidence to support them?

Yes, there is. In a Computer Prisoner's Dilemma Tournament, Robert Axelrod (1984) pitted many different strategies against one another in repeated interactions. Players could win mutual gains from cooperating with each other, or one could exploit the other, or both could fail to cooperate. What Axelrod found was that the most successful overall strategy was a simple tit-for-tat, in which a player starts by cooperating with other players and, after that, by reciprocating cooperation or retaliating against exploitation.

There are, though, important provisos that must be considered: A player always begins by cooperating, retaliates no more viciously than withholding cooperation, and does not hold grudges, forgiving past failure to cooperate immediately and starting cooperating again when another player shows he or she wants to cooperate.

Moreover, there is some additional evidence to suggest that, in order to prevent a situation of stable noncooperation, there may have to be a small number of people who are willing to cooperate no matter what, even to cooperate with known defectors. Yet there must not be too many such unconditional cooperators in any system because they would make malevolence pay off and, thus, threaten larger community goals (Kondo 1990).

If correct, these findings also reflect on another well-known principle, *lex talionis*, or the law of retaliation. Demanding "an eye for an eye, a tooth for a tooth" may discourage aggressors to some extent, but it may not be a good long-term strategy for winning the cooperation of other people, because it is too harsh. The withdrawal of cooperation often is sufficient retaliation rather than risking a new round of conflict by overt damage to others.

To take another example, ought rats to be worshipped and left alone to breed as Hindu mythology dictates? Or should rats be killed and removed from places of human habitation? There are good objective reasons why they ought to be destroyed and we can look to India for an example. First, through the fleas that they host, they help spread the plague that occasionally rises to epidemic proportions, killing hundreds of thousands of people. Second, they eat nearly a quarter of the farm produce, enough to feed the Indian people for three months. Here is a case where a religious belief is an anachronism so at odds with current scientific knowledge and so threatening to human well-being that it ought to be changed.

In sum, the religious source of a prescription in no way prevents it from being analyzed objectively. By so doing, however, we are no longer justifying the prescription by an appeal to religion. We have moved to a naturalistic and universalistic method. This is increasingly important as a global society is created in which humans consider themselves to be part of the whole of humankind, since global social interaction, communication, and identity invite some commonly shared standards of morality to govern them.

Fourth, and finally, religious beliefs have a role to play in mobilizing people for action to achieve preferable futures. If specified preferable futures have been justified by naturalistic means, then a search can be carried out in religious texts for values that support them. In this way religion can generate important backing for morality even in a modern, increasingly secular world (Lombardi 1988:66). When they learn how a given image of the future embodies the values espoused by their religions, people can be motivated by values that they already hold to work for its achievement. Hence, new theological research and debate relevant to the critical issues of our time, such as, for example, Badham's (1993) reinterpretation of Christian tradition in relation to environmental responsibility, are important.

The moral examples set by religious bodies themselves have contributed to the spread and acceptance of objectively based moral discourse since they sometimes justify their own value stance on an issue by grounding their reasons in the empirical natural and social science. Dillon (1993) gives several examples that involve the role of the Catholic Church in the mid-1980s debate in Ireland concerning the referendum on divorce.

In sum, religious justifications of preferable futures, despite the worldwide public belief in them, fail as objective, rational, and critical arguments. First, religious doctrines have been used to violate human freedom and well-being as well as to enhance them, often fanning the flames of intergroup hatred and warfare. Today, in various parts of the world, Muslims, Christians, Hindus, Jews, and members of other religious groups face one another in murderous conflicts.

Second, the disenchanted and skeptical modern mind simply does not find religious arguments convincing, because, standing alone, they rely on underlying supernatural beliefs that cannot be negated or confirmed. Nonetheless, religious values have some utility as part of critical, naturalistic moral discourse in at least four ways. First, they can be used to resolve disputes about what is right within a commitment-deducibility model, *if* disputants share a commitment to similar religious doctrines and are willing to accept them as authoritative. Ultimately, though, the commitment-deducibility model fails, because the commitment to the underlying religious values remains an act of faith (often involving a sacrifice of the intellect).

Second, within the means-ends model, causal knowledge can be used to design social action in order to achieve shared religious values.

Third, religions are useful as a storehouse of value assertions to be tested by other means, such as epistemic implication. Even though a value assertion may come from a source involving supernatural beliefs, its acceptance, rejection, or revision can be a consequence of the objective use of a naturalistic method.

Fourth, religions are useful as persuasive motivators calling people to action to work for particular futures. Thus, continued explorations and new interpretations of sacred texts are important in showing how religious beliefs and values relate to values that have been justified as preferable by naturalistic discourse. For example, various individuals and international groups increasingly are creating the knowledge base by which to formulate naturalistic reasons why people ought to value world peace and order, social justice and reconciliation, an equal and good chance for a long life of high quality for all peoples on Earth, compassion and understanding among peoples, the freedom and well-being of future generations, and the life-sustaining capacities of the Earth itself now and in the future. What support can be found in religious texts for such values?

The interfaith declaration, "Towards a Global Ethic," made by the Parliament of World's Religions which met in Chicago in September, 1993 is a step in the right direction. It foll ws and helps fulfill Hans Küng's (1991) call for a new world ethic, for an ecumenical theology for peace, and for an interreligious dialogue based on the desirability of the survival of human society, the responsibility of humankind for the future, and a coalition of both religious believers and nonbelievers.

Certainly, the use of religious justifications by fanatics and true believers, fundamentalist or not, who preach hate and death toward others ought not to go unchallenged by religious communities themselves.

Appeals to Law

A Definition of Law

Most—if not all—of the serious alternatives to religion as an arbiter of right and wrong are avowedly a matter of human—or some human's—

construction. No doubt they must seem puny to religiously devout people. After all, for people who believe strongly in God, what is a mere human's profane word compared to God's sacred word? Insignificant. To the contrary, for those people who believe that what passes for God's word is itself nothing more than another human construction, then nonreligious alternatives are no different in this way than religion. In fact, they may be more attractive precisely because they are avowedly naturalistic and invite human questioning and testing.

Governmental or state law is one such alternative. In contemporary Western societies it is admittedly a human construction. Beliefs in the divinity of political leaders and their law no longer compete effectively with the idea that law is made by humans for human purposes. This is true despite the fact that many religion-like beliefs have been transferred to the state and exist in modern political culture. One example is the idea, even in the United States where church and state are separated, that "national political history is built on a religious-based morality" (Williams and Demerath 1991: 417). Moreover, the similarities between political ideologies and religious beliefs, such as claims of transcendent and universal truth and goodness, have led some writers to speak of "political religion" (Apter 1963). Nonetheless, the state and its ideological foundations in contemporary societies rest primarily on natural, this-worldly beliefs rather than on supernatural, otherworldly beliefs.

State law comes the closest to replacing religion as the source of dominant legitimating beliefs in contemporary societies. Even where religion has great and overt influence on the state, as in the Islamic Republic of Iran, secular governmental law has come increasingly to dominate the collective daily lives of modern peoples (Unger 1976: 215).

Although anthropologists have located societies that function without government, they have found no societies that function without social order, some kind of political-like organization, and lawlike institutions (Moore 1986). Perhaps, by definition no human collectivity could be called a society without these features. If such a society ever did exist, it is doubtful if it could exist for very long. Small-scale, nonliterate societies have the rudiments of a legal system, even though they may require only that someone act to help resolve disputes according to commonly held standards (Schwartz 1986: 63–64). All human groups, organizations, associations, and societies, of course, have "laws" in the sense of rules governing the behavior of their members. For contemporary societies, however, the most important and pervasive law is that of the state or government.

Black (1976) defines law simply as governmental social control. Yeager (1991: 19) says that law refers to "all actions of government that seek to order the lives of a society's members, including the rules and processes that select and constrain such actions themselves." Yeager's definition, like Black's, includes the idea of governmental social control: administrative prohibitions and requirements and state actions that "influence the distribution of life chances in a political economy," such as welfare, farm supports, and military contracts.

The modern state claims a monopoly of the legitimate use of force and violence in society and its laws claim precedence over those of any other social institution. In Western societies in the modern era that claim is legitimated by appeals to the "will of the people," the most important source of new law being legislation enacted by democratically elected assemblies (Cotterrell 1984: 18). The rule of law is basic to the modern state.

Laws, Norms, and Values

Law and normative order. There are at least four general interrelationships between law and the normative order of society: (1) social norms may become laws; (2) Laws may become social norms; (3) laws and social norms may conflict with each other; and (4) laws may facilitate the creation of social norms by others.

These four interrelationships are mutually exclusive logically, but in the life of real societies they are not so separate, neat, or tidy. They are in constant flux. With social change, laws and norms change their interrelationships from various degrees of congruence to various degrees of conflict, sometimes in complex and confusing ways.

First, as law evolves in a society, it draws heavily on the norms, religious and otherwise, of that society. Custom, tradition, folkways, and mores are often absorbed into the law. Thus, in some societies, the law may be little more than an expression of the dominant patterns of custom, at least as it is believed they ideally ought to be if not as they really are in the actual behaviors of people.

Second, and more important today in large-scale societies, is the formulation of laws that define a "new set of behavioral standards, imposing them authoritatively" (Schwartz 1986: 64). Law has become a tool of governmental power and has been used to produce wide-scale planned social and economic change (Cotterrell 1984: 48). One example is civil rights legislation in the United States. Legislation, contrary to the customs at the time of some regional populations of the United States, mandated open housing regardless of race or religion, jury panels truly representative of the communities from which they are drawn, equal access to the vote for all adults, equal access to public places, antidiscrimination on the job, and equal justice before the law, among other things. Yet over time, the constant enforcement of such laws and the moral suasion of the law may result in a change in the normative behavior and judgments of the people so that they become more congruent with the law.

Other examples are laws aimed at the protection of consumer, environmental, and employee interests and the creation of such agencies in the United States as the Equal Employment Opportunity Commission in 1965, the National Highway Traffic Safety Administration in 1966, the Environmental Protection Agency in 1970, the Occupational Safety and Health Administration in 1970, and the Consumer Product Safety Commission in 1972. These laws defined many common business practices at the time as wrongful, created new standards of correct behavior for the future, and provided for major criminal penalties for violations (Yeager 1991: 12). Other examples can be found in housing law. Saltman (1975), for example, summarizes a substantial body of research literature on antidiscrimination that demonstrates how law can change not only behavior, but attitudes and beliefs as well, both directly and indirectly.

Obviously, such laws can influence behavior and even alter the norms of society, exerting pressure for change in the customs of particular groups, for example, standard practices of businessmen. Legislators, of course, did not enact these laws nor create these agencies in a vacuum. On the one side, there often was great business opposition. On the other, environmental and other groups were at work lobbying for what they perceived to be in the public interest. Also, public perceptions and values were involved. By the mid-1970s in the United States, we know from social survey data that corporate "illegalities such as price fixing and pollution often came to be considered at least as serious by the public as some of the more conventionally feared crimes such as burglary and robbery" (Yeager 1991: 4). Contrary to widespread public belief, sometimes morality *can* be legislated.

Third, laws and norms at any given time may conflict with each other. This may happen when social change results in new norms contrary to old laws or when new laws are written that conflict with present norms. To take a few examples: the law may contradict widely held religious beliefs, as when the National Conference of Catholic Bishops declared that abortion was still morally wrong in January, 1973 only two days after the U.S. Supreme Court declared it legal (Cecil 1983: 40); socio-economic development may create differentially developed geographical regions and diverse social classes with conflicting life styles; migration may bring into the country culturally and religiously diverse people; some aspects of society may change faster than the written law, for example, patterns of work and recreation vs. the so-called "blue laws" that forbade such things as working or shopping on Sunday or dancing or card playing anytime. Thus, a traditional consensus shared fully by all the people may cease to exist, and the law may be at odds with some segments of multicultural societies.

Some attempts to use law in a positive way to produce social change have been successful, even when law is in conflict with norms and even when powerful interests attempt to prevent legislation and to subvert its implementation when it becomes law. For example, considerable success has been achieved in combatting water pollution in the face of determined opposition of major business polluters whose past customs were being redefined as criminal. America's water is far cleaner today than it would have been without such environmental law. It would be even cleaner than it is, if there were more enforcement, more voluntary compliance, and fewer negotiated reductions in the standards of compliance (Yeager 1991). And it may be cleaner now than it will be in another decade if we allow such laws to be ignored or dismantled.

Even when the law goes against the popular opinion of the general public rather than only a particular subgroup, there are times when the law prevails, such as the U. S. Supreme Court's overturning the statutes obligating school children to salute the flag or in upholding the right of free speech of neo-Nazis, atheists, socialists, and communists (Schwartz 1986: 75–76). Not only the brute power of government is involved, but also moral suasion. As Bickel (1962) has pointed out, in such instances the Court makes the ideal of government under law meaningful and pronounces, clarifies, and protects basic moral values.

If norms and the law are in conflict, then the law may prevail or it may be ignored and evaded. A stunning example of the latter is the eighteenth Amendment to the U.S. Constitution, and the Volstead Act introduced in 1919 to implement it, that prohibited the manufacture, transportation, and sale of alcoholic beverages. As is well known, it did not prevent alcohol consumption.

Fourth, law facilitates the norm-forming process among various groups in society (Schwartz 1986: 64). For example, law can require disputants to seek agreement (as in the case of disputes between labor and management under some provisions of the National Labor Relations Act of 1935), it can foster agreements between parties whose relationship has disintegrated (as in the case of estranged husbands and wives under divorce law), and it can contribute to norm formation among group members (as in the case of researchers defining how they ought to treat their human subjects under the Protection of Human Research Subjects in the National Research Act of 1974) (Schwartz 1986: 91).

Conflict, integration, and legitimacy. The relationship between norms and law bears on the question of the legitimacy of law, in some instances supporting and validating law and in other instances undermining law. When there is near perfect congruence between norms—and we can add basic values—of society and law, both as it is written and practiced, then law is viewed as legitimate. Thus, the rule of law is accepted. When, however, there is conflict between the two, then people may judge the law to be illegitimate and withdraw their willingness to support and comply with it.

Sometimes, the law may represent the interest of some groups or classes in opposition to the interest of others. The well-known Marxist view, of course, is that in capitalist societies the state and its law serve the interests of the bourgeoisie against those of the proletariat, serving "only to consolidate and reproduce the political and economic power of elites" (Yeager 1991: 18). From this perspective, law is little more than a camouflage of power and a rationalization for tyranny and oppression.

Such abuse of law has occurred and may continue to occur at particular times and places, but the facts are somewhat more complicated. For example, the law may also side with one elite group against other elite groups, as in the case of differentially establishing import taxes that favor some businesses over others, for example, textiles rather than automobiles. Or it may pursue the public interest against the short-term economic interests of particular industries, as in the case of clean air acts that require manufacturers to reduce their air pollution. Or it may be used by disadvantaged groups against established and privileged interests, as in the case of the civil rights movement. Thus, the law may serve special private interests or the public interest, and it may be used to justify the oppression of people by the state or to protect the rights of people against the encroachment of others and even against the state itself. In large-scale contemporary societies it may do all of these things in one part of the legal system or another or at one time or another.

When the law unfairly serves special interests and is perceived as so doing, then it undermines its own legitimacy. If it loses legitimacy, then it tends to become an ineffective tool, even for pursuing the interests of a special group. Thus, although they are often too short-sighted to see it, even the sectors of society that are privileged by the law have a self-interested reason to see that the legal system appears just and that members of subordinate groups do not become disillusioned with it.

In a sample survey conducted in Chicago, Tyler (1990) found that people are more likely to comply with the law if they believe that the legal system is fair in substantive outcomes as well as in processes, that is, if legal authorities are neutral and honest, listen to the views of citizens, and treat citizens with dignity and respect. On the contrary, if the law fails to be fair, evenhanded, unbiased, impersonal, impartial, objective, exercised in the public interest, and equally open to everyone, then some people find it unacceptable and are less willing to comply with it.

But being equitable is only one of the values by which the formulation, adoption, implementation, and enforcement of law are judged. Law is also judged by whether it is rational, logically coherent, based on scientific fact, informed, stated publicly in advance, clear, internally consistent, moderate, stable, intelligible, based on persuasive reasons, predictable, not arbitrary, swift in producing results, efficient and economical, caring and sensitive in dealing with clients, and providing of individual and public safety (Schwartz 1986).

Everywhere the law is made by the few to be followed by the many. Everywhere it matters who those few are and in whose interests they act. Everywhere the law may arise out of both consensus and the interplay of different interests in conflict and political struggle. And everywhere the law itself is judged by the people whose acts it is intended to control. If the judgment is favorable, that is, if law lives up to values by which it is judged, then law contributes to social order and integration. If the judgment is unfavorable, that is, if law fails to live up to them, then law loses legitimacy and contributes to social disorder and fragmentation (Schwartz 1986: 99). Law has been, is, and can be both a tool of domination and a benevolent means by which peaceful compromise and negotiation result in beneficial self-direction for both individuals and the community (Moore 1986: 54).

From formalism to purposive law. The evolution of law with modern social development has resulted in law becoming more purposive. There has been a shift from formalistic legal reasoning, that is, mere deduction of conclusions from laws, to purposive legal reasoning, that is, deciding how to apply a law to achieve its purposes (Unger 1976: 194). As this has happened, legal analysis has tended to be transformed into policy analysis (Nonet and Selznick 1978: 51), with general goals and specific objectives stated in law and with the technical and institutional arrangements of their achievement more or less also specified by law and more or less open to a range of alternative administrative or judicial decisions.

From this perspective, modern law has become less past-oriented and increasingly explicit in embodying values whose achievement and fulfillment reside in the future. It has come to include valued goals and often specific means aimed at their future achievement. As a result, law in contemporary society increasingly is used as a tool less to confirm and duplicate the past in the present and more to change the present into a different and better future.

Consumer, environmental, and employee health and safety legislation, mentioned earlier, are examples. Legislation was passed setting general purposes, guidelines, and standards for the future. Agencies were created and given the responsibility for setting and achieving specific goals. And a capability for evaluating the results at various intervals in the future was created. Clearly, law in such cases has become an instrument for the design of the future.

We must add to this rather ideal account, however, that political struggle and pressure from special interest groups affect the atmosphere within which the laws are written, debated and voted on, implemented, and enforced. Such legislation often ends up serving the public interest less than some of the lawmakers had originally intended. Yet the conclusion is undeniable: the contemporary welfare state is, through the use of law, increasingly involved in steering and shaping society toward a future judged to be preferable to the present (Unger 1976: 193).

Law as Justification of the "Good"

The idea of "natural" law. Some of the conceptions of "natural" law that base law on some higher or universal standard serve to give law a claim to validity beyond mere human will. I add quotes to "natural" used in this sense, because it may mean nearly the opposite to what I have referred in earlier chapters as natural or naturalistic (meaning "of this world"). At one extreme at least, "natural" law arguments merge with religious belief in recognizing the work of a supreme being, some kind of supernatural force having commanded or willed the laws (Gibbs 1989: 399). A native Indian leader in Canada, for example, justifies his aboriginal rights by arguing that they derive from the Creator and, hence, are inalienable: "There is no tribunal on earth that can change the natural law, because it is outside our jurisdiction.... Aboriginal rights...are the law of the Creator" (Lyons 1985: 19).

We can treat definitions of "natural" law that are based on beliefs in the supernatural or on ineffable intuition much the same as religious beliefs. Their ultimate justification cannot be confirmed or denied, but they may be useful just as religious values can be.

When ideas of "natural" law are claims about the use of reason, the preconditions of social life, the fundamental nature of human beings, or universal patterns of human behavior, then these claims can be subjected to logical and empirical test, confirmation, or negation. We do not have to accept an entire theory of "natural" law in any metaphysical sense in order to analyze the cogency of such justifications.

Law and the commitment-deducibility model. Putting "natural" law arguments aside and acknowledging that the law is human-made, we can view law as a commitment-deducibility model of the judgment of legal right and wrong. Moreover, we can sometimes justify both our moral judgments of right and wrong and of preferable futures by appealing to the law, at least in democratic societies. For in democratic societies with freedom of inquiry, speech, and criticism, with equal access to information, with universal adult suffrage and fair, competitive elections, and with widespread citizen participation, there is a strong presumption that law is ultimately justified as being the will of the people, the outcome of a democratic due process that establishes law's legitimacy.

Additionally, being law-abiding itself receives a certain amount of respect from many people, out of conscious or tacit understanding of the contributions of law to the maintenance of social order and of the importance of social order to stable, secure, and purposive individual lives. Obeying the law yourself and encouraging other people to do so as well can often enhance individual well-being and freedom as well as social harmony.

Of course, law as an exemplar of the commitment-deducibility model is far less than perfect, partly because of the possible ambiguity and disagreement of interpretation of some laws and partly because many aspects of human behavior—from personal behavior (for example, whether or not you ought to attend your grandmother's funeral) to international relations among independent nation-states (for example, whether or not one state ought to give economic aid to another state) for which moral guidance is needed may be met with indifference by law. That is, not all possible behavior is covered by a law.

The other side of that coin is that many things are legal that you, nonetheless, ought not to do, such as, in the United States where they are legal, smoking tobacco or having more than two alcoholic drinks per day (on the grounds that doing so is bad for your health). Law gives you little guidance to choose among all the possible behaviors that are lawful.

Also, law, like religion, ultimately fails as a justification of the good within the commitment-deducibility model. Logically, the search for justification ends with some particular law. Who is to say that the law is morally right? There are stupid laws, unjust laws, and immoral laws. Henshel (1990: 37) describes a law in Louisiana that makes "a theater manager guilty of a misdemeanor if he allows people to be seated after a performance has started" and another in Arkansas that disallows erecting "a lunch counter on Decoration Day within a half-mile of a Confederate cemetary." And it wasn't until 1993 that North Carolina legislators repealed laws "against marathon dancing, capturing homing pigeons and disrupting a religious assembly by exhibiting a jackass near a church" (Rosenbaum 1994: 3E).

Absurd or anachronistic laws may be relatively harmless, more amusing than censurable. But take laws that may be immoral, such as South Africa's apartheid laws before their elimination. Or take an example from Jamaica. Before political independence in 1964, there were so-called bastardy laws in existence that severely limited the legal rights of children born out of wedlock. The function of these laws was to uphold a system of racial stratification in a colonial society by disinheriting "illegitimate" children, often brown-skinned children of white wealthy fathers and poor black mothers. Thus, "illegitimate" children of the wealthy classes were prevented from legally challenging the legal offspring of members of these classes for the land and wealth of their parents. After political independence, the new Jamaican political leaders judged these laws to be unjust and changed them, creating new equality between members of legal and "extra-legal" families and between legitimate and "illegitimate" children. They also banned the term "bastard" itself from legal documents (Cumper 1972).

In totalitarian countries where a small ruling group dictatorially issues proclamations defining lawful and unlawful behavior, laws may permit or demand injustice, even mass murder. It would be wrong to obey such laws. But how are we to know what is right when we question the morality of law itself? Obviously, we then must seek an answer outside of the law.

Even democratically promulgated law may be flawed in a variety of ways. It may represent mob hysteria, not reasoned critical judgment. It may represent the value priorities of special interest groups. It may be founded not on accepted scientific facts and theories, but on erroneous, though popular, beliefs, perhaps deliberate lies of its backers. Some laws may contradict other laws. Laws may reflect mere conventionality, the most trite and vulgar beliefs and values of the society...The list goes on and on. In the end, any given law may be morally wrong by some defensible external method of value judgment, even if it accurately represents the knowing will of the people.

Law and the means-ends model. With the growth of purposive law, there is considerable justification for looking at law not only as a codification of rules, but also as a set of goals to be achieved. Thus, the means-ends model is relevant to the use of law to justify the good. But such use is limited just as the commitment-deducibility model is, because the ends, like the commitment, cannot be validated *within* the model itself. Also like the commitment-deducibility model, the means-ends model has a strong claim to validity in democratic societies where ends are chosen through democratic processes and means that do harm to particular individuals are allowed, if at all, only with due process.

When law is aimed at the achievement of some goal, for example, clean air or water, the reduction of illegal drug importation, truth in advertising, safe automobiles, worker safety on the job, equal access to education, or any one of a thousand goals for which laws are enacted, the means-ends model is clearly relevant. Given laws that define such valued ends, the question becomes a factual one of what means are the most efficient and effective in achieving them (while, of course, doing the least damage to other valued ends).

In some cases, the means to achieve stated ends may be quite straight-forward and unexceptional, as when attempting to allow every adult to vote by eliminating the obstacles to voting such as literacy and property-ownership requirements, poll taxes, or other manipulations of voter registration requirements designed to prevent some particular segments of the population from voting. In other cases, we may not know the most effective means to achieve some end. Some social engineering may require complex knowledge of social causation that is beyond current social scientific understanding. Social scientists may not know what the efficient and effective means are to eliminate residential racial segregation, reduce institutional racism, or eliminate poverty while using limited resources, respecting human rights, and not interfering with family life any more than medical scientists know how to prevent or cure every illness. Thus, at any given time, the means-ends model is also constrained by the limits of whatever knowledge is relevant to achieving the legislated goals.

Finally, in actually making and enforcing law, though not in analytically applying it, the means-ends conception of law is further limited by the sometimes complex influences on the legislative process. For example, in the Congressional debates leading to new legislation regarding water quality in the United States, as Yeager (1991: 173–74) shows, laws can result from contradictory and irrational thinking as well as from "the rational calculation of means to ends." He shows that issues such as states' rights and federalism, "pork barrel politics, and presidential electioneering" entered in as well as contradictions between the environment and the economy (p. 147).

Somewhere in such a potpourri of conflicting interests, special pleadings, emotions, ideologies, misrepresentations, deliberate fanning of false hopes or fears, and private motivations (for example, personal envies, loyalties, prides, and hatreds), there is still room for a rational, objective, and critical analysis of the most efficient, effective, and equitable means to an end. In fact, such factors can often put greater pressure on researchers to be rigorous than does academic research, because rational and objective analysis dealing with the hot topics of public debate must be particularly sound to withstand the fiery attacks that may be leveled against it. But the compromise, negotiation, and power politics necessary to get any legislation passed and implemented can result in legislation considerably different from what might have resulted from a rational analysis of the best means to an end alone.

Law and epistemic implication. In theory, democratically created law, through informed public debate and rational-choice decision making, might approximate the results of epistemic implication. Laws are proposed; reasons are given to support the proposals; relevant evidence is evaluated; judgments and actions are taken. Listen to Yeager (1991: 327) as he concludes his analysis of the public regulation of private pollution: Like nearly every form of policy decision making, "environmental regulation must encourage honest and open inquiry based on intelligible fact finding and citizen participation, the sort of rationality that honors the virtues of honesty, persuasion, and clarity in civic discourse."

Such civic discourse—which is similar to critical discourse as proposed here—can be, and often is, distorted by the extraneous political elements mentioned above. The process is too frequently dominated by political alliances involving pressure groups that promise financial and other support to legislators if they vote as requested—or that threaten reprisals if they don't. In the United States, for example, reasoned argument about moral principles is seldom a key element in legislative deal making. It is of more importance, however, on constitutional issues that come before the courts (Dworkin 1994).

Also, law, like religion, can be a rich source of "ought" statements that can be analyzed and tested by the method of epistemic implication used by independent observers external to the legal system itself. Moreover, since legislators often give their reasons for creating particular laws, even if they are only rationalizations for decisions made on other grounds, and judges give reasons for deciding legal cases as they do, the legislative and judicial processes themselves yield a rich source of evidence to examine as well. We can ask whether the grounds given to support particular laws and legal judgments constitute serious, referentially and causally relevant, causally independent, and true evidence. If they do, the law is supported by the evidence and has survived efforts to falsify it; thus, it is reasonable to accept it. If they do not, it is falsified, but other grounds might then be sought. If no acceptable grounds are found, then the conclusion must be that the law fails to be supported by objective analysis and is refuted. Thus, a way of judging the validity of law outside of law is available through epistemic implication.

Summary

In sum, to some extent the law itself can function as a commitment-deducibility model. With the spread of purposive law it also can function as a means-ends model. Also, since reasons are given for and against legislation that ostensibly are considered and used as a basis of action to create law, it can function as epistemic implication as well. In each case, however, the resulting legislation may be flawed from an independent observer's perspective, because the outcome may owe more to self-serving political influences than to the logic and relevant evidence demanded by the models.

Yet in democratic societies there is the reasonable argument that, in the case of the first two models, the commitment and the ends respectively are not totally arbitrary. Rather, they are justified by being selected through democratic due process.

Compared with the commitment-deducibility and means-ends models, epistemic implication is the most powerful, plausible, and persuasive method available to independent observers by which to assess law, because the reasons underlying a given law can be more fully evaluated, beyond the logic of deduction and the efficacy of means. Epistemic implication also permits an indirect assessment of both commitments and ends themselves.

Law, obviously, is a powerful tool for futurists, both for futurists who are simply defining and analyzing preferable futures and for futurists who are actively trying to bring preferable futures into reality through producing social change. Where desirable laws are being violated by present practices, futurists can call for vigorous law enforcement and compliance with the law. Sometimes, they must do so in the face of the unwillingness to enforce the law on the part of law enforcement agencies themselves.

For example, in the United States the Reagan administration systematically assaulted many regulatory agencies, including, perhaps especially, those responsible for enforcing environmental laws. A citizen's environmental group, the Natural Resources Defense Council (NRDC), with a budget only 2 percent of the Environmental Protection Agency's (EPA) water enforcement budget, mounted more suits against industrial violators in 1984 than had the EPA. The NRDC took legal action against the 70 worst offenders out of 1,300 polluters it studied in fourteen states (Yeager 1991: 321).

Where present practices are legal but less desirable than possible alternatives, for example, present practices that damage the environment, futurists can work toward the creation of new legislation aimed at changing such practices by making them unlawful. Where present laws are not desirable, futurists can work toward changing them. The Manoa futurists, for example, under the direction of James A. Dator, have worked with the Hawaiian Judiciary trying to alter the usual court procedures to allow alternative methods of dispute settlement consistent with the norms of various ethnic communities in Hawaii.

Finally, for futurists the law is a field for investigation. How does the law shape the future of society? How does the law function—or fail to function—as an instrument in creating predictability in patterns of human interaction, in encouraging confidence that present expectations of the behaviors of others will be fulfilled in the future? How does the law create continuity among past, present, and future values? How does the law manage the contradictions among past, present, and future definitions of the good society, the incompatibility between the cohesive-building belief in immanence (that the present social order as it is is right and legitimate) and the legitimacy-undermining belief in transcendence (that there are possible futures that make the present appear badly flawed and in need of change)?

What are the possible futures for law itself? What effect will computer databases such as Lexis and Westlaw have in quantifying and systematizing judicial precedents? Can large-scale society exist with little or no law, a society of equals in a state of near anarchy (Black 1976)? Or is the rule of law in an open society humankind's best hope for effectively achieving group goals and avoiding either a future of fragmentation and impotence on the one hand or a future of totalitarianism on the other (Schwartz 1986; Nonet and Selznick 1978)?

Most important, perhaps, are questions of the future of international or global law: What laws will govern the relations among countries? How will conflicts between the sovereign laws of the various states and emerging global law be resolved? How will the public interest of the coming global society be incorporated into an international legal system? How will international laws be enforced? How will the crimes of states and nations, such as genocide, be prosecuted and punished?

Appeals to Collective Judgments of Group Members

The justification of goals and values according to appeals to the collective judgments of group members has a long history, going back at least to Aristotle who grounded justice in "common opinions" and including Kant's "common knowledge" theory of justice. It rests on the principle that, within any culture or subculture, values and norms exist that define the moral principles applicable to its own members. In any particular case, the futurist can attempt to justify his or her evaluation of alternative futures as more or less desirable for members of a particular group by using as standards of judgment the group's own values, choices, and normative behaviors. A justification of law based on the argument that law represents the outcome of democratic processes is a specific type of appeal to the collective judgments of group members where the "collective judgments" are measured by legislation and judicial decisions.

The collective judgments of group members, of course, define social conventions. They define the ordinary obligations, rights, and expectations of individual behavior in society as that society is organized by social roles and their relationships with each other. Fulfilling the societal expectations of legitimate social roles goes a long way toward doing one's moral duty.

Here, I limit my discussion to several lines of research, outside of law, involving collective judgments. They include: appeals to the history and charter myths of a group, appeals to surveys of public opinion, and appeals to the hypothetical judgments of imaginary group members. Each one can provide some basis for futurists' explorations of the preferable.

Appeals to History and Charter Myths

Members of collectivities—informal groups, formal organizations, or societies—find meaning and purpose in stories about their own history and in their charter or founding documents and myths, often reinforced by periodic commemorations such as the July 4th Independence Day observances in the United States. Such meaning and purpose define group or societal identity, embody basic values, and aid members of the collectivity in defining both the social boundaries and core cultural symbols of the group. Futurists can use such views of history and charter myths of a particular group or society as a standard by which to evaluate the desirability of alternative images of the future for that group or society. We can ask whether images of the future of a group or society actually embody the basic values of that group or society as these are exemplified in its constructed history and founding myths. We can ask, further, whether present contemplated actions provide effective means for attaining the group's basic values as congealed in their charter myths? Although the basic values contained in historical accounts and charter myths themselves are not validated, both the commitment-deducibility and means-ends model obviously fit such a procedure.

In his studies among native Indians of Canada, Menno Boldt (1980, 1981a, 1981b, 1982) investigated their images of their own future and their justifications of them. What he found, firstly, were native leaders from different tribal cultures who were trying to build a pan-Indian movement whose social scale matched that of the federal government and whose image of the future was based on a hope of a common, that is, pan-Indian, future.

Boldt points out, secondly, that the native Indians have been denied equality of treatment and opportunity; they have been refused entry into the mainstream of Canadian society; they have been excluded from meaningful participation in the political system; and they have been denied a satisfactory place in the Canadian history books as written by white Canadians. As a result, native Indian leaders have worked to create the collective power and structural changes necessary for native Indians to control their own future. They have done so by building overarching Indian loyalties and political mobilization at the national level. Also, they have proposed more autonomy for the Indian peoples, self-determination and separation from the larger society, more Indian control, for example, over the Department of Indian Affairs and Northern Development, over federal Indian policy, and over Indian lands.

Such a separatist movement, according to Boldt, can be prevented only by the complete decolonization of the native Indian peoples, by ending their political, economic, and sociocultural subordination. Boldt (1981a: 561) concludes that this "cannot occur without an honest transformation of both the social institutions and the attitudes of the dominant society, with a movement towards the acceptance of colonized racial-ethnic minorities fully, equally, democratically, and fraternally into the larger society."

But how can the past be used to create pan-Indian unity when it includes the facts of fragmented, quarreling, and warring tribal groups with different languages and subcultures? How can pan-Indian unity be promoted by the Indian past and founding myths when even the Indian present is fragmented, with Canada's Constitution Act of 1982, for example, defining aboriginal peoples of Canada as divided into different segments: Indian, both status (registered as Indian) and non-status, Inuit, and Metis, and with status Indians alone being members of 577 bands scattered across Canada (Boldt et al. 1985)?

The answer is that native Indian leaders draw selectively on the past, emphasizing the common bonds inherent in the traditional egalitarian values of all Indian tribes, their similar ways of relating to nature, and, perhaps most important, their "shared historical experience of oppression, deprivation and exclusion at the hands of the dominant society" (Boldt 1980: 19). All of these unifying facts can be documented, and the last is a shocking story of cruel and neglectful treatment of native Indians. Boldt found a growing pan-Indian political and cultural identity that was not so much replacing segmented tribal identities as co-existing with them.

More recently, Boldt (1993), in a brilliant contribution to public discourse in Canada, has challenged both Canadian Indian and non-Indian leaders to envision alternative and better future worlds for Indians. Boldt's work is an example of modern futures work at its very best.

Another example is Gunnar Myrdal's now classic use of charter documents and myths to justify an image of the future in his *An American Dilemma* (1944). Myrdal looked to America's early struggle for independence and to the contents of charter documents, such as the Declaration of Independence, the Preamble of the Constitution, the Bill of Rights, and the constitutions of the several states to define the values contained in what he labeled the "American Creed." These values, put briefly, include "the essential dignity of the individual human being, of the fundamental equality of all men [and women], and of certain inalienable rights to freedom, justice, and a fair opportunity" (p. 4). In the remainder of a long book loaded with documentation, Myrdal proceeds to show both how these high ideals continued to exist in American society and how American society had failed to live up to them.

For many African-Americans the realities of American life at the time meant degradation, segregation, inequality, and injustice. They had been practically excluded from participation in civil society; they could exercise few political rights in American democracy; they had little opportunity to earn a decent living; they could seldom get a decent education; and they were forced to the margins of American society. "From the point of view of the American Creed," Myrdal (1944: 24) says, "the status accorded the Negro in America represents nothing more and nothing less than a century-long lag of public morals. In principle the Negro problem was settled long ago; in practice the solution is not effectuated."

Myrdal's work is not without weaknesses. For example, he focused almost exclusively on the damaging effects of segregation and discrimination on African-Americans, ignoring the resilience of African-American institutions and the individual coping mechanisms that African-Americans had created for dealing with oppression. Moreover, his emphasis on integration and assimilation led him to overlook the positive elements of African-American culture (Jackson 1990).

Nonetheless, Myrdal's work was a powerful influence in shaping political and social change for more racial equality in the United States. Its strength resided in its call for the American people to live up to their own American Creed. American ideals, Myrdal argued, ought to win out in the future, shaping American social realities to conform to them. For justification, he appealed to the founding documents of American society which, he claimed, still defined the national conscience.

Appeals to Surveys of Public Opinion

Surveys of public opinion also can serve as a source of collective judgments and behaviors of group members. Every developed country today and many less developed countries have various national survey research agencies that regularly sample the opinion of people in the society. Moreover, many supranational and international surveys are available as well. Occasionally, such research focuses on measuring goals and values and can be used to construct standards of evaluation of the preferable for particular subgroups, whole countries, regions, or larger areas.

If used to measure people's preferable futures, survey data, as we saw in chapter 6 of volume 1, must be examined critically for reliability, validity, and relevance, since some surveys or polls, obviously, are more competently carried out than others. Also, it is not always a simple matter to find out what group members judge to be a preferable future. On some issues, people may not have clear and definite judgments. On other issues, their attitudes may be complex and difficult to measure or only more or less stable. On many issues, in order for people to have *meaningful* judgments of the preferable, they need access to information they may not have. Also, some people may change their opinions when they hear a public debate on the issues. Thus, there are inherent limits to validity in defining preferable futures using surveys. Yet, used with care and sophistication, survey data can be a revealing indicator of people's judgments about the preferable.

The examples given below are only two of many that could be selected. Some of the surveys briefly described in volume 1 also can serve as examples.

Jamaican leaders' preindependence goals. In Jamaica during 1958 and again in late 1961 and early 1962, I and my associates carried out studies of Jamaican leaders' beliefs and attitudes. These studies were done before political independence which was not to take place until August 6, 1962. Among the questions that we asked the leaders were several dealing with their images of the coming postindependence future of Jamaica and their preferences about them. With these data, we could compare attitudes of the waning, often white and sometimes expatriate, colonial elites with those of the waxing brown and black new national leaders.

The new national leaders were explicit in describing the future goals they hoped to achieve after coming to power in the new nation. One such goal had to do with ending the gross racial and class inequalities of the colonial stratification system. Nearly 500 years of foreign rule and 300 years of plantation slavery of Africans and the indentured labor of other racial and ethnic groups, had created a Jamaican society characterized by political, economic, and cultural inequality (Bell 1964, 1967; Bell and Oxaal 1964; Moskos 1967).

As new brown and black nationalist leaders looked forward to coming to political power, they intended—or so they claimed before independence—to create a new Jamaican society based on the equality of national citizenship to be shared by all Jamaicans, free and fair elections, equal political participation of all adults, equality before the law, the end of racial discrimination, the provision of equal educational opportunity for all, a reduction of gross inequalities of income and wealth, a higher level of living for the poorest Jamaicans, and a new and equal appreciation of the African contributions to Jamaican culture and history. They aimed both to increase the size of the economic pie and to divide it more fairly than it had been under British colonial rule.

An appraisal of Jamaican leaders' social legislation. Using their own preindependence statements of their goals, values, and preferred images of the future as the standard of judgment, let us appraise how well the leaders performed after they came to power. In 1974, I analyzed the social legislation that they had actually passed during their first twelve years of running the country (Bell 1977). Thus, I documented what Jamaica's new nationalist leaders had *tried* to do using their new control over the power of the state to create social change through purposive legislation. Moreover, Stephens and Stephens (1986) carried this preliminary appraisal of elite performance into the 1980s.

The answer? Yes, for the most part the leaders had kept faith with their preindependence images of the good society by their legislative acts. First, they lived up to the new constitutional provisions for a political democracy based on universal adult suffrage, carrying out mostly free and fair elections, although marred occasionally by political violence, voter intimidation, and bogus voting; they enlarged the voters lists by extending the franchise to all adults eighteen years of age and over, updated voters lists to include people formerly excluded unfairly, and redrew electoral districts so that the results in the distribution of parliamentary seats would better reflect the popular vote—all in an effort to increase the fairness and inclusiveness of political participation generally; and they maintained civil rights and public liberties (Bell and Baldrich 1983; Stephens and Stephens 1986).

Second, they passed social legislation *aimed* at raising the lowest levels of living and promoting more economic and social equality within Jamaican society. Such legislation dealt with public health care, a literacy program, housing, free secondary and university education, poor relief, minimum wages, workmen's compensation, a pension scheme (though modest in benefits), uniforms for primary school children, food subsidies, rent controls, equal pay for women, new mental health law and free education for the handicapped, new capital gains and inheritance taxes, compulsory recognition of trade unions, increased worker participation, and elimination of legal inequalities of "illegitimate" children (as mentioned earlier).

Third, they passed legislation *aimed* at stimulating economic development and creating more economic independence. Such legislation dealt with industrial development, reducing the control of foreign capital over the domestic economy, nationalization of bauxite multinational companies (up to 51 percent of Jamaican ownership), a State Trading Corporation, a skill-training program, a self-supporting farmers development program, the construction of small industries complexes, sugar cooperatives, a venture capital financing company to provide loans, a small enterprise development company, a national commercial bank, food farms (to reduce food imports), and a land-lease project which placed several thousand small farmers on land that they could work.

Thus, the new Jamaican leaders, *judged by the standards of their own preindependence definitions of preferable futures for Jamaica*, generally made serious, honest, and substantial efforts to live up to them according to the intentions of their legislative actions.

Having said this, I must add that, like people everywhere, there were some leaders who honestly disagreed with the preferable as defined by the majority, a few who were out as much for their own personal gain as for the public good, and some who were guilty of incompetence and mismanagement. Nonetheless, the new Jamaican leaders, on the whole, designed and implemented social legislation that was intended to fulfill their preindependence goals, values, images of the future, and, not least, their promises to the Jamaican people.

An appraisal of actual results. Was social legislation successful in achieving the intended results? What were the actual economic and social changes in Jamaica during the early years of independence? Did such changes also live up to the leaders' preindependence visions? To answer these questions we must look at relevant economic and social indicators in the postindependence period.

The answer is mixed, perhaps more negative than positive. Although there were some changes toward a more egalitarian society—especially in civil liberties, exercising political rights, and social and cultural inclusiveness—other social realities and, especially, economic conditions proved more resistant to change.

Political mobilization did occur. People's political awareness was raised, voter turnouts were high, and political participation increased. Some Jamaicans felt themselves to be part of the Jamaican polity for the first time (Stephens and Stephens 1986: 293)].

The percentage of people with both primary and secondary schooling increased; the percentage of young people attending school increased somewhat; there were dramatic declines in the infant mortality rate; income inequality may have been slightly reduced; public taxation and expenditure contributed to a small shift of real income to the lowest income groups, but the income distribution remained quite unequal in the mid-1970s; although median incomes increased, most of the increase was wiped out by inflation; there was some increase in proportion of the total land acreage accounted for by small farms partly as a result of Project Land Lease, but land inequality remained high. There was some success in reducing Jamaica's economic dependence on foreign capital, but trade dependence continued or increased (Stephens and Stephens 1986: 271).

Most important, perhaps, the overall economy deteriorated. This was partly because of conditions beyond the control of the Jamaican leaders, such as the prices and levels of production of sugar, bauxite, and alumina (which are exported) and oil (which is imported), the amount and conditions of loans and grants from foreign governments and international agencies, the amount of capital investment of multinational corporations (e.g., bauxite and aluminum companies), and bad weather that brought flooding in 1979 and a devastating hurricane in 1980. There were other circumstantial problems that faced the new national leaders as they took power: the small size of the state, the tradition of patronage (that burdened some government programs with unqualified and redundant workers), and too few competent managers and trained technicians (Stephens and Stephens 1986: 318).

Some mistakes, of course, were made by the new nationalist leaders as well. In the case of the People's National Party (PNP) drive toward democratic socialism, more state-sector investment rather than distributive programs, more care in foreign borrowing, and better monitoring of program implementation would have resulted in better economic performance. That might have prevented the decline of investment levels and the migration of professional and managerial personnel off the island (Stephens and Stephens 1986:319). Additionally, keeping Jamaica's distance from Cuba in foreign relations, instead of cozying up to Castro, and eliminating anti-American and antiimperialist political rhetoric would have removed important irritants both internally among the Jamaican capitalist and professional classes and among leaders in the United States.

By 1980, democratic socialism appeared to have failed and the opposition party, the Jamaica Labour Party (JLP), won 51 of the parliamentary seats, a sweeping majority. Yet Jamaica's young two-party political system remained intact and public liberties continued to be maintained. Moreover, many of the PNP's efforts to create higher levels of living for ordinary Jamaicans and a more egalitarian society were not dismantled by the JLP regime (Stephens and Stephens 1986).

Finally, the PNP was returned to power in 1989, not to reintroduce democratic socialism but, nonetheless, to continue its commitment to democratic governance, social and cultural equality, the struggle for economic development and growth, the reduction of poverty, and the elimination of gross and unfair economic inequalities. Members of the PNP returned sobered, however, by their earlier failures and the enormity of the task.

In this example, we see futurist-researchers using new nationalist leaders' own images of preferable futures as standards to judge the leaders' own subsequent actions. There is, obviously, a certain poetic justice in doing so.

The utility of the moral models. The commitment-deducibility model is useful: make a commitment to the leaders' own definitions of the good and then see if their actions and consequences are logical deductions of it. We saw that by their legislative acts the leaders for the most part intended to create the good society as they had defined it. The actual results, however, fell far short of the mark, partly because of their own mistakes, partly because of circumstances beyond their control, and partly because of the limited knowledge anyone has of carrying out such economic and social engineering.

In evaluating the actual results, of course, the means-ends model is relevant. Were the policies formulated to achieve the leaders' stated goals, even though they were consistent with them in intent, actually effective means to achieve them? Clearly, sometimes they were and sometimes they were not, but, then, economists and other social scientists do not always agree as to what policies are the most effective. The ultimate limitation in fitting means to ends in economic and social life may be the inadequate cause-and-effect knowledge of the social sciences.

Neither the commitment-deducibility nor the means-ends model, however, allow us to evaluate the leaders' preindependence images of preferable futures themselves. Did they, in fact, define the good society? To judge that we would need to specify some external criteria, for example by using epistemic implication applied to the leaders' own justifications (i.e., reasons, evidence, predictive grounds) or evidence drawn from other sources, to evaluate their views of the good future society toward which their efforts were directed. If I were now doing these Caribbean studies, I would add such an evaluation of the leaders' underlying values themselves, but I did not know enough then to do so.

Limits of opinion surveys: attitudes toward the market. The above example illustrates a case where the state was viewed by many leaders as a major instrument of planned economic and social change aimed at producing, among other things, both a larger economic pie (i.e., more goods and services per capita) and a more just division of the economic pie (i.e., a fairer—in this case more egalitarian—distribution of such goods and services). But there was disagreement in Jamaica about the relative merits of states versus markets in governing economies, and it mirrored a debate that was worldwide. As Robert E. Lane (1991: 3) says, this debate "has dominated most of the twentieth century." In fact, as I write, it still rages, even as most of the former state-run command economies in Eastern Europe and the former Soviet Union are being converted to market economies more or less along Western capitalist lines.

Since there is an infinity of possibilities between the extremes of totally state-dominated command economies and totally state-free economies, decision makers in these countries of transition face the debate again and again as they decide exactly how much and what kind of a role the state ought to play in given economic sectors as commander, stimulator, regulator, inspector, guarantor of conditions, protector of consumers, or punisher of abuses to achieve optimuum outcomes. Moreover, people of capitalist countries face similar decisions of possible changes in the goverance of their own economies, especially as they face problems of possible economic decline, foreign competition, issues such as crime and health care, or environmental degradation that may significantly affect their quality of life.

In a timely series of works, Lane has assessed the market experience. Among other things, he reviews many studies of public opinion that measure popular judgments of the justice of the market compared with the justice of the political system, especially in the United States where a great deal of research on the topic has been done. What he finds is that "Americans tend to prefer market methods to political methods" of governing the economy (Lane 1986:383).

His search of the relevant empirical social research reveals that the market compared to the political system is viewed by Americans as having many advantages. For example, Americans tend to believe that inequalities of the market encourage effort; that the market is bound by circumstantial necessity rather than (possibly arbitrary) political discretion; that its consequences result from people's own acts for which the people themselves, not government, are responsible; that its criterion of earned desserts enhances productivity while government's emphasis of equality and need do not (e.g., the market rewards achievement with income while the government punishes it with taxes); that the market produces while the government is a burden to production; that the market satisfies individual wants immediately (e.g., a new car) while the government produces collective goods with delayed and diffused gratification (e.g., a new highway or health care system); that being treated fairly is sufficient to justify the market but a fair outcome is demanded as well to justify the government; that the market is responsive to individual effort (e.g., hard work) while the political system is less so; that for the market self-interest is fruitful for the common good but for the polity self-interest derails the common good; and that the market provides opportunity and an open future while government planning closes options (Lane 1986).

After reviewing these and other beliefs and attitudes, Lane (1986: 387) concludes that on balance "the public tends to believe that the market system is a more fair agent than the political system." Thus, at least on the basis of the collective judgments of group members, we might conclude that a capitalist future based on the market is, therefore, legitimated where such views predominate. But Lane continues his analysis, inviting his readers to question whether such opinions are really true.

Most explicitly, Lane uses a means-ends model. He selects some ends, human life satisfaction and human development, for which he has a variety of justifications from survey research of people's preferences and attitudes, and he assesses both the positive and negative effects of the market on them. After reviewing an enormous body of social research, Lane (1991: 154) says, on the positive side, that "Markets are excellent devices for the efficient production of goods and services." Moreover, markets do provide some people with meaningful work, a sense of being effective, and being actively engaged with life (p. 488).

On the negative side, Lane (1991: 481) says that the market "is not much of an instrument for relief of pain or of psychological depression, let alone death, war, and oppression." Moreover, the market "has its own sources of dissatisfaction, unhappiness, frustration, anxiety, boredom, and depression," such as "loss of a job, selection among unsatisfying jobs, debt, bankruptcy, buying artificially obsolescent goods, externalities of pollution, and so forth" (p. 481). Markets also produce stress, insecurity, and disappointment.

Markets, he says, "are not designed for and have no special mechanism to promote human development" (Lane 1991: 154). Markets do not necessarily reward firms or individuals who develop themselves toward more complex thinking, a greater sense of personal control, nor increased self-esteem.

Even though *increases* in income give substantial short-term satisfaction, that fact leads to the misleading belief that *level* of income is the source of well-being. But it is a trap: working for more and more money is not a fruitful route to a sense of well-being. "Money," Lane (1991: 546) concludes, "does not buy happiness for individuals because it does not buy the things that make most people happiest, a happy family life, friends, enjoyment of work, and a sense of accomplishment therein." Many, if not most, of the sources of life satisfaction that substantially contribute toward well-being, as many surveys of public opinion have shown, do not go through the market.

In sum, Lane, among other things, (1) describes the beliefs and attitudes of group members concerning the market; (2) demonstrates that some are factually wrong; (3) proposes that markets ought to be judged not so much by the ends of material production and efficiency but more by the ends of human well-being and development (as defined by surveys of people's attitudes and values); and (4) judging the market experience by his proposed ends, he finds that the market as a way to govern the economy falls far short of the ideal.

If people were convinced by Lane's analysis, then, presumably, they would be likely to become less favorable to the market than many now are and more favorable to whatever system of governing the economy that would better achieve such goals. That is, their attitudes toward a market economy might change.

For people who value human life satisfaction and human development as worthwhile ends, Lane has given an important cautionary tale for our time. His conclusions and the detailed work on which they are based give pause to those of us who have been seeking justice, well-being, and human development through the market and they ought to give pause, too, to those peoples throughout the world now rushing headlong toward establishing unregulated market economies. Although communist command economies have collapsed in many places, the unbridled market, Lane demonstrates, may not be all that it is cracked up to be.

It is true that in the former communist countries of Eastern Europe and in the former Soviet Union there were inefficient and entrenched bureaucracies, the production of shoddy goods, occasional scarcities, and generally obsolete technologies. It is also true, however, that, generally, education, welfare, and public transportation were good and the level of employment was high.

Moreover, as even Americans have realized in the last few decades with the economic rise of Germany, Japan, Taiwan, and other countries, especially those following the Asian model of capitalism, institutional innovation involving the state's guidance of the market has been very successful. For the future, successful economies and societies may require a mix of market and state control, of private and public action and an interplay between the two. Fairly heavy doses of public direction and control have proved useful not only in education, welfare, health, and transport, but also in promoting research, developing new technology, and the retraining and relocation of workers (Stafford 1988).

A key variable, though, is the benevolence of the state, most surely guaranteed by a democratic system and public liberties. Market governance of the economy might almost always look better than state control to citizens of a repressive, totalitarian regime run by an oligarchy in its own interests, but it may not always be better than an economy controlled and regulated to some extent by democratic government.

Lane's tale concerning the attractions and failures of the market is cautionary, too, in highlighting some of the limits of using the collective beliefs and attitudes of group members as the sole defining criteria of preferable futures. There may be poetic justice in holding people to their own judgments and preferences, as we saw in the case of appraising the performance of Jamaican leaders. But, as Lane shows for some of the beliefs of Americans on which their preferences for a market economy rests, they can be wrong.

Appeals to the Hypothetical Judgments
of Imaginary Group Members

One of the best-known attempts in recent decades to define and justify the concept of justice is John Rawls's *A Theory of Justice* (1971). Rawls bases his judgments on a thought experiment, which in this case is an example of the use of *imagined* judgments of hypothetical group members to justify an "ought" assertion. The assertion being justified concerns the inequalities within a hypothetical society that are just or fair, inequalities, for example, of power, prestige, property, privilege, and participation, including such specific measures as education, training, occupation, income, wealth, and so on.

Although Rawls's book is long and complex and there are all kinds of extenuations, the underlying logic is straightforward. Rawls begins with the assumption that there are some people who are *rational choosers*. They are going to choose the nature and amount of inequality in some society of which they will become members in the future. His procedures are based on what these hypothetical choosers would rationally do. Through introspection, we generate and analyze hypothetical and speculative data from which we deduce what the rational choosers would choose.

Such choice does not take place in a vacuum. Rawls puts his rational choosers in what he calls an *original position*. That is, they must make their choice before entering the future society whose system of inequality they will be choosing.

Moreover, the choosers must make their choices with a *veil of ignorance* covering their coming social positions in the hypothetical society. That is, they do not know within the systems of inequality to be created in the future society whether they themselves will end up being advantaged or disadvantaged.

So, if you were such a rational chooser, how much inequality would you allow in a future society you are creating, if you do not know whether you will be benefitted or deprived in the system of inequality you create? If you don't know whether you are going to end up at the bottom, in the middle, or at the top, will you hedge your bets in designing the system of inequality itself so that, even if you end up at the very bottom, you will still have a decent and dignified life?

Among other things, Rawls concludes that, under such conditions, choosers will create a society with inequality, but the inequality they create will be only so great as to redound to the benefit of the least advantaged. The result, using Rawlsian logical deduction, is a society characterized by what might be argued are fair equalities and fair inequalities with no unfair equalities and no unfair inequalities. Both equalities and inequalities would be supported by a *social contract* as shaped voluntarily by his imaginary societal members, the rational choosers. Such choosers give "universal hypothetical assent" to a given amount of inequality and in so doing define that amount of inequality as just (Barry 1977).

Rawls's argument has a lot of intuitive appeal, although it has been widely criticized even as it has been widely acclaimed. His logical analysis is explicit and invites open debate. It is, thus, a step toward the objective justification of values. Standing alone, however, it invites empirical test. First, what do real people choose given the task Rawls sets for them? To answer this question, we can resort to opinion surveys, as discusssed above, or to equity research using small groups to be discussed in chapter 4.

Second, futurists can subject existing groups, organizations, and societies to study. Real social systems with real degrees of inequality can be evaluated as good or bad according to whether or not existing inequalities do, in fact, redound to the benefit of the disadvantaged.

Clearly, the means-ends model could be employed. Specify the end or goal: any inequality in society must redound to the benefit of the least well off. Then observe the social system under study to see if, in fact, a given type and amount of inequality actually redounds to the benefit of the disadvantaged.

Professional Ethics for Futurists

The Need for Professional Ethics

The questions of what to study, for whom to work, and what are appropriate standards of professional behavior raise practical questions of morality and ethics for the behavior of futurists themselves as they pursue their work as futurists, just as they do for any professional group: What ethical responsibilities do futurists have for the quality and consequences of their work? This is a much neglected topic.

Despite a concern for values in society at large, as exemplified by Rushworth M. Kidder's (1992, 1994) Institute for Global Ethics, there is little in the recent futurist literature about a code of professional ethics for futurists themselves. No written, agreed-upon standards of training, proper professional conduct, and ethical guidelines yet exist for futurists, despite the fact that futurists, as we saw in chapter 1, volume 1, are increasingly involved in professional activities as futurists: teaching, researching, publishing, consulting, and advising both governments and private organizations. Much less does any code exist that incorporates procedures of filing complaints, adjudicating or punishing cases of alleged ethical violations. Not much yet exists either to award accolades for exemplary behavior, although in 1993 the World Futures Studies Federation inaugurated three categories of awards for outstanding futures research on the part of individuals and organizations.

With a few exceptions, where professional ethics are discussed in the futurist literature, we are less likely to find an answer than a statement of a problem, that is, a plea for ethical guidance or an example of the need of it. Wachs (1987), for example, points out that forecasting has become a standard part of public policy formulation and action but that it is fraught with ethical dilemmas.

One exception occurred during the 1970s when there was a call for professional ethics for futurists among members of the World Futures Studies Federation (WFSF). For example, in 1975 Eleonora Masini and Knut Samset proposed that the WFSF should promote philosophical research "on the fundamental concepts and ultimate aims of futures studies, in order to establish a conceptual and ethical basis" (*WFSF Newsletter* June 1975). Among other things, they recommended that such an effort focus on "each generation's responsibility and limits of responsibility towards future generations," the obligations and responsibilities that futurists have as political actors in the future societies of the world, and "the need for each person in futures studies to state clearly his basic values, and the underlying presuppositions of his work." An Ethics and Future Studies Committee was formed with Axel Hörhager as sometime chair (*WFSF Newsletter* June 1977). After some debate, however, no code of professional ethics was ever adopted, the ethics committee no longer exists, and this important issue was apparently dropped from the Federation's active agenda (J. A. Dator, personal communication, 21 May 1992).

Unfortunately, it's too easy to find examples of what some people might judge to be horror stories in the growing body of futurist literature to show the need for ethical guidance. In a book whose title requires a double-take, *Population Control Through Nuclear Pollution*, by John Gofman and Arthur Tamplin "RAND suggested in 1966 that survivors of nuclear attack would be best off without the old and feeble, and U.S. policy should be to abandon them." RAND's response to what is perceived as a "morally repugnant but socially beneficial policy" is to endorse it (Dickson 1972: 73). We must ask, "socially beneficial" for whom?

During the Vietnam War, in Dickson's (1972: 67) opinion, RAND became so involved in Southeast Asia, from studies of bombing effectiveness to studies of the culture of the Montagnards along Vietnam's border that it was less an observer than a participant in the war, a participant whose contributions predominantly served to justify the war. There is considerable truth to this, and the need for ethical guidance is only made more urgent by pointing out that some RAND people opposed the Vietnam War and others, working on highly technical topics, had no intention of supporting it. After all, it was an ex-RAND employee, Daniel Elsberg, who leaked the Pentagon papers.

A persistent critic of systems and cost-benefit analysis, Ida R. Hoos (1978: 57–58), argues that the think-tank wheelers and dealers, like hired guns, have sometimes used their research armaments, such as cost-benefit analysis, to provide "a convenient rationale for just about any course of action. It simply depends on who wants to justify what."

But this does not have to be the case. For we have seen that objective and critical analysis of the moral dimension in decision making and policymaking is possible and can be made a part of the futurist professional role.

The time has come to create a formal code of ethics for futurists, including student futurists, with organizational procedures to implement it. Such a code would reinforce the responsibilities to peers and clients already existing in some parts of the futurist community, thereby encouraging improvement of the professional excellence of futurists and giving explicit support to the highest standards of ethical behavior. In what follows I sketch some of the ethical considerations that are preliminary to writing such a professional code and state a few principles that might become part of it. For the present, they can serve provisionally as ethical guidelines for student futurists for their own explorations into futures studies.

Professional Ethics Defined

Professional ethics, of course, refer to those virtues, values, prescriptions, or proscriptions that define proper behavior for a person occupying a particular occupational role requiring specialized training or learning, such as a doctor, lawyer, teacher, minister, and so on. They are codes of conduct that define both exemplary and prohibited behavior for members of a professional group, including their behavior toward their clients, be they patients, students, or parishoners. Often, such codes are written, formally approved by members of particular professional groups or organizations representing them, and enforced by some formal procedures by which grievances can be reported, investigated, and resolved.

Many futurists have memberships in nonfuturist professional groups and, presumably, their professional behavior is at least to some extent governed by the codes of these groups. Also, there is an informal and rather fuzzy code of ethics for futurists that rests on exemplars and horror stories of the behaviors of leading futurists of the past and present and on often casual and scattered conversations at meetings of professional futurists.

Professional Ethics and General Obligations

First, there are general obligations that futurists share with everyone. "Being a professional...in no way exempts a person from his or her ordinary obligations" (Tong 1986: 116). We owe everyone such things as honesty, respect, trustworthiness, not doing harm, and so on. Also, professionals continue to have moral obligations, as every citizen does, to the public welfare. Professional ethics define *additional* moral burdens that apply specifically to carrying out one's role as a professional.

Second, there are obligations that follow from the most general purpose of the futures field: to maintain and improve the well-being of humankind and the life-sustaining capacities of the Earth. Thus, whatever else he or she does, the futurist ought to engage in work that benefits humankind and he or she ought to be concerned about the public interest. As we saw in chapter 2, volume 1, futurists' distinctive obligation concerning the future invites them to speak for the freedom and well-being of future generations. The coming people of the future as yet have no voice and no power of their own.

Third, there are obligations that flow from futurist roles as scholar-researcher, teacher, practitioner, and activist. These obligations are to a variety of collectivities and individuals, ranging from society as a whole and the human subjects of futures research to students, colleagues, employers, employees, clients, and public authorities.

Paramount among such obligations is the search for truth, perhaps the most basic value of the futures investigator. There is a moral obligation, on the one hand, to test one's ideas empirically and logically as far as possible and, on the other hand, to report futures research results honestly. Standards defining excellence in doing futures research need specification, elaboration, and application.

Fourth, and finally, there are a variety of other general commitments, such as working to create and maintain the kind of society in which the open and free inquiry necessary for the proper conduct of futures research is possible, keeping the findings of futures research open to the public, and treating all people and human groups with respect and fairness, recognizing their human dignity.

When futurists do research on human subjects, for example, they are bound by the same standards as other scientists and practitioners not to harm their subjects in any way or to infringe upon their rights. Informed consent ought to be requested of such subjects before research is carried out that intrudes on their lives. Futurists ought to respect the privacy of their subjects and clients and they ought to keep their promises of confidentiality. They ought *not* to lie or deceive their subjects in collecting data or behave in ways that spoil the opportunities for other futurists who may want to collect data in the future (Punch 1986).

The Futurist as Consultant

Ethical guides from the policy analyst. One major role that futurists occupy is that of consultant or adviser for some organization or institution, such as a government, a business, or nonprofit organization. The futurist, for example, may serve as a policy adviser, function as an expert authority, carry out policy-related research, design policy alternatives for consideration by policymakers, or even advocate and publicly support and justify particular policy choices. Thus, the emerging code of ethics for policy analysts can serve as a guide to futurists in their role as consultants. Consultants are perceived as behaving unethically, for example:

- when their self-interests appear to have a higher priority than their client's goals, such as when consultants prolong their research for more money;
- when they serve the goals of some members of part of the organization for which they are consulting against other members;
- when they are too busy on other projects to do a proper job for the client or, for whatever reason, do poor work;
- when they withhold information from the client to benefit themselves or their friends;
- when they use insider information that they have learned from their client to benefit themselves;
- when they serve a competitor of their client;
- when they violate confidentiality;
- when they pad their expenses; or
- when they exclude the client from part of the decision process by withholding information (Payne and Desman 1987: 103–11).

Bayles (1981) argues that, above all, a policy consultant owes it to his or her client to be trustworthy and lists six virtues as part of a trustworthy professional's ethics toward clients: honesty, candor competence, diligence, loyalty, and discretion. These, of course, involve prima facie rules of behavior, subject to possible exceptions in particular situations where they may clash with other moral rules or valued ends.

The goals of the client. Some futurists solve—or, perhaps, avoid— the problem of making explicit value judgments and justifying them simply by accepting the goals or values of their clients. If their clients want to make more powerful, economical, and appealing widgets in the future, then some futures researchers accept those goals. Accepting the goals of the client is attractive because it is an easy, uncomplicated thing to do (assuming that the client really knows what his or her goals are). But it leaves the client's goals, and the values they represent, no more or less justified than before the futurist arrives on the scene.

Yet it is not without some moral justification for the futurist-consultant's behavior. For example, there is clearly an underlying moral commitment involved in "fulfilling a contract." The consultant freely enters into a contract, a mutual agreement, with the client. The client's definition of the "good" is embodied in his goals and is usually the basis of the client's interest in the services of the futurist. The futurist, thus, "contracts" to fulfill certain responsibilities that have to do with the client's goals. An important convention is keeping one's promises: "a person binds himself to do what he says he will do" (Harman 1977: 104). Additionally, a contract to do things allowed by law may be legally binding, thus adding the weight of the law as a justification for fulfilling it.

There is another ground for fulfilling one's promise as well. It involves the fact that a promise creates expectations about the future in the persons to whom the promise is made. They adjust their plans and future behavior accordingly and are usually disappointed, if not angry, when promises to them are broken. Keeping promises "encourages people to trust you in the future. If people stopped trusting you to keep your promises, it would become harder for you" to achieve your own future goals (Harman 1977: 153–54). Futurists who break their promises may sour clients not only on themselves but on all futurists. Thus, other things being equal, futurists ought to fulfill the contracts that they have made, both on pragmatic and moral grounds.

Another purpose of futures research is the clarification of goals. Thus, as part of making a contract, a futurist can inform the client that he wants to include in his research a clarification of the client's goals and explain why that is desirable from the client's perspective. Thus, the first job of a futurist-consultant may be to discover exactly what all the goals of the client are, both what the client says and what may be implicit, and the interactive consequences each goal has for others. When presented to the client, such a value analysis may or may not result in surprises and changes in a client's priorities. A client may very well have an overriding desire, *no matter what*, to make a larger profit by selling more widgets by making them more powerful, economical, and appealing.

An example of commitment to company profits and stockholder interests over the health and welfare of consumers may be found in the case of the Dalkon Shield, an intrauterine (contraceptive) device which had been manufactured by the Robins Company. By the mid-1970s about five million women in the United States and in seventy-nine other countries were using the device. The knowledge of serious and undesirable side effects finally led the Robins Company to suspend sales of the Dalkon Shield in the United States, but the company continued to sell it abroad for nearly a year. Moreover, the company failed to warn users of the dangers and failed to recall the shields already in use, even though its executives knew of its deleterious effects, which included spontaneous abortions, uterine perforations, premature brain damage to children, sterility, hysterectomies, and a higher pregnancy rate than anticipated (Cox

1985: 9). The company executives did not issue a recall until after being ordered to do so by a U.S. district court judge in February 1984.

There are many—far too many—similar stories, including the recent allegations that Dow Corning executives went ahead with the production and marketing of silicone gel breast implants even though saftey concerns were vigorously voiced by their own employees; that Upjohn may have withheld data about violent side effects from its sleeping pill, Halcion; and that Bolar mislabeled and adulterated eight different drugs (Etzioni 1992: 13).

Then, there is the widespread story, repeated by Geertz (1983: 175), that, early on, when faced with pollution controls on the cars that they manufacture, Toyota hired a thousand engineers while Ford hired a thousand lawyers. To mention a specific instance, in 1971, Henry Ford II and his then top executive, Lee Iacocca, went to see then-President Richard M. Nixon "to lobby privately against costly safety rules…'Safety,' complained Mr. Iacocca, 'has really killed all our business'" (*The New York Review* 18 September 1994: 9). One wonders how many people were killed or maimed in unsafe Ford cars, trucks, and buses, such as fourteen-year-old Shannon Fair who, along with twenty-three other children, was killed in May 1988 in a Ford school bus with a gas tank that was in violation of a federal safety law.

Taking into account other valued ends. At the risk of appearing to serve some interest other than that stated by the client, futures researchers can add a safeguard when fulfilling contracts. They can make sure that the actions that they recommend to achieve the client's goals are also examined for their consequences for other valued ends, both of the client and of society at large. That is, any proposed action which is a means to make more powerful, economical, and appealing widgets can also be evaluated for other valued goals and consequences. For example, do the materials going into the new widgets cause cancer, constitute a fire hazard, or increase heart attacks among their users?

Most clients do not want to harm others if they can help it, want to stay in business or to keep their nonprofit organization going, and, beyond survival, to thrive. Thus, they often welcome being informed of unintended or unanticipated consequences of their possible actions. Even if they are tempted to take risks with the public's health, usually they strongly desire to have a favorable public image and want to avoid any embarrassing violations of existing ideas of morality or legal regulations. The futurist-consultant can point out how the client's public image might be damaged if he or she decides to go ahead with some of the possible noxious means of creating better widgets, and how particular laws would be broken and what the consequences of getting caught breaking them are. Often, if the alternative consequences were clearly pointed out to him or her, a client would not choose to engage in unscrupulous acts even if such acts resulted in higher profits or other organizational benefits.

There is, for example, the well-known case of McDonald's response to the charges of unhealthy levels of fat in its food products. McDonald's reaction illustrates a company's willingness to change when unintended consequences come to be viewed as a threat to the public health. By 1991, the company offered cholesterol-free fries prepared in vegetable oil, reduced-calorie salad dressing, nearly fat-free milkshakes, fruit juices, fat-free and cholesterol-free muffins, whole-grain breakfast cereals, and a McLean burger containing fewer calories and less fat than a Big Mac. Thus, McDonald's acted to serve the values of health-conscious consumers who have been made aware of the increased risks of clogged arteries, heart attacks, and other damaging effects of a fatty diet. It also acted, please note, in its own best interests to maintain and expand its own markets, since some consumers will no longer accept a diet heavy in fat.

Examining the consequences of proposed action for valued ends other than the client's objectives makes the discussion of a client's preferred futures more sophisticated, more complete, and more realistic. It does not, however, in and of itself, provide a justification of the "other valued ends." How do we know they are valued and by whom? What makes such ends morally right? Nor does taking them into account in one's research guarantee that a client will even consider other valued ends in his or her decision to take action. How can clients be persuaded to consider the consequences of their actions for ends other than those for which they aim? Futurist-consultants must turn to other strategies of moral justification, such as epistemic implication, to find grounds for the values underlying their policy recommendations.

Alternative responses to wrong-doing: loyalty, voice, and exit. Adapting Hirschman's (1970) responses to decline in firms, organizations, and states, we can state three major alternative ways of behaving when futurist-consultants come to believe that their clients are betraying the public trust. The first is to remain loyal to the client. Keep silent. Lump it.

Simply ignore the possible ethical violation and let it continue without interfering.

But that is hardly the moral act if the public health and welfare are seriously threatened. As Tong (1986: 104) points out in commenting on Bayles's six virtues of a trustworthy professional, consultants can seldom be too honest, too frank, too competent, or too diligent. Yet they can be too loyal and too discreet. Being loyal to the client and being discreet might mean being silent and allowing the betrayal to occur. But is that the right thing to do? No, it is seldom fair, not even to the client. At least he or she must be told.

The second is for consultants to give voice to their critical judgments. They ought to explain them to responsible people within the organization, going to as high an authority as may be necessary. Internal dissent is a good moral choice, because it "is morally preferable to give wrongdoers a chance to mend their ways because they *want to* and not simply because they *have to* for fear of negative repercussions like public censure or imprisonment" (Tong 1986: 128). If that doesn't work, another alternative is to give voice to their beliefs by leaking the information to the press or some investigating or regulating agency, that is, whistleblowing. Tong (1986: 133) rightly says that leaking has its drawbacks as a moral act, because, if the leaker's identity is unknown, then he or she cannot be challenged adequately nor his or her sources checked.

Whistleblowers, of course, often pay a price for their ethical concerns. There are physical and emotional tolls that whistleblowers may face in abuse from their employers or co-workers (Glazer and Glazer 1989). For example, Charles D. Varnadore, a mechanic at Oak Ridge National Laboratory appeared on a CBS news program in 1991 to talk about cancer among Laboratory employees, including his own. Executives "of the Martin-Marietta subsidiary that runs the Tennessee lab rushed to do something about it. What they did, Mr. Varnadore said in a complaint to the Labor Department, was assign him to do busywork in an isolated room containing toxic and radioactive chemicals" (*New York Times* 9 February 1992: 67). Subsequently, the Labor Department ruled that Martin-Marietta had broken several laws and discriminated against Mr. Varnadore. His lawyer said that the employer's action bordered on attempted murder.

Nonetheless, leaking is sometimes a reasonable method of making an abuse public. After internal dissent has failed, Donald R. Soeken who has studied whistleblowing says, prepare a full statement of the wrong-doing, supply supporting documents, and release them anonymously to the press or to someone in authority outside the organization (*New York Times* 22 February 1987: 22). The revised False Claims Act of 1986 includes financial incentive for employees to give information about wrongdoing in cases of fraud against government agencies. It offers to such whistleblowing employees up to 30 percent of any money that the government recoups (which might add up to a considerable sum if one finds a case similar to that of the wrench worth twelve cents that General Electric sold to the Pentagon for $9,609 *each* [Clinard 1990]).

The third alternative is to exit the organization or the consulting rela-tionship, to resign. To be effective in influencing the client or employer, though, the exit may have to be made with a public statement about how the health and welfare of people are being or would be threatened by the wrongdoing of the client (Tong 1986).

Two former research scholars at the International Institute for Applied Systems Analysis of Vienna (IIASA) faced a moral problem because they knew that the results of a $10 million research project had been deliber-ately misreported and that the misrepresentation could affect public policy. A report, *Energy in a Finite World*, was published in 1981 by IIASA and concluded that fast-breeder reactors "would be cheaper than either coal or conventional nuclear power stations by the year 2005" (*New Scientist* 1984). Finally, the two scholars went public with their allegations that the study misrepresented the results and that the true findings showed the opposite, that "coal, rather than light-water or fast-breeder reactors, is the cheapest energy source up to and beyond the year 2030."

There are, of course, other options than loyalty, voice, and exit. In some extreme situations, subterfuge and even sabotage may be warranted. One case where they may have been appropriate is in opposition to the World War II Nazi efforts to exterminate Jews. Where massive crimes against humanity are being committed, subterfuge and sabotage may be the only weapons available to combat them. Obviously, such actions cannot be undertaken lightly, because they involve both violations of ordinary moral rules, such as trustworthiness and honesty, and great per-sonal risk.

In general, any expert serving as a consultant or researcher on a project who knows of an official misrepresentation has a moral conflict between his obligations of loyalty to his client or employer on the one hand and his commitment to truth and to the public good on the other. A futurist in such a situation must weigh the consequences in deciding whether or not to dissent, first by informing his client or employer of his beliefs and judgments, and, if that does not prevent the misrepresentation, then by making the allegations public. A futurist code of ethics endorsed by professional associations with established standing, if it existed, could provide important support for such actions.

As we saw earlier, some research may be so obviously of value that no justification may seem necessary before undertaking a commitment to work for a client. Even in cases of seemingly worthy goals and underlying values, however, futurists are best advised to be skeptical. They will want to know or to construct an explicit justification of the values defining their purposes and the proposed means of achieving them and they will want to subject such justification to critical analysis. They will want to do this not only to guard against their own and their clients' ethnocentrism or unconscious biases, but also as a part of their futures studies so that the foundations of any claims to describing preferable futures are made clear. Nothing can safely be taken for granted. Rather, all key value assumptions can be—and ought to be—explicitly stated and critically examined, as rationally and objectively as possible, not, however, as a substitute or obstacle to remedial action, but rather as a positive step toward such action.

Conclusion

In this chapter, I have examined a variety of practical strategies that are readily available for deciding what is a good and desirable future and for justifying such decisions. Such strategies are necessary since many decisions to act, and the moral choices involved in them, cannot be postponed for long, often not long enough for a full critical evaluation using a method such as epistemic implication. Time moves on. We cannot climb into a hole and avoid decisions and stop our lives. Moreover, even avoiding making a decision *is* a decision. We must act this way or that, or we must decide not to act. Thus, some rules of thumb or standards of judgment are required to guide us through both the daily small choices we must make as well as the important, long-term decisions that significantly shape our collective lives.

One thing I have asked in this chapter is how well the justifications of generally used moral rules and standards fare when compared to the three models of moral evaluation that I described in the last chapter. My aim, of course, is to encourage questioning and reflection about the moral rightness and foundations of such common rules and standards, especially by futurists as they attempt to create and evaluate their conceptions of preferable futures. Ongoing moral discourse within the critical realist perspective can result in improving moral rules of thumb.

Religion ultimately fails the test of rational and objective (naturalistic) analysis as a justification of the good. This is not to say, however, that religion is in any danger of becoming obsolete. No matter how much scientific knowledge and technology humans create to understand and control their physical and social worlds in the future, there will always be more to know and great mysteries to solve. As long as there are some people with unsatisfied needs in this world, there may always be some people who look forward to the next world of the "afterlife" for their fulfillment. Human beings have had beliefs about supernatural beings for at least 35,000 years (Harris 1989: 462). They may continue to have them for millennia to come.

Religious values and codes of behavior may or may not lead to good consequences as judged by other standards, including rational and objective ones. Throughout history down to the present day, fanatics of nearly every religion have shown themselves to be capable of the most despicable evils in the name of their religious beliefs. Additionally, religious justifications fail because they rely on faith in supernatural phenomena, such as belief in God's will, which transcend naturalistic efforts at logical and empirical verification or falsification.

Religion, however, has its uses in objective moral discourse. First, the commitment-deducibility model can be used to test the logical consistency between sacred values and some particular behavior in a specific situation. Make a commitment to the Koran, for example, and then deduce from it whether a given action is right or wrong. Second, using the means-ends model, futurists and others can select values from religious doctrine to serve as goals and, then, using causal knowledge, objectively design the most effective, efficient and equitable actions to achieve them. Third, and most important, may be the use of religious values as a source of moral assertions that can be tested by naturalistic, extra-religious methods, such as epistemic implication. Stripped of their sacred justifications, many—perhaps most—religious codes of morality may be judged as right and just on naturalistic grounds. Fourth and finally, religious values provide reasons that motivate people to action. Thus, their naturalistic justifications, when they exist, can be linked with their religious motivational force to encourage people to live according to them.

In modern societies, the most widely accepted secular alternative to religion in defining the good is the law of the state. Of course, state law and the normative order are not the same things, yet they more or less overlap, sometimes reinforcing one another and sometimes being in conflict. Laws may incorporate social norms and cultural values and they may also be designed to change such norms and values. Also, law has been used instrumentally as a means to change society, sometimes contrary to social conventions, for example, from guaranteeing people's right to vote and an equal opportunity to get an education to setting standards for safe automobiles and clean water.

Futurists can use the law within the commitment-deducibility model, by explicitly stating that some law is the standard by which the good will be logically judged in some situation. Of course, the commitment to the law as a standard itself remains unjustified. Where legislation is the result of democratic procedures, however, futurists have some argument for justifying their selection of law as the definition of the preferable for members of that society. For, presumably, in such situations the law also reflects the legitimate collective will of group members.

With the rise of purposive law, the means-ends model also becomes relevant. Given legislation aimed at the achievement of some goal, futurists can evaluate the efficiency and effectiveness of the means selected by using current knowledge of cause-and-effect relationships. They can also evaluate how using any particular means affects the achievement of other valued ends. Again, the ends, like the commitment, are not justified, except insofar as they represent the outcome of legitimate democratic processes.

Additionally, futurists can use epistemic implication to test the moral rightness of both the commitments people make to particular laws and the ends that laws specify to be achieved. Also, they can, in any particular case, explore how the law itself may work something like the critical discourse of epistemic implication, since both framers of the law and interpreters of the law give reasons for their intentions, anticipated consequences, and judgments. Such reasons can be taken as evidence and predictive grounds, and they can be subjected to rational and objective analysis.

Moreover, law, activist futurists ought to remember, is open to their own use. Where appropriate, they can request enforcement, suggest changes in existing laws, propose new laws, and work to eliminate old laws. For futurists, thus, the law is not only a framework of codes that helps justify the preferable, but also is both a subject of investigation and a tool that can be used to create a better future.

Another strategy by which futurists can evaluate images of preferable futures is the use of the collective judgments of relevant group members. The history and charter myths of groups often contain statements of the values and goals of the groups, even of whole societies, and these values and goals can be used as standards of judgment. Surveys of the opinions of relevant group members also can serve as standards of the preferable, as I illustrated in the case of appraising the postindependence performance of Jamaican leaders by using their own preindependence images of preferable futures.

Such methods are limited, though, by the fact that the underlying values used as standards of judgments are not grounded in any evidence other than the group's own judgments of the preferable. In the example of the evaluation of state or market governance of the economy, we saw that an investigator in an independent analysis found that some of the beliefs of group members were factually wrong and that the market as a means did not achieve adequately all the ends that group members wanted, especially if those ends included the most general and important ones of human life satisfaction and human development.

Rawls's theory of justice is based on a variation of this approach by using imaginary—rather than real—group members. In a thought experiment based on logical analysis, Rawls deduces how much inequality in a society would be created by rational people in an original position behind a veil of ignorance as to their future positions in the society. As far as it goes, it is persuasive, but it invites empirical social research to test some of the assumptions that underlie it. For example, how much inequality, if any, is really necessary to motivate people to extraordinary effort?

Finally, no agreed-upon, written, enforceable code of ethics governing the professional behavior of futurists yet exists. As a step toward such a code, I concluded this chapter with a review of some of the ethical issues that underlie such professional ethics. The ethical principles given, of course, are prima facie "ought" and "ought not" statements. They are, therefore, only guides. In specific situations, as we saw in chapter 2, we must consider what is the right thing to do *all-things-considered*. Thus, different—and possibly conflicting—values must be weighed as they bear on specific consequences. This is no easy task. Reasonable people, even when they value the same things, may weigh relevant values differently and, thus, reach different decisions as to what is right and wrong in a given instance.

In the chapter that follows, I continue the discussion of the ethical foundations of futures studies by considering the possible existence of universal human values. Are there values that people everywhere in all cultures share? If so, what are they and how did diverse peoples come to the same values? If there are universal values, can they provide a guide for futurists in their search for preferable futures?

4

Universal Human Values

Introduction

Cultural differences have been exaggerated during the last several generations. In fact, human societies and cultures have many features in common, including sharing some core values that are nearly universal. Some basic similarities in people's judgments of what matters, of what is right and what is wrong, exist among different peoples nearly everywhere. Furthermore, we have a reasonably good idea about what these similarities are and why they exist.

Futurists, of course, cannot justify a value simply on the grounds that it is nearly universal. First, some of the past conditions that produced a universal value and the norms of behavior exemplifying it may have changed. Under new conditions, it may no longer serve the best interests of humans, either individually or collectively. Thus, some human values today, perhaps near-universal and traditional ones that remain unquestioned, are anachronisms, because they were inherited from a past quite different from the present and even more different from the coming future. Like many other things, traditional values, too, may outlive their usefulness. Second, there are limits to accepting nearly universal values as justification of the good simply because of their universality, because, as we have seen, what *does* exist, even if it exists in all human groups, is not by itself a logical basis for concluding that it *ought* to exist.

Nevertheless, near-universals do not exist by chance. Thus, they give us insight about which values may have contributed to the survival and flourishing of human societies over the long haul of human evolution. They are clues to discovering which values are worthy of investigation and critical evaluation and a starting point to considering which values may have continuing utility for human well-being in the future and which may not.

For example, some basic human needs certainly have not changed in tens of thousands of years, such as needs for water, food, and shelter. Also, many of the preconditions of social life may have remained roughly the same, such as cooperation among people. Additionally, the environment, although greatly changed in some ways, remains the same in others, for example, the everyday-on-this-Earth laws of physics still apply and will continue to do so. Thus, examining nearly universal core values can provide robust hypotheses about what aspects of human life can be ignored only at the peril of endangering human well-being in the future.

Contrariwise, if we can identify values that in the past have led to the extinction of cultures or to harmful and less than optimal behavior, then we can formulate hypotheses about which values ought to be discarded.

In this chapter, I discuss (1) how the grounds supporting the belief in extreme cultural diversity and in the lack of cultural universals have eroded, (2) some human values that may be nearly universal, and (3) the possible origins of nearly universal values. Then, I give (4) more detailed examples of four human values about which a considerable amount of social research has been done, the core values of (a) knowledge, (b) evaluation itself, (c) justice, and (d) cooperation. These values not only have withstood the test of times past, but also may be of fundamental importance for the future well-being of humankind.

The Limits of Cultural Diversity and Relativism

Emphasizing the universality of values, of course, flies in the face of a long-standing anthropological tradition of cultural diversity and relativism. Modern anthropologists such as Geertz (1983), for example, often focus on the differences among cultures, practices that appear to peoples of other cultures to be strange and exotic, at first even incomprehensible. Indeed, it is important and useful to describe and understand such variations. To do so is a corrective to the errors of ethnocentrism, that is, the mistakes of condemning foreign cultural practices simply because they are foreign and of accepting the values of one's own group as correct without critically examining them.

Moreover, examining cultural differences in a comparative framework is a powerful method of building knowledge about the nature of culture and cultural development. What I have to say in this chapter about panhuman values and similarities in the human condition is not intended to disparage nor to usurp the study of cultural variation, but, rather, to add to it and to provide balance. After all, groups of people may be different in many ways and at the same time may be the same in many others.

The effort to investigate different cultures itself, of course, even while insisting on their incomparable differences as an extreme cultural relativist might, contains the assumption that there are enough basic similarities among different peoples that mutual understanding is possible. For example, no anthropologist has ever gone to another culture to study it and returned saying that it was so bizarre or incoherent that he or she was unable to comprehend it (Gellner 1981). People and their cultures are similar enough to allow human beings from one culture to go to other cultures and learn their languages and understand their ways. Even though there sometimes are difficult barriers of translation, cultures are similar enough for bridges of mutual understanding to be built.

Ethnocentrism, of course, is not the only source of error in understanding and accurately mapping the human condition. So, too, may be an exclusive focus on cultural differences, because it can mislead and distort in other ways. Stanley Lieberson (1985) has argued that social scientists may be missing many important principles by their general analytic strategy of looking for and analyzing differences. Such a strategy, for example, might never have resulted in the discovery of such a pervasive force as the law of gravity. Social scientists, Lieberson argues, typically would have studied the differences in the acceleration and speed by which different objects fell to the ground and would have formulated a series of explanatory propositions that explained the differences. They would never have come to what was common or universal in all objects falling to the ground, namely, gravity.

Take the necessity of eating and look at the world's different cuisines, for example. Even if we have sampled only a few of them, we are aware of the differences among the foods prepared by typical cooks of different nationalities. Contrary to what an extreme cultural relativist may believe, though, it makes sense to analyze, compare, and evaluate the differences, because it is more than simply a matter of each to his own. Objectively, some cuisines are more nutritious and healthy than others, given certain other aspects of a people's life style. Some, too, such as the grand cuisines of the Chinese and the French, are more elaborate, complex, perhaps lovingly prepared and enjoyable, although a considerable amount of individual preference, obviously, is learned and not innate (not many of us, for example, have acquired the Australian aboriginals' taste for the thick-bodied, sluggish larva of some insects known as "witchetty grubs.")

Whatever their differences, there are also basic similarities shared by different cuisines, for example, selecting what is edible and nutritious; peeling, skinning, cutting, or scraping off what is not to be eaten; adding seasonings of various kinds; cooking or marinating or drying; preserving some food in some way for later consumption; coming together in groups to eat following ritualistic patterns of behavior (partly what we in the West call "table manners"), and so on. The basic uniformities ought not to be obliterated by looking only at the differences. Moreover, the principle that "every problem is an opportunity" has few examples better than the way so many peoples throughout the world have transformed the universal human problem of having to eat to live into an opportunity of high enjoyment and pleasure.

Human values may be like language. There are differences but there are also similarities (Chomsky 1972). Languages have certain uniquenesses in phonology, grammar, and semantics that appear to make them mutually unintelligible. But these are superficial. At a deeper level they share universals that make them mutually translatable. For example, all languages draw their phonemes from a limited stock of phonetic features. All share similarities in the deep (cognitive) structure of grammars and in the sets of semantic features that separate concepts and meanings. "Thus the use of terms—the way the lexicon carves up the world—appears entirely arbitrary until the ethnolinguist discovers a framework of common semantic components" (Osgood et al. 1975: 4).

As Michael D. Coe (1994: 8) says, "Even though there are 4,000 to 6,000 languages today, they are all sufficiently alike to be considered one language by an extraterrestrial observer. In other words, most of the diversity of the world's cultures, so beloved to anthropologists, is superficial and minor compared to the similarities. Racial differences are literally only 'skin deep.'" There is a fundamental unity of humankind.

There is also the matter of variation within a country. For example, individuals differ in temperament and experience, because no one has exactly the same physical makeup and social environment as another individual. Compared to others, some people are more aggressive, depressed, irritable, hostile, mistrustful, intelligent, creative, strong, or beautiful. Every society contains both unusually talented people and especially disputatious and dangerous people (Edgerton 1992: 69).

Sometimes, variation within a country may exceed variation between countries. In a twelve-nation study done in 1965, for instance, about 30,000 accounts were collected of how individuals used their time as they pursued their daily activities (Szalai 1972). The researchers found that people of the same sex and employment status from different countries, even in the most disparate of the countries studied, used their time in ways that were more similar to one another than they were to other people within their own cultural settings.

Today, we know that cultural diversity in the world has been greatly exaggerated during the last two or three generations and that cultural relativism is a misleading doctrine. Exemplars that have sustained the belief in cultural diversity and relativism have been found wanting as restudy after restudy, usually more thorough and meticulous than the original, have been reported.

For example, research summarized by Donald E. Brown (1991), shows that, contrary to Margaret Mead's *Coming of Age in Samoa*, adolescence in Samoa was just as stressful as in the West; the matrilineal Trobriand Islanders, contrary to Bronislaw Malinowski's conclusion in *Sex and Repression in Savage Society*, did have an Oedipus complex; the Hopi's conception of time, contradicting the Sapir-Whorf hypothesis of cultural relativism and specific earlier research by Benjamin Whorf, is about the same as that in contemporary American society; and Mead's findings that male and female temperaments as understood in the West were reversed among a New Guinean people, as reported in *Sex and Temperament in Three Primitive Societies*, have been refuted.

Also, other formerly influential beliefs supporting the existence of extreme cultural diversity have been shown to be little more than myths. For example, people everywhere classify colors in about the same way and add new color terms to their languages in about the same order. That is, color classifications are not arbitrary. Neither is the link between facial expressions and emotions (Ekman 1980, 1982). A smile, for example, and many other facial expressions and body gestures, we now know, generally mean the same thing in all cultures. Modern researchers, as Brown (1991) says, have smashed these and other icons of cultural relativism.

Ronald P. Rohner (1986) shows that in all societies, parental warmth or rejection affects children positively or negatively in roughly similar ways. Melford E. Spiro (1992) demonstrates both that extreme cultural relativism is misguided and that a genuine cross-cultural science with commanding universals is possible. He argues that, despite some marked differences, non-Western peoples, like all humans, share so many traits and experiences they are simply part of a common humanity. They are "sister" and "brother" to us, not "other."

Of course, this is not to say that different peoples don't do some things differently and don't sometimes attach different meanings to the same thing. Differences in levels of technology alone account for many cultural differences, in ways of doing things even though ends may be similar, and this may go a long way in explaining why some peoples thrive while others merely subsist. Beyond that, some societies may be dysfunctional in some of their cultural patterns, including their priorities of cultural goals and values. As a result, they may become extinct, barely survive, or survive tolerably well but at levels below what would be optimal (Edgerton 1992).

Nor is it to say that the meaning people attach to words, gestures, and behaviors of others isn't relative to the frames of reference that they are using. No doubt much misunderstanding, even among people sharing the same language and culture, follows from the fact that in given circumstances different people may not share the same frame of reference. The late British comedian, Benny Hill, based a good deal of his comedy on the double meanings that arise from the use of different frames of reference. For example, Hill will have his character say of his wife, "She's got a black belt in cookery." (Pause). "She can kill you with one chop." Obviously, the "chop" can mean a blow using a Judo frame of reference from "black belt," or, using "cookery" as the frame of reference, a pork or lamb chop. But to say that meaning is relative to one's frame of reference, although it alerts us to the importance of discovering the appropriate frame of reference in any context, is commonplace. The cultural relativist claim of incomparability is a different matter.

Among the hidden perils of cultural relativism, Goldschmidt (1990: 234–35) includes, in addition to the denial of any universal moral values, "an implicit disrespect for our own culture" and "the assumption that the people of exotic cultures are happy with their own customs." On the last point, he continues by saying that it "is a strange notion that tribal peoples everywhere could somehow solve all the problems of community life and create a harmonious existence—something that has manifestly escaped

Western man through his long history." He says rightly that, after all, there are many negative and hurtful aspects of small scale, folk societies (see chapter 2).

In sum, the evidence rejecting the existence of universal or nearly universal cultural patterns is flimsy. We can speak superficially different languages, yet express the same thoughts, and we can believe in different gods, yet share the same values. Thus, we must consider the question of cultural similarities among people and the reasons for their possible existence.

Possible Universal Values: An Overview

What is a Universal?

By a "universal," I refer to a cultural trait or pattern of some kind, a practice, value, or institution that is shared by all known societies. Generally, I mean "near-universal," because I assume, first, that within any society there is deviance and not every single individual lives up to his or her society's moral codes and, second, that societies vary according to how well they satisfy the individual needs of their members and their own needs of societal survival. Nearly all existing societies, for example, may contain norms of behavior that ensure the adequate care of babies. But, for one reason or another, there may be a society that does not do so, thereby reducing the universal to a near-universal, and, we can add, condemning itself to eventual extinction.

Cultural traits and patterns need not always be absolutely identical to be considered universal or near-universal. They may be similar, frequently recurring, commonly shared, or convergent. They may, at the very least, possess resemblances. They may be simple facts of near identity, such as the fact that all peoples have norms and values involving reproductive activities. Or they may be functional equivalents, such as all peoples putting a value on proper child-rearing behaviors even though they may differ as to what they consider to be "proper."

Stinchcombe (1982b: 71–72) argues for the existence of "common categories" even when they may not be universal. For example, "foreigner" has some common characteristics everywhere, but also characteristics that are specific to a given culture: the Karimojong of Northern Uganda would kill a foreigner entering Karimojong territory, while a foreigner entering the United States might only get humiliated or given a limited period of visitation. Obviously, killing someone is totally different from humiliating someone, but in both cases there is a resemblance, "the principle of lesser elgibility is applied to foreigners."

The discussion of universals in human behaviors has a long tradition, especially among philosophers, dating back at least to Plato (Schoedinger 1992). Writers from Aristotle, Aquinas, and Locke to Berkeley, Kant, and Hegel to Heidegger, Russell, and Carnap, to mention only a few, have written on the topic. In recent years, Joseph Campbell (1968) has popularized the notion that mythology everywhere is the same beneath what he describes as "surface differences." Anthropologists, too, have written extensively about universals in general and they have drawn up several lists of possible universals (Kluckhohn 1953; Wescott 1970).

One such list, compiled long ago by Murdock (1945: 124) gives a total of seventy-three universals, ranging from such items as bodily adornment, cleanliness training, community organization, cooking, cooperative labor, cosmology, and courtship to puberty customs, religious ritual, residence rules, sexual restrictions, soul concepts, status differentiation, tool making, trade, visiting, and weaning.

In the daily newspapers and on television news programs we learn of bitter and violent religious, ethnic, and racial conflicts in many parts of the world, and we learn of the death and destruction to which they lead. Kurds in Turkey and Iraq; Croats, Slavic Muslims and Serbs in what was Yugoslavia; Armenians and Muslims in Azerbaijan; African-Americans and Jews in Manhattan; Basques and Castilians in Spain; Protestants and Catholics in Northern Ireland; Tutsi and Hutu in Rwanda and Burundi; the Tamil and Sinhalese in Sri Lanka; Sikhs, Hindus, and Muslims in India; Africans and East Indians in Guyana…the list goes on and on.

These clashes, often attributed to cultural and religious differences, are brought about not only by perceived differences, but also by *similarities* among such groups. For example, all people everywhere are capable of experiencing ingroup and outgroup feelings, expressing loyalty, defining their treatment by others as unjust, feeling righteous indignation and outrage, sacrificing themselves for their group, cooperating among themselves, exhibiting aggression and anger, hating others and seeking revenge, fighting and killing, and suffering because of the loss of loved ones. Understanding the basic similarities among peoples, as well as the differences, may help to understand and heal such conflicts.

Many different theories, terminologies, and views on the nature of universals now exist and they often define issues of disagreement among scholars. Most of these issues, however, do not concern us here, because we are concerned not with all near-universals, but only with those that are human values.

Prime Candidates for Universal Values

Depending on the level of abstraction and the forms of classification we choose, there can be innumerable universal values or virtues—and, of course, corresponding evils and vices. There exist endless numbers of lists, some that are very lengthy. Yet, as in the case of the utopian writers discussed in chapter 1, there are some generally similar values that occur time and time again on many different lists. Also, long lists of values usually can be organized by a smaller number of more general values. Thus, there appear to be some core human values about which there is wide agreement both over geographic space and time—from well before the birth of Christ up to the present. Let's look at some examples.

"Virtue" is one of the oldest ideas of moral discourse. Both MacIntyre (1984) and Pieper (1966) believe that the virtues as enunciated by Saint Thomas Aquinas in the thirteenth century constitute a nearly universal standard of morality. Aquinas's five primary virtues (with some secondary ones in parentheses) are temperance (restraint, moderation, and discipline), fortitude (perseverence and patience), justice as fairness (truthfulness and friendliness), prudence (the use of reason and objectivity) and charity (forgiveness and tolerance). These values or similar ones appear frequently on more recent lists.

For example, Boulding (1985) constructs a "G scale," that is, a scale or index to define and measure the good. It includes five basic variables that can be applied to entire societies as well as to individuals, whatever their cultural differences: (1) riches (e.g., wealth and economic welfare); (2) justice; (3) freedom; (4) peace, and a residual category; (5) the quality of life (by which he means health, education and learning, opportunities for family life and sexual behavior, work environment, church and religion, beauty, and the character and quality of human persons themselves, e.g., whether or not a person is kindly, generous, trustworthy, honest, helpful, friendly, courageous, reliable, etc.).

Lasswell (1971, 1977) lists eight broad values that derive from his conception of human dignity. Each one is a good candidate for being universal. They are: shaping and sharing of power, enlightenment, wealth (sufficient but not enormous), well-being, skill, affection, respect, and rectitude. Lasswell views them as categories that are general enough to subsume most other lists of values, to encompass, for example, the long list of rights enumerated in the Universal Declaration of Human Rights of the United Nations (see below).

In addition to honesty, trust, and sharing with others, Campbell (1965) has suggested other contenders for universal values that derive from the preconditions of social life, such as industriousness, surplus production, abstinence from indulgence, loyalty, and respect for both authority and knowledge.

A somewhat overlapping, but more general, list of values has been given by Hemming (1974: 20): integrity, fairness, truthfulness, honesty, cooperation, honoring obligations to others, willingness to sacrifice one-self for the group, courage, loyalty, caring for one another, and self-control. Additionally, we ought not to forget the values of flexibility and a refusal to overspecialize, both of which permit adaptability to a wide range of environments and the ability to respond to a great variety of challenges (Ferkiss 1974: 131).

Two contemporary futurists, Willis W. Harman and Peter Schwartz (1978), after emphasizing the need of futurists for some value propositions to guide their work, suggest three sets. The first is survivability, including adaptability, resilience, self-healing, and learning. The second is what they call "the perennial values of human civilization," including individual freedom, equal justice under the law, democratic liberation from oppression by institutions, reverence for and oneness with nature, a sense of community and brotherhood. The third is that which is compatible with "whatever can be discovered to be man's most fundamental nature," which, unfortunately, they leave unstated. For these authors, futures are desirable to the degree to which they are compatible with or achieve these three principles.

After years of carrying on hologeistic studies, that is, studies taking the range of cultures throughout the whole world into account, often using the massive data sets contained in the Human Relations Area Files, Raoul Naroll (1983: 47–49) formulates a set of four core values that he proposes as the value foundations of a future global society:

1. Peace (world peace, the reduction of armed aggression and warfare among all peoples, some form of world law and its enforcement without killing people).

2. Humanism (making people, each individual, the measure of both the good and the true, the ultimate good being the earthly happiness of humankind).
3. Decency (including the idea of brotherhood and sisterhood extended to all humankind, people helping each other).
4. Progress (especially the growth of powerful knowledge, that is, knowledge that helps people to control their lives).

More recently, Rushworth M. Kidder (1994) took a moral and intellectual safari around the world and asked twenty-four prominent men and women a single question, "If there could be a global code of ethics, what would it contain?" Although his respondents included a diversity of different people from different societies, he found considerable consensus on eight core values:

1. *Love* (including caring for all people, mutual assistance, and compassion for others).
2. *Truthfulness* (including being honest, keeping your promises, not lying, and not behaving deceitfully).
3. *Fairness* (including justice, fair play, even-handedness, following the golden rule, equality [but note below that sometimes inequality is fair], and equity).
4. *Freedom* (including liberty and democracy).
5. *Unity* (including fraternity, cooperation, community, group allegiance, and oneness with others).
6. *Tolerance* (including limits in imposing your values on other people, respect for the dignity of each person and the right of everyone to have ideas. Remember, though, as we have seen, there are limits to the *behavior* that ought to be tolerated).
7. *Responsibility* (including both taking care of yourself and of other people, and having a concern for community interests).
8. *Respect for life* (including the prima facie proscription, "Thou shalt not kill.")

Kidder's respondents mention other values—courage, knowing right from wrong, wisdom, hospitality, obedience, and stability—but did so less consistently. Also, they express concern about three crosscutting contemporary issues: racial harmony, respect for women's rights and equality, and the protection of the environment.

One noteworthy program of research on global values that involved an international group of scholars took place during the 1970s. It is known as the World Order Models Project (WOMP) of the Institute for World Order (now the World Policy Institute). The primary aim was to propose, document, and analyze a set of values that can be widely accepted as goals for a "model of a preferred world" (Falk 1975; Kothari 1974). Over a number of years, many researchers contributed to the WOMP effort, and designed ways that the proposed global values could be achieved (Falk 1977, 1983; Galtung 1980).

One culmination of WOMP appeared in 1991 with the publication of Michael J. Sullivan III's *Measuring Global Values*. In it Sullivan uses more than 100 indicators to measure five global values: peace, economic well-being, ecological balance, social justice, and political participation. He then proceeds to evaluate national policies and the state performance of 162 countries, ranking them as to how well they have achieved each of the values.

Other studies and reports dealing with basic or core values could be described, but we have reviewed enough, I think, to make the point that there is considerable similarity in those things that people throughout the world value. Different scholars may categorize them somewhat differently, different respondents may use different words for them, both may use somewhat different classification schemes or different degrees of abstraction and generality, but the conclusion is sound: A similar set of basic values appears to exist among people nearly everywhere.

Are Changes Occurring in Basic Values?

In one of the most ambitious attempts to measure values and changes in values crossnationally, Ronald Inglehart (1990) reports survey data for over twenty-five countries, including multiple data collections within the same countries from 1973 to 1988. In all, he analyzes over 200 separate studies involving more than a quarter-million respondents. His major contention is that in countries where material well-being and physical security have been the standard for decades, that is, in advanced industrial societies, traditional "materialist" values of physical sustenance and safety have been decreasing in importance while "postmaterialist" values such as individual autonomy, innovation, self-expression, beauty, and a tendency to challenge—rather than blindly accept—authority have been increasing. That is, top priority is shifting from the basic physical necessities of life to those things that will enhance the quality of life. This generational shift is supported by the data.

Inglehart claims, further, that this new axis of polarization—materialism vs. postmaterialism—rather than traditional left-right differences now explain people's responses to such "new" issues as environmentalism, nuclear power, and women's rights.

But does this shift from materialist to postmaterialist values in advanced industrial societies mean that basic universal or pancultural values are changing? Perhaps not. First, from Inglehart's data we note that many people, even in advanced industrial societies, continue to express materialist values. Thus, the change he documents is by no means a complete shift in values on the part of all people in industrial societies.

Second, as Wright (1991: 893) has argued, even within many of the postmaterial values there is a materialist aspect. For example, a clean and pretty environment may be an aesthetic goal but it also has survival value. Also, opposing nuclear power is partly a matter of appealing to thoroughly materialist cost-benefit analysis.

Third, and most important, postmaterial values are partly contingent upon the adequate satisfaction of survival values. If you have a satisfactory job, food to eat, a spouse and children, reasonably good health, a home, and so on, you take such things as the base from which you seek additional things, such as self-realization. In such a circumstance, you can value self-realization without having to choose between, say, eating and expressing your artistic talents. But when people face not having food to eat or a place to live, they judge self-realization to be of little immediate importance. As the old blues refrain puts it, "You don't care 'bout the water till the well runs dry."

Thus, if we postulate different levels of values—for example, survival, comfort, and self-fulfillment—in a hierarchy similar to that suggested by Maslow (1968), we can understand how a growing proportion of people in an advanced industrial society with a high level of living come to exhibit self-fulfillment values. Many people in such societies have a relatively high and secure level of personal safety and economic well-being. Thus, their survival and comfort needs are largely satisfied. This does not mean that survival and comfort are not important to them. It simply means that for people with enough food to eat and decent homes in which to live in safe neighborhoods, self-fulfillment becomes a more prominent goal of human endeavor. Moreover, good health (beyond mere survival) continues to place highly in value studies (Perkins and Spates 1986), because people realize that it is not only a good thing in itself but also a precondition for the achievement of other goals.

In the future, if generally high levels of living are achieved, then the exploration and elaboration of aspects of an individual's self-realization, especially in relation to the self-realization of others, may become of great importance for the further development of human values and potential. But more than two-thirds of the Earth's population today do not live in advanced industrial societies and for most of such people the struggle for survival and a modicum of comfort takes precedence over self-fulfillment.

Also, the relatively high levels of living that have characterized many (but by no means all) people living in advanced industrial societies during the last few generations is in no way guaranteed in the future. It remains exceptional in the course of human experience. And it remains precarious and dependent on complex political, economic, and social structures that may or may not continue to function adequately. A worldwide crisis—political, economic, health, agricultural, climatic, or nuclear—or social disruptions and breakdowns within societies might reduce all of the Earth's people to a preoccupation with survival. For without some minimal satisfaction of basic needs, the pursuit of higher order values—and even life itself—ends.

Nevertheless, some basic human values have changed and, given changing conditions, some others *ought* to change, if human societies are to flourish in the future. We must question and retain a reasonable doubt about what human values are the most appropriate for achieving the freedom and well-being of the human community, now and in the future (see chapter 6).

A Reaffirmation of The Universal Declaration of Human Rights

On December 10, 1948, the United Nations General Assembly adopted The Universal Declaration of Human Rights. It incorporates most of the provisions of the Declaration of Rights and Duties of the World Citizen that pioneer futurist H. G. Wells drew up in 1940–42. In June 1993 at a World Conference on Human Rights meeting in Vienna, it was reaffirmed by representatives of most of the Earth's states, a larger and more diverse group than the original adopters in 1948.

The U.N. Declaration is important as a statement of possible universal values because, being based on worldwide critical discussion and considerable consensus, it carries the moral authority of a legitimate international organization and sets a consensual law-like standard for the rights of all people. There remains, of course, much to be discussed and agreed upon—for example, differences regarding the priorities that ought to be given to civil and political rights versus economic and social rights. Moreover, spurred on by China, Indonesia, Syria and Iran, forty Asian countries diluted the global unity concerning standards of justice and fairness by insisting on allowing for regional peculiarities and various historical, cultural, and religious backgrounds, in what could have been an attempt to disguise wrongdoing in a claim of exception.

Nonetheless, the U.N. Declaration is a promising step toward the specification of universal global morality. It recognizes the inherent dignity of all people and brings everyone into a global moral community as full members. In the summary of some of its provisions, which I give below, note the recurrence of most of the candidates for universal values discussed earlier.

The thirty articles of the Declaration flow from the "recognition of the inherent dignity and of the equal and inalienable rights of all members of the human family" which "is the foundation of freedom, justice and peace in the world." The Declaration affirms, among other things, the unity of human beings, the right to life, freedom from slavery and torture, equality before the law, the right to privacy, freedom of movement, a right to marriage and a family, a right to own property, freedom of thought and expression, peaceful assembly, participation in government, social security, a right to work, a right to rest and leisure, a right to health and well-being, a right to education, a right to participate in cultural life, and duties to the community including recognizing and respecting the rights and freedoms of others and "meeting the just requirements of morality, public order and the general welfare in a democratic society."

The Declaration might be faulted by some philosophers as well as practical people because in some of its articles it appears to go beyond minimalist notions, proposing not just a right to a human life but a right to a *good* human life (Griffin 1986: 226–27). For example, such provisions as protection against unemployment, the right to an adequate standard of living, social security, education directed to the full development of the human personality, and so on may be considered too extensive. Such rights, admirable as they are, can be set against what is possible and practical, especially in many poor countries that cannot now afford to provide all of these economic and social services. Thus, as a statement of economic and social rights, the Declaration can be taken as an image of a future toward which people can—and ought to—strive as their resources permit.

Taken as a statement of political and civil rights, however, it defines the standard of behavior that all individuals and governments now can be—and ought to be—expected to exhibit.

Some countries, obviously, have done better in living up to the Declaration than others. Some have horrendously failed. Today, one or another of its articles is violated by most of the national governments of the Earth. In some countries, people are still imprisoned for their beliefs, torture remains official government policy, and slavery still exists. These political and civil violations ought not to be tolerated.

Taken as a statement of general values, the Declaration gives a powerful voice to an international standard of morality that defines the good as we ought to behave toward other people and the evil as we ought not.

Global Ethics: A Parliament of the World's Religions

As mentioned in chapter 3, in September 1993 at a Parliament of the World's Religions meeting in Chicago, more than 200 leaders representing more than 100 of the world's religious faiths signed a declaration, "Towards a Global Ethic." The declaration was the result of two years of work by scholars and theologians. The religious leaders viewed their declaration as a beginning effort to create a global ethic for all humankind that can be "affirmed by all persons with ethical convictions, whether religiously grounded or not" (p. 3). Acknowledging the U.N. Universal Declaration of Human Rights, they wished to support what the U.N. Declaration had proclaimed as rights by confirming and deepening it ethically.

Among the values supported in "Towards a Global Ethic" are individual responsbility, treating others as we wish them to treat us, respect for life, treating all other people with dignity (without regard to distinctions of age, sex, race, skin color, physical or mental ability, language, religion, political view, or national or social origin), patience, understanding and acceptance of one another, forgiveness, solidarity and relatedness with other people of the world, kindliness and generosity, caring for others, compassion, love for one another, equality between men and women, nonviolence, economic and social justice, peace and global order, nature-friendly ways of life, respect for human rights and fundamental values, constancy and trustworthiness, truthfulness and honesty, moderation and modesty, loyalty, safety and security, freedom as long as no harm is done to others, tolerance, and sexuality that expresses and reinforces a loving relationship lived by equal partners.

Among those things that are devalued are abuses of the Earth's ecosystems, prejudice, hatred, theft, greed, arrogance, mistrust, hostility, violence, envy, jealousy, resentment, terror, oppression, torture, mutilation, killing, ruthlessness and brutality, lies and deceit, swindling and hypocrisy, demagoguery, fanaticism and intolerance, opportunism, domination, and degradation.

Again, we see the similarity among these values, both positive and negative, and the other lists which were generated from a variety of sources—as far into the past as Thomas More and beyond. Thus, despite the diversity of religious faiths of the signatories to this document, we find evidence of values which the world's people hold in common. Also, we find some additional moral support for a set of universal or near-universal values.

Let us now turn to the question of how values that appear to be shared by people nearly everywhere came into being, despite the apparent world diversity of cultural beliefs and social environments.

Origins of Human Values

An Evolutionary View

Human values are not arbitrary or capricious. Their origins and their continued existence are partly found in the facts of human biology and the interaction of human bodies and minds with their physical and social environments. That is, the very nature of human beings as biopsychological entities shapes and constrains human behavior within the physical and social situations that they function. It shapes, too, humans' beliefs about the world and their evaluations of various aspects of it.

Variation in human behavior, including random variation, proposes many attempted solutions to fulfilling the conditions of human survival and well-being. On the one hand, those behaviors that allow humans to survive and thrive, both as individuals and as groups, tend to be reinforced, selected for retention by circumstances, and become valued by group members. On the other hand, those behaviors that threaten human survival and well-being tend to be discouraged and discredited by poor results. They tend to become devalued. Inferior or failed patterns of behavior, if not the groups practicing them themselves, tend to die out. Both the hidden hand of unintended and unanticipated consequences and the conscious decisions of human design are involved. Myths, rituals, mystical beliefs, and religions as well as institutionalized patterns of social rewards and punishments, both material and nonmaterial, develop and support valued behaviors and discourage devalued behaviors.

Thus, over the course of human development, what works tends to last. What doesn't work tends to die out. What works better tends to replace what doesn't work as well, although dogma and ritual concerning past ways of doing things can slow the adoption of new ways and what works just well enough is often the enemy of what would work better. What works one place may be similar to what works at another place, because similar evolutionary principles of variation, selection, and retention are constantly at work as people with similar needs and capacities attempt to solve similar problems.

Of course, it often is a complicated and slow process. As Boulding (1985: 26) points out, some cultures with errors of matters of fact reinforced by their value sets have existed for long periods of time. The Aztecs believed that it was necessary to sacrifice human beings in order to make the corn grow. But, eventually, if the Aztecs did not do some things that were technically correct to make corn grow rather than relying on technically incorrect human sacrifice, the corn would not grow. Moreover, we have evidence from pyschological experiments that lead us to believe that purely arbitrary cultural norms cannot be perpetuated indefinitely. The collective effect of people's own observations can eventually erode a functionless arbitrary belief (Jacobs and Campbell 1961: 657).

When we speak of social and cultural evolution, we are talking not so much about natural selection, that is, the workings of reproductive success or failure, but about social and cultural selection. Social practices and cultural traits can be born and die out all within the lifetime of particular individuals, since humans can change their beliefs and behaviors.

Human values are not simply a matter of personal belief nor are they simply a matter of particular social and cultural traditions (Lombardi 1988). They fundamentally rest, rather, on nearly universal patterns of human judgment that have arisen because of basic similarities in human nature, the prerequisites of social life, and the nature of the physical world.

Origins of Values in Human Nature

Biological-psychological origins. Human beings cannot exist without having certain of their needs met. They must have air, water, food, sleep, and personal security. Moreover, there are other needs that, although they are not absolutely necessary for the bodily survival of individuals, contribute to individual survival and are necessary for comfort and flourishing. These are needs for clothing, shelter, companionship, affection, and sex. The last, of course, although not necessary for the survival of an individual, is necessary for reproduction and, hence, the continued survival of the human group.

Thus, there are many constraints placed on human behavior, if individuals and groups are to continue to survive and to thrive. These are *not* matters of choice. They are factual conditions that must be met that derive from the nature of human beings. *How* they are met involves some—often considerable—leeway of choice, but, obviously, these needs set limits to the possible. Practices of drinking only sea water, eating only rocks, and breathing only carbon monoxide will not sustain human life and humans having sex only with sheep will not reproduce human life.

Human beings do not come into the world devoid of a means of evaluation. Before culture and learning take hold, even though they begin almost immediately at birth, the human body and brain are programmed with a variety of sensors, such as taste, smell, sight, hearing, and touch, and of drives, such as hunger, thirst, and sex. We know that infants have the ability to be afraid and that fear conditioning is fundamental to an individual's safety. We know, too, that the neural site of human fear is in an almond-sized section of the brain called the amygdala.

Individuals feel pain and pleasure, even before they have become persons, that is, before they have become social and cultural entities. Without having to be taught, they seek pleasure and avoid pain. Thus, as a result of the basic design of the human body and brain, people have some basis for evaluation, some built-in criteria for believing that some things are good and that some things are bad.

For example, a hunger pang, being thirsty, suffocating, a bitter taste—such things, our sensations tell us, are bad, while a stomach filled with food, a drink of clean water, a breath of fresh air, a taste of something sweet—such things, our sensations also tell us, are good. Such built-in sensations provide a primitive set of useful guidelines for the welfare of an individual organism and a foundation for the origins of more complex human values. All normal human beings share these basic biological and psychological needs and drives.

Empathy appears to be a human trait visible from the earliest point in human development. For instance, when newborn babies hear other babies cry, they cry too (Rest 1986: 7). Thus, being concerned for the plight of other people may be wired into human nature through the capacity to put oneself in the place of the other.

It is true that some writers may overemphasize the biological origins of human values, such as Pugh (1977) for example, and may underestimate the possibilities of learning and the ultimate neutrality of the human central nervous system as to what it learns. For people are organisms built for learning and they are capable of learning nearly anything, even though what they learn may give them immediate pain or be of long-term harm to them. Social and cultural practices can—and sometimes do—override natural reactions to innate sensations and may lead people to avoid pleasure and seek pain, even death in defense of the group for example.

Yet Pugh (1977) and others are right in stating that there are limits to social and cultural domination of biology and psychology. The basic conditions of human biopsychological survival must be met for enough men, women, and children for any group to continue to exist and for human development to continue to take place.

Other values, such as those we place on money, develop secondarily, in part from the reinforcement they receive from the satisfaction of basic biological drives. Receiving and classifying sensory data, remembering and refining, transforming reflex action to rational thought, learning routines and placing habits under rational control are all part of the process of originating and reconfirming values and of going beyond conditioned responses and unconscious learning. For example, almost "all the experiments which purport to show behavioral changes as a result of operant conditioning can also be explained as a purely rational response to learning experience which changes the animal's world model" (Pugh 1977).

Origins in higher-order needs and capacities of individuals. I am here making an arbitrary dichotomy, because in reality there is no clear demarcation between biopsychological needs and drives and higher-order needs and capacities. Rather, there is a continuum, running from the most basic needs of sheer biological survival to such capacities as the ability to reason, to attribute meaning to things, and to decide to act in one way or another. Moreover, some of the higher-order needs and capacities may themselves, in fact, rest upon biological structure. Diamond (1992), for example, claims that what makes us uniquely human is the larynx. The great leap forward in the development of human culture that took place about 40,000 years ago, he says, was the result of changes in the human ability to control spoken sounds, which itself was dependent upon laryngeal anatomy.

Even if such dependence exists, however, it remains useful for the sake of analysis to treat the extremes of such needs and capacities separately, since they differ both in how constraining they are on the range of possible human behaviors and in how much they provide opportunities for discovery and invention. For example, you cannot live without oxygen, period. Your capacity for language, however, permits you to do a lot of different things: speaking Cantonese or French, or composing a sonnet or writing an advertisement for beer.

Lombardi (1988) starts his effort to understand human values with basic physical needs and wants. Thus, he includes in his conception of "human welfare" such things as those that lead to sheer physical survival (e.g., health, use of limbs); he moves next to physical well-being (e.g., absence of pain, opportunities for sex and exercise); he moves further to emotional or psychological well-being (e.g., absence of phobias, satisfaction of emotional needs) and, finally, he moves beyond that to aesthetic and intellectual pleasures (e.g., musical and dramatic performances, learning how the solar system works). Thus, he includes a range of levels of needs, from those that are absolutely necessary for biological survival to those that promote intellectual understanding of the world. All are equally derived from the nature of human beings.

He adds to the considerations of human welfare another set of considerations dealing with human freedom. He derives these considerations, too, from the nature of human beings, specifically from the capacities of people as rational beings, as beings who make decisions and choices. Thus, decision-making abilities imply the ability to develop options (e.g., needs for educational training and equal access to jobs and resources), the ability to deliberate and choose (e.g., needs for having relevant and accurate information and truth telling), and the ability to carry out a decision once it has been made (e.g., needs for absence of force, threats, or other interference) (Lombardi 1988: 21–22). In a nutshell, it is in the nature of human beings to be choosers, and choosers need freedom to choose in order to exercise this capacity.

This is not to appeal to unbridled individualism, however, since humans "can only acquire the ability to act from the positive actions of others and they from others and so on" (Doyal and Gough 1991: 76). That is, individual freedom and autonomy exist within a network of social norms that govern social interaction and cooperation with other people and individual achievements rest upon the foundations of contributions of others.

Much of human morality, then, is related to the type of being humans are, from biological and psychological characteristics to higher order capacities of reasoning and choosing. If humans were invulnerable and immortal, injunctions against murder would be unnecessary. If humans did not rely on communication of knowledge and information from others, lying would not be a moral issue. "The capacities and limits of human beings provide the basis for our moral values" (Lombardi 1988: 6).

Here we confront the contradiction of the utopian socialists directly, namely, the plasticity of human beings on the one hand *and* the rigidities and limits of human beings on the other. In the short term of human lifetimes, any randomly selected normal newborn baby from anywhere on Earth and of any race can learn the language and culture of the people who raise it, whether in Afghanistan and Albania or New Zealand and Zimbabwe. Started early enough, any normal human can learn reasonably well anything any other human can learn and, in addition, may invent and understand things no other human ever did before. Within limits, humans are plastic. They are capable of being molded by others and learning from their own experiences. Moreover, they also mold themselves, because they have self-generated purposes and carry out self-originated plans of action. Thus, within limits, humans are capable of observing and knowing the world for themselves, of creating new reactions, and of inventing themselves.

Yet there are constraints and limits, some very narrow such as the length of time people can live without air. There are, obviously, many things humans cannot do or can do only with damage to themselves, from flapping their arms and trying to fly after jumping off a tall building to breathing water. Such human limitations set moral limits, too. For, as we have seen, you cannot be expected to do what you cannot do. And, prima facie, you cannot be expected to do what you can do only with harm to yourself.

Origins of Values in the Preconditions of Society

Overlap of human nature and social life. Since similar beings face similar problems of group living, we can expect and explain even more similarities in human values and norms than by human nature alone. Although the boundary separating them may be a bit fuzzy since they overlap and interact, we can make a distinction between the nature of humans, especially their biopsychological nature, and the preconditions of social life.

Some needs of human individuals, such as needs for love, approval, emotional support, and communication are inherently social, because they can be satisfied adequately only by interaction with other humans. At the stage of infancy, of course, individuals are totally dependent on other people. As adults, people's lives can be enriched by their direct as well as indirect interaction with others. Such interaction satisfies not only such needs as affiliation and communication but also the survival needs for food, clothing, and shelter. An individual may be able to obtain such necessities acting alone, but the cooperative efforts of a group and a division of labor are nearly always far superior than is one individual working alone, for example, in hunting, providing protection from beasts and hostile groups, building shelters, or carrying out large-scale community projects. Human nature includes the fact that humans are social beings.

Prerequisites of group living. But social life itself shapes human values, too. In the course of the evolution of society there has been a selective retention of only some of the logically possible variations in human values as organized norms, rights, and obligations. There are both prerequisites and consequences of group life and they exist equally for all humans who attempt to live in groups. Morality importantly functions to make social life possible, to permit and encourage people to live and work together (Baumeister 1991: 39).

Moreover, morality is not a matter of mere group survival. Morality also allows people and their societies to flourish (Haan 1983: 232). Through the cooperation and mutual regulation that it provides, morality promotes the synergetic effects of organized and coordinated human effort that allows individuals and societies to thrive (Haan 1983: 244). Just as it is likely that there is a word for "nose" in every language because of the structure of the human face, it is also likely that there is a word for "cooperation"—and many other human values—because of the structure of human society.

Greed, pride, dishonesty, covetousness, cowardice, lust, wrath, gluttony, envy, thievery, promiscuity, stubbornness, selfishness, egocentrism, and disobedience, among many other human dispositions, constantly threaten the survival or well-being of society (Campbell 1975). Such dispositions are as much universals as are the societal efforts to control them, possibly because they once, long ago, had survival value. But with the growth of society, they became obstacles to the cooperation necessary to carry on orderly community life, especially large-scale, complex community life. In no society do parents "teach their children to be selfish, greedy, angry, stubborn, envious, or disobedient; instead, they search everywhere for means to limit or eliminate these characteristics in their children." But they never do so with complete success (Edgerton 1992: 70).

Generalizaing from the efforts of many scholars, we can say that the persistence of a society depends on its ability to provide adequate social mechanisms (1) for the production, distribution, and consumption of goods and services; (2) for the social control, supervision, and coordination of its members through authority systems; (3) for the bearing and early physical care of children; (4) for the education and training of children to occupy adult roles and for children's socialization into the society; (5) for orientations (magical, religious, or scientific) toward the unknown and for justifications of the society's core beliefs, values, and ways of behaving; (6) for recreation and play; (7) for the giving and receiving of affection among its members; and (8) for the allocation of adult roles (e.g., the division of labor) and for the conferral of status among its members.

Societies, of course, are diverse in how well they perform these functions, and that depends, at least in part, on how well each is legitimated by moral codes.

Every living person has duties and obligations to others according to the age, sex, and other social roles he or she occupies. Every living person experiences changes in such social roles throughout life (e.g., from young to old), has social ties of kinship to other people, learns from others, is rewarded or punished according to the presumed rightness of his or her behavior, has certain rights, and so on. Summarizing some of these facts, David Braybrooke (1987) says that in all cultures there are some activities that everyone must understand and participate in and he lists as examples such social roles as those of parent, householder, worker, and citizen. And there are many others.

Thus, in successfully surviving societies it is not surprising that we find similarities of values, such as honesty, trust, and sharing with others (Campbell 1965). For among all peoples everywhere, such values flow from role relationships that share some similarities and such values make various aspects of group life possible. Honesty and trust, for example, are necessary for many types of social learning to take place. Sharing with others was a key value and behavior pattern in small-scale societies, especially among hunting and gathering and rudimentary farming societies, where successful outcomes of individual efforts were chancy. Without such values as generosity, reciprocity, and the redistribution of foodstuffs among group members, many individuals—and possibly the group itself—would not survive.

Trust may be of particular importance in maintaining group life. For example, there is a general trust that concerns the everyday expectations people have of how other people ought to behave in their relationships. There is a trust that deals with expectations of others as being technically competent. And there is a trust concerning expectations that people will fulfill their direct moral responsibilities for the welfare of others, for example, caring for family members (Barber 1983).

But distrust is also necessary for the maintenance of social order. For example, rationally based expectations that someone will not carry out a technically competent performance or will deliberately fail to fulfill an obligation can be beneficial, both by preventing one's exploitation and, more important, by motivating action to create mechanisms of social control, such as law, that aim to hold people to being trustworthy (Barber 1983).

Imperatives may be proscriptive as well as prescriptive. Examples are incest taboos between mother and son, father and daughter, and brother and sister. Although there are a few exceptions in the case of brother-sister incest, for example, in ruling groups in ancient Peru, Egypt's Ptolemaic dynasty, Hawaiian royalty, the emperors of China, and several East African kingdoms, for ordinary people everywhere incest taboos exist (Harris 1989). Moral codes define incest as wrong.

Also, the exchange of goods and services is part of the glue that binds groups together, it is universally valued, and it generally enhances both individual and group well-being. Mutual giving and taking allows each party to an exchange to have something he or she wants and might not otherwise have. In the past, small foraging bands of people risked extinction if they did not establish peaceful and cooperative relationships with neighboring groups. To promote peace, such bands often exchanged their most valuable possessions, their sons and daughters in marriage (Harris 1989: 204). People construct moral codes to govern such relationships.

The "free-rider" problem. One frequently mentioned objection to this view of the social origins of human values in the preconditions of group life is the so-called "free-rider" problem, the cheat who does not share his or her goods and labor with others but who expects others to share with him or her. If too many people in any group or society become cheats, obviously, then the social organization of that group or society is in danger of collapse and its well-being—perhaps its very survival—is threatened.

There are several ways, however, that people acting collectively in societies attempt to deal with the free-rider problem and each one further contributes to the reinforcement of certain societal values. The first way is the "preferential association of the naturally cooperative. The cheat is left out in the cold" (Snell 1988: 209; Boorman and Leavitt 1973). People associate more with other people who cooperate with them and, in the extreme, ostracise those people who do not. Thus, networks of mutual aid and exchange of goods and services are established and maintained among those who are willing to play by the rules of reciprocity.

The second is a system of justice in a society under which a cheat is punished and cooperative behavior is rewarded. Justice—or fairness or fair play as it appears on several of the lists of universal values given above—is, thus, a selective principle, encouraging some forms of behavior and discouraging others. Nearly all societies contain such a system of justice, rewarding people who contribute to society and punishing people who do society a disservice (Snell 1988: 248). In the extreme case, cheats are killed. I elaborate on justice or equity in individual relationships later in this chapter.

The third is teaching new members of the society that cheating is wrong. Moral education is a part of what infants and children are taught, directly and indirectly, by their parents and other adults and a part of what they learn in their interactions with peers as they are socialized into society. Thus, a cheat must defy the norms, violate the ideals, and contradict the moral exemplars of society. To do so risks not only the disapproval of other people, but it also risks the pangs of conscience (Snell 1988: 225).

Cheats risk their own peace of mind and happiness, because each rests to some extent on their self-respect and feelings of self-worth.

Moreover, a person's self-respect and feelings of self-worth depend in part on a person's imagined judgment of him- or herself by other people. "Good" and "bad" refer both to moral judgments and to pleasant and unpleasant feelings. In teaching children what is morally good and bad, society incorporates humans' inborn capacities to feel good and bad (e.g., sensations of pleasure and pain) and links them with moral judgments. Children learn to use the same words to refer both to obeying rules and to feeling good (Baumeister 1991: 39).

Other factors contributing to moral behavior that have been suggested include understanding how cooperation functions and what one's own stake is in building a moral world (Dewey 1959; Piaget 1965), the identification with something greater than oneself (such as one's country), empathy, and the experience of living in just and caring relationships (Rest et al. 1986: 14).

Egoism and altruism. Selfishness exists everywhere people exist. People are often egoistic, being motivated by the ultimate goal of increasing their own individual welfare (Batson 1991: 7). Perhaps, it could not be otherwise, even for the functioning of society, because without someone's self-interest to serve there could be no guidance as to what to do. Imagine, for example, if all people tried only to serve the interests of others but there were no other people with self-interests. Like two persons poised before a doorway, each waiting for the other to pass through first, to use the classic example, no one could move forward at all unless one person was willing to put him- or herself before the other.

From this perspective, it is perfectly correct for people "to regard their own good as morally relevant and justifiable." In fact, it is not possible to take all parties' claims into account adequately without all parties being able to make their claims known (Batson 1991: 7). Perry (1978: 22) captures the interplay of self-interest with the interests of others this way: "Your interests are best and most immediately served by you, and mine by me." In other words, we can each serve each other best by letting each of us serve him- or herself. Benevolence, then, is partly permissive. Sometimes, we ought to help each other, but, most important, we ought to abstain from hurting each other. Thus, we ought to follow our own inclinations in ways that also make it possible for other people to follow theirs.

Although the term "altruism" was not coined until the nineteenth century by Auguste Comte, the issue of caring for others for their sake rather than our own had been raised earlier both by the Greeks and by Judeo-Christian groups (Batson 1991: 61). The dominant view in Western thought has been that altruism is exceptional and that human beings are basically self-interested. In fact, "all major theories of motivation—Freudian, behavioral, and even humanistic theories—is quite clear: Everything we do, including everything we do to benefit others, is ultimately done for our own benefit" (Batson 1991: 3).

Yet altruism, genuinely wanting to help others, has been widely observed and, in fact, appears to be as ubiquitous as egoism. People everywhere on Earth engage in some behavior that is apparently nonselfish: giving to charity, volunteering to work for youth clubs and hospitals, voting to support welfare to the poor, donating blood to strangers, saving for future generations, and so on (Collard 1978: 3). Among the most dramatic examples of altruism in modern times, perhaps, were the actions of the many rescuers of Jews from the Nazi Holocaust. For example, during World War II in one French village alone, Chambon-sur-Lignon, Protestant villagers hid 5,000 Jews from the Nazis at costs to themselves that included jeopardizing their own safety, a story that was made into a 1987 film, "Weapons of the Spirit," by Pierre Sauvage.

Altruism is a complex and multiply determined phenomenon, yet some possible explanations for it exist. First, some of it may be enlightened and far-seeing self-interest. Some people are able to think in terms of delayed gratification and long-term future gains. Thus, they are willing to make contributions in the short run without commensurate benefits for themselves until much later. Sometimes, according to some people's religious beliefs, "much later" does not come until some supernatural afterlife in heaven, a reward from God. But often it is simply a matter of predicting fairly accurately what the long-term material or psychological benefits for oneself will be for behaving generously toward other people.

We may be unwilling to call such behavior "altruistic," since from an actor's perspective some selfish reward exists. But, whatever it is labeled, the benefits of such enlightened behavior for other people and group cohesion are the same. (A corollary, of course, is that at least some socially destructive and apparently malevolent behavior results from misguided self-interest where the consequences, especially the long-term ones, when fully considered, actually redound to the harm of a selfish actor.)

Moreover, according to Batson (1991: 6–7), being truly altruistic, that is, pursuing the ultimate goal of increasing another's welfare, may involve cost to the self or it may involve self-benefit. Even if it involves self-benefit, it is still altruistic as long as self-benefit is not the ultimate goal. For example, your spouse is nice to you because he loves you. You are so pleased that you are extra nice to him. He wins too, but that was not his intention in the first place. Self-sacrifice is not necessarily involved in altruistic behavior.

Second, some altruism derives from the respect and admiration that individuals receive for their service to other people or to society at large, a distinctly social phenomenon. Everywhere, society gives approval, admiration, respect—that is, esteem and prestige—for outstanding individual efforts that contribute to the group (Harris 1989: 366). To be sure, such rewards may be ephemeral and not at all of the same order as the individual sacrifices involved, but they are important motivating factors for individual behavior that puts group welfare ahead of one's own. Again, this may not be altruism in the strict sense, since a primary motivation may be the payoff to the actor exhibiting the behavior, even though the payoff is not material. But from a sociological perspective it is important in understanding individual contributions to societal well-being.

Third, some altruism follows from social control of the cognitive and emotional processes that produce an individual's response to others and his or her self-feelings, both learned principles and rules on the one hand and emotional reactions on the other. The socialization of individuals into society tends to produce individuals who feel guilt or shame, who empathize and sympathize with the plight of others, and who feel anxiety, stress, and distress in reaction to the plight of others (Eisenberg 1986). Batson (1991) formulates an empathy-altruism hypothesis and tests it in a number of social-psychological experiments which provide convincing evidence that empathic "emotion evokes altruistic motivation to have the other's need reduced" and that "the ultimate goal of this motivation is to increase the other's welfare, not one's own" (p. 90). This behavior appears to be altruistic in the strictest sense of the term.

In sum, the norms of a group and its mechanisms of social control interact with the individual's own self-intersts, self-image, self-other expectations, and capacities for empathy to reinforce positive social values and prosocial behavior.

Fourth, altruism results from the social evolutionary process of selection whereby groups are advantaged if they contain members who are willing to sacrifice themselves for the group. As Snell (1988: 208) reminds us, Charles Darwin wrote in *The Descent of Man*, "When two tribes of primeval man, living in the same country, came into competition, if...the one tribe included a great number of courageous, sympathetic and faithful members, who were always ready to warn each other of danger, to aid and defend each other, this tribe would succeed better and conquer the other." In such a case, the values of courage, sympathy, and faithfulness are being selected by the evolutionary process.

Fifth and finally, helping others is also a power exchange that gives an advantage to the helper. Even if the helping behavior is done for the purest of reasons, there is a byproduct whereby "the donor has augmented his or her power while the recipient forfeits power" (Worchel 1984: 392). This fact may help explain why Dorothy Parker's comment, "No good deed ever goes unpunished," has some truth to it. Indeed, helping "is not always received with gratitude and warmth" by the recipient who may end up disliking the helper. Thus, people don't want to be *given* justice, for example, so much as they want to take an effective and meaningful part in the dialogue that produces it (Haan 1983: 244). Yet, Parker's cynical witticism notwithstanding, for most people most of the time, one good deed deserves another, reciprocity reigns.

Individual and group well-being. Very often an individual's personal well-being is consistent with the well-being of the group, especially from a broad, long-term perspective. Thus, some behavior may be egoistic and altruistic at the same time. It is in many instances perfectly moral to follow the directions of your own best interests not only for your own good but for the good of others as well. For example, you may want to go to a motion picture or to the beach, rather than go to work as you are supposed to. But you go to work, because you need your job and want to continue eating and paying your rent. You did the right thing, the moral thing, both in light of your own long-term best interests and in light of your obligations to society.

When personal well-being and society's well-being collide, as they must upon occasion, then the situation invites analysis. First, do they really collide? What action contributes to your personal well-being in the given case in the long run? What is society's claim to its welfare being served or not by your acts? Second, if an apparent conflict continues to exist after such analysis, then the opposing actions can be subjected to an examination of relevant reasons and evidence that support them, using some objective method such as that of Keekok Lee's epistemic implication. In the end, you must decide how to act *all things considered*, including taking into account the judgment of your acts by other group members, that is, their admiration or disgust, what that judgment is worth to you, and whether or not their judgment rests upon sound grounds.

There may be no easy solution. For example, most parents when raising their children face many situations in which they must choose between the welfare of their child on the one hand and his or her freedom on the other. Should they do what they truly believe is good for their child or respect a firm decision by the child to do something that the parents believe is bad for the child? (Lombardi 1988: 22). Competing value assertions in given situations may each have good reasons and convincing evidence to support them. In this example, the good of the child's welfare conflicts with the good of the child's freedom.

We can only speculate that over the long, old road of societal evolution, when a particular individual's interests conflicted with society's survival (and, thus, the long-term interests of most individuals in the society) that the groups and societies that continued to exist were the ones that selected and retained values that enhanced the survival of the group or society itself.

Finally, it is in society's interest to minimize destructive conflict among its members. Morality can harmonize conflicting interests, by preventing conflict when it threatens, removing conflict when it occurs, and advancing to the benefits of positive cooperation. Morality gives us ways of solving the problems created by conflict, whether such conflict is within ourselves or between different persons (Perry 1978: 19).

Origins of Values in Interaction with the Physical Environment

A third major source contributing to the development of globally shared values is found in the nature of the containing physical environment itself. As we have seen, all people have certain similar basic needs and all people face similar problems of the construction and maintenance of social interaction with other people through time, the preconditions of social life. All people also exist in natural environments that, whatever their differences of climate and topography, are subject to similar physical and chemical principles (e.g., gravity, the nature of air, fire and water, and mundane things as objects sharing length, weight, volume, etc.).

Being as it is, the natural world permits only so many solutions to similar problems, sometimes very few at similar levels of technology. Hunters, fishermen, gatherers, and farmers, if they are to be successful, have to learn about realities relevant to their activities of hunting, fishing, gathering, and farming. How do game animals behave? How can they be captured or killed? What can we know about their habitats that is useful to their capture? What tools or equipment are useful to catch them? How must boats be constructed so that they will float and so that they can be steered? When and how must seed be planted and how must it be nurtured to grow fruit or vegetables? When is the right time to harvest? How can fire be started and kept going? How can a spear be thrown over a long distance and still hit a moving target? How can fields be irrigated? How can the power of the wind be harnessed to sail boats or draw water from the Earth? Such knowledge and technology, as they are formulated and accumulated partly through trial and error, become valued.

Builders face the limitations of the materials they use and the principles by which they can be transformed and shaped; and they face similar engineering problems that must be solved to allow buildings to stand firmly and endure. Of course, in different climates and terrains, there are many differences in available materials—an igloo made of snow as shelter will not work in Samoa. But the forces of physics and chemistry are present and work equally well everywhere on Earth. Building a bridge, an arch, a roof, or a wall present certain generic problems of engineering that have limited solutions.

Take *pi* for example, the ratio of a circumference of a circle to its diameter. Everywhere in the world it is the same: 3.14+. Anyone, regardless of his or her language and culture, who conceives of the possibility of such a ratio, who can draw a circle, who can measure its circumference and its diameter, and who can conceptually relate the two will reach roughly the same conclusion about the size of *pi*. For it is in the reality of circles and the relationship between a given circle's circumference and diameter that it is so. Thus, humans have the capacity to observe reality and, as a result, to change their ideas about it and their behavior toward it. If they do not change their ideas and behaviors, they may endanger their survival or well-being. In the case of what we now call *pi*, humans understood it as early as 2000 B.C. (Beckmann 1971).

When humans recognize the sun as the giver of life, it is understandable that they come to value, even worship, it. When humans learn that seed corn is necessary to grow corn, they come to value it. The same can be said of literally thousands of things. The way reality is not only helps shape humans' conceptions of it, but also helps shape their evaluations of it. As we saw in chapter 2, beliefs can change attitudes and values. Thus, people come to value those things that, within the realities of the natural world as they experience them, they believe contribute toward their freedom and well-being, whether such realities have to do with getting food or begetting children.

This summary of the origins of human values is not to say that values never change. Certainly, the increasingly human-made environment in which group life takes place and the consequences of technological development may create pressures toward reshaping some values as social evolution continues.

Nor is it to say that there is no variation in the way values are manifested. We have already considered the general value of respect for authority that exists everywhere, even though it may be expressed in a variety of ways. At least some cultural diversity is simply an expression of alternative ways of affirming basically similar underlying values. This is not to say either that every person in every society shares the same values and behaves properly according to them. In fact, every society can find its own survival problematic and faces the question of determining the right set of values, transmitting them to new members, and making sure that people behave according to them by creating some mechanisms of social control.

The other side of the coin is that every society may change for the better as a result of the innovative behavior of creative individuals who violate some of the norms of their society and convince others to change their traditional ways.

What is the Role of Religion in the Origin of Values?

In chapter 3, I noted some similarities in values among the world's major religions, and, earlier in this chapter, I reported on the shared values in the declaration, "Towards a Global Ethic," attested to by leaders of the world's major religions. This is not to say, of course, that there are no differences in the major religions. Their differences range from overarching perspectives—for example, ascetic Protestantism's mastery of the world, Confucianism's accomodation to the world, and Hinduism's flight from the world—to details too numerous to list. Yet the religions that emerged in the thousand or so years before and somewhat after the birth of Christ are founded on many similar values, such as, for example, the golden rule.

What explains these similarities? Is it that moral principles of behavior originated from religious doctrine, that is, this action became right and that action wrong because people believed that God or Allah or the Bible, Koran, or Torah said so? Probably not. Rather, in the development of morality, the causal connection went in the opposite direction: religious injunctions became what they did because they were influenced by moral codes that already existed. That is, the morality came first and religions, as they were being created, defined, and organized, incorporated them into religious doctrines. As Meeks (1993: 212) says about the early Christians, their "lists of virtues and vices were not much different from those common in popular morality."

Baumeister (1991: 197) questions whether moral rules were derived from religious beliefs and revelations. If they were, he asks, then why didn't different religious faiths (having different gods, different prophets, and different doctrinal bases) produce widely different moral rules? But they didn't. Their moral systems are actually similar. From what we have seen of the origins of values, it is plausible to believe that religions simply accepted the existing rules as they were in the societies that surrounded them.

They did so, however, selectively. The moral rules adopted by such religions included not only some ancient and preexisting moral principles but also some new emphasis that was being forged within the same crucible of social conflict and change that gave rise to the new religions themselves. For example, the early Christians, while adhering to lists of virtues and vices basically "interchangeable with those of other moralists of the time," nonetheless made greater reference to sexual misdeeds and added idolatry as a vice (Meeks 1993: 68).

Harris (1989: 444) says that the religions of love and mercy "arose in response to the failure of early states to deliver the worldly benefits promised by their kings and priests." They arose at a time of brutal and costly wars, of food shortages, of the rise of cities, of rigid inequalities of social rank, and of widespread poverty. These religious doctrines, thus, incorporated both existing values of a people coping with the maladaptations of one social order, often old and dying, and the visionary hopes of another social order, struggling to be born.

Morality, as Reiman (1990: 310) says, "was always the voice of reason, but since the irresistible authority of that voice was heard while its source was not understood, it was, in the childhood of humankind, personalized, its authority hallowed." But we humans are no longer in our childhood. In today's world, we may still rely on the word of God for many comforts, but we can find justifications for our moral beliefs in a naturalistic worldview.

Toward that end, I gave in chapter 2 three naturalistic models of moral analysis, in chapter 3 some practical strategies for judging the good, and in this chapter naturalistic hypotheses about the origins of values in human nature, in the preconditions of social life, and in the nature of the physical environment. Below, I continue exploring this line of reasoning by selecting four values that are both important and nearly universal for fuller discussion. They are knowledge, evaluation, justice, and cooperation.

Knowledge

Knowledge is so obviously useful to human beings that it hardly seems necessary to discuss it. It is so commonplace and taken for granted that it is often overlooked in listings of universal values. Its importance is captured in the adage, "Knowledge is power." Indeed, it is knowledge that allows human beings to make their way as successfully as they do in the physical and social worlds in which they live. And "it is knowledge which has made human beings the most powerful creatures of all" (Musgrave 1993: 1).

Knowledge—including, of course, the idea of truth on which it rests—has been recognized by some writers since the beginning of written records. Condorcet, as we saw in chapter 1, made knowledge a central concept and value in his theory of social change, and, in the twentieth century, George Orwell gave it a central place in his dystopia, *Nineteen Eighty-Four*. In his novel, Orwell shows that the truth matters; he depicts the evil consequences for a society of a denial of objective reality, where the truth goes down "the memory hole." Thus, in the world of *Nineteen Eighty-Four*, the Ministry of Truth concerns itself with producing lies, and the principles of Ingsoc—Newspeak, doublethink, and the mutability of the past—reign supreme.

Some philosophers specify three different kinds of knowledge: (1) knowledge of recognition or identification, that is, knowledge of things or objects sometimes referred to as "knowing-of" or "knowledge by acquaintance"; (2) knowledge of how to do things, that is, "knowing-how"; and (3) knowledge of statements or propositions, that is, "knowing-that" or propositional knowledge (Musgrave 1993: 6).

Perhaps, of primary importance is recognition or identification. Human beings function by being able to locate themselves accurately in relation to other things in the world, including in relation to other human beings both within and outside of their own group. They function, also, by being able to recognize the nature and meaning of other things and other people in relationship to themselves. Who am I? Who are we? Who are they? What is this? What is that? These are questions all normal, healthy humans eventually ask. Accurate answers are important in deciding what behavior in what situations is appropriate. Such decisions affect people's survival and flourishing. Hence, it is understandable that accurate knowledge of recognition or identification comes to be valued.

Geertz (1983: 59), though he has explicit reservations about generalizing to the point of creating a universal "everyman," nonetheless acknowledges that the concept of person "exists in recognizable form among all social groups." At least "some conception of what a human individual is, as opposed to a rock, an animal, a rainstorm, or a god, is...universal," although, as he points out, the specific conceptions involved may vary quite a lot from one group o another.

In order for humans to make their way in the world, they need to recognize and discriminate. We may think of the act of "discrimination" when it refers to treating a particular individual as only a member of some category of individuals as unfair. It may well be unfair, immoral, and, indeed, unlawful in many societies when the categorization is irrelevant to the purposes for which discrimination is used, for example, refusing to employ a qualified person in the United States only because he or she is of a particular race, gender, or age.

Yet the human ability to recognize different things in the world, to generalize from the experience with some objects to probable future experiences with entire classes of objects, and to choose to behave differently toward different classes of objects (including people) as a result of that knowledge of recognition clearly is essential for behaving appropriately and effectively. As Axelrod (1984: 94–95) says, being able to recognize other people and discriminate among them "may be among the most important abilities because it allows one to handle interactions with many individuals without having to treat them all the same." For example, accurately knowing whom to trust and whom to distrust, as we have seen, is crucial for making our way effectively in the social world.

Additionally, humans function more effectively when they know how things work. If you don't know and if you don't care about the nature of the physical and social world around you, your welfare and even your very existence may be threatened. This leads, of course, to a general respect for all knowledge and a particular concern for knowing what causes produce what effects. Also respected are the relevant technical skills for adapting to and manipulating the world.

Furthermore, knowledge involves creating, storing, and disseminating new information and organizing it into new patterns, but it also involves discovering obsolete information and patterns and eliminating them from belief systems that underlie current practices. Thus, people formulate principles, state propositions, and enunciate relationships in order to synthesize, organize, preserve, select, and communicate knowledge to other people. They do so, also, in order to scrutinize, criticize, improve, and expand their knowledge. Humans generally value accurate representations, word-pictures, maps, and models of the nature of the physical and social worlds, because they contribute to human understanding and give meaning to human activities.

Finally, knowledge is fundamental to evaluating, to making moral judgments. We have already seen that ignorance can lead to inhumane and hurtful acts. Getting the facts right is a first step. As British sociologist A. H. Halsey says, "Knowledge is the precondition for good morals" (Kidder 1993: 4). If you do not know who is who, what is what, what causes what, how things work, where people and things are, and so on, you cannot judge whether actions are good or bad. You wouldn't even know what the factual consequences of a given act would be. Clearly, although it may be conjectural and fallible, human knowledge about the world is an important factor contributing to human survival and flourishing.

Evaluation

Another value that is universal is evaluation itself. Like knowledge, it, too, is so obvious that it is often taken for granted and omitted from lists of values and it, too, may be of everlasting importance.

Recognizing and identifying various aspects of physical and social reality and learning about cause-and-effect relationships—that is, knowledge, as we have seen—is clearly important for human survival and well-being. So, too, is the ability to evaluate such things correctly, to assess their degree of goodness or badness. For example, we may know how to do or create something, but ought we to do so? We cannot decide without making a value judgment.

People value making value judgments accurately about whether or not recognized and classified objects and people or the causes and effects they produce are good or bad, benign or threatening, safe or dangerous, edible or poisonous, and so on. For some things out there in reality *are* good to breathe, to drink, to eat, to grow, to step on, to judge time by, to float on, to rest on, to make a fire with, to make clothing with, to make a shelter with, to talk with, to love, and so on. and some things definitely are *not*. Knowing which is which can be a life or death matter. Thus, knowing and valuing to some extent merge, since we need to judge what is worth paying attention to and knowing about, and we also need to judge what is really desirability and what is not. Both have factual components.

Because there really are right and wrong judgments about whether things in the world are safe or threatening, beneficial or harmful, it is possible to use such objective methods of value judging as Lee's epistemic implication. When people and groups make the wrong judgment and act on it too often, their well-being and even survival may be imperiled. Thus, evolutionary processes tend selectively to reinforce some value judgments and not others.

The work of psychologist Charles E. Osgood and his associates (1975) on cross-cultural universals of affective meaning supports the contention that evaluation itself is a major human value. These researchers collected data on about forty subjects in each of some twenty-five cultures who were asked to judge 600 concepts against thirteen semantic differential scales. The countries included a wide range from, among others, Afghanistan, India, Hong Kong, Iran, and Japan to the United States, Costa Rica, and Mexico to Belgium, Finland, France, Germany, Hungary, Italy, and Turkey.

The semantic differential scales involved asking subjects to judge a series of concepts (e.g., my mother, the Chinese, modern art, sex, dream, sin, anger, etc.) with a series of bipolar seven-step scales defined by verbal opposites (e.g., beautiful-ugly, useful-harmful, hard-soft, rigid-flexible, nice-awful, sturdy-delicate, strong-weak, etc.). Often a single concept was "placed at the top of a page and judged successively against a series of scales:

MY FATHER

*good*__ : __ : __ : __ : __ : __ : __ *bad*

*weak*__ : __ : __ : __ : __ : __ : __ *strong*

etc." (Osgood et al. 1975: 40–41).

Osgood and his associates show that human beings tend to use the same qualifying or descriptive framework in giving affective meaning to different concepts (p. 6). They show that the meanings attributed by human beings to various aspects of the world can be summarized in a relatively few dimensions, the three most important being *Evaluation* (things are good or bad), *Potency* (things are strong or weak), and *Activity* (things are active or passive). Everything from a hurricane (in most instances, bad, strong, and active) to the behavior of a particular father (let's say good, strong, and active, but it could be bad, weak, and passive—or some other combination of the three—contingent on the behavior of some particular father) can be so classified. They contend that most of what people mean when they express affective meaning is captured by the general concepts of evaluation, potency, and activity and that such meaning constitutes cultural meaning.

The three concepts provide a universal frame of reference that people everywhere use to identify things and people around them. Osgood and his associates conclude from their data that these three dimensions of cultural meaning are linked to both people's emotional and motivational states. Also, studies of children show that evaluation, potency, and activity are already dominant in children's meaning structures by the time they reach seven years of age (Osgood et al. 1975: 60).

Additionally, evaluation has the special property of incorporating a value judgment and may be the single most important dimension both in defining people's meaning of things and in contributing toward their survival and well-being. Young children generally acquire the ability to attribute evaluation earlier than they acquire the other dimensions of meaning.

This is not to say that Osgood and his associates found no cultural differences. Although evaluation, potency, and activity were the most important factors of cultural meaning, other factors of lesser importance sometimes appeared as well. For the Japanese, for example, the researchers found a fourth, aesthetic, factor, defined in part by scales such as *beautiful-ugly*, *graceful-awkward*, and *delicate-rough*. Even for the three major factors, the dominant metaphors used to represent them varied by culture. For example, American English-speakers defined evaluation in part as sensory experiences (e.g., *sweet-sour*), Lebanese Arabic-speakers did so in terms of *merciful-cruel*, Finnish speakers as *light-gloomy*, Indian Hindi-speakers as *ambrosial-poisonous*, Japanese speakers as *comfortable-uncomfortable*, and Mexican Spanish-speakers as *friendly-repelling* (Osgood et al. 1975: 32). Although such metaphors of good-bad "are denotatively quite distinct, they are used affectively in the same way and represent a common 'evaluative' factor" (p. 33).

The data collected and reported by Osgood and his associates provide considerable support for believing that there are pancultural dimensions of meaning. They support, too, the belief that the most important dimension is evaluation, the capacity to judge whether something is good or bad. Thus, along with knowledge, the capacity of evaluation itself—and being accurate in such evaluation—may be among the most basic of universal values.

Justice

Every known society has some system of social stratification, some systematic inequalities in its distribution of property, power, prestige, privilege, and participation among people in different social positions (Berelson and Steiner 1964). Likewise, every known society has ideas about justice that include judgments about which of those inequalities are morally right and which are morally wrong.

Judgments of the moral rightness or the fairness of specific equalities or inequalities are complex and not thoroughly understood. Yet there have been many studies of them and the results reveal some recurring explanatory factors, some useful conceptual distinctions, and some underlying principles. Let's begin by way of illustration with a brief description of some work, often known as "equity theory and research," and, then, make whatever qualifying or additional comments that seem necessary to reflect other research traditions.

Equity Theory and Research

Research on judgments of justice or equity in a relationship has been carried out for decades. Usually, it has been conducted using individuals or small groups who are under the supervision of a group of investigators in a laboratory setting where the stimulus is introduced by the investigators. In such a setting extraneous variables are eliminated or controlled and an experimental group can be compared to a control group. The responses being studied are often actual behaviors of the subjects as well as their beliefs or attitudes.

Because so much of the research has been done on Americans—especially American college students—the results of equity theory and research must be viewed with caution as an example of the universality of a principle of justice. Yet some research has been done in other cultures and societies and some of the empirical results and theoretical propositions are supported by cross-cultural data. Thus, while agreeing that much more research is needed on non-American and non-Western subjects, we can explore some of the findings of equity research as hypotheses concerning the possible universality of a principle of justice.

Conveniently, Walster and others (1978) have summarized such research. Let's begin with a definition of equity as it is often used in such research: "An equitable relationship exists if a person *scrutinizing* the relationship concludes that all participants are receiving equal *relative gains* from the relationship" (p. 10). Simplified, the "equity equation" is:

$$O_a/I_a = O_b/I_b$$

where: O_a is the outcome (reward or costs) for individual a.

I_a is the input (contribution or liabilities) for individual a.

O_b is the outcome (reward or costs) for individual b.

I_b is the input (contribution or liabilities) for individual b.

For individuals in a relationship, what the equation says is that equity exists when the outcome (e.g., the income from a job) of person a divided by the input (e.g., amount of responsibility on the job) of that same person a is equal to the outcome (e.g., income) of person b divided by the input (e.g., responsibility) of person b. In this circumstance, each person receives equal relative gains (or losses) from the relationship.

Thus, there may be great inequalities of outcome, that is, in rewards or punishments of one kind or another (e.g., income), that are judged as fair according to the equity equation, as long as they are commensurate with (i.e., proportional to) the inequalities of inputs (e.g., responsibility). For example, people who have more skills, work harder, do more dangerous work, or make a more important contribution than others would be judged as being treated fairly if they received commensurately larger incomes than others with fewer skills, who work less hard, do less dangerous work, or make less important contributions. Human subjects in laboratory experiments where they are asked to judge the fairness of many different outcomes and inputs of people in a variety of situations often use such logic.

Inequalities of reward or punishment, however, that are not compensated for by inequalities of inputs result in judgments of unfairness. People are defined as overbenefited or underbenefited (i.e., exploited), depending on whether or not they are getting *relatively* higher or lower rewards than they "deserve" compared to their relative inputs or contributions. That is, it is the equality or inequality in relative gains or losses that determines whether or not a relationship is equitable or inequitable (Walster et al. 1978: 15).

Research findings show that individuals feel distressed when they find themselves in an inequitable relationship, sometimes even when they are overbenefited but especially when they are exploited. People often react to being treated unjustly not only with a sense of dissatisfaction, but also with resentment, anger, and moral outrage.

There appears to be a general tendency for people to attempt to restore equity to a relationship that is judged as being unjust. They can do this by actually changing the costs and rewards that people pay or receive, so that the ratios become equal. This creates a just relationship.

Or they can create what has been called "psychological equity" by mentally manipulating the *assessments* of inputs or outcomes. For example, they can discount the contributions of an exploited person so that he or she no longer appears underbenefited. To do so, of course, may distort reality, often in a self-serving way. It may, however, permit the continuation of relationships that others (e.g., independent, third-party scrutinizers of a relationship) would judge as unfair.

At least some of the norms of equity as discovered in laboratory research may derive from some of the prerequisite conditions of social life, which explains why they may represent nearly universal principles. Although individuals try to maximize rewards for their own selves when they can, groups maximize their collective rewards by constructing systems for equitably distributing rewards and costs among individual members. People develop norms of equity for their societies and teach these norms to their members, promoting a consensus about them. Such norms of equity encourage some individual behaviors and discourage others and they tend to be institutionalized and supported by sanctions (Walster et al. 1978).

Everywhere, inputs and outputs may be seen in relative terms. Everywhere, there are overbenefited and underbenefited persons in some relationships. Everywhere, people in relationships judged to be inequitable may experience some degree of emotional distress, whether as exploiter or, especially, as exploited. Everywhere, groups generally reward people who treat others equitably and generally punish people who treat others inequitably. Everywhere, there may be fears of retaliation on the part of exploiters and self-concept distress when persons perform acts that their society defines as unjust. And, everywhere, exploited people ought not to accept their exploitation quietly; rather, they ought to express their grievances because that may be an effective way of redressing injustice (Walster et al. 1978: 41).

The weight of the evidence supports these generalizations, although it may be true that different societies place different weights on justice as compared with the weights they place on other values. The Japanese, for example, have no word for "fair," at least none that is used in exactly the same way as in English. Rather, the values of honor, respect, politeness, harmony, and the avoidance of conflict are important and tend to suppress claims for justice (Kidder and Muller 1991). Yet each of these values may have a justice component mixed in them when viewed in reciprocal relationships. For example, how much respect is due one person in a relationship compared with another? Who ought to bow lower than whom in what situations? Clearly, such social forms may result in underbenefited and overbenefited persons and have an element of "fairness" in them. (The Japanese have no word for "hot flashes" either, but that does not mean that Japanese women never experience them.)

Walster and her co-authors (1978: 15) say, "In the end, however, equity is in the eye of the beholder." That is to say, equity ultimately depends upon someone's—or some group's—assessment of the relative inputs and outcomes of different individuals involved in a particular set of relationships. Yet we can take issue with this, because "the eye of the beholder" is shaped both by culture and, ultimately, by both human nature and the requisites of group life and is, thus, both molded and constrained. Moreover, the criteria by which people are to be compared, both inputs and outcomes, can be stated, critically examined, and often objectively measured.

Moreover, often the beholder's eye sees only through a filter constructed by the powerful individuals and ruling groups of society. Such ruling groups tend to monopolize community goods and justify their doing so by evolving a social philosophy designed to persuade themselves and others of the equitableness of a grossly unequal allocation of resources. Unfortunately, both exploiters and the exploited can convince themselves that the most inequitable of relationships is fully fair, even when it is not (Walster et al., 1978: 220).

Yet we must ask, why is it necessary for exploiters and the exploited to evolve such a social philosophy? Why don't the powerful simply take by force and the weak submit without such rationalizations of injustice, without trying to make what is unjust appear to be just? The answer is a general recognition of a value of fairness or justice in creating social cooperation, both by the exploiters and the exploited, and the general sense of distress that people feel when it is violated. The value of justice is served, even as it is being violated, when people try to persuade themselves and others that their unjust actions are just. *"L'hypocrisie,"* as La Rochefoucauld said, *"est un hommage que le vice rend à la vertu"* (Hypocrisy is a homage that vice pays to virtue).

Elaborating Equity Theory

There are some issues that have been neglected by equity theory and research as summarized by Walster et al. that have been discussed by other researchers (Deutsch 1986; Folger 1986):

1. Many equitable microrelationships, such as the ones studied, do not necessarily add up to a just society, even in the judgments of the same people. Every person in a society, conceivably, could be in an equitable relationship with other people, yet the macrosystem of social justice in the society at large may be judged to be unjust. Justice on the individual level does not necessarily result in macrojustice, because at the societal

level there are additional considerations to take into account before a judgment can be reached, such as the overall distribution of resources that is desirable, the range of inequality that is optimal for the freedom and well-being of societal members, and minimum standards that define a decent level of living below which no one in the society ought to be expected to live. There is some evidence (Hermkens and van Kreveld 1991), for example, that at the individual level of income differences people prefer equity as defined above (i.e., proportionality), but at the societal level of income distribution they prefer more equality (i.e., a leveling of income differences).

2. Equity theory in the narrow sense focuses almost entirely on the contributions a person makes to an exchange, that is, on merit. Yet there are alternative justice principles that people use with good reason (Folger 1986).

From a wide range of research studies, we find, for example, a long, diverse, and rather untidy list of criteria actually used by respondents in their judgments of what is just or fair. For example, some people say that differences in income are justified by differences in education, that is, more education justifies more income. Other criteria justifying one or another inequality (or equality) are as follows: training, experience, ability, skills, contributions to society, quality of performance, achievement, physical arduousness of a job, psychological stress of a job, degree of responsibility, unpleasantness of the job environment, accustomed level of living, customary privileges, past deprivation, market value (supply and demand), honesty and loyalty, moral worth, seniority, degree of danger or risk, willingness for self-sacrifice, number of hours worked, industriousness, cooperativeness, ascribed characteristics such as sex and race, size of family, family background, and personality characteristics.

Three general principles that continually recur appear to be merit (rewards proportional to contributions), need (rewards proportional to legitimate needs), and equality (rewards distributed equally). But there are others, such as reciprocity and willingness to cooperate. Some research (Deutsch 1986) has shown that systems of reward based on equality or need promoted cooperative feelings among participants more than did systems of reward based on the prinicples of winner-takes-all or proportionality which tended to promote competitive feelings.

3. Equity theory in the narrow sense focuses mainly on distributive justice and fails to take account of procedural justice. There is consider-

able evidence that people may accept outcomes that they may otherwise judge to be unfair if they judge the procedures by which the outcomes were produced to be fair. Outcomes, for example, in which the people affected by them have been allowed to have a voice are more likely to be considered fair than those in which they have had no voice (Folger 1986).

4. Equity theory in the narrow sense may be too focused on scrutinizing the relationship between the inputs and outcomes of one person and those of another. The situation may be considerably more complicated than that. It may also involve a comparison between a person's actual present outcomes and his or her own past outcomes. If one's own present is judged as better than one's own past, then a person may feel satisfaction with improvement in his or her own situation.

Equally important, perhaps more important, is a comparison between a person's actual present outcomes and his or her expected future outcomes. There is a "what-might-have-been," futures-oriented aspect to a person's evaluations of his or her outcomes in life that may also govern reactions to them. A person builds up expectations of some outcome as a result of some set of activities and partly evaluates the reality by using such expectations as a standard of judgment. If what-might-have-been is judged to be much better than what-turns-out-to-be when some specified future becomes the present, then a person may feel unjustly treated (Folger 1986).

Moreover, the likelihood of future amelioration of a present unjust outcome can alter one's reaction to it. That is, the same amount of inequity in the present often is interpreted quite differently depending on different images of the future. For example, if you didn't get a bonus this week, but you fully expect one next week, you may not be upset. The future looks rosy, so forget a minor setback in the present. If, however, you don't expect a bonus next week either, nor the week after that, then you may be distressed. Thus, "two people may respond differently to the same level of current inequity if they have different impressions of what the future holds" (Folger 1986: 148).

5. Whatever the comparative basis for an equity judgment—another person or persons, one's own past, or one's anticipated future—resentment may vary as a function of whether there was an acceptable reason or an intolerable reason for an inequity (Folger 1986: 150). For example, employees for a firm may expect to be paid on the first of the month, but they are not. There is a discrepancy between their legitimate expecta-

tions and an actual outcome. Yet whether they react with resentment and anger or not depends on the weight they give to the reasons the firm's manager offers them for the lack of payment. In this case, an example cited by Folger (1986: 151), the company's records had been destroyed by fire that morning, so that it had been impossible to prepare paychecks but they will be prepared as soon as possible. Resentment and anger would certainly be lessened by that explanation, compared with the news that the firm not only was not going to pay the workers but was closing down and filing for bankruptcy. Thus, if people do not receive what they believe they are entitled to, their reactions will vary depending on the reasons why they did not (Folger 1986: 159).

6. Finally, there is a difference between what people may deserve in one sense and what is fair in another. For example, in situations of scarce resources a fair distribution may give each person considerably less than he or she deserves.

Stages of Moral Development

The work of Lawrence Kohlberg (1981, 1984; Colby and Kohlberg 1984), Rest et al. (1986), and others shows that there may exist a universal process of moral development. Kohlberg, working from both the empirical tradition of the French psychologist, Jean Piaget, and the philosophical tradition of ethical analysis, posits a developmental process involving five, possibly six, stages. Justice, according to Kohlberg, lies at the heart of moral development.

For Kohlberg (1981: 143–45), the principles of justice are the forms by which moral conflicts are resolved. Such principles are centrally organized around justice as equality and reciprocity. They are the reasons that justify moral (i.e., just or fair) action.

Kohlberg empirically grounds his theorizing in studies of the same group of seventy-five young males over a period of about twelve years, from when they were aged ten to sixteen until they were aged twenty-two to twenty-eight. His work has been supplemented by research in other cultures. The subjects in various studies have included people of several different religions: Catholics, Protestants, Jews, Buddhists, Muslims, and atheists. To date, other researchers have confirmed, modified, or disagreed with his conclusions. On balance, despite some qualifications and revisions, his conclusions appear to have held up reasonably well. Certainly, there is overwhelming evidence supporting the existence of a general developmental process of moral judgment (Rest et al. 1986: 29).

Kohlberg (1981: 123) contends that "the same basic ways of moral valuing are found in every culture and develop in the same order." He argues that observed differences in moral commitment and reasoning between individuals and cultures are differences in stage or development status, not in morality itself. That is, different people may be in different stages and whole societies may contain different combinations of people in various stages. But the basic process of moral development is everywhere the same, although not all advanced stages may be present in particular societies. Stages five and six, for example, appear to be absent in nonliterate and semiliterate village culture.

Briefly, Kohlberg's six moral stages can be characterized as follows:

Stage 1: Obedience and the avoidance of punishment. Doing right depends on external authority.

Stage 2: Serving one's own needs or interests while recognizing other people's needs or interests (including the idea of reciprocity, the exchange of favor for favor). Doing right still depends on external authority.

Stage 3: The need to be a good person in your own and others' eyes and being mutually loyal in long-term relationships. Doing right is living up to the expectations of others.

Stage 4: A concern with larger social institutions and society as a whole. Doing right is fulfilling one's obligations and being concerned about the welfare of the group.

Stage 5: A rational obligation to be impartial in upholding values and trustworthy in fulfilling voluntarily-made contracts, recognizing that some general rights such as life and liberty transcend law and majority opinion. Doing right is both fulfilling one's freely agreed to obligations and a rational calculation of the greatest good for the greatest number.

Stage 6: Universal principles of justice, the equality of human rights, and respect for each individual's human dignity are most important, more important even than law. Doing right flows from a rational belief in the validity of universal moral principles and having a personal commitment to them.

With respect to society's moral norms, stages 1 and 2 are preconventional, stages 3 and 4 are conventional, and stages 5 and 6 are postconventional perspectives.

Kohlberg no longer claims that stage 6, which has an underlying deontological or rule-oriented philosophy, has an empirical basis, so that stage 5, in fact, may be the highest stage. Stage 5, which is based on a utilitarian-teleological or consequences-oriented philosophy, is more compatible with Lee's epistemic implication than is stage 6, and Robert E. Carter (1984) contends that stage 6 is not logically more useful than stage 5.

One well-known critic of Kohlberg is Carol Gilligan (1982) who focuses on the fact that Kohlberg based his original work only on males. Gilligan, studying females, questions Kohlberg's central definition of morality as justice. She claims that women are less likely to respond to moral questions in terms of justice than Kohlberg's men subjects and more likely to respond in terms of caring and responsibility, although she recognizes the interplay of justice and caring among both men and women.

Subsequent research, however, has not generally supported her contention of a gender gap in making moral judgments. "Gilligan's view that women appear less sophisticated in justice concepts than males is not at all supported" by some other research (Rest et al. 1986: 178). Although some women respondents do identify moral reasoning that minimizes concerns of caring and connectiveness as masculine (Haste and Baddeley 1991), the major conclusions seem to be that both sexes have access to both justice and caring modes of moral reasoning and that there are more modes of moral discourse—including a caring mode—than a model of justice reasoning alone would imply.

Although it is certainly not the only value that ought to be considered, the principle of justice is, nonetheless, a powerful value in studying, proposing, or evaluating preferable futures. Since inequalities are ubiquitous in human societies, there is always the possibility that they are being judged as unjust with resulting feelings of dissatisfaction, resentment, and anger. Such a judgment and such feelings on the part of members of a society can negatively affect their performances and contributions to the society, undermine their beliefs in its legitimacy, and even threaten its continued existence.

Futurists can strive to determine exactly how much relative inequality of what kinds between what people is really necessary to get organizational jobs done or, at the level of whole societies, basic social functions performed, for example, in production, distribution, socialization of the young, decision making, and dispute settlement. With adequate research, an objective and rational answer may be found. That is, how much relative inequality of what kinds is fair, based on an objective analysis of the functions of relative inequalities among people in society? This remains an open question that futurists can address as they imagine, construct, propose, and evaluate images of preferable futures. How much equality or inequality is functional? How much of each is, therefore, just? Are the dominant societal myths justifying inequality true or false? How far can we move toward an extremely egalitarian or an extremely inegalitarian society and still expect people and societies to flourish?

One part of the answer to such questions may be found in the relationship between people's sense of justice and their willingness to cooperate. Beliefs that the equalities and inequalities of the world are right, that things are fair, and that procedures work as they ought to increase the chances that people will be motivated to make their contributions to society and to cooperate with others. Let's turn to some research on cooperation to see what we can learn about its causes and consequences.

Cooperation

Cooperation, of course, is not necessarily a good thing. But, then, few things are. Water is essential for humans' biological survival, but too much of it at one time can kill by drowning. In the case of cooperation, it depends in part on who is cooperating with whom for what purposes. Cooperation among gangsters and members of the Teamsters' union at New York's John F. Kennedy International Airport for the purpose of getting illegal payments for the movement of freight, for example, may be good for them but is bad for the rest of us who must pay inflated prices for the transport of such freight. Yet cooperation is as essential for the functioning of social organizations and society as water is for the human biological organism.

Research on cooperation illustrates that individuals do not necessarily have strictly opposing interests, but, rather, can all gain by working together. Moreover, *the key to cooperation is believing that there is a future to influence by the reaction of other people to one's own behavior*. Cooperation is stable only when the future is important relative to the present; if the future is heavily discounted, then cooperation suffers. It evolves most surely from the possibility of a long-term set of repetitive social interactions with the same set of other individuals, where individuals meet—*and expect in the future to meet*—each other again and again (Axelrod 1984).

A now classic study in the evolution of cooperation is that of Robert Axelrod (1984). He carried out a series of studies in which experts in game theory submitted programs for a Computer Prisoner's Dilemma Tournament.

For readers who do not know what the "Prisoner's Dilemma" is, I give the following brief description, as it was defined in Axelrod's studies. The Prisoner's Dilemma is a game that involves two persons confronting each other at a time. Each of the players has a choice, either to cooperate with the other player or to defect (fail to cooperate). If both defect, both do worse than if both had cooperated. But the players cannot discuss the situation. Thus, they cannot work out an agreement beforehand. The dilemma is that each one must make his or her decision without knowing what the other person will do. They only know that after a first meeting, after which each knows what the other player did on their earlier meetings. Axelrod scored the game as follows:

Both cooperate = reward = 3 points each.

Both defect = punishment = 1 point each.

One defects, the other cooperates = 5 points for the defector and 0 for the cooperator ("the sucker").

Note that defecting all the time in order to protect yourself from being a sucker doesn't get you very far if the other player defects too. Taking turns exploiting each other does not get as many points as both players cooperating. For example, two encounters of cooperation net each player 6 points, while two encounters of taking turns at exploitation nets each player only 5 points.

The "prisoner" part of the dilemma comes from the classic version of the game in which the scoring is different, with the players winning or losing not points, but years in prison (the "loser" in this case having the most years in prison). The situation is similar to two persons being apprehended for committing a crime and each being interrogated separately, not knowing whether the other person was going to confess or not.

Just as in real life, the Prisoner's Dilemma is not a zero-sum game. By cooperating, players can both "win," that is, both can be better off than they would be by not cooperating. But if you cooperate and the other person does not, then you lose badly.

Axelrod asked the experts to submit strategies for playing the game. Some strategies were quite simple and some were quite complicated, but all decided to defect or cooperate depending on some assessment of the past behavior of the player being encountered. These strategies, then, met each other in Axelrod's computer tournament, not once but many times. That is, his tournament was an *iterated* Prisoner's Dilemma. Axelrod also added the twin of a strategy to see how it would do when meeting itself and a random strategy that defected or cooperated according to a table of random numbers (no systemic behavior whatsoever).

Additionally, Axelrod played a second game, telling the experts the results of the first game, including which strategy had won, and then asking them to make any improvements in their strategies they wished. In addition, he made other computer studies, including one in which unsuccessful (low-scoring) strategies were progressively eliminated from the game and successful (high-scoring) strategies were allowed to proliferate, through many generations. Thus, as the game progressed, it evolved, with each strategy having to face more and more successful strategies and fewer and fewer unsuccessful strategies.

In the first game involving entries meeting each other randomly in a round-robin tournament, the winner was the simplest strategy. It was tit-for-tat. It started with cooperation at its first meeting or encounter with another strategy and then at the next meeting with that strategy it did simply what the other player did on his or her last move. It was not very exploitable, since, when it met a defector, it defected the next meeting; it did well with its own twin, and on repeated meetings with cooperative strategies it always cooperated.

The second game included sixty-two entries from six countries, including both professionals, as before, plus a larger number of computer hobbyists. This time some strategies were even more elaborate than in the first game, including several attempts to improve on the simple tit-for-tat decision rule that had won earlier.

Tit-for-tat won again! It won yet again in the generational-evolutionary game, being the most successful rule by the one-thousandth generation. That is, it was the best survivor in the long run (Axelrod 1984: 52).

"Nice guys and dolls finish first." For tit-for-tat is a nice strategy. It was never the first to defect, always giving other strategies the benefit of the doubt by cooperating with them on the first meeting. It always cooperated when it met cooperative strategies, never holding grudges. By the rules of the game, it never responded more viciously than failing to cooperate when it met a strategy that defected. Such nice strategies accounted for almost all of the most successful strategies.

Tit-for-tat won, however, not because it beat the other individual players with which it was repeatedly paired, but because it encouraged the cooperation of other players, allowing it *and* the other player with whom it was matched to do well (p. 112). Moreover, Axelrod (1984: 39) says that an even nicer rule, if it had been in the tournament, would have beaten tit-for-tat, namely one-tit-for-two-tats.

Axelrod (1984) shows that cooperation can emerge even in a situation without central authority and even where each individual aims to do well for him- or herself. What evolves is a strategy of reciprocity based upon a variety of related principles which include, as examples of what can be learned from an analysis of this sort, the following imperatives:

1. Do not be envious of the success of others, because most of life is not a zero-sum game; thus, the more another person gets, the more you may get.
2. Never be the first to fail to cooperate, because your own behavior may be echoed back to you.
3. Reciprocate both cooperation and failure to cooperate, the first to maximize cooperation and the second to prevent both your exploitation and the exploitation of others by teaching the exploiter that he or she cannot get away with it. Reciprocity, as mentioned earlier, is a better foundation for morality than the unconditional cooperation implied in the golden rule.
4. Be forgiving. Remember your past experience with particular individuals and act accordingly, but, when a former adversary is ready to cooperate, then forgive the past, and cooperate. Otherwise, you may end up in a relationship of permanent retaliation in which everyone loses (a condition that appears to characterize a number of places throughout the world where long-standing ethnic conflicts continue, e.g., from Bosnia to Sri Lanka).
5. Do not be too clever, because if you are, then other people cannot figure out what you are doing and may fail to cooperate because they find your behavior incomprehensible, hence unreformable.
6. Teach people the facts of cooperation theory, because people who are willing to look toward the future and who care about the future can understand the advantages of cooperation; as a result, the evolution of cooperation can be speeded up (Axelrod 1984).

Futurists can find additional principles in Axelrod's work to help them promote cooperation. For example, make interactions among people more durable and frequent, point out long-term incentives for mutual cooperation, teach people to care about each other and teach them the mutual benefits of reciprocity, improve people's recognition abilities (who am I dealing with and how ought I to treat him or her?), and teach people to remember the history of their interactions with other people (Axelrod 1984). Obviously, because of their aims, futurists wish to promote only that cooperation that is intended to achieve worthy purposes.

Axelrod's work, of course, is part of a much larger inquiry into the nature and conditions of cooperation that is being carried on by many different social researchers. How many of his results we can safely apply in our daily lives remains to be seen, but they suggest that individual interests can be mutually served through cooperative acts. There is, for example, evidence from other sources that some general principles of cooperation may be widely applicable. One source is the Mondragon cooperatives in the Basque region of Spain which for more than forty years have flourished. Today, they are a vital, successful, and resilient network of more than 170 worker-owned-and-operated cooperatives employing some 21,000 workers (Morrison 1991; Whyte and Whyte 1988). The principles of cooperation appear to work in real life.

We are, of course, learning more about the sources and functions of cooperation all the time. Kondo (1990), for example, has found that both normative and moral behavior that goes beyond the rationality of the tit-for-tat strategy may be necessary to move a group permanently out of a situation of stable noncooperation. As I said earlier, there may have to be a small number of people who are willing to cooperate no matter what.

Conclusion

In this chapter I questioned the validity of the view that different cultures are so different from one another as to be incommensurable. I questioned, too, the more modest view that great cultural diversity exists in the world, with every culture having little in common with other cultures. I showed that many early icons of cultural relativism have been falsified and that the amount of cultural diversity has been overstated. Just as the dogma of cultural relativism, as we saw in chapter 2, is morally bankrupt, so, too, the dogma of incomparable cultural diversity appears to be factually wrong.

Contrary to the tenets of recently dominant views of cultural diversity, human universals or near-universals do exist. They include values, and some good candidates for near-universal human values are knowledge, education, honesty, truth, integrity, evaluation itself, justice, cooperation, loyalty, freedom, a sense of community or brotherhood, industriousness, sufficient wealth or riches, peace, health, opportunities for family life and sexual behavior, love and affection, kindness, friendliness, generosity, caring for other people, reciprocity, courage, reliability, respect, power, participation, trust and trustworthiness, self-control, moderation, fulfilling one's obligations to others, adaptability, respect for life, respect for the life-sustaining capacities of the Earth, and living a meaningful life.

Such universal or near-universal values can be classified in a variety of ways, including those that have to do with survival, comfort, and self-realization. At the highest level of abstraction, it is useful to think of them as considerations either of human welfare or freedom.

This is not to say that societies do not differ, nor that the differences are not important. Rather, it is to say that societies *do* importantly differ, but most significantly in how well they have succeeded in living up to an underlying set of common human values, how well, for example, they have created social arrangements that contribute effectively to the welfare and freedom of their members.

Near-universal values exist because of evolutionary processes. Namely, three broad sets of factors and their interactions have tended to select and retain certain values and eliminate others throughout the long course of human development. The first is the nature of human beings, both at the biopsychological level and at the level of higher order human capacities, such as appreciation of beauty and satisfaction of intellectual curiosity. Adhering to certain values (e.g., sharing with others to satisfy hunger) can make sheer biological survival possible. Adhering to other values (e.g., the search for knowledge) can help make human life thrive.

Second, there is also a basis for universal moral values in the prerequisites of society that face all people who attempt to live in human groups. Both the individual and collective payoffs from group living are dependent on values such as trust, trustworthiness, honesty, justice and cooperation. Although not everyone in a society must share such values and exhibit them in his or her behavior, the vast majority must do so enough of the time so that routine and repetitive social interactions among people—what we call "society"—will be sustained over time.

Third, the nature of physical reality itself, the natural environmental context within which people pursue their projects, contributes toward a convergence of human values. Certain fundamental aspects of physical reality, for example, gravity, are basically the same everywhere. Thus, essentially similar beings pursuing goals that include similar ones of survival and flourishing come to somewhat similar beliefs and evaluations since they function within many similar physical constraints and opportunities.

Of particular importance for human well-being may be the values of knowledge, evaluation itself, justice, and cooperation, and we examined each of these in some detail to try to understand why they are of importance and how they function.

Near-universal values have withstood the test of time. They have contributed to the survival and well-being of the human species and they have been forged out of the millennia of human existence. They have been shaped by trial and error and human ingenuity as humans pursued their purposes. They have endured in those human societies that have lasted. They have endured despite tremendous changes in agriculture, industry, settlement patterns, science, technology, and belief systems about the nature of reality.

Thus, they invite respect and consideration as futurists evaluate the past, the present, and the images of alternative futures that they and others construct. Certainly, basic values ought not to be dismissed or taken for granted. Any present society and any proposal for the future in which a near-universal human value is consistently violated must be viewed with skepticism.

Yet because a human value is nearly universal in and of itself does not make it right. Some other justification for believing rationally that a value is good is necessary beyond the observation that it exists nearly universally. For many traditional values and the cultural practices they spawn are mediocre, less than optimal solutions to problems of human surviving and flourishing. Also, even where optimal solutions may have existed, conditions can change, thereby possibly making past solutions maladaptive. Moreover, the coming future may contain challenges to the human condition that will require new and different cultural values and practices if future human society is to flourish. Thus, although nearly universal values are excellent sources of finding candidates for the global ethics of the future, each one invites critical and objective assessment.

Some human values have changed, some ought to have changed, and some ought to be changed still more. In fact, the human future may depend on two contradictory capacities: (1) recognizing, understanding the need for, and abiding by most near-universal values, and (2) continuing to make changes in other values that fail our tests and that appear to be inappropriate to changing conditions. Hence, there is a need for further inquiry and worldwide discourse exploring the question of what human values are the most appropriate.

Are there better ways of doing things than the ways we are now doing them? Are there changes taking place among people, human societies, and the natural environment that make some long-standing universal human values no longer of positive use? Might some existing human values be counterproductive in the world as it is and as it is coming to be in the twenty-first century and beyond? If so, which ones? What values ought to replace them? What do living people owe to future generations of people? What do they owe, if anything, to past generations?

I'll take up these and other questions in chapter 6. But first, there is a prior question that deserves our attention: What is the most important human value of all?

5

The Quantity of Human Life

Introduction

In this chapter, we will consider the preeminent human value, human life itself—the quantity of time that humans can expect to have as living beings. Also, we will discuss the quality of life, partly because it is of value in its own right and partly because it contributes to the quantity of life: generally, people live longer when their quality of life is good.

The length of human life—that is, the quantity of life that individuals have on average—has varied through time in the past, with a clear trend toward having longer lives. Also, it varies today by geographic space. There are important differences, for example, in the number of years people can expect to live comparing the major regions of the world and the 190 or so nation-states into which they are divided. People born in some countries can expect to live on average nearly twice as long as can people born in other countries. Human life expectancies vary, too, by socioeconomic position within countries. Using gender and racial data for the United States, I illustrate the diversity of life expectancies of different subpopulations within a country.

Given the priority we place on the value of human life, what attitude ought we to take toward abortion? What value ought we to place on nonhuman forms of life? How ought we to respond to the quantity of human life in the sense of the sheer number of people on Earth, for example as measured by the projected increases in the human population for the years ahead?

Clearly, such questions raise some perplexing contradictions and moral ambiguities. Take, for example, the value we place on the length of individual lives versus the value we now place on the total number of people on Earth in the future. On the one hand, we work toward lengthening the lives of all living people for as long as there is any hope of a reasonable quality of life for them, expanding each person's quantity of life. On the other hand, many people today are convinced that we must work toward limiting future growth in the total human population, restricting the quantity of human life in that sense.

A Master Value: The Quantity of Human Life

One human value may be supreme. It is the value of human life itself. The late American comedian, Groucho Marx, is reported to have overheard a man complain, "Life is difficult!" Groucho turned, puffed on his cigar, flicked the ashes off and asked the man, "Compared to what?" (Szalai 1980: 18).

Groucho had it right, because without life, nothing else is possible in this world (and we have no guarantee that there is another one). Death means that you have no future. Thus, you ought to value life, because without life, you cannot be anything, do anything, or care about anything. Death is oblivion (Baumeister 1991: 273, 275).

We have already mentioned the martyr who chooses to give his or her life for others. It is the supreme sacrifice precisely because life is so precious. Yet there are situations in which it may be necessary for some members of society to sacrifice their lives so that others may live. Heroes are honored and dead heroes are remembered in the minds of the living by stories, monuments, and histories, reinforcing the value of the individual lives of the living and of the survival of the society. Sometimes people face terrible choices in life and having to choose between some lives and other lives is one of them. Even—perhaps especially—life-sacrificing actions often reaffirm the value of life itself.

It is widely believed, both among secular humanists and the vast majority of the devout of the world's major religions, that all humans ought to value human life, both their own lives and the lives of other humans; that they ought to value the continued survival of the human species; and that they ought to value maximizing the chances of each person living out his or her normal life span, now and in the future.

These "ought" statements, of course, are prima facie statements. *All things considered*, you might decide to take the life of some sociopath who is attacking you and your family with intent to do bodily harm, if all else failed to stop him or her. You might decide to serve in your country's military services and, as a result, you might be asked to kill or you might be killed in a war. If you were to experience great pain, suffering, and disabilities and if you faced no chance of leading a life of acceptable quality, you might prefer to be dead than alive. In such circumstances, *all things considered*, you might rationally and objectively decide that the right thing to do was to take a life, even your own. All such cases require examination of the specific details before an all-things-considered judgment to act is made. Surprising things can happen in life, even in what appear to be the most hopeless circumstances. Therefore, choosing to take a life deliberately is a last, desperate act that can rarely be justified.

Theodore J. Gordon et al. (1979: 183) reach a proposition in which we can have justified belief. They say "that life is of great value, that preserving life has an extreme (not an absolute) claim on us, and that we should pay a great price—in money, effort, and pain and suffering—to preserve it." This is not to say, however, that we ought to pay *any* price. Thus, this proposition is consistent with the view that at some point in the effort to add years to our lives we can pay too high a price in increased suffering or decreased quality of life for it to be worth it.

Death, as we understand it today, is a pefectly normal event, a natural part of human existence. From the biological perspective, a timely, even a "good," death is one that comes when a person has lived a long life, not one prematurely cut short by accident, war, homicide, or disease. The biological clock, according to this view, runs down eventually. When it does, it is time to die. From the sociological perspective, a timely or "good" death is one that occurs when one's life work has been completed, when one's moral obligations to significant others have been fulfilled, and when one's dignity is unimpaired by unbearable and degrading pain (Gordon et al. 1979: 178–90).

Granting considerable truth to each of these views, however, tells us little about the actual age at which people normally expect to die at different times and places. As we shall see, the average length of life has changed dramatically through history and it remains problematic as advances in life-extending technologies continue to be made that allow more and more people to live longer lives. Moreover, the aging process may turn out to be a disease, as some medical professionals already are beginning to believe (Gordon et al. 1979: 191). This implies that aging might be slowed, even prevented or cured.

There are some people who view death as an illusion, merely a gateway to another life or someplace where one will find true happiness. Such views, often religious, are contrary to our contemporary scientific knowledge and unsupported by any serious evidence (Gordon et al. 1979: 29).

Most people—including those with views such as the above—most of the time do in fact choose life over death. Moreover, they ought to. One of the earliest lessons learned by humans in the course of their development was the value of life. As William Graham Sumner (1960: 17–18) said in his classic, *Folkways*, "If we put together all we have learnt from anthropology and ethnography about primitive men and primitive society we perceive that the first task of life is to live." So it is for all of us today and so it will be for all the people of all the coming tomorrows: *The first task of life is to live.*

The Quality of Human Life

The second task of life may be to live well. Although living itself—that is, the sheer quantity or length of individual lives—is basic to all experience, what that experience is in its specific details matters greatly to people. Such details describe the full contents of a life. Living well is to live modestly rather than luxuriously in the material sense, but to live richly in social relationships, knowledge, and understanding of self and others, self-development, personal achievements that contribute to society through family, community, and work, and in finding worthy purposes and meanings in one's life. Such things are captured in the concept of the "quality of life."

Research on the quality of life can be viewed as an outgrowth of the general effort to obtain objective indicators of the economy and society and the changes in them. Ogburn's work on social trends discussed in chapter 1, volume 1 is one of the earliest examples of the modern movement to create a social accounting and to prepare social reports, going beyond economic indicators. Since that time, most national governments, many local governments, and international agencies, especially various units of the United Nations, in addition to private organizations, have funded reports on social indicators in an effort to assess the present status of their own or other countries' populations and to describe the trends of change.

During the past two decades or so, a considerable number of researchers have tried specifically to measure the quality of life of people, usually comparing individuals, localities, and, especially, whole countries at roughly the same time and sometimes comparing the same units through time (Andrews and Szalai 1980; Miles 1985; Mukherjee 1989; Slottje et al. 1991). "Quality of life" refers "to the more or less 'good' or 'satisfactory' character of people's life" (Szalai 1980: 8). It has been measured using descriptive measures ranging from the relative number of physicians or hospital beds, daily per capita calorie supply, and percentage of a population with access to clean drinking water to literacy rates, rate of secondary school enrollment, and personal security to the existence of political rights and civil liberties, economic prosperity, and energy consumption per capita in a locality or country.

It has also been measured using surveys of people's own opinions, such as how satisfied they are with their overall lives or, specifically with some aspect of their lives, such as their marriage and family life, health, neighborhood, friendships, jobs, leisure, housing, amount of education, and level of living. Such studies measure some of the more subtle aspects of quality of life, coming closer to deeper, more personal meanings (Andrews 1986; Campbell et al. 1976).

Both types of approaches involve objective measurements in the sense that data are specified and collected using systematic methods open to the replication of others. Both also have a so-called "subjective" aspect, since the indicators selected are not only descriptive but also judgmental. Such a judgment is sometimes made by the research team whose members decide, using theory or general agreement, that scoring high or low on some particular indicator is good or bad, that is, contributes to or detracts from the quality of life. For example, having a high literacy rate in a country is judged as good, while a low literacy rate is undesirable. At other times, the respondents' own judgments are measured and used to evaluate their own quality of life, the justification being that the concept necessarily involves some degree of personal satisfaction or dissatisfaction on the part of the people whose quality of life is being studied. In some studies both sorts of evaluations are used.

However measured, such resulting indexes are usually labeled "quality of life," "well-being," or "life satisfaction," with some other, related and often overlapping indexes being named "social development," "human development," or, emphasizing the opposite (negative) pole of the index, "human suffering."

One valid criticism of studies of quality of life is that they often fail to take viability and adaptability adequately into account (Wilkening 1974).

That is, focusing on "well-being" and "satisfaction" may ignore the sustainability of the productive and distributive forces that contribute to a given level of well-being and satisfaction. We need to ask how viable they are in the long haul and whether they permit growth and development. Also, we need to ask the related question of how adaptable they are to possible changing conditions. Present well-being and satisfaction are not necessarily good if they lead to impoverishment and dissatisfaction in the future.

There are obvious cases where the quantity and quality of life for a particular person may be in conflict, for example, when a person's life can be lengthened only at the cost of his or her quality of life (as in the cases of radically disabling surgery or of keeping brain damaged people alive, though in a vegetative state, by heroic technological means). Under certain circumstances, people of any age may be so damaged and miserable, and, hence, have a quality of life so low, as to be intolerable, making lengthening their lives of questionable value. Although life may be the preeminent human value, reverence for human life without regard to its character is irrational (Behnke and Bok 1975).

Some indicators of the quality of life include items that measure the quantity of life. In an index used by fifteen OECD countries, for example, six of twenty-five indicators deal with some aspect of life expectancy and a seventh concerns child mortality (Scheer 1980: 154). Even when quality of life indicators do not include life expectancy and related health measures, they are nonetheless empirically correlated with the quantity of life when each is averaged over whole populations and subpopulations. Generally, people live longer when they enjoy a higher quality of life (House 1986), a fact that Condorcet had noted before the end of the eighteenth century in his *Sketch*. That is obviously the case regarding satisfying people's basic human needs, but it is also the case regarding the satisfaction of higher order needs as well (Berkman and Syme 1979).

Other things being equal, for example, people live longer when they are better educated, have comfortable levels of living, enjoy freedom to pursue their projects, have friends and loved ones with whom they interact regularly, are happy and satisfied with their lives, have meaningful work, have hope for the future, feel competent and effective, enjoy high levels of self-esteem, are committed to goals beyond their own personal welfare, and have a strong sense of community (House 1986; Sagan 1989). Thus, for populations as a whole, the quantity and quality of life are highly correlated. Obviously, there can be no quality of life whatsoever without some quantity of life.

Below, I examine the distribution of average length of human life through time and across geographic and social space. How well, I ask, has the human species done and how well is it doing in achieving the preeminent human value of life itself? Moreover, since human life expectancy is also an important indicator of human well-being, we can reach some general conclusions about the spread of human lives of high quality.

First, however, we must consider the concept of "life expectancy" in more detail.

The Expected Length of Human Life

"Life Expectancy" Defined

A concept widely used by demographers is "life expectancy." It tells us how long on average people of any age will live "if the age-specific death rates for a given period were to remain constant and were to apply throughout the experience of an entire generation" (Palmore and Gardner 1991). It is typically based on the actual mortality rates at all ages (how many people per 1,000 people of a given age died in the year) attributed to a population in a calendar year (for example, the death rate of 0-year-olds in 1995, of 1-year-olds in 1995, of 2-year-olds in 1995, etc.). Such age-specific death rates are applied to a hypothetical group of persons until all the persons in the group are dead. Such an imagined collection of people (usually specified at the start of the calculations as 100,000) is known as a "hypothetical birth cohort."

The resulting life expectancies, thus, are based on factual information, that is, the current mortality experience of an actual population, but they do not describe the actual experience of a real birth cohort (Bennett 1992: 438). They do allow valid comparisons of the survival chances of people in different societies and groups, because the life expectancies so calculated are not influenced by the age structure of the population or by migration.

In order to describe the experience of an real birth cohort, we would have to trace the actual deaths of a group of people born in a given year until the last one of them had died, probably more than 100-plus years (Bennett 1992). Such generation or cohort life tables, as they are called, are appropriate for an historical analysis of populations now extinct but they are of little use for planning for the future of people now alive or yet to be born who, we assume, may be living under quite different conditions than did people of the last 100 years. Thus, life expectancies based on current life tables are more useful than those based on generation life tables for present decision making. They are also an excellent example of a futurist tool.

For instance, when current life tables are applied to existing numbers of real populations of people of particular ages, we can answer such questions as: How many elementary, junior high, and senior high schools will be needed to accomodate the number of children expected to have survived in given future years? How many hospitals, retirement residences, and nursing homes will be needed to accomodate expected numbers of older aged people ten, twenty, or thirty years from now? In order to cover costs, how much must be charged in premiums or otherwise set aside to provide a death benefit by insuring the lives of people of given ages? Life expectancy data combined with the age distribution are useful in planning most aspects of the economy and society, including the future demand for various products and services and the future size of particular consumer or client populations.

In table 5.1, I give life expectancies for various ages for the population of the United States in 1990. These data tell us the average number of years of life remaining at the beginning of each age. For example, at birth (age 0) persons born in the United States can expect to live on average a total of 75.4 years if the age-specific death rates for 1990 in the United States applied throughout his or her lifetime. From the table, we can see that, under that assumption, for children aged 5, life expectancy is 71.2; for persons aged 20, it is 56.6 years; for persons aged 30, it is 47.2 years; etc. As we shall see, whether you are white or black, male or female makes a considerable difference and you can expect on average to have fewer or more years to live than the number shown in table 5.1.

Such life expectancies for a country or a region give one possible scenario of future average lengths of lives for people of different ages living in that country or region. It gives only one possible scenario, though, because the assumption that current age-specific death rates will remain constant throughout all the individual lives of the real people that make up a cohort may be wrong. For example, natural disasters (such as earthquakes or widespread flooding), the occurrence and spread of new dis-

TABLE 5.1
Life Expectancies by Age Groups, United States, 1990.

Age	Life Expectancy
0	75.4
1	75.1
5	71.2
10	66.3
15	61.3
20	56.6
25	51.9
30	47.2
35	42.6
40	38.0
45	33.4
50	29.0
55	24.8
60	20.8
65	17.2
70	13.9
75	10.9
80	8.3
85	6.1

Source: National Center for Health Statistics (1994: 14).

eases (such as AIDS), and human conduct (such as wars, terrorism, genocide, or destruction of the environment) may increase death rates above
what were assumed in computing the life expectancies.

Contrariwise, death rates may decrease after a life table is constructed
as a result of such things as physical engineering (for example, safer
design of automobiles and highways), changes in life styles (for example,
people ceasing to smoke), social engineering (for example, improvements
in the delivery of health services), and advances in medical science (for
example, cures for heart diseases and cancers). During the past two centuries, as countries developed economically and socially, life expectancies based on current life tables have tended to underestimate the actual
average length of life for real cohorts of people because of the long-term
trend toward lower mortality rates, especially at younger ages.

"Life Span" Defined

"Life expectancy," as we have seen, is the length of time that people can expect to live under particular physical and social conditions.

"Life span" refers to something different. For several generations of demographers, it has been defined as the length of time that people could expect to live under the most ideal conditions for their health and happiness, that is, totally free of all exogenous risk factors. It has been thought that the human life span has a limit and that it is determined by the biology of the human organism itself.

Human bodies may be genetically programmed for a total length of life, even under ideal physical and social conditions, of about 115 years, with an average possibly as high as 100. The relatively few people certified and documented to have lived beyond 115 constitute statistical outliers (Olshansky et al. 1990). Over the last 50,000 years or so, if not longer, there has probably been relatively little change in the human life span.

Yet there has been a remarkable increase in human life expectancies, and most of it has occurred in very recent times. That is, most of the increase in the length of human lives has occurred not because of increases in the life span, but because more people are living closer to some possible limit of 115 years. Compared to the past, today relatively fewer people are dying at young ages and relatively more people are living out more and more of the life span.

Changes in Average Length of Life

The evidence about human longevity for prehistoric times is fragmentary and based largely on archeological exploration, including the examination of fossil remains. Thus, caution is warranted in reconstructing prehistoric life expectancies. According to our best estimates, prehistoric man and woman lived on average no longer than eighteen years, with only a small chance of living beyond the age of forty. For example, 95 percent of Neanderthal men, who lived about 150,000 to 100,000 years ago, died before reaching age forty. From 35,000 to 8,000 years ago in the Near East, the average length of life was not much better; about 90 percent died before age forty (Howells 1960).

We have better information about ancient men and women. Surveys of Greek skulls, for example, from about 3500 B.C. show a small and slow rise in average length of life, along with increases in body size, a reduction of arthritic conditions, and improved teeth up to about 300 B.C. Then, there was a decline during the medieval period, with life expectancies rising again after 1400 A.D. About 400 B.C. in Greece the average length of life at birth was probably about thirty years (Thomlinson 1976). This does not mean, of course, that there were no old people alive then. Rather, it means that many people died at young ages, while relatively few lived to old age, resulting in an average of about thirty years.

From recorded ages of death of Egyptian mummies during the Roman period, Pearson (1901–1902) calculated that an Egyptian aged ten had less than a 10 percent chance of surviving until age sixty-eight. That is, ninety-one out of every hundred ten year olds died before he or she reached age sixty-eight. Since women were underrepresented, since few entries for the first year of life were recorded, and since the mummies probably were of a higher—and therefore longer-lived—class, Pearson's calculations may not be valid for the entire Egyptian population. At birth, an average Egyptian of the time probably could expect to live no longer than 22.5 years.

In Rome, as in ancient China and various other places, population counts, often for purposes of taxation or military conscription, were made. Also, the Romans kept numerical data on duration of life, had life insurance, and used life tables to calculate annuities. But even such data are not very reliable: taxes, for example, didn't apply to everyone and sometimes were avoided; military conscription only affected adult males; and deaths of infants, women, and the poor were often not recorded (Petersen 1975: 398). Among other sources of data are Roman tombstones from which John D. Durand (1960) estimated that, during the first and second centuries, inhabitants of the Roman Empire at birth could expect to live between twenty-five and thirty years. But this may be an overestimate because deaths of children and women were probably underrepresented in his sample of tombstones. It is likely that life expectancy at birth for Romans in Italy may have been as low as twenty years (Petersen 1975: 417).

During the Middle Ages in England, life expectancy at birth may have been at most about thirty-three years. For example, for members of the English royal house born before 1348, "the year that the Black Death struck England, the expectation of life at birth was generally slightly above 30 years. It fell during the plague period to 17, and then rose very slowly over the next 75 years again to something over 30" (Petersen

TABLE 5.2
Life Expectancies at Birth for the United States by Year,
with the Decennial Increase and Cumulative Gain

Year	Life Expectancy (Years)	Decennial Increase (Years)	Cumulative Gain (Years)
1900*	47.3		
1910*	50.0	2.7	2.7
1920*	54.1	4.1	6.8
1930	59.7	5.6	12.4
1940	62.9	3.2	15.6
1950	68.2	5.3	20.9
1960	69.7	1.5	22.4
1970	70.8	1.1	23.5
1980	73.7	2.9	26.4
1990	75.4	1.7	28.1
1992	75.8	0.4 (for 2 years)	28.5

Source: National Center for Health Statistics (1994: 19–20); the 1992 figure is from *The New Haven Register* (16 December 1994: A7).

*Data prior to 1940 for death registration states only.

1975: 419). From the thirteenth to seventeenth centuries, fragmentary data suggest that in Europe life expectancies at birth ranged from twenty to forty years (Yaukey 1985: 114).

In Breslau in Silesia, where births and deaths were recorded since 1584, average length of life for the period 1687–1691 was 33.5 years (Halley 1693). Before 1789 in the states of Massachusetts and New Hampshire, it was 35.5 years (Thomlinson 1965). In Massachusetts it went from 38.3 years in 1850 to 46.1 years in 1900–1902 for men and from 40.5 to 49.4 for women (Dublin et al. 1949: 48). For 1838–1854 in England and Wales, it was 40.9 years. In the United States for 1900–02, it was 49.2 years.

In recent times for more developed countries, records have been more widely and reliably kept. For an illustration of the recent trend toward longer life, look at the life expectancies at birth for the United States given in table 5.2 above:

As can be seen from table 5.2, in 1900 Americans' life expectancy at birth was 47.3 years. By 1992, it had increased by more than 60 percent, that is, it was 28.5 years greater. By then, newly born Americans on average could expect to live 75.8 years.

The above summary account of declining mortality and increasing life expectancy gives an erroneous impression of orderly and steady change. The facts are quite to the contrary for much of the period. There were periodic disasters and increases in death rates, periods during which hundreds of thousands of people died. These periods were caused by famines and chronic food shortages; epidemic diseases including the plague, smallpox, cholera, and typhus; lack of sanitation, contaminated water supplies, and inadequate sewer systems; and war and other breakdowns in the social order.

Death rates soared during such periods and people were often reduced to bestial behavior, sometimes ignoring any values other than survival. People sometimes ate leaves, roots, dogs, cats, even their own children. Cannibalism was common, some people digging up and eating freshly buried corpses. Prison inmates attacked new prisoners and ate them. People stole anything that could be bartered for food. Famine was accompanied by the breakdown of society (Thomlinson 1965: 79).

Comparison of Life Expectancies by Region and Country

Although more and more people on Earth today are living beyond the early years of life and dying at older ages, there remain great discrepancies in life expectancies for different peoples living in different regions and countries. That is, some peoples seldom, if ever, experience famines, dangerous lifestyles, inadequate public health facilities, or lack of modern individual medical care, while other peoples suffer one or more of them.

An overview of regional differences in life expectancies can be see in table 5.3. People born in the early 1990s in North America or in Northern, Western, or Southern Europe, could expect to live to age seventy-six. For people born in eastern and middle Africa, however, it is only fifty-one, a difference of twenty-five years. Other regions have intermediate positions.

The inequality in average length of life is actually considerably greater among different populations and subpopulations than shown in table 5.3, because the regions defined there are gross categories that hide many differences. Thus, it is worth looking at table 5.4, where life expectan-

TABLE 5.3
Life Expectancy at Birth (in Years) by Region (early 1990s)

Region	Life Expectancy (Years)	
Africa		55
Northern Africa	62	
Western Africa	52	
Eastern Africa	51	
Middle Africa	51	
Southern Africa	64	
Latin America and the Caribbean		68
Caribbean	68	
Central America	69	
South America	68	
North America		76
Asia		64
East Asia	71	
Southeast Asia	63	
South Central Asia	58	
Western Asia	67	
Europe		73
Eastern Europe	69	
Northern Europe	76	
Southern Europe	76	
Western Europe	76	
Oceania		73

Source: "1994 World Population Data Sheet." Washington, DC: Population Reference Bureau.

cies for both men and women are given by country as of about 1991. Note three things from table 5.4:

First, the more developed countries generally have populations with relatively long expectations of life while the less developed countries have populations with relatively short expectations of life. Note that the diversity is much greater than that shown by the regional comparisons only. People in developed countries such as Japan, Hong Kong, Sweden, Switzerland, the Netherlands, Norway, Australia, Greece, France, the

United States, among others, can expect to live a long time, well into their seventies and even in some cases into the beginning of their eighties (e.g., women can expect to live 82.1 years in Japan, 80.9 years in France and Switzerland, 80.4 years in Sweden, 80.3 in Australia, etc.).

People in less developed countries, however, can expect to live much shorter lives, in some cases as much as thirty to forty years shorter, particularly in Africa south of the Sahara (South Africa being an exception). Different peoples are diverse not in their desire to live, but in how well they have been able to fulfill that desire.

Second, women generally live longer than men, sometimes considerably longer. Some of the differences are explained by social factors, such as the 13.2 years that women live longer than men in El Salvador where a civil war had been going on for some years. Also, there may be characteristics of modern life that give women an edge, perhaps related to social stress falling more on the shoulders of men. But the generality of the finding suggests that women may be biologically programed for a somewhat longer life than men, other things being equal. About 1991, for example, women could expect to live longer than men by 6.8 years in the United States, 8.5 in the former Czechoslovakia, 8.0 in Finland, 8.8 in Hungary, 9.2 in Poland, 8.1 in France, and longer by somewhat lesser amounts in most other countries.

Third, there are some exceptions to the sex difference in life expectancies favoring women. In countries where women are most subjugated, then women's advantage in life expectancy tends to be small and sometimes, as in Bangladesh, Iran, the Maldives, and Nepal, even reverses, with men living somewhat longer than women. The comparative disadvantage of being female in some countries compared to others also can be seen in the life expectancies by sex in Algeria, Guinea, Tunisia, Afghanistan, Bhutan, India, Iraq, Pakistan, Yemen, Papua New Guinea, and the Solomon Islands, among other countries. Generally, where women have no longevity gap over men, women's mortality connected with pregnancy and childbirth is relatively high.

Differences in Life Expectancies within Countries

Nearly all states today contain some degree of socioeconomic, ethnic, and racial diversity. Often, such diversity is a basis of inequalities, including inequalities in living conditions and opportunities for such things

TABLE 5.4
Life Expectancy at Birth (in Years) by Country and Gender (about 1991)

Country	Life Expectancy (in Years)	
	Men	Women
Africa		
Algeria	61.6	63.3
Angola	42.4	45.6
Benin	43.9	47.1
Botswana	52.3	59.7
Burkina Faso	45.3	48.8
Burundi	46.7	50.1
Cameroon	52.0	55.0
Cape Verde	59.0	61.0
Central African Republic	45.2	50.4
Chad	43.9	47.1
Comoros	53.5	54.5
Congo	49.4	54.7
Côte d'Ivoire	50.3	53.7
Djibouti	45.4	48.6
Egypt	62.9	66.4
Equatorial Guinea	44.4	47.6
Ethiopia	43.4	46.6
Gabon	49.9	53.2
Gambia	41.4	44.6
Ghana	52.2	55.8
Guinea	42.0	43.0
Guinea-Bissau	39.9	43.1
Kenya	55.9	59.9
Lesotho	55.5	60.5
Liberia	52.0	54.0
Libyan Arab Jamahiriya	59.1	62.5
Madagascar	52.0	55.0
Malawi	43.5	46.8
Mali	55.2	58.7
Mauritania	44.4	47.6
Mauritius	65.6	73.4
Morocco	59.1	62.5
Mozambique	44.5	47.8
Namibia	55.0	57.5
Niger	42.9	46.1
Nigeria	48.8	52.2

TABLE 5.4 (continued)
Life Expectancy at Birth (in Years) by Country and Gender (about 1991)

Country	Life Expectancy (in Years)	
	Men	Women
Réunion	67.9	77.0
Rwanda	45.1	47.7
St. Helena	—	—
Ascension	—	—
Tristan da Cunha	—	—
Sao Tomé and Principe	—	—
Senegal	46.3	48.3
Seychelles	65.3	74.1
Sierra Leone	39.4	42.6
Somalia	43.4	46.6
South Africa	57.5	63.5
Sudan	48.6	51.0
Swaziland	42.9	49.5
Togo	51.3	54.8
Tunisia	64.9	66.4
Uganda	43.2	46.1
United Republic of Tanzania	47.0	50.0
Zaire	49.8	53.3
Zambia	50.7	53.0
Zimbabwe	55.1	58.6
North and Central America and the Caribbean		
Anguilla	—	—
Antigua and Barbuda	—	—
Aruba	68.3	75.4
Bahamas	67.5	74.9
Barbados	67.2	72.5
Belize	69.9	71.8
Bermuda	68.8	76.3
British Virgin Islands	—	—
Canada	73.0	79.8
Cayman Islands	—	—
Costa Rica	72.9	77.6
Cuba	72.7	76.3
Dominica	—	—
Dominican Republic	63.9	68.1
El Salvador	50.7	63.9
Greenland	60.4	66.3

TABLE 5.4 (continued)
Life Expectancy at Birth (in Years) by Country and Gender (about 1991)

Country	Life Expectancy (in Years)	
	Men	Women
Grenada	—	—
Guadeloupe	66.4	72.4
Guatemala	55.1	59.4
Haiti	53.1	56.4
Honduras	61.9	66.1
Jamaica	70.4	74.8
Martinique	67.0	73.5
Mexico	62.1	66.0
Montserrat	—	—
Netherlands Antilles	71.1	75.8
Nicaragua	64.8	67.7
Panama	70.1	74.1
Puerto Rico	69.7	78.5
Saint Kitts and Nevis	65.9	71.0
Saint Lucia	68.0	74.8
St. Pierre and Miquelon	—	—
St. Vincent and the Grenadines	—	—
Trinidad and Tobago	66.9	71.6
Turks and Caicos Islands	—	—
United States	71.8	78.6
U.S. Virgin Islands	—	—
South America		
Argentina	65.5	72.7
Bolivia	56.6	61.2
Brazil	62.3	67.6
Chile	68.1	75.1
Colombia	65.5	71.1
Ecuador	63.4	67.6
Falkland Islands	—	—
French Guiana	—	—
Guyana	60.4	66.1
Paraguay	64.4	68.5
Peru	62.9	66.6
Suriname	66.4	71.3
Uruguay	68.3	75.3
Venezuela	66.7	72.8

TABLE 5.4 (continued)
Life Expectancy at Birth (in Years) by Country and Gender (about 1991)

Country	*Life Expectancy* (in Years)	
	Men	Women
Asia		
Afghanistan	41.0	42.0
Armenia	69.0	74.7
Azerbaijan	66.6	74.2
Bahrain	66.8	69.4
Bangladesh	56.9	56.0
Bhutan	45.6	46.6
Brunei Darussalam	70.1	72.7
Cambodia	47.0	49.9
China	68.0	70.9
Cyprus	74.1	78.6
Democratic Kampuchea	47.0	49.9
Democratic Yémen	49.4	52.4
East Timor	41.6	43.4
Georgia	68.1	75.7
Hong Kong	74.6	80.3
India	55.4	55.7
Indonesia	58.5	62.0
Islamic Republic of Iran	55.8	55.0
Iraq	77.4	78.2
Israel	74.9	78.5
Japan	76.1	82.1
Jordan	64.2	67.8
Kazakhstan	63.9	73.1
Democratic People's Republic of Korea	66.2	72.7
Republic of Korea	66.9	75.0
Kuwait	72.6	76.3
Kyrgyzstan	64.3	72.4
Lao People's Democratic Republic	47.0	50.0
Lebanon	65.1	69.0
Macau	75.0	80.3
Malaysia	67.5	71.6
Maldives	66.2	65.2
Mongolia	60.0	62.5
Myanmar	58.9	63.7
Nepal	50.9	48.1

TABLE 5.4 (continued)
Life Expectancy at Birth (in Years) by Country and Gender (about 1991)

Country	Life Expectancy (in Years)	
	Men	Women
Oman	66.2	69.8
Pakistan	59.0	59.2
Philippines	63.1	66.7
Qatar	66.9	71.8
Saudi Arabia	66.4	69.1
Singapore	73.5	78.0
Sri Lanka	67.8	71.7
Syrian Arab Republic	64.4	68.1
Tajikistan	66.8	71.7
Thailand	63.8	68.9
Turkey	62.8	68.0
Turkmenistan	61.8	68.4
United Arab Emirates	68.6	72.9
Uzbekistan	66.0	72.1
Vietnam	63.7	67.9
Yemen	49.8	50.2
Europe		
Albania	69.6	75.5
Andorra	—	—
Austria	72.6	79.2
Belarus	66.8	76.4
Belgium	72.4	79.1
Bulgaria	68.1	74.8
Former Czechoslovakia	67.3	75.8
Denmark	72.2	77.7
Estonia	64.7	74.9
Faeroe Islands	73.3	79.6
Finland	70.9	78.9
France	72.8	80.9
Former German Democratic Republic*	69.7	75.7
Former Federal Republic of Germany	71.8	78.4
Gibraltar	—	—
Greece	72.2	76.4
Hungary	65.0	73.8
Iceland	75.7	80.3

TABLE 5.4 (continued)
Life Expectancy at Birth (in Years) by Country and Gender (about 1991)

| | Life Expectancy (in Years) | |
Country	Men	Women
Ireland	71.0	76.7
Isle of Man	—	—
Italy	73.5	80.0
Latvia	64.7	74.9
Liechtenstein	66.1	72.9
Lithuania	66.6	76.2
Luxembourg	70.6	77.9
Malta	73.8	78.0
Monaco	—	—
Netherlands	74.0	80.2
Norway	74.0	80.1
Poland	66.1	75.3
Portugal	70.0	77.3
Republic of Moldova	65.5	72.3
Romania	66.6	73.1
Russian Federation	63.5	74.3
San Marino	73.2	79.1
Slovenia	—	—
Spain	73.3	79.7
Sweden	74.9	80.4
Switzerland	74.1	80.9
Ukraine	65.9	75.0
United Kingdom	72.7	78.3
Former Yugoslavia	69.1	74.9
Oceania		
American Samoa	—	—
Australia	74.4	80.3
Christmas Island	—	—
Cocos Islands	—	—
Cook Islands	63.2	67.1
Fiji	60.7	63.9
French Polynesia	65.8	71.1
Guam	69.5	75.6
Marshall Islands	59.1	63.0
Nauru	—	—
New Caledonia	—	—
New Zealand	72.4	78.3

TABLE 5.4 (continued)
Life Expectancy at Birth (in Years) by Country and Gender (about 1991)

Country	Life Expectancy (in Years)	
	Men	Women
Niue	—	—
Norfork Island	—	—
Northern Mariana Islands	—	—
Pacific Islands	—	—
Papua New Guinea	53.2	54.7
Pitcairn	—	—
Samoa	61.0	64.3
Solomon Islands	59.9	61.4
Tokelau	—	—
Tonga	—	—

Source: United Nations (1994: 116–26). *From United Nations (1990: 174–84).

as a good education, a job, and adequate health care. One outcome of such inequalities, of course, is that the life chances of members of various social classes or other groups are different, a fact that is mirrored in their different life expectancies. Even within more developed countries, the life expectancies, not just of men and women, but of other subpopulations can be very different. Where people are disadvantaged politically, economically, and socially, they tend also to have shorter life expectancies than privileged groups within the same society.

It is beyond the scope of this book to take up this question in its comparative aspects, but one example will illustrate the point. In the United States in 1990, 12.1 percent of the population was classified as African-American. African-Americans, of course, were only one of the identifiable racial-ethnic groups in the United States, but I take them as an example of one group that contains a relatively large number of disadvantaged people. Some other groups in the United States, such as Native Americans, may be even more disadvantaged than African-Americans.

In table 5.5, I give life expectancies at birth for both African-American and white men and women for three different periods, 1900–02, 1969–71, and 1991. Note that women have longer life expectancies than men among both African-Americans and whites at each time period. But let's look at the racial differences. In 1900–02 white women could ex-

TABLE 5.5
Life Expectancy at Birth (in Years) for White and African-American Men
and Women, 1900–02, 1969–71, and 1991, United States

Gender and Race	Life Expectancy		
	1900–02*	1969–71	1991
Women			
White	51.1	75.5	79.6
African-American	35.0	68.3	73.8
Men			
White	48.2	67.9	72.9
African-American	32.5	60.0**	64.6

Source: National Center for Health Statistics (1995: 2). **From NCHS (1993: 2; the figure for African-American males in 1969–71 in 1994 and 1995 publications is incorrect).
*Death registration states only.

pect to live 16.1 years longer than African-American women, and white men could expect to live 15.7 years longer than African-American men.

In 1969–71, the racial differences were considerably smaller but in the same direction, the advantage for whites being 7.2 years difference for women and 7.9 years difference for men.

By 1991, there was a small additional relative gain for African-American women, their life expectancy having risen to 73.8 years, but that was still 5.8 years below the life expectancy of 79.6 years for white women. African-American men, although they gained 4.6 years in life expectancy compared to their own 1969–71 figure, lost relative to white men. In 1991, they remained 8.3 years behind the life expectancy of white men.

Even in 1991, taking both gender and race into account, white women at birth could expect to live 15 years longer than African-American men.

The Future of Life-Extending Technologies

Increasing life expectancy. The inequality in length of life for people both among and within countries may be one of the half-dozen or so most important moral issues facing humankind today. For how can we morally justify unequal life expectancies that regularly and systematically give some disadvantaged people ten, twenty or even thirty or forty fewer years to live on average than other people largely because of the accidents of birth? Being born in a low or high social class, a disadvantaged or advantaged ethnic or racial group, or in a poor or rich country contributes greatly to a person's chances of having a good and long life. Since life is our most precious possession, is it morally defensible to deny it to anyone unnecessarily? Our answer can only be no.

Yet we *are* denying it unnecessarily. We already have the technical knowledge to increase life expectancies dramatically in less developed societies where life expectancies at birth are relatively low. We could add as many as thirty years to the average longevity in the worst-off societies by eliminating famine (there is plenty of food on Earth to feed everyone but it is maldistributed: food now goes to waste in the more developed societies), by providing up-to-date medical technologies to further control infectious and contagious diseases (3 million children a year could be saved by immunizations alone), by reducing unwanted pregnancies and by delivering proper preventive and curative medical care for people of all ages including pregnant women and young children (the lives of one million women who die every year from preventable reproductive health problems could be saved) (Brown et al. 1992: 4). Moreover, such gains in life expectancy would be additional years of active life, mostly free of illness and disability. Good health not only adds years to a life, it also adds increased quality of life.

Even in the economically advanced societies, there is room for improvement on such factors. In the United States, for example, hunger strikes as many as 4 million children from low-income families, with an additional 9 million-plus at some risk of going hungry (*New Haven Register*: 21 July 1995: A3).

More difficult to deal with are intractable problems of social conditions such as poverty (nearly one-fifth of the Earth's population survives on less than one U.S. dollar per day), illiteracy (about one billion adults on Earth cannot read or write), lack of education (more than 100 million children of primary school age are not in school), lack of safe water to drink (1.2 billion people are affected) (Brown et al. 1992: 4–5), unhealthy life styles, neighborhood and ethnic violence, unsafe work and home environments, and human behavior that makes the environment less livable, ranging from the destruction of rain forests and the ozone layer to the pollution of air and water.

These are largely problems that can only be solved through social engineering and management combined with relevant scientific and technical knowledge. The physical scientific knowledge is largely available, although not entirely as in the case of global warming, for example, where technical experts still disagree about forecasts and timetables. In every case, these problems challenge both the human capacities for organizing responsible individual and collective action and our knowledge of the human sciences. They are social as well as physical problems that invite social solutions, while using relevant technical knowledge. When these problems are solved adequately, further gains will be made in human longevity.

People, mostly through no fault of their own, do not have equal access to life-enhancing information, treatment, and conditions. Fetuses developing in their mothers' wombs, obviously, are helpless to control their own environment; babies have little choice about the nature of the care they receive; and young adults are more or less beneficiaries—or victims—of their opportunity or lack of opportunity for education, their subcultures, and their socioeconomic circumstances.

This is not to minimize individual responsibility of each individual for him- or herself. Such responsibility is fundamental, only partial at young ages but increasing as people grow into adulthood. When people damage themselves by their own behavior—from overeating and smoking cigarettes to taking drugs and living lives of violence—they lessen not only our sympathy for their plight but also society's legitimate obligations to them.

Both the helpless and the willfully reckless are part of the challenge of the future. Can we invent and enlarge the opportunities for more and more people to take control of their own lives in positive, life-affirming ways and open up more possibilities for everyone to benefit from the life-extending technologies currently available? Can we educate effectively, so people will acquire the knowledge, skills, and moral principles of behavior that allow them to make choices that lead to productive, long lives of good quality for themselves and others?

Increasing life expectancies where they are now low is a matter of more and more people surviving to live out the human life span as we now understand it. It is also a matter of continued research and development in public health behavior and medical technology so that still more gains can be made, even in the more developed societies. For example, new increases in life expectancy might be made through prevention, diagnosis and treatment of cardiovascular, cerebrovascular and malignant

neoplastic diseases and through organ transplantation, nonbiological pros-
thesis, and further improvements in both life-style and the environment,
including health and safety in the workplace (Gordon et al. 1979: 3).

Increasing the life span. At the frontiers of knowledge, much more
may be possible. We may be able to increase the human life span itself.
For example, Gordon et al. (1979: 3–4) forecast life span-extending technologies, such as dietary control or supplementation, that actually slow
down cellular aging processes, and they foresee others that slow the aging of key organ systems, that slow "programmed aging" such as hor-
mone-induced aging, and that regenerate human tissue. Such technologies
and, eventually, further advances in genetic engineering may allow control of the fundamental rate of aging itself.

Breakthroughs in the present barrier of the human life span, were they
to occur, would be of possible benefit to people in all societies. Such life
span-extending technologies, however, are not likely to produce rejuve-
nation, that is, making the old any younger. Rather, they are likely to
produce retardation of the aging process. Thus, they will be of greatest
benefit to people who have not yet aged. Their effects would appear only
slowly, probably not until well into the 21st century, as young people
who begin to receive benefits from such technologies reach older ages
(Gordon et al. 1979: 6).

The distinction between life expectancy and life span will probably
continue to be useful for some time, although eventually it may become
blurred. Life expectancy-extending technologies and life span-extending
technologies may each have some effect on both life expectancy and the
life span. For example, any process that tended to increase life expectancy by eliminating death due to heart disease also might increase the
life span in some individuals, for example, those whose failing cardiac
function resulted in reduced oxygen and nutrient supply to tissues (Gordon et al. 1979: xxii).

The applications of life-expectancy extending technologies to allow
people to live out their life spans could result in people living an average
of 85 or more years in nearly every country on Earth, somewhat more in
the most developed societies. Probably not much higher than that, however, even in an optimistic scenario, because accidents would still occur
and possibly murders and wars as well.

Using the most optimistic assumptions of the application of both life
expectancy-extending *and* lifespan-extending technologies as they may

be by the year 2000, however, Gordon et al. (1979: 3) make a more favorable forecast. For example, they find for the United States that the size of the total population would stabilize shortly before the year 2200 and the average length of life at that time could be as high as 180 years.

There are a few people, such as Christian Scientists, who reject most treatments of modern scientific medicine, both life expectancy and life span-extending technologies, as interfering with God's plan, and others who reject them as being against nature. Yet most people, whether religious believers or not, view most life expectancy-extending technologies, as desirable. Many of those same people, however, regard life extension through lengthening the life span itself as morally questionable, an example of human hubris that is an affront to their God or human meddling in what is—and ought to remain—a natural process. Humans ought not, according to this view, try to change what is commonly regarded as natural or sacred by some artificial means. Such a view also may preclude many other medical procedures, from test-tube babies to genetic manipulation to prevent disease (Gordon et al. 1979: 28, 178–79).

But such a view is untenable. Carried to extreme it would mean that no medical intervention would ever be warranted, whether life expectancy or life span extending. Although the possibility of human lives as long as 150 or 180 as a normal occurrence appears incredible to us now, it may be regarded as quite natural two hundred years from now. Thus, a conceptual and attitudinal revolution in human thinking about what is a natural and normal death may be required. This, in turn, invites changes in our judgments about what human medical interventions are appropriate under what circumstances. There will remain, no doubt, some point where a death will still be regarded as timely, but it may be at a far older chronological age than at present. It may occur, though, when nothing more that is reasonable and humanly possible can be done to prolong a life at an acceptable level of quality, given the medical knowledge of some future time.

It is beyond my purposes to pursue this topic here. Entire books could be—and have been—written about the possible consequences of human longevity in the future, some writers viewing it with alarm and emphasizing predictions of crisis and disaster and others emphasizing the positive benefits and opportunities. In casual discussions, some people may say, "Oh, I would never want to live that long," just as my great-grandmother once said she would never ride in an infernal "horseless carriage." (In the last years of her life, my grandmother loved nothing more than going for a Sunday drive in the family car.) Remember the mayor of Bangor, Maine, described in chapter 3 of volume 1, who said that the new time zones in 1883 for standardizing train schedules was a violation of God's immutable laws, time zones that we now take for granted. Such attitudes, to say the least, are subject to change with knowledge and understanding.

Having more people live longer and relatively more old people in the population in relation to the young could have many benefits for all humanity. Individuals could expect to have more of that precious value, life, and of that scarce resource, time. Moreover, their added years can accurately be thought of as coming in the middle years rather than at the end of life, because they will mostly be years of vigor and good health. Not only death, but many of the infirmaties of old age will be postponed. Even now, for people of good health, to grow older is generally a blessing.

Additional benefits could flow from the new possibilities for personal and social development and cultural evolution. Unlike biological evolution where the continued existence of people is not necessary beyond the point of their reproduction, social and cultural evolution can benefit from the contributions of the old, experienced, and the wise as much as, if not more than, those of the young, inexperienced, and the rash. Given the facts that social and cultural heritages continue to grow and that proper socialization and adequate education, therefore, take longer and longer, great contributions cannot be made until later in life in some fields of human endeavor. This may be particularly true in creatively managing the great events of history, in shaping the political and moral organizations of nations and supranational entities that are dedicated to peace, freedom, and well-being, and in improving social institutions.

In sum, I have emphasized what *might* be possible for the extension of human life under the optimistic assumptions that relevant research and development will continue, that adequate knowledge and treatment will be widely distributed throughout the entire human race, and that no major catastrophes, human-made or otherwise, will occur. These assumptions may turn out to be true. Then, again, they may not.

It partly depends, of course, on how we humans see our choices, on what we decide we ought to do, and on what we actually do. If we do act to reduce war, murder, and other human-inflicted damages to each other, if we do act to preserve the life-sustaining capacities of the Earth and to create and widely apply life-extending technologies, then future humans will have a good chance to have long lives of good quality.

A Global View of Population Growth

As I write, there are more than 5.5 billion people on Earth. If present growth rates continued, there would be 10 billion people by 2030, 20 billion by 2070, and 40 billion by 2110. Of course, such a high growth rate over an extended period is highly unlikely and could not continue. For it would exhaust the life-sustaining capacities of the Earth and force drastic reductions in size, if not extinction, on the human race (McFalls 1991: 34).

From figure 5.1, note that human population growth has had a very, very long fuse and a recent, sudden explosion. Over the three to five million years since hominids began to evolve, their total numbers were mostly relatively small. There was a tremendously long period of small ups and downs in the growth of the hominid population with relatively little change except for very slow and staggered growth over the long term. The population probably never exceeded 10 million people before 8000 B.C. (McFalls 1991).

Throughout this long prologue, death rates were relatively high and mostly beyond human control. People struggled to live, created cultural values and practices to support life, and invented religions that invoked divine assistance to encourage people to reproduce and to make food supplies plentiful. If they did not do these things, they died out. Even if they did, they sometimes died out anyway.

Generally, birth rates were high, balancing the high death rates. They were necessary for group survival. Because people tended to breed up to near their biological limits, population growth or decline was tied to variations in the largely uncontrollable and variable death rates.

About one million B.C., there was a small explosion in the human population in response to the use and making of tools, after which a new balance of births and deaths was achieved.

Then came an even greater change, the agricultural revolution. It began slowly about 8000 B.C. with the beginning of farming and animal husbandry. Death rates in some areas began to fall. From that point on humans began to be able to control some of the causes of their death, starting

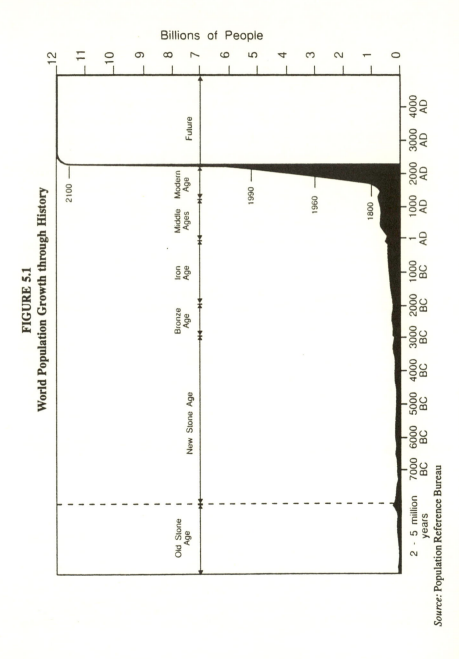

FIGURE 5.1
World Population Growth through History

Source: Population Reference Bureau

with the reduction of famine and better nutrition. Increasingly, it became possible to better achieve the age-old human value of life against death.

The most dramatic reductions in the death rates, however, did not occur until after 1750 as the effects of the industrial revolution began to be felt in England. As the industrial revolution began, birth rates generally remained high, also reflecting age-old values supporting high fertility rates. Over the millennia, such values had importantly contributed to human survival. It must have seemed idiotic—probably immoral and sacrilegious—to question them. As death rates, especially at first infant mortality rates, continued to fall in industrializing countries, the growing gap between high birth rates and lowering mortality rates resulted in an explosion in population size. A larger and larger percentage of children was living to maturity. Finally, the long-burning fuse of human population growth had ignited.

After about 1750, country after country in the then-developing world experienced a demographic transition, which is diagrammed in figure 5.2. This account, I hasten to add, is an ideal model and oversimplifies the facts. Demographic changes and their causes are complex and in different localities specific events and the sequence of changes in birth and death rates differed. Nonetheless, the overall result was a tremendous increase in human population.

Simply put, the first stage is a period of high birth rates and high death rates, with a relatively stable population and short life expectancies. The second stage is a period of falling death rates, but continuing high birth rates, and a population growing at an increasing rate of increase and having lengthening life expectancies. The third stage is also a period of rapid growth, but with a lowering rate of population increase, as death rates bottom out and birth rates begin to fall. Finally, the fourth stage is a period in which a new population balance is reached with relatively low death rates and low birth rates and with relatively long life expectancies.

In the fourth period, death rates tend to be pushed to the lowest level possible and they tend to be relatively steady, eventually moving up slightly as more and more people live closer to their life spans to die at higher age-specific death rates of older ages. At this point, population growth is linked not to variations in uncontrollable death rates as in the first stage but to variations in the now largely controllable birth rates. Population growth in such societies becomes a collective consequence of individual

FIGURE 5.2
The Stages of Demographic Transition

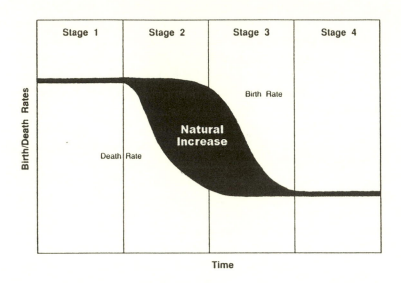

Source: McFalls (1991: 33)

choices which are made in a new cultural context informed by the facts of low infant mortality and generally long lives. Clearly, at this point the reproductive values, choices and decisions of individuals and groups become major factors in the future course of population growth.

All of this unprecedented change started very recently when viewed against the long period of human development, within the last 300 years. Following England, came other countries in Northern and Western Europe, North America, Australia, and New Zealand. Then came Eastern and Southern Europe. Then Japan and the former Soviet Union went through the transition (Yaukey 1985: 114). In the period following the demographic transition in a given country, life expectancies end up being relative high but improvements in them begin to slow.

By 1650, the Earth's human population had expanded about fifty times, from 10 million to 500 million.

The next 150 years added another half-billion people, so that in 1800 the total population had reached one billion.

It took only 130 years to reach two billion, which it did in 1930.
In only thirty more years, by 1960, it reached three billion.
Fifteen years later, by 1975, it reached four billion.
It reached five billion in 1987, only twelve years later (McFalls 1991: 33).

For the more developed countries that went through the demographic transition early, the causes of declining mortality at first were associated more with economic and social development than with advances in medicine and disease control. Increased ability to produce food and to store it safely and transport it were important factors, reducing local famines and improving nutrition. Public sanitation, sewers, clean water supplies, and personal hygiene had a role. By 1900, bio-medical science, almost entirely as a result of the "germ theory of disease," contributed to further declines in the death rate. For example, both smallpox and the great pox (syphilis) were virtually eliminated.

Birth rates in the developed societies declined partly as a result of the same changes in social organization and economic life that permitted declining death rates. Industrialization and urbanization, for example, altered family life and the economic importance of children. Birth rates may have declined partly as a result of the declining death rates themselves. For once infant mortality was significantly reduced it was no longer necessary to give birth to so many infants in order to have some children live to maturity.

For less developed countries, the control of infectious and contagious diseases, especially since the end of World War II, has played a much larger role in reducing mortality and in increasing life expectancies than it did in Europe and North America. Social and economic transformations have played a smaller role.

Although life expectancies have been increasing in most developing countries, there remains considerable room for improvement. Also, birth rates, and, consequently, population growth, although slowing in many places, remain relatively high. Today, only about one-third of the Earth's population has gone through the demographic transition and has reached a new balance with relatively low death *and* low birth rates. The Earth's population is still growing at a rapid rate. Yet in many of the less developed countries—from Bangladesh and Thailand to Colombia and Kenya—people are adopting the use of contraceptives, and fertility appears to be declining at a more rapid rate than it did earlier in Europe and

America even without comparable economic and social development (*New York Times*, 2 January 1994: 1, 8).

Recent scenarios of future global population growth put the lowest forecast at more than 8 billion people by 2030, assuming extremely low levels of fertility and relatively high levels of mortality; they put the highest forecast at nearly 11 billion, if fertility levels are slow to decline and mortality levels are low (Lutz 1994b: 26)

Cause for Celebration or Alarm—or Both?

If human life is the most important human value, then both the lengthening of individual human lives and the sheer growth of the human population during the last three centuries can be seen as triumphs, perhaps the greatest of all human achievements (Simon 1981: 163). Rightly, they are causes for celebration. Throughout much of human existence, the same factors that resulted in people living longer also resulted in a growing population, a mathematical necessity unless birth rates drop immediately by some amount proportionate to longer lengths of individual lives. More human life is good, both more years for each individual to live and more people to live those years.

Both increasing longevity and an excess of births over deaths contribute to population growth. But in the long view, longevity tends to have a depressant effect on growth, because older people are beyond the childbearing ages. Thus, women living into their late forties and older ages no longer continue to bear children. The effect of fertility on growth, however, continues to be great because of its multiplier effect, since each child may have several children in the future who, in turn, will have several more, and so on (Lutz 1994b: 13). If the Earth is overpopulated, then this is another reason to serve the value of life not by adding new births beyond the replacement level, but by increasing the longevity of those people who are born.

These two valuable things—longevity of individual lives and increasing the total number of people—have been positively correlated historically, because they have common causes. Yet they are becoming opposed to each other. In the future, we can achieve one only at some cost to the other, because the carrying capacity of the Earth is limited, as we saw in the discussions of Meadows et al. (1972, 1992). The growth in sheer numbers of people on Earth is already damaging the quantity and quality of individual lives in some regions and will increasingly do so in more and more regions. Unless the high rate of adding new babies to the human population is controlled, we humans eventually might face a painful reduction in human life expectancy as a result of the breakdown of the social order and the deterioration of the life-sustaining capacities of the Earth.

Human population growth will reflexively affect itself, because, beyond some point, it cannot be sustained at a high level, even with low levels of living. It threatens the very survival of humankind. Many writers (Ehrlich and Ehrlich 1991; Hardin 1993; Kennedy 1993) agree with these cries of alarm.

Some writers, however, disagree. They include, for example, Julian L. Simon (1981, 1995) who has argued persuasively with considerable empirical data that such cries of alarm are false. He documents that natural resources generally have become *less* scarce over the long run. For example, the costs and prices of most natural resources have been going down relative to human work time. Also, the known reserves of most natural resources have increased in recent years, for example, tin, manganese, zinc, lead, copper, bauxite, oil, chromite, iron, potash, and phosphates. They have increased, despite their extraction and use, because of discoveries of heretofore unknown deposits, new technologies that made access to some supplies economical, and recycling.

Simon also shows that for the Earth as a whole per capita food production has been increasing; total agricultural land and yield per acre have been increasing; and many kinds of pollution are less than they were. He claims that energy is not finite but potentially inexhaustible. He argues that the more people there are, the higher the level of living in the long run, because with more people comes more knowledge, ingenuity, and enterprise. People are, for Simon, the ultimate resource: "skilled, spirited, and hopeful people who will exert their wills and imaginations for their own benefit, and so, inevitably, for the benefit of us all" (Simon 1981: 348). These views of Simon, incidentally, are similar to those expressed by Condorcet, who was confident that "overpopulation" could be solved by reasoned human action.

There is considerable truth to Simon's arguments. Certainly, given current data, he is correct to say that from a global perspective there is no reason to panic. Unless some natural catastrophe occurs, the Earth is not going to collapse in the immediate future. Even Meadows et al. and many other concerned citizens agree: there is time for humans to adopt policies that will create sustainable economies and societies. Yet there are several flaws in Simon's thinking that cloud the rosy impression that he gives.

1. As Simon knows, despite the trend toward increased longevity, the majority of the people on Earth, including some people in the most economically advanced societies, are not coming close to living out their full life spans. Simply delivering effectively what we now know about sanitation, medicine, nutrition, etc., as we have seen, would allow most of the people on Earth to live many more active, vigorous years than they now do.

As they did so—that is, as longevity increased—population growth would continue simply because more people were being kept alive longer. Even if birth rates dropped radically, another several billion people probably would be added to the human population, especially in countries that now have young populations where up to a third or more of the people still have their reproductive lives ahead of them.

Simon (1981: 337) sets up a choice between level of living on the one hand and total number of people on the other, and he concludes that it is right to choose more people, even if it means people had to live at a lower level of living than they otherwise would. But this thinking creates a false choice, erroneously pitting mere material things vs. human life. In fact, the choice is one of life vs. potential life, that is, years of life of existing people vs. the sheer numbers of sperm that might fertilize an ovum and that might become an individual.

Justice argues that priority ought to be given to eliminating the arbitrary inequality in length of life of living people, both now and in the future, by acting so as to lift life expectancies to the level of the longest lived populations. This task ought to take precedence over using resources to deal with the consequences of rapid population growth, for example, nurturing and educating massive numbers of children many of whom would face short and miserable lives. What is required is adding by human design a tiny fraction to the countless numbers of sperm (the typical man may produce five trillion in his lifetime) that already fail to fertilize an ovum. Certainly, there is no cause for rosy complacency about high birth rates when some people now alive—including young children—face early deaths unnecessarily.

2. Simon tends to look only a relatively short time into the future, the next forty years or so. On such a short time scale, he may be quite right

about his optimistic view. For example, at one point he explains how the expected future supply and demand of a material affect its current price, and therefore automatically take into account future generations (Simon 1981: 150). Thinking a few years ahead—even up to thirty or forty years ahead—we can understand how this might work. But 200 or 500 years ahead? Whose current behavior is shaped by dreams of profit that far into the future, much less thousands of years ahead? Clearly, deferred gratification based on the profit motive has its time limits and they are very short range when considered according to the time scale of human existence, past and possibly future.

Also, there are some problems that take a long time before their negative consequences are visible, such things as global warming and ozone depletion. Yet to remedy the possible future negative effects, present action may be necessary. Moreover, some such problems are by their very nature global and require collective action which may take a long time to create. There is no justification for complacency concerning such problems.

3. There are many potential threats to quality of life and life expectancy that are local and immediate. Such threats require action now. Deforestation, for example, may be debatable as a global problem for the near future, but it is a local problem in many areas of the planet right now (Rudel 1993). To take another example, there may be no reason for immediate panic that the entire human race will die out if some children in various parts of the world are exposed to toxic substances that eventually shorten their lives or reduce their mental and physical capacities. Even though many such children may show few—if any—immediate symptoms, there *is* reason to panic if you are a parent of such an exposed child. His or her quantity and quality of life may be negatively affected.

Exaggerated warnings may be counterproductive and dangerous, as Simon (1981: 143) says, but he nonetheless fully acknowledges that all humankind is indebted to people who have worked to publicize and correct pollution problems.

4. Finally, I confess that I share many of Simon's optimistic views. But I am not at all certain of them, because they are contingent on many shaky assumptions about how present and future humans will behave. If, indeed, people act in informed and intelligent ways to increase human well-being, as Simon assumes, then there is a reasonable chance that human society will thrive in the future. If people can learn to live in peace and harmony, cooperate with one another, invest in research and

development and in education, develop new and useful ideas, create more powerful and effective technologies and social arrangements, behave competently and morally, sufficiently defer gratification, reduce poverty and unemployment, eliminate hunger and starvation, and care for all people everywhere and the life-sustaining capacities of the Earth, then, barring natural catastrophes or new incurable diseases, the human future indeed may be rosy.

But it is by no means certain—perhaps not even likely—that people will behave in these ways. Each person is not only "the ultimate resource," but also a potential ignoramus, psychopath, or genocidal fanatic. There seems no limit to the human capacities for wisdom or stupidity, or for good or evil. A lot depends on the care, nurturance, and opportunities to learn people receive when they are young. And a lot depends on the kinds of social institutions people create. For example, there has never been a famine in a democratic country with a free press despite shortages of food, while people have starved under authoritarian regimes—perhaps up to 30 million in Mao's China during the "Great Leap Forward" (Sen 1981).

Thus, we can hope that people will behave so as to benefit both themselves and all humankind, but there is no guarantee that they will. Simon, obviously, knows this, but he gives a general impression that these things are near certainties, or that the wise and the good will necessarily outweigh the stupid and the evil.

A prudent response may be to believe that there are serious problems, to define them, to call attention to them, and to search for and to suggest solutions to them, as in the example of Meadows et al. Acts designed to create freedom and well-being will not simply occur automatically, especially if people are encouraged to believe that there are no problems. Such acts may—at least some of them surely must—require conscious and deliberate thought. In fact, most of the rosy picture than Simon paints, from increased resources to examples of lessened pollution, is factually based on the consequences of planned human intervention.

From the perspective of the long-term sustainability of human life on this planet, the Earth may already be overpopulated. There is, however, no need to panic and we can continue to honor the ultimate value of human life. For example, we can—and ought to—continue to add years to the lives of living people. But we ought to reconsider the appropriateness of some traditional human values for the future, including reproductive values—a topic to which I return in chapter 6.

Abortion

The Abortion Debate as a Clash of Worldviews

Is it morally right to kill a fetus growing and developing in a woman's body? To be consistent with the value of human life as an ultimate touchstone for morality, we conclude that the prima facie answer is no. But it is not that simple, because there are at least two lives involved, the pregnant woman's as well as that of the fetus. Moreover, the current debate about abortion is more than a debate about the status of the fetus. It is also a clash of worldviews. For example, Kristin Luker (1984: 10) says that the abortion debate involves "our most cherished beliefs about the world, about motherhood, and about what it means to be human."

First, the abortion debate is about personhood and the sanctity of life. Nearly everyone agrees that the fetus is located on a continuum from a single cell (an egg or a sperm) to a newborn human infant. Nearly everyone agrees, too, that fetuses have heartbeats by about the twenty-fourth day of pregnancy but that they do not breathe until birth. Nearly everyone agrees, furthermore, that persons have rights and nonpersons do not.

But everyone does not agree whether or not the fetus is a person. For pro-life militants, the fetus is a baby and abortion is murder. For pro-choice militants, the fetus is not a baby and abortion is acceptable contraception. Moreover, Luker (1984) shows how the abortion debate is a struggle to define personhood that goes well beyond the moral status of the fetus and relates to all individuals who may have to be kept alive by advanced medical technology—from brain death and kidney dialysis to heart and other organ transplants. Both medicine and law, according to Luker, urgently need decision rules about who is a full-fledged member of the human community.

With respect to a fetus, Harold J. Morowitz and James S. Trefil (1992) ask, when does humanness begin? They give a context for their answer based on the evolution of the human animal and how humans differ from other forms of life. What sets us apart, they contend, is our highly evolved cerebral cortex. Therefore, since the cerebral cortex does not make the connections to the rest of the nervous system that enable us to receive and process information until about the end of the second trimester of pregnancy, they conclude that the developing fetus does not acquire humanness before that time.

Second, the abortion debate is no less than a debate about the role of women in society, that is, the proper place of motherhood in a woman's life, and even cultural definitions of sexuality and children. Modern contraception, for example, the "pill," and easier and safer abortion have empowered women to schedule their pregnancies and "subordinate childbearing to an entire life plan." These, in turn, have accelerated social changes that have tended to validate the role of career women, while devaluing the roles of mother and wife. Pro-choice women tend to see childbearing as secondary to their fulfilling their potential as human beings, while pro-life women view pregnancy and childrearing as the proper moral center not only of their own lives but also of the lives of all women. From this perspective, the "right-to-life movement is an attempt to form a moral cartel to use state power to define the social role of women." It aims to make sure that family roles have greater priority than career roles for women and that women's work within the home is fully honored (Barry and Popkin 1984: x–xi).

Third, changing technology had a role in changing abortion from a private dilemma to a public phenomenon. For example, with modern technology, the fetus is visible very early in the pregnancy, newborn babies have excellent chances of living into adulthood (hence fertility is less valued), and proper medical abortion procedures are safe, effective, and widely available (Luker 1984: 1, 5). Also, technology may have a role in changing abortion back to a private decision. Technology already developed, for example, the so-called "morning-after pill," RU-486, may make the abortion debate moot. Such technologies and others, as they become available, may remove the abortion question from public debate.

Abortion as a Personal Decision

Understanding the abortion debate as a clash of worldviews does little to help individuals make personal moral decisions in particular cases. For that, we must review additional factors. We can use the values of freedom and well-being to assess *both* the life of the fetus and the life of the woman carrying it. Additionally, we can evaluate ancillary factors, including those that may be unique to given situations. Thus, we can ask whether a woman has good reasons to support her choice to abort or to carry her fetus to term. By "good reasons" I refer to evidence or predictive grounds that meet Lee's five criteria as described in chapter 2. A wide range of objective and subjective (though objectively measured) conditions might qualify as good reasons.

For example, some writers condone abortion when the woman's life is endangered by continuing the pregnancy. Why the preference for the woman's life over the fetus's? Because, adherents of this view answer, if people must make that hard choice, then take into account that the woman is a fully formed person, both biologically and socially. The fetus is neither. Thus, while considerations of welfare apply to both the woman and the fetus, considerations of the capacities for freedom, personal autonomy, informed judgment and choice only apply to the woman at the time a decision to abort is made.

Also, other people may depend on the woman—parents, a husband, siblings, and other children perhaps—while no person yet depends on the fetus in the same way, that is, within routinely patterned networks of social interaction and within sets of reciprocal obligations. Take into account, as well, society's investment in the woman which is considerable, while it has practically no investment in the fetus. Remember, too, that the woman may be pregnant not by her own voluntary actions but as a result of incest or rape. Finally, assess the chances that the woman might die during a difficult pregnancy leaving her baby, possibly prematurely born, without a mother to love and raise it; then, the mother's life has been lost and the baby's quality of life would be precarious from the outset.

Some writers condone abortion as morally right when the woman wishes an abortion and is very young, still a child herself; has not finished her education; cannot financially support a baby; has no spouse to help raise the baby; is not psychologically suited to be a nurturing mother; or is told by attending physicians that the fetus is defective and that the baby will be born with mental or physical disabilities.

Other reasons may also apply. Each individual case is unique and must be evaluated on its own merits. In the end, the woman must decide, weighing the facts of her situation and taking into account her own moral judgments and those of other people who matter to her.

In her decision to abort, ironically, a woman may in fact honor motherhood in her understanding of the overwhelming responsibilities of motherhood and in her desire to be a good mother, while realizing that she may not have at that time the resources—physical, psychological, or material—to be the mother she expects herself to be.

The moral issue of abortion is difficult because there are often good reasons from both the pro- and antiabortion viewpoints. The fetus's life, for example, is always a consideration that deserves some moral claim and the more developed it is, that is, the nearer it is to normal birth, the more consideration it ought to receive. Thus, a woman who is eight months pregnant ought to have more moral obligation to her fetus than a woman who is six weeks pregnant. Also a factor is the responsibility of the woman when her pregnancy resulted from her own autonomous and free choice. Like everyone else, she ought to hold herself accountable—and society ought to hold her accountable—for her own informed actions, but, this, too, is a prima facie, not an all-things-considered imperative. Finally, we can ask, as we did in the case of having the baby, if an abortion would have deleterious consequences for the freedom and well-being of the woman. For example, a woman might find it difficult, perhaps intolerable, to live with the knowledge that she had "killed her baby," if that is the meaning that abortion has for her.

One of the strongest correlations—in this case a negative correlation—found in the worldwide comparative study of cultures is between the severity of punishment for abortion in a society and parental acceptance of a child ($r = -.76$) (Rohner 1986: 110). That is, in societies where penalties for abortion are most severe, children are least likely to be loved and accepted after birth. Cold and rejecting parents damage their children. Thus, preventing a pregnant woman from having an abortion and forcing her to have a baby may be to deny that child the love and affection of its parents.

In any given case the well-being of the fetus and the freedom and well-being of the pregnant woman may be in sharp conflict. The consequences of such a clash may be that some reasons both for and against abortion are good reasons and cannot be refuted. Both sets of reasons may be objective and rational. Thus, in such cases being objective and rational may not result in a clear cut judgment that one ought to do one thing or another. Furthermore, as if the issue of abortion isn't already complicated enough, the prospective father's rights, responsibilities, freedom, and well-being have some legitimate claim to be considered in the decision to abort or give birth.

Clearly, there are complicated moral issues involved in the decision to abort or not. But whose decision ought it to be? Each case may burden the pregnant woman socially and psychologically, obviously affects the fetus she is carrying, and possibly burdens members of her family and the father. All of us as members of society and the human species have a right, if not the duty, to enter into the critical discourse about the morality of an action. But do we also have the right to interfere with the freedom and well-being of a pregnant woman in the name of the well-being of an as-yet-nonexistent person? As I write, American law says that we do not, especially in the early stages of pregnancy before the fetus can live on its own without heroic medical intervention, which occurs about the end of the second trimester of pregnancy.

Given the perplexities of the abortion debate and its link to the changing role of women in society, we can expect continued political debate and struggle about the abortion issue in the immediate future, until medical science and technology make the moral dilemma moot or until cultural definitions and attitudes toward the liberation of women change more fully. We can hope that such debate will be openmindedly aimed at enlightenment and carried out with civility, logical analysis, and attention to the relevant facts. What is clearly immoral is for the debate to become fanatical, with activists of either side dehumanizing and vilifying their opponents—or even murdering them.

If there were a need for more people in the world, that would be another good reason to support the moral claim of the antiabortion side of the argument. But there is no such need in the present, as we have seen, nor will there be in the near future according to our best population forecasts. In fact, the exact opposite is the case. There are too many people on Earth already and the current rate of population growth is too high to sustain even a modestly good life for all living humans in the future.

The Value of Nonhuman Forms of Life

Humans, of course, are not the only living things on Earth. What value, then, ought we humans to place on other forms of earthly life? The answer seems clear. Humans are—and ought to be—concerned about the welfare of the Earth's animals and plants. There are two, possibly three, reasons.

The first is simply that the welfare of human beings depends upon the welfare of many other forms of life. This is so well known that it hardly needs elaboration here. Humans depend upon plants for everything from shade and housing materials to clothes and food. They depend on plants, also, for one of the fundamental life processes on Earth: the photosynthesis of carbon dioxide and water into carbohydrates and oxygen. Humans depend upon animals for many things also, including food, clothing, companionship, and work of various kinds—from power and transportation to hunting and herding.

Thus, the evidence to support the value proposition that humans ought to be concerned about the welfare of other animals and plants flows, first, from enlightened self-interest. Those animals and plants on which human welfare depends ought to be allowed to flourish to some optimum point for their human uses. We ought to be less concerned about other animals and plants, for example, insects that damage food crops or carry disease and plants that poison grazing animals, and we may even want to eliminate them from particular environments. But even in such cases we need to proceed with caution, because our knowledge is limited and we may inadvertently destroy animals or plants for which future generations might find a use. We also need to proceed with caution to make as certain as possible that unintended consequences of our efforts don't damage human welfare, for example, unintentionally poisoning water supplies with pesticides.

This argument can be extended to all things that are of use to human beings, including nonliving things. That is, it can be generalized to encompass all of nature. For example, it can be used to support judgments to create and maintain unpolluted environments, stop wasteful use of natural resources, prevent destruction of arable land, and so on. Humans need soil, air, water, forests, grasslands, seas, the fauna, and the flora. Human "life moves afloat on a photosynthetic, nutritional biocurrent, with organic life in turn dependent on hydrologic, meteorologic, and geologic cycles." Life does not stop at our skin. It "is an affair of natural resources" (Rolston 1981: 127).

This argument is limited by being "humancentric." It relies on a view of all things as instrumental for the well-being of humankind. Going beyond humancentric reasons, we can find a second reason that justifies believing that humans ought to value the welfare of animals that is based upon their intrinsic worth. Louis G. Lombardi (1988), as we have seen, justifies the inherent worth of human beings by appealing to considerations of welfare and freedom as these derive from human capacities. If his argument is correct, then basic moral considerations ought to be extended to some degree to animals, because the features of human nature that lead to considerations of welfare and freedom are shared to some degree with other species.

Other animals are not moral beings and, thus, do not understand the difference between right and wrong, although some of them—dogs, cats, and horses, for example—certainly understand and respond to the approval and disapproval of their human companions. But it is beyond question to say that other animals share more or less the needs and desires of humans as physical beings. Many, if not most, animals share the capacities to feel thirst, hunger, and pain.

According to some writers, even plants can be included in that all life may have some claim on moral consideration. We do not cut down a tree, for example, without a reason. All living things are what Paul W. Taylor (1981) calls teleological centers of life. As such, they deserve some consideration and care.

But there are important differences. All living things—plants, animals, and humans—share vegetative capacities. Some—animals and humans—are also active and conscious. And some—humans—are also moral agents. Some beings, thus, can experience welfare and freedom in more ways than others. Therefore, they are due more moral consideration than others. Many animals, for example, cannot interact with us humans at the level of responsible agents (Lombardi 1988: 101). Moreover, distinctions among animals are justified as a basis for unequal treatment, if they are relevant to the treatment. For example, the "hopeless illiteracy of a chimpanzee is a fine reason not to admit it to Yale, but if we're about to strap it down and cut into its brain, the question isn't whether the chimp can read, but whether it can suffer" (Wright 1990: 27).

Some humans have responded to this argument or similar ones by becoming vegetarians, advocating animal rights, trying to prevent human cruelty to animals, or attempting to reduce any unnecessary animal suffering. Also, in general, such people destroy and take from plants and animals only what is necessary for their own survival and well-being and attempt to create conditions for the replacement of what they take.

A third argument is a cosmic one. Everything in the universe and on Earth, including everything living and nonliving, had a common origin in the exploding star of creation. We humans, therefore, share some degree of identity with everything in existence. Also, we do not know in a cosmic sense what this experiment in space, time, matter, and life is ultimately about and we do not know what the fate of the human species will be or what it ought to be. In such a state of ignorance, prudence may be the best policy when dealing with nature and with the life forms, the ecosystems, and the natural resources of the Earth.

However ignorant we are, humans nonetheless are the most conscious, most knowledgeable, and most powerful beings on Earth. As such, we have a moral obligation to be the guardians of the life-support systems of the Earth and protectors of all life: human, animal, and plant. Thus, the ideal of stewardship may be a good guide for human behavior, replacing and reusing what we can and avoiding gratuitous destruction of nature (Schnaiberg 1995).

Conclusion

In this chapter, I have tried to confront basic questions of life, its value and meanings, and, leaving religion and other supernatural beliefs aside, to give objective answers. I have appealed to the idea of humanity and to reason, to scientific and secular humanism. Like religion, humanism is a total worldview. Unlike religion, humanism is not theocentric but anthrocentric, and it seeks perfection—or as near to perfection as is humanly possible to get—in *this* world.

From this perspective, the purpose of human life begins with the struggle for life itself, for existence in this one real world. We ought to want to live because without life nothing else is possible in this world, nothing else matters. Thus, the quantity of life is the preeminent human value, both individual longevity and the total number of living human beings *in the long run* stretching into the indefinite future.

Beyond sheer existence, the purpose of human life includes seeking a life of high quality, that is, a good and meaningful life. But what is a good and meaningful life?

From these chapters on the ethical foundations of futures studies, we are justified in believing the following: A good and meaningful life is a life that exemplifies most fully in its living some combination of the core human values that lead to the freedom and welfare of human beings. Such values include concerns for life, health, personal security, economic security (but not enormous wealth), diligence, peace, justice, education, love and affection, family life and sexual behavior, respect for authority and knowledge, moderation and modesty, loyalty, courage, cooperation, honesty and truth, generosity, helpfulness, friendliness, trust and trustworthiness, receiving and giving dignity, individual autonomy constrained only by the necessities of group living and genuine concerns for fair play and a fair distribution of freedom and well-being for all, benevolence toward others, and self-fulfillment. Lives that embody these values—or most of them—are lives of high quality and tend to maximize individual satisfaction and happiness as well as social harmony.

People live best who live for others as well as for themselves. Thus, embracing these values means wanting them for others as well as one-self. In the case of life, health, economic security, justice, and education, for example, this must be stated, because at least in the short run it appears that we could achieve these things for ourselves while denying them to others. But for many other values, the element of sharing is a part of the definition of the value itself. For example, being generous, cooperative, helpful, forgiving, friendly, and loving contain within them the element of caring interaction with other people.

The average length of human life has increased over the past 300 years and many people in the more developed parts of the world now live relatively long lives. But even though recent decades have seen increased longevity in the less developed countries, life expectancies remain unequal when comparing countries. People in some countries can expect to live no more than forty-five or fifty years on average, while people in other countries can expect to live well into their mid-seventies and early eighties.

Also, the inequality of life expectancy within a country may be nearly as great as that among countries. Underprivileged subpopulations, even in economically advanced countries such as the United States, have life expectancies lower than others within the same country.

Inequalities in life expectancies constitute one of the most pressing moral problems of our day, because life is the supreme human value and because we have the knowledge, the technologies, and the organizational capacities to add years to the lives of disadvantaged peoples everywhere, both at home in our own countries and throughout the world.

In addition to the possibility of raising minimum levels of life expectancy for the world's disadvantaged peoples, we can expect, with continued research and development, new technologies to increase life expectancy still further and even to extend the current limits on the human life span. Two hundred years from now, it might be possible to extend human lives up to 180 years with the added years being years of vigor and good health.

Throughout the long period of human development, many of the same factors that contributed to increasing individual longevity also contributed to increasing the total size of the human population. These two accomplishments may be among the greatest achievements of the human race and, certainly, are cause for celebration.

They are, however, no cause for complacency. For these two good things may no longer be positively correlated. They now appear to be increasingly at odds, with continued increases in population growth threatening the life-sustaining capacities of the Earth and the conditions that permit long lives for individuals. If population growth is not curtailed, then it is probable that human suffering and misery will increase and human lives will become more brutish and short.

I argued that, although there is no need for panic, there is an immediate need to consider action to restrain the rate of population growth. We are justified in believing that the quantity and quality of human life are best served in the long term by concentrating our efforts on increasing the length of individual human lives for all people on Earth. To achieve this, additional changes in human reproductive values may be necessary (see chapter 6).

On the face of it, abortion is antilife. It is morally wrong. But a decision to abort or not is not that simple, all things considered, because there are at least two lives involved, not only the life of the fetus but also the life of the pregnant woman. There are often sound, objective reasons for deciding both for and against the moral rightness of abortion. Thus, it is a tough moral choice in which any decision may violate some reasonable moral judgment. In any event, the debate is not helped by extremists or fanatics from either side. Rather, it invites civil exchange of ideas and efforts to understand the legitimacy of the moral judgments on *both* sides. Both "pro-choice" and "pro-life" activists might find common ground working together to promote family planning and to prevent unwanted pregnancies, thereby eliminating the need for an abortion decision.

Humans ought to value and protect nonhuman forms of life, because (1) the welfare of humans depends in part on the welfare of many animals and plants; (2) some of the capacities of human nature that lead to considerations of freedom and well-being apply also to animals (e.g., they can experience suffering) and even to plants (e.g., in some sense they struggle to live); and (3) humans' cosmic ignorance ought to lead to prudent (nondestructive) behavior when it comes to other life forms and the life-sustaining capacities of the planet. We do not know all the consequences of our present acts and we do not know what humans might need in the future that we don't think we need now.

In the next, and final, chapter, I raise the question of what human values ought to be changed as the human community enters the twenty-first century. Such values are beacons that can guide the human community into the future and that help futurists shed light on the relative desirability of different images of the future. Also, I ask why the present generation ought to care about the freedom and welfare of future generations.

6

What Human Values Ought to be Changed?

Introduction

In this chapter, I conclude the discussion of human values that we began with the utopian visions of Thomas More. I do so by considering the possibility that some human values ought to be changed. If you recall, in chapter 4, I suggested that the human future may depend on two contradictory capacities, recognizing and abiding by most universal human values and continuing to make changes in other values in response to changing conditions.

These changing conditions include the recent rapid growth of the Earth's human population, the increase in the scale and intensity of human interaction and interdependence to encompass the globe, and threats to the life-sustaining capacities of the Earth from human behavior. In view of such changes, are there human values—however serviceable they may have been in the past—that ought to be changed? Are there any human values and customary practices based on them that today are outmoded, appropriate for past conditions but dysfunctional for present and future conditions? Are there more appropriate values that ought to replace them? In contrary cases, are there some long-held universal values that ought to be strengthened and held even more strongly in the future? The answers may be yes.

We'll discuss some candidates for change in this chapter: the values of the length of individual lives, reproduction, great wealth vs. sufficiency, women's lives, aggression and violence vs. peace, ethnocentrism vs. a world moral community, and, finally, the value of caring about future generations.

I propose that the coming global society may succeed only if it also becomes an inclusive moral community that embraces the world, a global community where all people have at least some degree of caring for the freedom and welfare of all other people everywhere and where no peoples are demonized and dehumanized, where no human groups are defined as the alien "Other."

Moreover, a successful human future may also require that presently living generations learn how to value the well-being of future generations. They may have to learn to care and to make present sacrifices for people not yet living, to act in ways that appear, at least on the surface, to be contrary to their own immediate self-interest. Thus, I conclude this chapter by trying to answer these questions: What obligations do present people have to future generations? If there are any such obligations, are they as great as present obligations to past generations? Why should present people care about future people?

The Value of the Length of Individual Lives

Although all human societies already reinforce the value of the length of individual human lives, we humans ought to consider placing still greater value on human life in this sense. We ought to expand the preeiminent human value so that all persons born anywhere on Earth have an equal right and opportunity to live out their full life spans as it is defined by the technological limits of the time and within the limits of maintaining an acceptable quality of life.

Since it was the burden of chapter 5 to justify belief in the fundamental importance of the length of human lives, I will not elaborate this proposal here.

The Contingent Value of Reproduction

Also, we have already discussed reasons to change human reproductive values. They have already changed radically in many countries and ought to change everywhere toward valuing low birth rates to the point of no more than an average of one child per person so as to achieve, eventually, near zero-population growth. This is now an old story, as we all know, its most famous author being Thomas Robert Malthus who published *An Essay on the Principle of Population as it Affects Future Improvement of Society, with Remarks on the Speculations of Mr. Godwin, M. Condorcet, and Other Writers* in 1798. But it must be told again and again if we humans are to achieve a good chance for a long and good life for every baby that is born: It is no longer a positive contribution to human welfare to "increase and multiply."

Some effective means of birth control ought to be made available to women everywhere. As many as 100 million women in the world already want such services but have no access to them. Other women ought to be taught how and why they ought to use them. Some people—both men and women—still need to be taught that children are not simply facts of nature nor gifts of God, but rather the consequences of their own acts that can be—and ought to be—regulated by their own choices. Then, women of every society and every social class could plan if and when to have a child.

The use of coercion to enforce a population policy, whatever its purpose, of course, is immoral and ought to be avoided. Some excesses, including compulsory sterilization and forced abortions, have occurred in recent years in China, for example, which have marred its efforts to reduce fertility. Obviously, such brutal actions violate norms of freedom. Education, collaboration, voluntary choice, and allowance for diversity are the only moral solutions. Additionally, we must recognize that any social policy, including policy regarding reproductive values, may turn out to be misguided.

To the extent to which men's virility and status are linked to having a large number of children, we can work to change these beliefs and values by means of critical discourse. To the extent that women's status is viewed as properly being no more than that of a breeder and caretaker of children, we can raise questions about the validity of the beliefs and values that support such a view in relation to alternative views of equal opportunity for careers and self-realization for both men and women.

The greatest amount of human life, in the sense of more humans having lived totally in the long run, may be achieved only by controlling the total human population size now and in the future so that human and other forms of life will be sustained on Earth for hundreds of thousands of years more, perhaps indefinitely until the end of time. Thus, taking a long view, limiting births on the one hand and extending the lives of living persons on the other combine to produce the greatest possible quantity of human life in terms of total number of years of human lives lived.

We are justified in believing that people's values can change from high to low ideal conceptions of human fertility, because they have already done so for many people in the developed world who have passed through the demographic transition and they are so changing elsewhere as well. Just as many people in economically advanced societies have learned to curb the millennia-old human craving for fat, which was functional under conditions of scarcity but which under conditions of constant availability results in the deadly clogging of human arteries, it would be beneficial to learn to change our reproductive behavior. If reason is to prevail, we must look at the facts and our presumptively true predictions of future disasters resulting from continued rapid growth in the Earth's human population and engage people everywhere in considering them.

Let us, however, add an important proviso. Obviously, there must exist a minimum number of living people in the world for the human species to continue to survive. As far as our understanding of present human reproductive behavior goes and as far as presumptively true predictions of future population growth indicate, we ought to reduce population growth in the near future for the long-term advancement of freedom and welfare of members of the human species.

But what if our understanding is wrong and our predictions turn out to be terminally false? What if some dreadful disease, natural disaster, social chaos and war, or presently unimaginable development kills off people by the hundreds of millions and threatens the very survival of the human species? What if something like a trend toward smaller sperm counts turns out to be true and accelerates to the point of reducing pregnancies dramatically below replacement levels? Then, of course, values supporting high fertility might once again become a positive contribution to human well-being, and women, under those circumstances, might once again be encouraged rightly to engage in behavior resulting in high fertility.

The decision to promote zero population growth or not, thus, is contingent. Yet it is not a matter of mere individual preference. Nor is it a matter relative to the diversity of cultural traditions either. It is, rather, a matter of evidence, predictive grounds, and objective value judgments affecting the well-being both of individuals and of all of humanity.

The Value of Sufficiency

Curbing wasteful consumption in the economically advanced societies may be as important for a successful human future as curbing birth rates and population growth in the less developed societies (Arizpe et al. 1994: 5). To take just one example, in 1990 the North (Europe, the former Soviet Union, and North America) with only one-fifth of the world population produced two-thirds of the total carbon emissions which, of course, contribute to global warming. Per capita emissions in the North are six or seven times greater than in the rest of the world (Lutz 1994a: 56–57). Thus, global warming is a problem of high consumption per capita in some parts of the world as well as one of sheer numbers of people in others.

As Garrett Hardin (1993: 202) reminds us, the impact of any group or nation on the environment is a consequence not only of its population size, but also of its per capita affluence, as measured by its level of consumption, and of the environmental damage that is done by the technologies it employs in supplying that consumption.

Although the greater consumption of the developed countries may be partly justified and offset by their greater contributions to future generations through the empowerment provided by their scientific and technological achievements, waste and consumption of material goods for their own sakes are impossible to justify morally, especially if they contribute to environmental degradation.

The human values of frugality, saving, avoiding waste and excess, eschewing indulgence, abstaining from random and pointless destruction, and sharing with others are old and widely held. Reexamining them today from the perspective of the goals of creating a sustainable society and contributing to the well-being of future generations, we find that they remain serviceable and lead to values of moderation and material sufficiency.

Great material wealth is not necessary for long and happy lives. In fact, it can be detrimental if it allows overindulgence and excess. Gary Gappert (1979, 1982) describes a possible "Emersonian future" for economically advanced societies in which the human potential movement will flourish, acceptable alternatives to traditional work will exist, conspicuous consumption and waste will not be tolerated, and educational opportunities will be broadened. In fact, he believes that in American society a transition to a "post-affluent" society may already be underway.

In any event, for the sake of a flourishing human future, a reduction in population growth in poor countries ought to go hand in hand with a reduction in the growth of per capita consumption among affluent groups and nations (Arizpe and Veláquez 1994).

The Value of Women's Lives

The Current Status of Women

Both in absolute terms and relative to men, the status of women has improved in several ways during the last few decades. Women have made gains with respect to health and education nearly everywhere, although more so in some regions than others. They have made gains, too, in employment in some regions, such as Latin America and the Caribbean (especially in urban areas) and in Eastern and Southeastern Asia. There have been some increases, too, in women's participation in governments, in parliaments for example, and in business at middle management levels, although their representation remains well below that of men. As we saw in chapter 5, nearly everywhere, women's life expectancy exceeds that of men at every age. Moreover, between 1970 and 1990, women's life expectancy at birth increased faster than men's in every region in the world (United Nations 1991: 55).

Despite these improvements in their status, the world's women remain disadvantaged compared to men, in some regions severely so. For example, in 1970 the number of illiterate women was 543 million. By 1985, it rose to 597 million. For men, the comparable numbers are 348 and 352 million (United Nations 1991: 1). Thus, in 1985 there were 245 million more illiterate women than men in the world. In formal schooling, women still lag behind men in many regions, even in primary and secondary education, for example, in Southern Asia and sub-Saharan Africa.

Everywhere, the workplace tends to be segregated by sex, with women being more likely to fill clerical, sales, domestic service, teaching, caregiving, and subsistence agricultural positions. Men, in contrast, tend to work in manufacturing, transport, management, administration, and politics. Within industries, women tend to fill the lower-level positions. In education, women predominate as teachers at the lower grades while men predominate as professors at institutions of higher education. In the home and in the fields, women's work may be unrecognized and unpaid (United Nations 1991).

Worldwide, women hold only between 10 and 20 percent of managerial and administrative jobs and less than 20 percent of the manufacturing jobs. Women's nonagricultural wages average 30 to 40 percent lower than men's, with some countries reaching nearly 50 percent lower, and the gap may not be narrowing substantially (United Nations 1991: 5). When it comes to the top ranks of power, policy and decision making, women are barely visible. They account for less than five percent of "the world's heads of state, heads of major corporations and top positions in international organizations." Even in the United States, where women are relatively well-off compared to men, only two of the top 1,000 corporations are headed by women (United Nations 1991: 6, 5).

In many countries, girls and women receive less nutrition, health care, and other support compared to males. In a few countries, some widows are still burned to death, dowry deaths still occur, and female infanticide may be still practiced in some rural areas. Moreover, abortion of female fetuses may be on the rise. For example, "of 8,000 abortions in Bombay after parents learned the sex of the foetus through amniocentesis, only one would have been a boy" (United Nations 1991: 11, 1). In chapter 2, we have already considered systematic female genital mutilation. In addition, rape is common as a weapon of war, as in Bosnia; forced prostitution exists, as among Burmese women in Thailand; and in some countries violence against women, including wife beating, is both accepted and pervasive. These and most other sex discriminations, of course, derive from cultural values and practices that often reflect local traditions and religious beliefs.

According to the American Civil Liberties Union and the Human Rights Watch in a report they issued December 1993, the United States is in violation of Article 26 of the International Covenant on Civil and Political Rights. American women, the report says, face systematic and entrenched discrimination in conditions of employment, compensation, education, and access to occupations.

The Liberation of Women

International efforts aimed at women's equality have a long history, going back at least to the 1946 United Nations Commission on the Status of Women. More recently, in 1979, the U.N. General Assembly adopted the Convention on Elimination of All Forms of Discrimination against Women. It became an international treaty on September 3, 1981 after it had been ratified by twenty countries. By June 1, 1990, 102 states had ratified or acceded to it and fourteen others had signed but not ratified it. Forty-five states, however, had neither signed nor acceded to it. Even more recently, in 1985, 157 countries approved The Nairobi Forward-looking Strategies for the Advancement of Women (United Nations 1991).

These two documents set the international agenda for policies to create equality and freedom for women. The Convention, for example, calls for women's basic rights and freedoms: the abolition of women's slavery and prostitution; the rights to vote and hold political office; the right to change or retain their nationality and that of their children; equal access to quality education in all subjects and at all levels; equal employment opportunities, promotion, vocational training, job security, benefits, and equal pay for work of equal value; adequate health services, including family planning; equal access to financial credit; the right to participate in recreational and cultural activities; equal rights to choose a spouse; and so on (United Nations 1991: 115). The Nairobi Strategies document calls on governments to play key roles in achieving these aims through specific actions.

We must recognize, however, that achieving equality may not always benefit women. In the economically advanced societies, for example, compared to women, men are more likely to commit suicide, to be victims of violent crime, to hold hazardous jobs, to die in wars, to be homeless, and to be in prison (Farrell 1993). With equality, women may end up less well off than they are now, unless, of course, equality is achieved by reducing the incidence of these personal and social ills among men rather than by increasing them among women. Each is at least to some extent preventable, and gender equality, if achieved in this way, would benefit men, women and the entire society.

Why Should Women be Liberated?

Values concerning the status of women ought to be changed everywhere on Earth to create opportunities for women to choose and to pursue meaningful lives equal to those of men. There are several reasons that provide evidence for this value proposition.

First, women as members of the human race deserve equal treatment and equal opportunities with men. Considerations of justice lead to the conclusion that women have the same rights and responsibilities as men do. Arguments supporting the morality of male privileges and dominance and of female deprivations and submission, although often supported by local or national custom and religion, simply cannot be justified objectively and rationally. To the contrary, arguments supporting equality for members of both sexes can be so supported, and, indeed, they are no different from those that support equality of opportunity for members of different races, religions, and ethnic groups. They have been affirmed, as we have seen, in both national laws and international agreements.

Second, some of the predictable consequences of the liberation of women would be beneficial for all humankind, both for women and men. The most obvious and probably most important would be to slow population growth. If women everywhere were to have equal opportunities to pursue occupational careers and activities of their own choice, then they could be freed from lifetimes devoted primarily to the cycle of pregnancy, the risks of childbirth, and caring for small children. Such freedom would result in lower fertility rates. Generally, both within and among regions, where women's status is lowest and most miserable, fertility rates are highest.

The liberation of women would reduce fertility levels in two ways.

1. It would allow women in less developed areas to implement the reproductive goals that they already have to reduce the number of their childbirths. For example, we know from the World Fertility Survey that most women in many developing countries do not want to have any more children. Yet, because of the cost, inaccessibility or custom, they are not using any method of birth control (United Nations 1991: 61).

2. Allowing and encouraging women to pursue life goals and careers other than motherhood and child care would reduce their fertility levels still further. As more and more women chose their own educational programs and occupational careers on an equal basis with men, many of them would delay the age at which they get married, choose to have their first child at a later age, stay single or divorce their husbands more often, and aim to have totally fewer children in their lifetimes than they would under present conditions.

If policies leading to the liberation of women did result in signficant declines in fertility levels, then that alone would seem justification enough for pursuing them. But there may be a variety of additional benefits as well. Healthier women are more likely to have full-term pregnancies and strong children, getting the immediate next generation off to a better start. Better-educated women could improve sanitation and nutrition for the child or two that they did have and for their husbands. Healthier and better educated women would make better and more productive workers, help reduce poverty, have the knowledge to understand both the need for and the effective methods of environmental protection, and give better care and education to their children. All of these benefits appear to be dual in nature, helping both present and future people.

The Changing Status of Women and the Need for Compassion

Since women are now better off in the more developed regions than they are in the less developed regions, would worldwide efforts to liberate women be a form of ethnocentric bias and cultural imperialism? Would it simply be yet another example of the mostly Western world forcing its own values and policies on third world peoples? That has been the charge, for example, made by some critics of mainstream feminist theory. Some authors condemn feminist criticisms of such cultural practices as veiling and female circumcision as being "neocolonialist."

Such criticisms come partly from postmodern writers who, as we have seen, tend to reject universalist or global ethical systems and argue that cultures and societies cannot be meaningfully judged on the same scale of values. They can, according to this view, only be judged in their own terms, that is, by their own conventions, customs, and traditions (Abaza and Stauch 1988; Barrett and McInstosh 1985; Moghadam 1994).

We have already reviewed the errors in such views, the mistaken dogmas of both cognitive and ethical relativism, and the illogical jump from the "is" of the factual observations of cultural and value diversity to the conclusion that there "ought" to be such diversity. What I have tried to show is that being objective is not absolutism, that testing cultural values is to question them—which is the very opposite of ethnocentrism (i.e., accepting one's own group's values uncritically). Moreover, the women from developing countries who attended the Fourth World Conference on Women in Beijing in 1995 "dismissed as nonsense the criticism of those who say that the agenda of the meeting was created by and for Western feminists" (*New York Times*, 10 September 1995: E1).

Yet the charges of ethnocentrism and the other critiques of the feminist program may point to the need for understanding and compassion as people act to produce what they consider to be benefical changes in women's lives. They ought to recognize that human societies everywhere are already in various stages of a worldwide revolution concerning the status of women and the role of motherhood and that this revolution is causing immediate distress as well as creating opportunities for the future.

Clearly, change leaders ought to move forward not as militant extremists secure in the certainty of their beliefs, but as prudent and thoughtful people open-mindedly testing their beliefs and willing to change them if necessary. Some men and women, even in economically advanced societies, feel threatened by the changing status of women. Some women, as we saw in chapter 5 in the discussion of abortion, are outraged by what they perceive as the degradation of their own life plans of wife and mother. A social and moral chasm has developed between women who have options outside the family and women who do not. The sanctity of life and of the family, in the eyes of some men and women, may be at stake as the status of women changes (Luker 1984).

Thus, consideration ought to be given not only to the liberation of women so that they can adopt new, powerful, and prestigious roles in society, but also to honoring the traditional roles that women have played and that some women are still playing. We do not know what functions the family may have in the future, the possible roles of men and women in it, the future meaning of parenthood and motherhood, and how babies and young children will be loved and nurtured. We do know that these things are fundamentally important in human development. The liberation of women might mean that these necessary tasks of creating and educating new members of human society will be done more equitably and effectively, to the benefit of both young and old and of men and women. It would be sad if it meant that they would be done worse in the future than they now are and that the roles of wife and mother—or, more generally, spouse and parent—were devalued.

In sum, although the world's women have experienced considerable gains over the last few decades, they remain more or less disadvantaged compared to men with respect to many aspects of life, from illiteracy and employment to top decision-making positions. Efforts ought to be made to give women an equal chance with men to have meaningful lives and careers of their own choosing, not only for the benefit of women themselves but also for the benefit of all humankind, for the double benefit of enhancing the well-being of both present and future generations.

The Value of Peace

During most of human existence, the Earth's population, as we saw in chapter 5, was never larger than 10 million people. Moreover, groups in different parts of the Earth were relatively isolated and independent with no means of rapid communication and transportation, and people had very low levels of weapons technologies. Under such conditions, individual and collective violence against members of other groups never threatened the freedom and welfare of the whole human race.

But the situation has changed. With the emergence of an interdependent world, with modern technologies of communiction, transportation, and destruction, with a total population of more than 5.5 billion and still growing rapidly, and with the consequences of human behavior affecting the life-sustaining capacities of the planet itself, humans are today all linked together. Moreover, current technological developments are increasing the scope and frequency of social interaction and making the global society more intensely interknit every day. Writing from a Birmingham jail, Martin Luther King (1964: 79) got it right, not only for Americans of his time, but for all of the Earth's people today, in our time: "We are caught in an inescapable network of mutuality, tied in a single garment of destiny. Whatever affects one directly, affects all indirectly."

Human beings everywhere are increasingly chained to a common fate. Today, violence against other groups can threaten the freedom and well-being of us all. It can threaten the survival of the entire human race. Moreover, the twentieth century, one of the most violent, bloody, and warring centuries in history, has culminated in the growing realization that modern weapons of war are so vastly destructive that they cannot be used successfully in an instrumental way. They have made large-scale war a case of everybody loses, vanquished and victor alike (Burk 1995).

There are several ways to encourage the reduction of aggression and violence. One is to work toward changing the nearly universal, culturally sanctioned emphasis on manliness in the sense of toughness, aggressiveness, and stoicism. Gilmore (1990) says rightly that these ideals of manhood under certain environmental conditions have been factors in successful societal adaptation and community survival. Today, though, they are largely misdirected, given the growth of global interdependency and the mutual payoffs of global cooperation.

There will remain room for manliness in the future, if it's "societal nurturance" function is redirected away from aggression, hostility, and destruction (and possibly from toughness and stoicism too) and toward the constructive ends of cooperation and caring for others on both local and global levels. For the majority of men, protecting people and providing security could come to mean not bloody fighting, but peaceful negotiation, compromise, and the fulfillment of agreements.

Yet, realistically, we must recognize that there are hostile people who will not play by the rules of treating other people with dignity and respect and there are people who will not abide the necessary self-constraints to allow other people their fair share of freedom and welfare. Such people ought not to be allowed to control the human agenda for the future. Since in an interdependent global world, we cannot ignore them, they must be taught humanity's core values and how to behave according to them.

If they cannot or will not learn and if they engage in aggressive and violent behavior aimed at harming others, then they must be removed from society as sociopaths, that is, people "who cannot respond to moral imperatives" and "are rightly judged to be mentally defective" (Ferkiss 1974: 121). They must be put where they can do no harm. If force is required to do this, then so be it. There "are situations where violence and evil can only be countered by violence" (Ferkiss 1974: 273). It ought to be as little as possible but as much as necessary. Also, it ought to be exercised legitimately, sanctioned by democratic institutions and by due process of law, and carried out competently.

Even more important, of course, are mechanisms for the control of aggressive and violent behavior of collectivites, such as states, on the world scene. The values of peace, international cooperation, and collective security need to be strengthened, legitimated by international law, and institutionalized through international organizations such as the United Nations. Aggressive and coercive collective behavior ought not to receive respect and it ought not to be allowed to flourish. We don't have to resign ourselves to the gloomy forecasts of the future that foresee inevitable world conflicts, such as Samuel P. Huntington's (1993) vision of a coming clash of European, Islamic, and Confucian civilizations (which, incidentally, he bases in part on the false assumption of irreconcilable differences in human values).

James Burk (1995) sees some hope of limiting and preventing the use of armed force on the world stage in three current trends of international institution building. The first is the trend in international law. For example, since the Partial Test Ban Treaty of 1963, sixteen other treaties that limit the use of nuclear, biological, or chemical weapons have been negotiated and ratified. Some are legally binding, multilateral agreements, such as the Nuclear Non-Proliferation Treaty of 1968, the Biological

Weapons Convention of 1972, the Inhumane Weapons Convention of 1981, the Treaty on Open Skies of 1992, and the Chemical Weapons Convention of 1993. These and many other initiatives, including attempts in the United Nations General Assembly to ban nuclear weapons completely, are indications of a recognition of an international common interest in the reduction of state violence. An emerging moral consensus, a developing customary law, and an increasing international cooperation all aim to prevent the use of weapons of mass destruction.

The second is the increase in number and density of multinational institutions dedicated to the collective control of armed conflict. Such institutions include the International Committee of the Red Cross that has worked to protect people from violent atrocities of their own governments by invoking human rights law. They also include various agencies of the United Nations, for example, the General Assembly resolutions of December 1960 precipitated by the French atrocities in Algeria. They include, too, the increased attention given to war and human rights abuses, both by the mass media (e.g., CNN's role in publicizing the massacre of the Kurds) and human rights monitoring organizations (e.g., Helsinki Watch and Amnesty International). Today, large-scale atrocities receive worldwide attention and the moral condemnation of the emerging international community.

Additionally, they include multinational peacekeeping efforts under the banner of the United Nations. During the cold war, there were fiften UN peacekeeping missions. Since then, between 1989 and 1994, there were twenty-five (Ratner 1995). Although the results of some of these efforts have been mixed, they nonetheless are indications of a growing multinational consciousness about the importance of keeping the peace and a willingness to make some serious attempts to do so. They show "how states may come together to identify a common interest in limiting the use of armed force in intrastate conflicts" (Burk 1995: 18).

The third trend in relevant international institution building is the continuing effort of world powers and international agencies to encourage the spread of democracy. Although there is no guarantee that the historical correlation will continue into the future, the past record shows that democracies tend not to wage war on one another. Moreover, the more democratic a state is, the more likely it is to reach a negotiated peace in an early phase of conflict (Burk 1995). Thus, the more polities that are democratic, the more likely that both interstate and intrastate war will be avoided and that peaceful cooperation and conflict resolution will prevail.

Although we have a long way to go before we have created a world community that is capable of preventing all armed conflict and adjudicating a just peace among the various peoples of the world, there are, as the above examples illustrate, efforts being made by many different parts of the international community to achieve this goal. There is a growing understanding that international cooperation and peace can create a situation in which everybody wins and that attempting to reduce aggression and violence is the morally right thing to do.

For some time to come, there may be a continuing need for some aggressive, tough, and stoic behavior among the future local police and global peacekeeping forces whose legitimate job it would be to prevent aggression. They would use deadly force, however, only after informal controls and nonviolent efforts to maintain order and personal safety, keep the peace, and achieve compromise had failed. Like today's United Nations' blue-helmeted "peace soldiers," their chief skills would be diplomatic.

The Value of a World Moral Community

At least part of the explanation of why people systematically treat some people decently and other people abominably is to be found in the existence of ethnocentrism, including people's conceptions of the boundaries of social groups and of their membership and identification with them. Perceptions of "ingroups" and "outgroups" and prescriptions about how members of each ought to be treated are universal. In fact, who is to be counted as another human being and therefore deserving of our respect is frequently limited to ingroup members and special trading partners. Outgroup members are frequently stigmatized and treated like nonhuman "others," not worthy of respect or dignity. Us vs. Them defines the civilized vs. the wild brutes, the good people vs. the barbarians (Davies et al. 1993). Where mutual patterns of revenge and raiding exist, then killing, kidnapping, stealing, and destroying property often occur.

This is not to say that physical violence does not occur among members of the same group or even among members of the same family. It obviously does and not infrequently. But such within-group violence does not have the same kind of legitimacy and righteous justification, calculated planning, cultural support, and systematic hostility about it as does between-group violence. Moreover, within-group violence is aimed at some unique individual and specific behavior, while between-group violence is aimed at an entire class or category of people.

For most of human existence, people's memberships in relatively small groups defined the limits of their duties and obligations to others. What was valued was not owed to others generally, but was owed specifically to particular other people within one's ingroups, members of one's family, extended kin group, village, and to a lesser extent trading groups. Groups could survive, and often could only survive, by exchanging their children with neighboring groups as marriage partners, thereby providing links of mutual caring and hostages intended to encourage intergroup peace and cooperation. Or, if such peaceful relations broke down, they treated members of outgroups as enemies, which may have occurred much more frequently during the later Neolithic when some writers believe that the increase in numbers of people began to press on the carrying capacity of the land (Carneiro 1978: 210).

We in the modern world have many group memberships and identities. We belong to many overlapping groups at different levels of social scale. We belong to neighborhoods, to towns or cities, to subnational regions (e.g., states in the United States), to countries, to supranational regions (e.g., Europe), and to the human species as a whole. For example, some of us are simultaneously Woodward Parkites (a neighborhood), Fresnans, Californians, Far Westerners, citizens of the United States, North Americans, and human beings—and that is not to mention the voluntary, business, or union organizations or the occupational, age-sex, familial or other groups to which we belong.

Studies of race and ethnicity, religion, social class, the corporation, and especially the nation-state show that individuals can develop strong emotional allegiances, loyalties, and emblematic identities based on their memberships in or their attachments to large-scale collectivities, just as they can to small groups (Bell and Freeman 1974). In fact, in today's world the nation-state is the preeminent institution demanding the highest loyalty of its citizens and we are all familiar with the intense feelings of patriotism it can engender. If people are capable of creating bonds of belongingness and identity with other people through such large-scale units as nation-states, then they are also capable of expanding these bonds still further to the global community of humanity.

As a French social scientist (Varenne 1977: 231) found when he studied an American community some years ago, many modern people already see themselves as human beings first and foremost. It is their deepest and most universal reality. They realize that all people, under their apparent diversity, are human beings and thus there is a fundamental unity among them. Indeed, we are now witnessing not only the increase in the scale of society to the global level, but also the emergence of a global consciousness among many individuals.

Even states are capable of forming international communities that develop collective identities, loyalty, common interests, and feelings of solidarity. Alexander Wendt (1994), for example, argues that self-interested motivated power struggles and wars are not the necessary relationships among states. Rather, states have common interests, shared threats (e.g., fears of an environmental catastrophe), and economic interdependencies. Moreover, different states interact along many different dimensions, not to mention the people-to-people and institution-to-institution interactions involving a variety of organizations from universities to multinational corporations (Burk 1995). NATO and the European Union are current examples.

Who ought to be included in our largest human community of concern today and in the future? If the trends toward a global society and toward human behaviors that have global effects continue, then the answer is: Every human being on Earth. Expanding our community of moral concern, of course, is not so much a matter of changing our values as it is a matter of enlarging the scope of application of those values.

Yet, even then, we would still owe our highest priorities to ourselves, because our sense of self-worth and self-interest gives us purpose and a basis for cooperating with others. Next, we would still owe a high priority to our small family circle of loved ones, because they fulfill our needs for passion, intimacy, and commitment. We would still owe a special debt of concern, too, to our close friends, neighbors, co-workers, and the small communities in which we live, because they can enrich our lives with a network of face-to-face mutual caring. After that, our priorities ought to include an ever widening circle of concern, not only encompassing other people of our nationality, our social class, our race, or our religion, but eventually all members of the human species. For all of our fates are ultimately linked together. Moreover, every human being both deserves an equal opportunity to have freedom and well-being and has a responsibility to help maintain such equal opportunity for all. Every human being counts as a person.

We know from psychological research that individuals "favor the group that offers them a positive social identity." Thus, individuals allocate outcomes in favor of their "own group members and not in favor of members of outgroups. This favoritism is present even when the difference between in- and outgroup is based on irrelevant input criteria, such as having different colors of caps" (Vermunt and Steensma 1991: 8).

This favoritism may be overcome, however, by at least two factors. One is giving people the responsibility and the motivation to care for others, because such caring people are not inclined to exclude others from receiving their fair shares. Another is by building social networks across existing group boundaries, because such networks tend to reduce behavior that excludes others. Moreover, from other research (Lerner 1980: 189) we know that, generally, people are not out simply for all that they can get for themselves. On the contrary, although they care about what they consider they deserve for themselves first, they are concerned also about justice for others (as we saw in chapter 4).

A possible model for defining the relationship between the self and society can be found in Indian culture. It is there conceived more as a reinforcing unity or symbiotic relationship rather than as divided into separate and opposing entities as in most Western thought. Most Indian philosophical and religious traditions include the value of service to others as a way of achieving the ultimate good. They view the whole of humanity as interrelated and incorporate the belief that the universe, too, is one's relation. In the Upanishadic doctrine of ever-expanding ego or self, for example, a person begins with concern for one's own self, gradually expands one's ego to encompass one's community, and ultimately embraces even the entire world (Sinha 1984: 450).

The long-term trend toward an increase in the scale of society may continue to encourage the expansion of the community of moral concern. Various possible future political arrangements may support it. Global unification, if and when it comes, may be based on strong centralizing institutions. More likely, it may correspond to a loose confederation rather than a strong unitary state. In either case, free and open discussion, full participation of all parties, and democratic decision making are the only answers to lasting unity.

The Basque nationalists, for example, have an image of the future that includes "the disintegration of the European historical states, including even those of such long tradition as France, and their substitution by a united Europe based on ethnic-linguistic-historical fatherlands or regions rather than states, reversing the process of national unification that took place through the last few centuries" (Blasco 1974: 370). Such an erosion of the authority of the nation-state combined with generally smaller-scale, semiautonomous, and socially inclusive units banded together in a supranational democratic federation of global scale may prove to be a viable alternative for the future political organization of the entire Earth.

In any event, whatever its importance in the present, we do not have to believe that the nation-state will be around forever as the most dominant and demanding political organization in our lives. As Karl W. Deutsch (1963) says, human beings existed long before nation-states did and they probably will exist long after them.

Given the human barbarities that exist in the world today, the horrible things that human beings have done and are doing to each other in the name of one group allegiance or another, this image of a future world as a moral community may be highly improbable. Indeed, creating a global society not of aggression and violence, but of peace and law, human dignity, mutual caring, civil discourse and compromise about the appropriateness of various core values, and cooperative collective action to achieve freedom and well-being is a herculean task.

Yet it may not be enough. In addition, a thriving human future may depend on humans expanding their community of moral concern still wider to include not only all presently existing humanity, but also generations of people into the future. It may depend on present humans making sacrifices for future generations.

The Value of Caring About Future Generations

When asked to make sacrifices for future generations, some members of the present generation may reject the request with the retort, "What have future generations ever done for me?" They have a point, of course, because the usual motivations for cooperation and mutual caring among people, such as reciprocity and exchange, are absent. A present sacrifice for the well-being of future people appears to be a one-way street. Obviously, people who will live 500 or 1,000 years from now can do little or nothing of material worth for present people who, by then, will be long dead.

Confronting such a view, how do futurists justify their concerns for the future and their distinctive commitment to speak for as yet voiceless future people? More important, how do they persuade the present generation to share their concern about the future and take present, possibly costly, action for the well-being of future people? Why, for example, should present people save a forest now at the cost of their own livelihood for the sake of possibly providing a better life for people who may be living 200 or 500 years from now?

Let's examine some reasons given by philosophers for the value assertion that present generations ought to care for the freedom and welfare of future generations.

Do Future Generations Deserve to Live?

Humankind today has enormous power to affect the future, power that is unprecedented in history. We are capable of destroying the human future and destroying it forever. Although our descendants may have different tastes than ours in music and poetry, or in sports or other amusements, they will need clean air and water, nutritious food, and an environment free of ultraviolet and nuclear radiation. But we now know that these necessities of future life are in jeopardy (Partridge 1981a: 2).

What ought we to do? One alternative is to do nothing for future generations. We could simply cease our present efforts at conservation and could carry on wasting, polluting, dumping, exhausting, burning, and destroying the Earth and its plants and creatures. Let posterity take care of itself when—or if—the future comes. Who cares about as yet unborn people who might or might not be alive on Earth 500 or 5,000 or 10,000 years from now? Who other than a few wacky futurists would want to think that far ahead anyway?

Perhaps, we ought to go further. Maybe the human race deserves to die. There is so much suffering in the world that it may be immoral to keep bringing new people into it only to add to the suffering. Even humans' best, most enlightened efforts will not relieve all the human suffering on Earth, and most of the suffering that they can eliminate will not be relieved at once or even within several decades.

Then, too, much human behavior is loathsome. People are sometimes greedy, stupid, cruel, ruthless, malicious, stingy, narrow-minded, unreasonable, and mean. They are sometimes downright evil in their behavior toward others. After millennia of human experience, there are still human beings everywhere on Earth bent on hating, killing, torturing, maiming, raping, starving, cheating, or somehow hurting other human beings. Look at Bosnia, Rwanda, Somalia, the Sudan, Liberia, Sri Lanka, the streets of some of the world's largest cities, including American cities...the list goes on and on. If we knew that such human abominations would continue or would grow, if, for example, "we knew that future generations would inevitably descend into bestiality or a Hobbesian war of all against all, it might be reasonable for us to put an end to the species deliberately" (Kavka 1981: 118).

But we do not know these things. We insulate ourselves from the human evil of the world—and there is no evil other than *human* evil—by remembering the good that some humans have done and are doing. We recall the heroes and exemplars of human history; the religious teachings of love, compassion, and justice; the sacrifices our parents and grandparents made for us; and the comradeship, affection, and love of our family, our friends, our neighbors, our teachers, and our small communities of mutual caring. The human condition is constituted in such memories.

More important, the human condition is constituted in hope. The meanings of our lives depend importantly on our images of the future. Without the possibility of a future, there is nothing left but despair. Thus, if we give up on the future, we also give up on ourselves. The ancient prophecy remains true: Where there is no vision, the people perish.

Grounds for Caring about Future Generations

Moral relationships among generations are complex and have only recently become a topic of concerted philosophical effort. For example, Peter Laslett and James S. Fishkin (1992) point out that justice over time did not exist as a subject of analysis much before the 1970s and certainly not before the 1960s. In 1971, John Rawls's *A Theory of Justice*, which we discussed briefly in chapter 3, was important in bringing the topic of obligations to future generations into modern philosophy and Derek Parfit's *Reasons and Persons*, published in 1984, is credited with advancing the topic further. Yet there may not as yet exist any fully adequate account of justice over time (Laslett 1992).

Nonetheless, there are several specific arguments that provide evidence for the value assertion that present generations ought to care for the well-being of future generations, even the well-being of far-future generations with whom they cannot share a common life. I summarize some of them below:

1. *A concern for present people implies a concern for future people.* No clear demarcation exists between one generation and the next, thus a concern for people living now carries us a considerable way toward caring about future people. We care—and we ought to care—about our own well-being. Some part of the near future includes ourselves. Therefore, caring for the near future is partly a matter of caring for ourselves, which each of us bears as a primary responsibility.

Moreover, we care about our children and grandchildren, nieces and nephews, and young cousins, if we have them, because we love them. They will care about their children and grandchildren and they, in turn, will care about theirs. Thus, the chain of human connection and caring continues unbroken into the future. For the members of any generation, at least some members of the next generation and even of the generation after that are already alive. Thus, if we care about them now, then our present caring includes their future well-being and their future concerns (Laslett 1992).

The chain of obligation through time, moreover, means that we of the present generation wrong our existing children by making it difficult for them to fulfill their own obligations to their offspring in the future. Thus, our high-consumption life styles, if they are at the expense of our children's ability to meet their future obligations to their children, are morally wrong.

This justification meets Lee's five criteria of acceptable evidence; it is serious, referentially relevant, causally relevant, causally independent, and empirically true.

2. *Thought experiments in which choosers do not know to which generation they belong rationally imply a concern for both present and future people.* Let's perform a thought experiment following Rawls's (1971) theory of justice. Let's assume that we have some people who are rational choosers in an original position who have a veil of ignorance covering their knowledge of when they will live, in the present, the near future, or the far future (Barry 1977: 2–3). That is, people don't know when they will live and we ask them to choose how each generation ought to behave, consuming now or saving and preparing for the future.

Clearly, there is a question of possible equality or inequality in this experiment. It concerns differences among people of different generations. Choosers will have to decide how to create both present and future worlds so that they will not regret living in any generation. For example, if they demand too much saving in the present, then they may suffer if they live in an early generation. But, if they fail to save enough and consume too much in the present, then they may suffer if they live in a later generation as a result of resource depletion and damage to the environment (Barry 1978: 239).

If our choosers are indeed rational, then their choice must allow for the well-being of both present *and* future generations. Thus, we ought to care about the well-being of future people because that is what rational people would choose to do if they did not know what generation they were in. This is assuming, of course, that people will not want to create a time, now or later, when it is impossible to live a satisfactory life for themselves.

With regard to questions of social justice, however, we need to be concerned, also, about distributing present sacrifices for the well-being of future generations equitably among presently living persons. Thus, some special consideration ought to be given to the well-being of presently disadvantaged people (Green 1977). For by consuming less, disadvantaged people pay a disproportionately high price for the well-being of future people.

This justification meets the first four of Lee's criteria, but fails the fifth because there is no empirical test in the strict sense. It is, after all, a thought experiment. It would be possible, however, to conduct a laboratory study in which human subjects were asked to make such choices in a hypothetical situation. The results would provide some empirical grounding—or refutation, depending on the choices made—but I don't know of any such studies having been done.

3. *Regarding the natural resources of the Earth, present generations have no right to use them to the point of depletion or to poison what they did not create.* The present generation, certainly, owes it to future people not to poison naturally self-renewing resources such as air, soil, and water (Baier 1981: 181). No human being produced these things, therefore everyone has a right to their use, including members of future generations. No one has the right to deny their use to others. Thus, the members of the present generation have an obligation to future generations of leaving the Earth's life-sustaining capacities in as good a shape as they found them or of providing compensating benefits of life-sustaining worth equal to the damage that they do.

As Peter C. Yeager (1991: 130) points out, environmental protection has become a question of moral rights, "for example by linking the principle of equality of opportunity to the right to a decent environment, without which opportunity is compromised." This argument meets Lee's five criteria. The empirical support, of course, depends on general logical deductions of human rights—especially of life itself—from the facts of human nature. A moral concern for the environment was clearly manifested at the meeting of the United Nations Earth Summit in Rio de Janeiro in 1992. A step was taken toward creating a set of "Earth Ethics" in agreements signed by 178 countries.

A cautionary note needs to be added. Fanaticism remains fanaticism even if it is in the name of a good cause such as saving the environment. No ethical person can condone aggression and violence, killing people, or willfully destroying property. Thus, we can only condemn the tactics of some environmental groups that include guerrilla acts such as spiking trees that endanger the lives of loggers. The ecosabotage of groups such as Earth First! is no substitute for civil debate, and legal and political action.

4. *Past generations left many of the public goods that they created not only to the present generation but to future generations as well.* Every generation is an heir to the legacies of past generations. Public goods from highways and television stations to school buildings and libraries to political and economic institutions to works of art and science were created by past people and were inherited by present people. Such goods are part of the human heritage. No ger eration has the right to use up or destroy the existing human heritage, whether material, social, or cultural, so that it is no longer available to future generations. Thus, the present generation owes to future generations their share in these public goods (Baier 1981: 181; Weiss 1992).

To do the right thing, either present generations ought to act as stewards of their cultural heritage preserving or renewing it or they ought to replace it with works of equal or higher value.

One way in which present generations can compensate future generations for both the natural resources and the public goods that present people use up is to leave to future generations increased knowledge and technology, and therefore power, to deal with the changed world that they face (Partridge 1981a: 3). In the discussion of the damage that present generations do to the future well-being of coming generations, this point is often overlooked. Present generations can help make future generations better off as well as worse off. They can do this not simply by conserving resources, but by using them to create knowledge that will bring new resources into being and to develop new technologies to use them (e.g., there was no great demand for gasoline until after the invention, development, and spread of the internal combustion engine that used it for fuel).

Ernest Partridge (1991: 16) points out that the present generation might morally use up the Earth's existing fossil fuels, if it did so in ways that included developing replacement fuels such as biomass, photovoltaic cells, fusion reactors, or whatever possible fuels we cannot now imagine. In this way, the present generation can leave as much and as good, though different, resources for their successors as it had.

Some resources are renewable (e.g., solar energy) or reusable (e.g., aluminum). But knowledge, as Gregory Kavka (1981: 119–20) says, is both. It can be used without being depleted. It can be used as it continues to be shared with others and to grow itself. And it can be used to increase the supply of other resources, too, including the Earth's physical resources. Kavka is referring especially to scientific and technological knowledge, but I see no compelling argument for such a limitation. All human knowledge, conceived very broadly to include art, literature, music, the social sciences, and philosophy as well as science and technology, could contribute positively to the well-being of future generations.

Moreover, I would include in the beneficial legacy that the present generation can leave: (1) foresight capabilities through the expansion of futures studies. With foresight, as every futurist would agree, we can more intelligently plan for our own future and better prepare the future of coming generations. And (2) critically examined, elaborated, and objectively justified moral codes by which alternative futures can be evaluated as to their desirability. For wisdom can come not only from better foresight but also from more appropriate values: humans need to know what they want, to want the things that will in fact contribute to their present and future freedom and welfare, and to know and to be able to explain why they ought to want them. Both foresight and moral judgment, for example, are needed in making decisions about the development and use of technology so that the results will be beneficial and not harmful.

Kavka (1981: 120) recognizes that the present generation faces vast investments in the development of currently poor countries. In order to stabilize the global population, for example, and to give every living human being a good chance at a long life of high quality, our generation may have to use what appears to be more than our fair share of resources. Kavka gives two justifications that would allow us to do so. The first is simply to make an exception. We must create the initial conditions that permit long and good lives for everyone and this may be a one-time-only extraordinary investment until every country has gone through the demographic revolution and, thus, has reached the point of slow or no population growth.

The second is to balance the books by considering the benefits of our spreading positive values into the future, such as, to continue the examples given here, values supporting individual longevity, low birth rates, sufficiency, the equality of women, the value of peaceful cooperation rather than aggression, and a sense of moral community that encompasses all of humanity. This strategy substitutes something of value for the extra resources we use.

Kavka says, with respect to the threat of overpopulation, that we can view the pronatal values and practices that our ancestors handed down to us as a *negative* resource. Thus, our extra use of some other resources would be justified if we eradicated this negative resource. All things considered, he continues, we would be leaving our descendants no worse off than we were. If our generation (or even the next one) could succeed in doing this, then, other things being equal, future generations would be considerably better off than they would be otherwise.

If each generation added to the store of human knowledge and wisdom, then the human species not only would increase its chances of having a future, but would also increase its chances of having a desirable future for millennia to come. Greater knowledge makes possible both the use of resources and the growth of resources.

The arguments presented here about the rights to cultural heritage meet Lee's five criteria of acceptable evidence. The arguments about the legacy of knowledge and other compensations do also, but the "evidence" constitutes "predictive grounds" as I explained them in chapter 2, that is, expected future outcomes of present behavior and, thus, they are at best only presumptively true.

5. *Humble ignorance ought to lead present generations to act with prudence toward the well-being of future generations.* Generally, moral responsibility grows with knowledge and foresight. If we know that the consequence of shooting a rifle aimed at a man is that he will be killed or

badly hurt, then that knowledge makes us responsible for our act. Yet ignorance can create moral responsibility too. Because there are many things about the planetary life-support system that we find complex and mysterious, humble ignorance morally requires us to act with respect and restraint (Partridge 1981a: 2).

Even though human knowledge has grown phenomenally during the last several generations, human ignorance, as I said earlier, remains vast. We do not understand everything about the biosphere. We have not observed and classified all—or even most—of the forms of plant and animal life on Earth, even as some species are becoming extinct. We do not know what may be of use to future generations. We do not know what the human destiny is or might become. Weighted with such ignorance, the present generation ought to act prudently so as not to threaten the future survival and well-being of the human species. As Brian Barry (1977: 3) says, it would be a cosmic impertinence to do otherwise.

This argument follows from the discussion of "good intentions and good results" in chapter 2 and meets Lee's five criteria, although the "evidence" rests on predictive grounds. In this case, the predictive grounds have to do with the harm we might do to future people by acting imprudently out of our ignorance.

6. *There is a "prima facie obligation of present generations to ensure that important business is not left unfinished"* (Bennett 1978: 68). By "important business" Bennett refers to human accomplishments, especially exceptional ones in science, art, music, literature, and technology, and also human inventions and achievements of organizational arrangements, political, economic, social, and cultural institutions, and moral philosophy. The continuation of these achievements, obviously, depends upon the continuation of the human species. They depend, too, on a quality of life that is sufficiently high so that at least some future individuals will be free from mere survival activities and able to concentrate their energies on such ventures.

The human story to date has only been partially told. We do not know what its ending will be. Nor do we know what it ought to be. The narrative of humankind disappears into the future. So far, although it has included many despicable acts of evil, it has also included many wonders of accomplishment, from architecture to poetry and from acts of grace to acts of courage. Surely, we can learn to live sufficiently well in the present while at the same time creating conditions for the human story to continue, allowing for the possibility of future discoveries and inventions that we cannot now imagine.

This reason for caring about future generations meets the first four of Lee's criteria, but it appears weak on empirical support. It may be true that important business ought not to be left unfinished—perhaps by the definition of "important." Yet it seems less persuasive than some of the other reasons, especially when compared to the first reason concerning the empirically demonstrable chain of human connection among generations from parents, to children, to grandchildren, and so on.

7. *The present generation's caring and sacrificing for future generations benefits not only future generations but also itself.* Once again, we recognize "that a concern for others benefits one's own character" (Rolston 1981: 126). Elaborating on this theme, Partridge (1981b: 204, 217) suggests that a need for self-transcendence may be a basic fact of the human condition. Self-transcendence includes caring for the future beyond one's own lifetime. People lacking in self-transcendence are socially and morally impoverished compared to self-transcendent people. It is through being concerned for other people, both living and as yet unborn, that a person achieves self-enrichment and personal satisfaction.

The idea of a human need for self-transcendence speaks to the despair of the modern, secular peoples of the world. Losing faith in many traditional values, modern humans have elevated selfhood and the cultivation of identity into core values. Having done so, they have made themselves particularly vulnerable to a sense of despair and pointlessness as they face death, because death brings an end to the self that has given life most of its meaning. Our ancestors, by contrast, drew meaning from cultural values that were larger than the self and that would outlive them (Baumeister 1991).

Genuinely caring about future generations and taking effective action to benefit their well-being may be answers to the contemplation of one's own death and the feelings of futility it produces. By an act of informed will, we can enlarge ourselves, not only by our memories of the past but also by our anticipations of the future. Thus, we can strengthen ourselves by creating a community of hope, as Robert N. Bellah et al. (1985: 153) have called it, connecting "our aspirations for ourselves and those closest to us with the aspirations of a larger whole and see our own efforts as being, in part, contributions to a common good." We may learn that meaning can be found by contributing to the possibly infinite flowing of the river of life (Rolston 1981: 126).

This argument, though emotionally appealing, may be based more on wishful thinking than on solid evidence. Thus, more research is invited before we can agree that this reason meets Lee's fifth criterion of empirical truth. Yet we do know that doing good tends to make us feel better about ourselves. After death, nothing may matter to us anymore. Yet within our own lifetimes knowing that we have contributed something beneficial to the human future might contribute to our sense of peace and tranquility and ease our knowledge of the coming oblivion of death.

Discounting the Future

Generally, economists discount the future, while philosophers do not (Cowen and Parfit 1992). We can find some truth in each point of view. What is needed is balance, a concern both for the immediate present *and* for the future. The interests of both present and future generations need to be taken into account.

One good reason to discount the future somewhat is its uncertainty. We know less about the future than we do about the past and the present. "A bird in the hand is worth two in the bush" because if you give up the certain one for the uncertain two you may end up with none. Alternative scenarios about what the future will be are necessarily contingent and cannot all come true. Many scenarios may not even come close to what the future will actually be like when it arrives.

Moreover, the more distant into the future we go, the more uncertain it may become and, possibly, the more negligible are the effects of present acts. For example, the present generation cannot control the actions of intervening generations of people, so present planning for the far future is subject to unknown possible interventions. Yet we must judge each case on its own merits, because there are some things that we can predict with reasonable accuracy, even into the far future. Nuclear wastes, as far as we now know, will be dangerous for tens of thousands of years; and some human acts, such as those that destroy species, will have permanent effects (Cowen and Parfit 1992: 159).

Also, the present generation cannot even be certain that future generations will need what it may save for them (Passmore 1981: 51). Then, too, the present generation could even make future generations worse off by its misguided efforts to benefit them since present knowledge is so limited.

Finally, future generations may be so much more knowledgeable and powerful than the present generation that they may be quite capable of taking care of themselves.

But there is another side of the coin. Even in our own lifetimes, if we never act to benefit our own futures, we may live to have an impoverished future ourselves. If we never sacrifice in the present by deferring gratification, then we may have nothing left for our future. For example, if we never study and learn, if we never defer playing for work, if we never put off a pleasure now for a greater pleasure later, if we never save for our retirement, if we never plan, then we may never accomplish anything of worth in our own lives and may live with regret and suffering in the future. In like manner, if present generations never concern themselves with the well-being of future generations, then future generations may end up powerless to survive at all, much less thrive.

At a discount rate of five percent per year, one death this year is equal to over two million deaths 300 years from now. Although economists may find this to be an acceptable trade-off, philosophers may find it morally repugnant. A human life is a human life, whether now or in the future. And a duty is a duty. The time dimension of a duty (present or future) does not matter (Partridge 1981a: 8). Also, despite our ignorance, we now know that many of the consequences of current human behavior *are* damaging the environment and *are* hurting present people and we now know that they will continue to hurt people at least into the near future.

The best policy may be one of giving first priority to the alleviation of present suffering and maximizing the freedom and welfare of living people, making it possible for members of the present generation to live out their life spans in good health and happiness. But we ought to do so with a genuine concern about the consequences of our actions, both intended and unintended, for the well-being of future generations as well.

The interests of present and future generations do not always clash. Often they merge and both can be beneficially served by the same actions. For example, reducing pollution, recycling, restoring the environment, preventing wasteful uses of resources, distributing food, expanding the delivery of health services, educating people, lowering high-birthrate reproductive behavior, inventing and disseminating effective contraceptives, liberating women, creating institutions to promote peaceful and democratic governance and to ensure justice, investing in public goods of transportation and communication, reducing loud noise levels, investing in research and development, maintaining social order and peaceful change, teaching the benefits of cooperation, spreading the values of concern for the global community, etc. may be "double benefit" forms of action (Passmore 1981: 56–57). Often, they help present generations *and* they probably will help future generations as well.

We ought to behave now so as to keep as many options open for the future as possible. Other things being equal, we cannot harm the interests of future generations by "our leaving them more choices rather than fewer" (Barry 1977: 275). Certainly, we do not want to make the Marxist mistake of doing certain harm to present people in the name of future happiness that may never come, as we saw in chapter 1. Nor do we want to make the mistake of living for today with no thought of the future. Present happiness in exchange for probable future misery is a false choice, because without hope for the future, as we have seen, the present itself becomes meaningless.

Thus, a balance between the interests of present and future people is the moral choice, with a strong preference for those actions that have the double benefit of helping both present and future people have a longer and better life (Kim 1994). Given the basic needs of both present and future people (e.g., for clean air, water, and soil), we ought to be especially concerned about the life-sustaining capacities of the Earth and the continued existence of plants and animals, both now and in the future.

Finally, it is not unrealistic to hope that people everywhere on Earth will work together to achieve justice for future generations. Many examples already exist. Some national constitutions, for example, contain provisions for preserving the natural environment, from Albania and Bahrain to Switzerland and Thailand. In the United States, the constitutions of Hawaii, Illinois, and Montana do so too. Additionally, national cultural treasures are protected by the constitutions of forty-five countries (Weiss 1992).

The Outer Space Treaty of 1967 provides for the use of outer space "for all humankind." The Moon Treaty of 1979 also declares that the moon and its natural resources belong to all humans. Other precedents for global cooperation include the 1959 Treaty of Antarctica, the 1972 London Ocean Dumping Convention, the 1972 World Heritage Convention, the 1982 World Soil Charter, the 1985 Vienna Convention for the

Protection of the Ozone Layer, and the 1987 protocol on chlorofluoro-carbons and halons. These are signs that distant threats can be antici-pated and responded to with concern for future generations (Weiss 1992).

Obligations to the Past

I have addressed the question of whether or not we of the present generation have obligations to future generations. After reviewing seven reasons, I concluded that, indeed, we do. Justice over time, however, can extend not only into the future, but also into the past. Thus, another question immediately comes to mind: Do we also have obligations to past generations?

Given current philosophical thinking, the answer is, perhaps yes, some, but they are not nearly as many nor as compelling as our obligations to future generations. Thus, the past can be morally discounted in a way that the future ought not to be. The difference in our commitments to the past and the future derives directly from the facts, as we saw in Volume 1, that the past has already happened and we can do nothing now to change it and that the future is yet to come and importantly depends on present actions. Morally, we cannot be expected to do that which we are unable to do, and we cannot change the past.

Yet the living do, in fact, fulfill many commitments to the dead. They bury them, honor them, carry out their wishes (e.g., follow the directions of their last wills and testaments), tell their stories, carry on their unfin-ished work, remember them, and otherwise acknowledge and mark their existence and accomplishments. Fulfilling such commitments to past people, as in the case of caring for future people, can result in benefits to the living (Partridge 1981a).

There are two reasons why we ought not to give as much concern to the dead as to the living and the unborn. The first is that nearly all that mattered to the dead happened in their lifetimes and now cannot be changed (Kavka 1981: 111). The second is that, even when the desires of the dead concerned future states of affairs, they themselves are no longer around to react and experience any satisfaction or disappointment in seeing them fulfilled or left unfulfilled. Thus, the desires of past generations now dead can be discounted, even ignored, in our moral decision making.

Neither of these reasons, obviously, applies to presently living people who can act, react, and experience satisfaction. Nor do they apply to future people who someday *will* be able to do these things (Kavka 1981: 111). Thus, the difference in their temporal location *does* constitute a reason for favoring both present and future people over past people. But it "does not constitute a reason for favoring present over *future* people" (Kavka 1981: 111). Both present and future people, as we have seen, have rightful claims on the Earth's natural resources and cultural heritages.

When the beliefs and values of our dead ancestors clash with the freedom and welfare of present and future generations, then they ought to be abandoned and replaced by new beliefs and values that do contribute positively to human well-being, now and in the future. By thus changing our beliefs and values, one major obligation to past generations will be served: we will have helped to ensure that human life has a future, that the river of life will continue to flow.

There is at least one special case that deserves separate consideration. It is when present people may deserve compensation for the effects on them of past, perhaps ancient, wrongs to their forebears. In the United States, for example, ought African-Americans today be somehow compensated for the forced slavery and transportation of their ancestors and ought Native Americans be compensated for the theft of land and life from their ancestors? (Sher 1992: 48).

Although we cannot right all the wrongs of history, some compensation may be fair, going back one or more generations. But George Sher (1992) argues that the fairness of compensation fades with time. One reason is that the more time that has elapsed between the past wrong to an ancestor and a descendent's present circumstances, the more likely it is that a descendent's present circumstances are the result, not of the past wrong, but of his or her or other people's intervening actions.

Of paramount importance, to continue the examples, are the wrongs that may be being done to African-Americans or Native Americans today in their own lifetimes. Present and recent acts of unfair discrimination and neglect against any group of people demand our present concern and invite immediate redress.

Conclusion

In earlier chapters, we identified some universal human values and elaborated a few, for example, knowledge, evaluation, justice, cooperation, and, especially, life itself. We concluded that in many cases, such time-honored values remain beneficial today and probably will remain beneficial in the future. Yet there are important exceptions. The human future may depend not only on recognizing and living by most universal human values, but also on changing some.

In this chapter, I proposed several human values that may be good candidates for change as we enter the twenty-first century:

1. Even more value than it is now given ought to be placed on longevity, extending the length of individual human lives.

2. Given the continued growth in the human population, reproductive values ought to be changed to a target of no more than one child per person on average.

3. The value of sufficiency ought to receive more emphasis than it does now, reducing luxury and wasteful consumption, especially in the more economically advanced societies.

4. As a high priority, the value of women's lives ought to be increased, so that women will become fully equal to men in the opportunities to have lives of their own choosing.

5. The value of aggression and violence against other human beings ought to be replaced by the value of peaceful cooperation.

6. Exclusivist and ethnocentric values and practices are counterproductive in today's complex and increasingly interdependent global society; they ought to be replaced by caring for others on all levels of social scale, up to and including the world community.

Although ethnocentrism throughout most of human history may have contributed to the survival and thriving of human groups, today it threatens human life. We ought to replace such behavior by values of inclusivism and universalism, by enlarging the community of human concern to all peoples. Dehumanizing people by defining them as "members of an outgroup" or "alien others" ought to be devalued to the point of total elimination. Instead, we ought to encourage the global consciousness and conscience that are now growing among some people nearly everywhere, creating a world moral community.

Caring about yourself, your family, your friends, your neighbors, and your local community ought to continue to be of first priority. But caring for and sharing with more distant people, both geographically and socially, is both an effective way of creating a secure world for yourself and your small community and the morally right way of treating other people.

We can promote discussion and we can encourage the caring, mutually beneficial policies and acts that flow from such discussion, sweeping aside the barriers that prevent the inclusion of outgroups into the larger oneness of humanity. We can expand the powers and increase the effectiveness of the United Nations or some other kinds of democratically legitimated and enforceable international authority and the institutional mechanisms of international law (Moynihan 1990). Also, we can create a democratically constituted world police force—in order to provide security from vicious people and nations who will not play by the rules of peaceful negotiation and compromise to solve conflicts of interest. We humans can unite globally to prevent genocide, violence, victimization, and brutality (and the unnecessary and tragic losses of life and property and the destruction of nature that goes with them) while encouraging human responsibility and ensuring human rights.

7. Moreover, we can—and ought—to increase the scale of our consciousness, our caring, and our sharing still further, not only in space but also in time, to include the freedom and welfare of future generations.

We ought to enlarge our community of human concern not only to include all people currently alive on Earth, but also to include future generations. We ought to work to establish a World Court for Future Generations, along the lines proposed by Bruce E. Tonn (1991) for the United States, whose responsibility would be to safeguard the lives of future generations by monitoring and evaluating present actions. Why ought we to do so? I reviewed seven reasons that various philosophers have given:

- Because of the chain of intergenerational connection, a concern for present people implies a concern for future people.
- Thought experiments in which choosers do not know to which generation they belong rationally imply a concern for both present and future people.
- Regarding the natural resources of the Earth, present generations have no right to use to the point of depletion or to poison what they did not create.
- Past generations left many of the public goods that they created not only to the present generation but to future generations as well.
- Humble ignorance ought to lead present generations to act with prudence toward the well-being of future generations.
- Present generations have a prima facie obligation to ensure that important human business is not left unfinished.

- The present generation's caring and sacrificing for future generations may benefit not only future generations but also itself.

The moral choice appears to be a balance between the interests of both present and future generations: an obligation, first, to strive to create the conditions that permit an equal and good chance of every presently living person to live a long and good life, and, second, an effort to leave future generations at least as well off as we of the present generation, so that they, too, can live long and good lives. Being morally responsible means caring both for ourselves and for others, now and in the future.

Further, because the interests of present and future generations do not always clash but sometimes are convergent, we can search for those present acts and policies that contribute to the well-being both of present and future people. Such "double benefits" often come from acts that maintain and enhance the life-sustaining capacities of the Earth. They also can come from research, technological development, and scholarship, giving both present and future people increased knowledge, and, therefore, increased power to control the conditions of their own lives.

Additionally, they can come from advances in futures research and in moral discourse so that present and future people will have both the foresight and the good judgment to use technological developments for life enhancing-purposes and not for destruction.

From a variety of sources, including surveys of students from nine countries around the world, Allen Tough (1993b) asked what people of the future need from us in the present. He summarizes his results in seven points: We in the present are asked by hypothetical future people to work toward (1) peace and security; (2) a planet capable of supporting life; (3) the avoidance of catastrophes that would harm human civilization; (4) effective democratic governance addressed to a long-range, global perspective; (5) knowledge; (6) nurturing care of children; and (7) lifetime opportunities—from childhood to late adulthood—for learning.

Most of what I have read and learned in preparing to write this book confirms this "message from the future." Indeed, we know that future people need these things from us and, indeed, we ought to work now to bring them about.

Epilogue

Finally, I have reached the end of my task and the time for a summing up. In these two volumes, I identified some prominent futurists, described the major features of the new field of futures studies, elaborated a theory of knowledge appropriate for investigating the future, gave a few exemplars and methods of futures research, enumerated some near-universal human values and assessed them objectively, showed how such values underlie images of desirable futures, and proposed that some traditional values be reassessed and possibly changed in order to meet the changing conditions of the twenty-first century.

In volume 1, I began by reviewing several strands of the futures field's recent history and development, from the well-known work on social trends and technology assessment of William F. Ogburn to the mostly forgotten work of the social psychologist, Nathan Israeli. I discussed the spread of national planning, nation-building in the new states, operations research and the think tanks, Daniel Bell and the Commission on the Year 2000, *The Limits to Growth* and the Club of Rome, H. D. Lasswell's developmental analysis and the invention of the policy sciences, and evaluation research. I also described some futurist organizations, publications, conferences, and other indicators of the rise of the futures movement. Of course, my brief review is by no means complete; a proper history of the rise of futures studies remains to be written. Yet nonfuturists, I hope, have gained some appreciation of the scope, content, and promise of the contemporary futures field.

The most general purpose of futures studies, I pointed out, is to maintain or improve the freedom and welfare of humankind, both now and in the future. Futurists' distinctive contributions include prospective thinking and giving present voice to the well-being of future generations. Futurists aim to discover or invent, examine and evaluate, and propose possible, probable, and preferable futures. They study images of the future held by various people. They explore the knowledge and ethical foundations of futures studies. Through their constructions and apprais-

315

als of alternative images of the future, futurists also help to interpret the past and orientate the present. For beliefs about what future is coming importantly contribute both to our understanding of the past and to the meanings that we give to the present.

Additionally, futurists organize knowledge and appeal to values as they design or evaluate social action aimed at adapting to or controlling the future. Some people may recoil at the idea that the future can be or is being "controlled." Yet, whether we like it or not or whether we intend it or not, our present actions *do* contribute to creating the coming future. Therefore, futurists encourage people to recognize this fact, to be more conscious of the consequences of their own actions, and to be more deliberate and responsible in their decision making. They urge people to pay attention to such consequences, including unintended consequences, because they may produce part of the future world in which all of us, and our children and grandchildren will have to live.

Futurists also believe that people have the right to participate in the decisions that affect their own future and, therefore, they work to spread the knowledge and to create the organizational arrangements that make genuine democratic participation and decision making possible. Futurists want to create what philosopher John Dewey called a "community of deliberation," a community of democratic discourse and decision about desirable futures and the means to achieve them.

Sometimes, futurists become active advocates, spending part of their time communicating and promoting a particular image of the future. They do this openly, taking part in public debate.

How do futurists know that they know what they claim to know? I answered this question by discussing three major aspects of the knowledge foundations of futures studies: underlying assumptions, theories of knowledge, and specific methods of futures research.

Modern futures thinking and research rest on a set of interrelated assumptions. I gave nine key assumptions, starting with the assertion that time is continuous, unidirectional, and irreversible. Other key assumptions are: Not everything that will exist has existed or does exist; that is, since future time will be new time, new things may exist that have never existed before. Futures thinking is essential for intelligent and informed human action. The most useful knowledge for deciding how to act is "knowledge of the future," because we need to know the consequences of our actions *before* we decide on taking the actions that will produce them.

But, because the future is unobservable and nonevidential, this creates an epistemological paradox for futures studies.

Additional key assumptions are that the future is not totally predetermined; that, therefore, the future remains more or less open to human will and action; that interdependence characterizes the world, and, thus, that futurists adopt a holistic perspective and a transdisciplinary approach to understand it properly, especially when organizing knowledge for decision making; and, finally, that some futures are more desirable than others.

I also gave three general assumptions that futurists share with some other scholars and scientists. They are that people are goal-directed beings bent on pursuing their projects; that society includes not only persistent patterns of repetitive social interaction, but also expectations, hopes and fears for the future, and decisions; and that past realities existed and present realities exist, quite apart from the human knowing of them, and that a future reality likewise *will* exist.

This last general assumption provides the focus for chapters 4 and 5 of volume 1 in which I gave an epistemology for futures studies. Following some of the later writings of Thomas S. Kuhn, I described a transdisciplinary matrix for futures studies, specifying fifteen shared beliefs and practices that define the group commitments of futurists. Although futures studies shares some features of both art and science, I showed that futurists, like scientists and unlike artists, have an obligation to seek the truth. I concluded that futures studies is a transdisciplinary action and social science. This is not to say, of course, that futures studies does not have its intuitive, imaginative, and speculative aspects. It certainly does, just as do both art and science.

The futurist paradox mentioned above concerns how we can know the future when the future has not yet become present reality, when it is not yet evidential. In answering this question, I reviewed competing theories of knowledge that have affected futures studies. The modern futures movement developed at a time during which the positivist theory of knowledge—in fact, science more generally—was under attack. Thus, the recent development of futures studies took place during a period of epistemological disarray and conflict. Some futurists have worked in the positivist tradition, while others have rejected positivism and adopted some or all of the postpositivist views of postmodernism. Other futurists simply ignored such philosophical questions altogether or casually adopted some mixture of both views.

I explained some of the major features of positivist and postpositivist theories of knowledge, giving the strengths and weaknesses of each. I argued that, although postpositivism, quite rightly, has corrected some of the faults of positivism, neither theory is fully satisfactory. Instead, I proposed a post-postpositivist theory of knowledge known as critical realism as being most appropriate for the futures field.

Critical realism is post-Kuhnian and part of the larger humanistic culture of critical discourse. To some extent it is a synthesis of positivist and postpositivist views. Unlike positivists, though, critical realists assert that plausibility, not certainty, is the most that can be claimed by science and that knowledge is provisional. Unlike post-positivists, critical realists believe that the way external reality really is decisively affects our beliefs about it and that conjectural knowledge is possible. Critical realists believe that there are causes and effects independent of the human mind and that it is often possible to know them objectively. They claim that it is reasonable to believe in assertions that have withstood serious efforts to refute them. Moreover, I contended that, within a critical realist theory, beliefs about the nonfactual future can be justified objectively in basically the same way as beliefs about the factual past and present.

Yet, because the past and present have an evidential reality that the not-yet-existent future does not share, I added some epistemological principles specifically for futures studies. Thus, I proposed that futurists incorporate into their theory of conjectural knowledge concepts such as posits, surrogate knowledge, presumptively true (or false) and terminally true (or false) predictions, the reflexivity of self-altering prophecies, and the "what if?" of counterfactual (as well as factual) thinking. Later, in my discussion of values, I also proposed incorporating the concept of predictive grounds as part of the evidence to test the validity of value judgments.

In chapter 6, volume 1, I moved from the abstract and philosophical to the concrete and methodological. There, I described the third major aspect of the knowledge foundations of futures studies, methodology, and evaluated some major methods of futures research. We considered the pragmatic prediction of one variable by others, the extrapolation of trends using time series analysis, cohort-component methods, survey research techniques, the Delphi method, simulation and computer modeling, gaming, monitoring, content analysis, participatory futures praxis, social experimentation, and ethnographic futures research.

The scenario, of course, is the preeminent method of futures research and it is involved to some degree in all the other methods. Stories are the most characteristic products of futures research, stories about what the future can be or could be, about what it is likely to be, about what it ought (or ought not) to be, or about what we ought to do to create a desirable future or prevent an undesirable future. Futurists tell stories, but they often base their narratives on logical inquiry and disciplined empirical investigation.

In volume 2, I turned to the topic of the ethical foundations of futures studies, the question of what the future ought or ought not to be and how we can make and validate such judgments within the limits of naturalistic inquiry. Pursuing this topic leads us, of course, to the age-old exploration of the nature of the good society. We are led to ask: What kind of future ought we to want? What values are the right values to use as standards to judge what is good, right, and moral about human behavior and society? What is evil, wrong, and immoral? Such inquiry takes us to a fundamental level where values themselves are evaluated.

Futures studies is not a "value-free" science. Rather, it is concerned with both the true *and* the good. It is an action and human science whose purposes include not only the description and explanation of what was, what is, and what will be, but also include the investigation and achievement of what ought to be, the preferable. Just as people and organizations cannot make intelligent decisions to act without knowing the future consequences of their actions (a prediction problem), they also cannot do so without having some valid way of deciding how desirable or undesirable those consequences will be (a value judgmental problem). Unfortunately, to date futurists have not made significant progress in justifying their beliefs in the moral rightness of the values that they use. Thus, I devoted all of volume 2 to this issue.

I began my quest for the nature of the good society and some valid grounding for value judgments by examining a few major utopian writings, starting with Thomas More and ending with Karl Marx. Given the enormous quantity of utopian writings over the years—not to mention the voluminous works in moral philosophy—we barely scratched the surface in our discussion. Yet we saw that, indeed, utopian writers base their images of a better or perfect society on some specified human values, such as individual happiness and social harmony.

Their justifications differed, however, ranging over appeals to God, nature, human nature, society, the "people," reason, and science. The long-term trend has been away from appeals to God and toward some combination of the other appeals as they have been redefined by the modern use of reason and scientific knowledge. This has been accompanied by a trend away from the belief that a perfect society can be achieved only in some otherworldly place and toward the belief that humans can create their own desirable—if less than perfect—world here and now on this Earth.

We saw that many of the utopian writers rightfully belong in the history of the human sciences. Some of them, for example Condorcet, the utopian socialists, and Marx, conceived of themselves as doing social analysis and left us protosocial scientific works. Others, even the most obviously fictive in their orientation, such as Defoe and Sade, include implicit categories of social analysis in describing their "perfect" societies and in their critiques of the imperfections of actual, existing societies.

In their efforts at social engineering, some of these writers pointed the way, also, to social experimentation and applied human science. For example, the utopian socialists created small-scale, planned communities and Marx inspired large-scale efforts of directed social change in entire societies. Unlike mainstream social scientists of the last few generations, utopian writers explicitly struggled to incorporate not only the true, but also the good in their social theories and blueprints for a better society. That they most often failed, sometimes disastrously, encourages us to be prudent, cautious, and openminded in our own, contemporary efforts to plan social change, but it does not discredit the effort to construct a better society.

We saw that there was a dramatic shift in utopian writing at the end of the eighteenth century, especially with the work of Condorcet. Before Condorcet, most utopias had been located in the present, that is, contemporaneous with then-existing real societies, but at a different geographical place. After Condorcet, most utopias were set at a different time, the future. Thus, Condorcet has a good claim on the title of "The First Futurist."

Facing the question of making value judgments not only explicitly, but also objectively, reliably and validly, I gave three models or methods of testing moral decisions: commitment-deducibility, means-ends, and Keekok Lee's epistemic implication. Although each method may be helpful in resolving value conflicts and ambiguities, only epistemic implication is fully satisfactory.

Each of the first two models ultimately fails, because the commitment in the first case and the selection of ends in the second remain untested. Using epistemic implication, however, we can assess indirectly both commitments and ends themselves by examining the reasons given to support them, that is, by making serious efforts to refute them. Since it is reasonable to believe in unrefuted reasons, we reach, by implication, an objective judgment about the rightness of the specific values underlying images of preferable futures.

I placed epistemic implication firmly within the critical realist theory of knowledge. Doing so allows us to use the same basic philosophical postulates (i.e., fallibilism) to justify our beliefs about the past and present, about causes and their effects, about truthlike assertions concerning the possibilities and probabilities of alternative and contingent futures, and about the validity of the values and moral judgments on which we base our assertions about the desirability of alternative futures. That is, using critical realism, we can objectively test our propositions about both the true and the good, bringing the good back in to the human sciences *but doing so explicitly and with rigor and discipline*.

To say that value judgments can be objectively tested or validated is, as I write, an unorthodox belief. It runs counter to the dominant academic dogmas of the day. Although I am well aware of the reluctance of some members of scholarly and scientific communities to accept this view, I believe that eventually it will prevail. For I have seen that it works, that it can be taught to others, and that there are signs of change, both among scientists and philosophers. Also, there is a growing recognition of the common need to find some objective and universal procedures for resolving conflicts without the use of force, especially among peoples of different cultures. Most important, perhaps, are scholarly honesty, trust in rationality, and public verifiability. Although there are lags, if a view is right, eventually it will overturn even long-held and cherished beliefs (and, usually, more quickly than it took the Catholic Church to acknowledge that Galileo's views were correct).

I evaluated several widely used practical strategies for making moral judgments, from religion and law to the collective judgments of group members. I showed the strengths and limitations of each in relation to the three moral models that I had described earlier. Each of the practical strategies has some utility in making moral judgments, and religion may be of special importance in motivating people to act rightly. I concluded that law in democratic societies, even with its many limitations, can come closest to approximating the procedures of epistemic implication. Moreover, democratic legislation provides a legitimate means by which social change aimed at creating a desirable future can be implemented. Thus, for futurists, the law, although not infallible, is both a framework of codes that helps evaluate claims as to what is preferable and a tool that can be used to create a better future.

Also, as part of the discussion of practical strategies, I pointed out that no agreed-upon code of ethics yet exists governing the professional behavior of futurists themselves, guiding them as they seek to behave rightly in the role of futurist. Thus, I listed some of the ethical issues that ought to be addressed by such a code and proposed some ethical principles for futurists to consider as they move toward formulating and formally adopting ethical guidelines for their profession.

In my discussion of human values, I questioned two major tenets of cultural relativism. The first is the belief in ethical relativism, the contention that, since every culture has its own distinctive cultural values and practices, cultures cannot be evaluated by any external ethical criteria or universal standards. The second is the belief that cultural diversity is so great that comparing cultures is virtually impossible or meaningless.

Both beliefs, I concluded, are flawed. In the first instance, I showed that we can ask whether or not a culture positively contributes to the survival and flourishing of its population, to the physical and mental health of its members by satisfying their needs, and to their life satisfaction and happiness. I showed that, contrary to long-standing assumptions among some anthropologists, traditional beliefs and practices do not always do so. Rather, they sometimes produce fear, violence, and suffering, even murder. Sometimes, as in the case of clitoridectomies, traditional practices involve mutilation and child abuse. To those who believe that such judgments are ethnocentric, I pointed out that to question human values is to make them problematic, the very opposite of ethnocentrism. All values, including yours and mine, can be—and ought to be—questioned.

In the second instance, I showed that cultural differences were exaggerated in the past and that the major studies on which the belief in incommensurable cultural diversity rested have been refuted. I demonstrated that the world's cultures have a great deal in common with one another and that many universal or near-universal human values exist. They range, to take only a few examples, from respect for life, honesty, truth, loyalty, trust, courage, and freedom to peace, health, love, kindness, generosity, self-control, and moderation.

Moreover, we have reasonably good explanations of why such near-universal human values exist. They have resulted from evolutionary processes. First are those processes involved in the similar nature of human beings, both at the biopsychological level and at the level of higher order human capacitices. Second are those involved in the prerequisites of social life, because social life would be impossible without some shared values, such as trust, trustworthiness, honesty, justice, and cooperation. Third are those involved in the nature of physical reality itself which is in important respects basically the same everywhere (e.g., gravity). Thus, similar beings pursuing similar goals of survival and flourishing come to many similar beliefs and evaluations as they function within similar social and physical constraints and opportunities.

I selected a few core human values for more detailed examination: knowledge, evaluation itself, justice, cooperation, and the value of human life. Because of its preeminent importance, I devoted an entire chapter to a discussion of the last, the value and meanings of human life. Putting religion aside, I appealed to scientific and secular humanism and concluded that the first purpose of life is to live. We ought to want to live, because without life we can be nothing and we can do nothing. Death is oblivion.

The second purpose of life is to live a good and meaningful life, which I defined generally as living according to core human values, the right values that contribute not only to our own life satisfactions but also to the well-being of other human beings now and in the future. People who live best live for others as well as for themselves. They take primary responsibility for themselves to be sure, but they also accept some accountability for the well-being of the communities to which they belong. They tend to accept and to do their duty, fulfilling their obligations to others. Especially important are the small face-to-face groups within which most of their daily lives are lived. Of lesser priority, but also important, are the duties to the many multileveled and diversified organizations within which their small communities exist, embracing, at the highest levels, collectivities of great social scale—up to and including all of humanity. Caring for others contributes to creating a world in which others will care for you.

The extension of individual human lives during the last few generations constitutes one of the greatest of all human achievements. In the developed countries of the world, newly born individuals can expect to live well into their mid-seventies and even into their eighties. Even in the least developed countries, there have been recent gains in longevity. More and more people nearly everywhere are living longer and longer. Largely, this great achievement in increasing the length of people's lives has been made during the last hundred years or so, despite the massive wars, genocides, and self-damaging behaviors of one of the most violent and destructive centuries in human history. We have to wonder how much more could have been accomplished without the carnage of the twentieth century.

It is possible that this trend toward longevity will continue into the future, adding decades of vigorous life to the average person. Both life expectancy and the life span might be increased. But, then again, they might not. Society as we know it might collapse, leaving members of the human race with lives that are "solitary, poor, nasty, brutish, and short." Today, as I write, in Russia death rates have gone up and people are dying younger than they did a decade ago. This serves to remind us that the future of the length of human life is contingent. It depends on many things that we cannot now know, such as the possible appearance of some new incurable diseases or some monstrous natural catastrophe, for example, a large meteor hitting the Earth. Probably, it mostly depends on what we humans do, in advancing medical knowledge, for example, but also in creating the conditions for cooperation and peace that make human efforts for social betterment possible. Ethnic, racial, and nationalist fanaticisms continue to wreak death and ruin, and the challenges of mass poverty, illiteracy, ignorance, unemployment, and undernourishment keep a billion or more of the world's people on the edge of survival.

In some countries today, children can expect to live twenty or thirty, even forty years fewer than children in other countries. Moreover, within countries—even within countries that have long life expectancies—some people, especially poor and subordinate subpopulations, can expect to live fewer years than more advantaged people in the same countries. Such inequalities in life expectancy of innocent children are shocking and morally unacceptable, because we already have the knowledge and technology to eliminate most of them.

One of the recurrent themes of this book has been the doomsday future possibilities of continued population and economic growth. Although

I concluded that there is no cause for panic, there is reason for people to begin reinforcing some old values and practices and changing some others, and for doing so now. The carrying capacity of this Spaceship and Time Machine Earth is finite. Except for its energy source, it is fundamentally a closed system and cannot maintain present levels of growth indefinitely.

The human future may depend on recognizing and living according to many age-old human values, such as knowledge, truth, honesty, integrity, justice, cooperation, loyalty, freedom, industriousness, health, love, kindness, generosity, forgiveness, respect, trust, self-control, moderation, and many others. But it also may depend on changing some values—perhaps holding some even more strongly than we now do—in response to changing conditions. Such changing conditions include resource depletion, pollution and environmental damage, the large and still rapidly growing human population, the increase in the destructive power of weapons of war, and the tremendous increase in the scale and intensity of human communication and interaction throughout the globe. If we humans fail to change in some significant ways, then the results may be devolution and anarchy (Laszlo 1994), mass misery and death.

Thus, I proposed some specific changes in human values and practices. These proposals are not the only changes that ought to be considered. No doubt, there are others. Moreover, they are contingent; we must constantly monitor and periodically review our goals and plans of action, being ready to revise them as necessary as we identify changes in relevant conditions. Future circumstances may need quite different responses than these. Given our present foresight, however, I offered the following seven recommendations:

(1) Even more value than at present ought to be placed on extending the length of individual human lives. Priority ought to be given, first, to applying existing knowledge to increase life expectancies where they are now low, so that all people everywhere will have a good chance of living out most of the human life span as we now understand it; and, second, to increasing life expectancies still more, beyond even what they are today, for the most long-lived people, and to extend the life span itself, making these new potentialities equally available to all peoples everywhere. (The cost of doing these things is not beyond possibility. A significant shift in spending throughout the world from weapons of destruction to education and health care would be a sufficient start.)

(2) At the same time, reproductive values ought to be changed everywhere, through voluntary choice and education—including education concerning everyone's individual responsibilities to society and humankind—toward valuing low birth rates, to no more than one child per person; (3) sufficiency ought to become highly valued while wasteful consumption and luxury ought to become devalued, especially in the more economically advanced societies, reinforcing age-old values of moderation and abstinence from indulgence; (4) the freedom and welfare of women ought to be valued as much as that of men, so that women will have equal opportunities with men to lead lives of their own choosing; and (5) the practices of aggression, violence and warfare, though possibly useful—even necessary—in the past as defense against the attacks of other people, ought to be devalued and replaced by the value of peaceful cooperation.

Additionally, (6) millennia-old practices of social exclusivism and ethnocentrism ought to be discarded. They are dysfunctional. In today's world, individuals and the small communities to which they belong are all interdependent. They not only depend on each other, but also on multilevel hierarchies of supranational and special purpose regional and global organizations. Today and in the coming future, it is contrary to our own freedom and welfare to create outgroups and dehumanize people as the alien Other. It is contrary to our personal interests to avoid community responsibility and not to care about the human rights of other people, both friends and strangers alike. It is contrary to our personal interest, too, to hate and to destroy, because to do so breeds more hate and destruction that may circle back to us or to our kin, neighbors, and close friends.

Rather, we ought to value inclusivism and caring for others. We will all win the most in quantity and quality of life, if we can unite globally to prevent aggression and encourage peaceful negotiation and compromise. We and others will benefit, if we can enlarge our community of concern to include all of living humanity and, thereby, help to create a world moral community.

Finally, (7) we ought to enlarge our community of concern still more to include the future. As part of our present responsibility, we ought to care for the freedom and welfare of future generations. In chapter 6, volume 2, I gave seven reasons why we ought to do so, several of which remain unrefuted and meet the five criteria of epistemic implication. The moral choice, I concluded, is a balance between the interests of both present and future generations, striving, first, to create conditions for an equal and good chance of every living person to live a long and satisfying life and, second, to leave future generations at least as well off as we of the present generation.

These proposals, stated baldly, may sound impractical. Yet I have shown that they are real possibilities. Efforts are now being made to achieve them. In some cases—for example, life expectancy, birth control, women's status—important gains already have been made in some parts of the world. In all cases active organizations exist that are dedicated to their achievement. Both regionally and globally, international agreements have been made and ratified. Transnational groups are functioning regarding mutual defense, protecting the environment, monitoring and ensuring human rights, and promoting economic and social development for sufficiency and sustainability. Governments, religious institutions, charitable foundations, and thousands of voluntary and civic groups are involved.

How successful will they be? We do not know. Certainly, the cup of long life, decency, and opportunity in the world today is no more than half full. In order to fill it to the brim, people of goodwill have much work to do. There are many obstacles to be overcome, not the least of which is the existence of ignorant and indifferent people. They are joined by other people who are consumed by selfishness, greed, hate, desires for vengeance, plans of aggression, anger, mendacity, cravings for power, self-loathing, and every evil that ever existed—plus some, no doubt, that are beyond present imagination. Additionally, they are aided and abetted by some people who think only in the short term, of immediate gratifications, with little or no serious thought of the consequences of their actions even for their own individual futures weeks or months ahead, much less the futures of their children and grandchildren many decades ahead. Perhaps most important, the organizational and institutional structures that frame the flows of communication, influence and collective action for the common good of humanity, such as the United Nations, require considerably more development and widespread participation and support.

But there is as much cause for hope as for despair. The cup *is* partly full and, over the last century, it has been getting more full. Parts of the world are already largely what Max Singer and Aaron Wildavsky (1993) refer to as zones of peace, wealth, and democracy, where life expectancies are long, birth rates are low, women are achieving equality, and civil discourse as an ideal predominates. Moreover, in such zones people tend to care about protecting the environment, creating and maintaining cooperative global interconnections with other peoples, and ensuring the well-being of future generations. Among some groups, there are signs of supporting the values of moderation and sufficiency. Of course, the struggle to control the future is by no means finished in such zones, but, despite many setbacks, the winds of change during the past century have blown toward such values and give us hope that they will spread and prevail.

There are also zones of turmoil, war, and development, as Singer and Wildavsky say, where life is cheap and where peace, harmony, and civil discourse are no more than distant dreams. In such zones, the present struggle to control the future is often furiously violent, but a process is well under way in them that will result in most of the world's societies becoming just, orderly, peaceful, democratic, and wealthy. Yet, at best, these authors envision a twenty-first century in which "billions of human beings are doomed to have their lives cut short or mutilated by poverty, tyranny and violence" before the process is complete (p. xiii).

Throughout these two volumes, I have described many images of the future, from Ogburn's vision of technological progress, Kahn's life after nuclear megadeaths, Meadows et al.'s. projections of possible overshoot and collapse of human society as we know it, and Lasswell's garrison-police state to Mau's study of Jamaican leaders' images of the future, Polak's analysis of visions of the future of entire civilizations, Textor's probings into the future of Thailand, Condorcet's future society of reason, freedom, and equality, and Marx's communist future, among many others.

The contemporary futures and futures-related literature contains hundreds of images of the future for our time that, for lack of space, I have been unable to describe here. Whether they are likely or unlikely, desirable or undesirable, or small- or large-scale, these alternative images of the future constitute a rich tapestry of possibilities, probabilities, and preferences to inform the thinking, choosing, and acting both of ordinary people in their personal lives and of public leaders in making collective decisions that may affect us all. For images of the future, as we have seen, help people steer themselves and their small groups, large organizations, their nations and their societies, and even the entire global society through time toward the goal of the best possible future.

The number of alternative possibilities for the future is enormous. The future could contain astounding advances in genetic engineering; information technology; communications; robotics that will reduce the dehumanizing routine and repetitive tasks that some people now have to perform and that will lead to a redefinition of both work and unemployment; undreamed of knowledge of the physical and social worlds; human potential, such as altered consciousness, control of emotions, body and mind control through bio-feedback, super-learning, deeper wisdom, and synergistic social organizations; abundant energy resources; fairness in human relationships; democratic participation and decision making in all groups and societies; guaranteed human rights and commensurate responsibilities for everyone; and the continued increase in the scale of society, including the possible evolution of human life into outer space.

Or it might contain none of the above. Things can get worse as well as better; zones of violence can spread to zones of peace as well as vice versa. There is no guarantee that the human experiment won't fail, resulting in high death rates and population decline, brute struggles for survival, mass starvation and deprivation, a war of all against all, uncontrolled hostility and violence, the loss of knowledge and technology, primitive living conditions, and dramatic increases in human suffering.

What will the future bring? Futurists claim that it importantly depends on the choices that people make and the actions that they take. Futurists try to contribute to the making of informed and wise choices by carrying out systematic studies of possible, probable, and preferable futures and by spreading information, formulating plans, and taking part in public discussions about what constitutes the most desirable future. Futurists aim to challenge people's thinking by encouraging them to examine critically their current routines of behavior, to consider alternatives, to search for currently unrecognized possibilities, to question their goals and values, and to become more conscious of the future and the control they may have over it. Clearly, futures education is needed, raising alternative images of the future to people's consciousness and spreading understanding of both their origins and their consequences (Riner 1991).

Today, futures studies exists as a loosely unified set of professional activities, an emerging community of futurists, and a growing body of shared purposes, assumptions, principles, methods, substantive knowledge, and values. It has already contributed importantly to policy deliberations and it can do so still more in the future. As I write, futures studies, although still a young and mostly untried field, appears to be entering another period of high productivity and intellectual progress, as it moves toward maturity. Although poor work has not yet been driven to the periphery, futures studies now contains many examples of both innovative ideas and sound, rigorous scholarship and research.

To be a futurist is to accept a special responsibility not only to investigate alternative futures, but also to work toward a desirable future. In the near term it is to work for the well-being of presently living people and in the far term for the well-being of the coming people of the future. It is to carry forward the great utopian traditions by exploring the meaning of the good society and how it can be achieved, insisting that reason includes not only technical competence but also moral learning and judgment. It is to seek the truth openmindedly and to dedicate oneself to the inherent dignity and value of each and every human life. It is to work toward democratic participation and civil discourse in public debate and in making the decisions that will shape the coming future. It is to work toward creating a community of moral concern that will include all of humanity. It is, furthermore, to work with the many social movements and organizations that aim to achieve human freedom and welfare for the various peoples of the world and the orderly social relationships that make them possible. And it is, finally, to dedicate at least a part of one's life to add in some small measure to human happiness and social harmony, both now and in the future.

Whether or not the futurist message will be heeded in the years to come remains to be seen. What is without doubt is that the future is now being prepared, largely by the human actions that have been taken, that are being taken, and that will be taken—including your actions and mine. Although we humans do not know our destiny, some future for our small planet is coming, whether or not we are ready for it. Spaceship and Time Machine Earth keeps traveling on and on, carrying us toward our common fate. Will the human experiment end in the hate, anger, and violent destruction that now threaten us? Or can we seize our opportunities, play active roles with knowledge and virtue, and write a human future of compassion, peace, love, cooperation, and justice in the book of time?

* * *

I conclude by reprinting below a pledge that describes some things that each of us can do for future generations in our daily lives. It was written by futurist Allen Tough (1993: 91):

A Pledge to Future Generations

Although humanity is far from perfect, it is definitely worthy of my respect, affection, compassion, and nurturance. I am fully aware of the pain, suffering, ignorance, selfishness, and greed in the world, but I do not condemn human civilisation nor write it off as hopeless. I believe that a satisfactory future is possible if enough people care about future generations, understand today's options, and make appropriate choices.

For me, it is very important that humanity and other life on our planet continue to evolve in positive directions. Nothing is more important than the continued flourishing of human culture and society over the next few decades and beyond. Because I care deeply about humanity and its future, I do my best to live up to the following principles.

1. I care about the well-being of future generations. Their needs are just as important as those of today. When I am making a major choice in my own life, when I am facing a significant ethical or moral question, and when I am involved in policy-making or decision-making, I take into account the needs of the next two or three generations. No short-term or narrow goal should be allowed to jeopardise humanity's long-term future. My choices support the principle of equal opportunity for each future generation: we should not cause their opportunities and well-being to be less than ours.
2. I choose paid work or volunteer work that makes a positive contribution to humanity's flourishing. I do my work with conscience—and with respect for the well-being of future generations and our planet.
3. I play my part in halting the deterioration of our environment and I support efforts to achieve a sustainable relationship with our planet. I try particularly hard to avoid actions that might reduce the ozone layer or increase global warming. I understand that people who own and consume more than they really need do even more harm to the environment than the desperate efforts of the poorest one-fifth of the world's population to survive.
4. I understand and support humanity's urgent need to halt population growth in all countries. In my own personal decisions, I am strongly influenced by this. I take highly effective steps to avoid pregnancy except when I have made a careful and thoughtful decision to have a child.
5. Because the institution of war causes so much harm over the years, I speak up against all wars, terrorism, organised violence, and arms manu-

facturing. Better ways exist for handling conflicts, greed, anger, and the urge for revenge. Because I believe the world's storehouse of weapons should be kept below the level capable of ending civilisation as we know it, I spport campaigns for a huge reduction in nuclear, biological, and chemical weapons.

6. Through words and actions, I support some of the additional goals and directions that will help human civilisation to survive and flourish over the next few decades. Examples of positive goals and directions include the following:
   - the health and well-being of children;
   - understanding and cooperation among diverse cultures;
   - a deeper understanding of the universe and our place in it;
   - a more profound body of knowledge related to world problems and our future;
   - widespread human rights, civil liberties, and political participation;
   - a designated spokesperson for future generations in all political and military decision-making;
   - experiments with innovative policy-making and governance.

7. I support local organisations, political parties, government policies, and international organisations that foster these six principles. I oppose those that do not take seriously our responsibilities to future generations.

8. When deciding how to spend my money and time, I seek an appropriate balance between my own needs and those of future generations. Instead of choosing luxuries and activities that harm the environment, I focus on my most significant underlying needs, such as relationships, learning, giving, contributing, vigorous health, a spiritual connectedness to nature, and other simple joys in life. I do not use material goods to meet my psychological and social needs.

9. I continue learning about the world's problems in some depth, and about our various potential futures ranging from highly positive to extinction. I face my feelings about these problems and possibilities, and avoid becoming stuck in hopelessness and paralysis. I speak up to counter misinformation and untruths, but I also keep an open mind to new ideas and perspectives.

10. I live in a decade during which some of the most important choices in the history of human civilisation will be made. I happily join others in facing the heroic challenge of this decade—to move from our present catastrophic path to a new path that will dramatically improve our prospects for a flourishing future.

References

Abaza, M. and G. Stauch. 1988. "Occidental reason, Orientalism, and Islamic fundamentalism." *International Sociology* 3, No. 4 (December): 343–364.

Adam, Barbara. 1988. "Social versus natural time, a traditional distinction re-examined." Pp. 198–226 in M. Young and T. Schuller (eds.), *The Rhythms of Society*. London: Routledge.

Ajzner, Jan. 1988. "Modern society as a moral community (back to Aristotle)." Paper read at the annual meetings of the American Sociological Association, Atlanta, GA (August 24–28).

Alger, Steven F. 1972. "Images of the Future and the Two Cultures." Unpublished Ph.D. dissertation, New Haven, CT: Yale University.

Alonso, William and Paul Starr (eds.). 1987. *The Politics of Numbers*. New York: Russell Sage Foundation.

Amara, Roy. 1981a. "The futures field: searching for definitions and boundaries." *The Futurist* XV (February): 25–29.

———. 1981b. "The futures field: how to tell good work from bad." *The Futurist*. XV (April): 63–71.

———. 1981c. "The futures field: which direction now?" *The Futurist*. XV (June): 42–46.

———. 1984. "New directions for futures research—setting the stage." *Futures* 16 (August): 401–404.

———. 1986. "Letter to the editors." *Futures Research Quarterly* 2, No. 3 (Fall): 5.

Anderson, Elijah. (1976) 1978. *A Place on the Corner*. Chicago: The University of Chicago Press.

Andic, Fuat M. (1985) 1990. "Human resources in the Caribbean." Pp. 153–161 in S.B. Jones-Hendrickson (ed.), *Caribbean Visions*. Frederiksted, VI: Eastern Caribbean Institute.

Andrews, Frank M. (ed.). 1979. *Scientific Productivity: The Effectiveness of Research Groups in Six Countries*. New York: Cambridge University Press, and Paris: UNESCO.

———. (ed.). 1986. *Research on the Quality of Life*. Ann Arbor: The University of Michigan.

Apter, David E. 1963. "Political religion in the new nations." Pp. 57–104 in C. Geertz (ed.), *Old Societies and New States*. New York: The Free Press of Glencoe.

Arblaster, Anthony and Steven Lukes (eds.). 1971. *The Good Society*. New York: Harper & Row, Torchbook.

Arens, W. 1986. *The Original Sin: Incest and Its Meaning*. New York: Oxford University Press.

Argyris, Chris, Robert Putnam, and Diana McLain Smith. 1985. *Action Science*. San Francisco, CA: Jossey-Bass.

333

Arizpe, Lourdes, M. Priscilla Stone, and David C. Major. 1994. "Rethinking the population-environment debate." Pp. 1–9 in L. M. Arizpe, M. P. Stone, and D. C. Major (eds.), *Population & Environment.* Boulder, CO: Westview Press.

Arizpe, Lourdes and Margarita Veláquez. 1994. Pp. 15–40 in L. M. Arizpe, M. P. Stone, and D. C. Major (eds.), *Population & Environment.* Boulder, CO: Westview Press.

Axelrod, Robert. 1984. *The Evolution of Cooperation.* New York: Basic Books.

Babbie, Earl. 1973. *Survey Research Methods.* Belmont, CA: Wadsworth.

————. 1986. *The Practice of Social Research.* Fourth Edition. Belmont, CA: Wadsworth.

Badham, Roger A. 1993. "Constructing a theology of the environment." Pp. 42–58 in H. F. Didsbury, Jr., *The Years Ahead.* Bethesda, MD: World Future Society.

Baier, Annette. 1981. "The rights of past and future persons." Pp. 171–183 in E. Partridge (ed.), *Responsibilities to Future Generations.* Buffalo, NY: Prometheus Books.

Banfield, Edward C. with the assistance of Laura Fasano Banfield. 1958. *The Moral Basis of a Backward Society.* New York: The Free Press.

Barber, Bernard. 1983. *The Logic and Limits of Trust.* New Brunswick, NJ: Rutgers University Press.

————. (ed.). 1987. *Effective Social Science.* New York: Russell Sage Foundation.

Bardis, Panos D. 1986. "Futurology and irenology: will the world be at peace in 2000 A. D.?" *International Journal of World Peace* 3, No. 2 (April-June): 117–124.

Barnes, Barry. 1974. *Scientific Knowledge and Sociological Theory.* London: Routledge & Kegan Paul.

Barney, Gerald O. (study director). 1980. *The Global 2000 Report to the President.* The Council on Environmental Quality and the Department of State. Washington, DC: U.S. Government Printing Office.

Barrett, M. and M. McIntosch. 1985. "Ethnocentrism and socialist-feminist theory." *Feminist Review* No. 20: 23–47.

Barry, Brian. 1977. "Justice between generations." Pp. 268–284 in P.M.S. Hacker and J. Raz (eds.), *Law, Morality, and Society.* Oxford: Clarendon Press.

————. 1978. "Circumstances of justice and future generations." Pp. 204–248 in R. I. Sikora and B. Barry (eds.), *Obligations to Future Generations.* Philadelphia, PA: Temple University Press.

Barry, Brian and Samuel L. Popkin. 1984. "Foreword." In K. Luker, *Abortion and the Politics of Motherhood.* Berkeley and Los Angeles: University of California Press.

Barthes, Roland. (1971) 1976. *Sade, Fourier, Loyola.* Trans. by: Richard Miller. New York: Hill and Wang.

Batson, C. Daniel. 1991. *The Altruism Question.* Hillsdale, NJ: Lawrence Erlbaum Associates.

Bauer, Raymond A. 1966. *Social Indicators.* Cambridge, MA: MIT Press.

Bauman, Zygmunt. 1976. *Socialism: The Active Utopia.* New York: Holmes & Meier.

————. 1987. *Legislators and Interpreters: Modernity, Post-modernity and intellectuals.* Ithaca, NY: Cornell University Press.

Baumeister, Roy. F. 1991. *Meanings of Life.* New York: The Guilford Press.

Bäumer, Bettina Dr. 1976. "Appendix: empirical apperception of time [in India]." Pp. 78–88 in *Cultures and Time.* Paris: The Unesco Press.

Bayes, Thomas. (1764) 1958. "An essay towards solving a problem in the doctrine of chances." *Biometrika* 45: 296–315.

Bayles, Michael D. 1981. *Professional Ethics.* Belmont, CA: Wadsworth.

Beckmann, Petr. 1971. *A History of Pi.* New York: St. Martin's Press.

Beckwith, Burnham P. 1984. *Ideas about the Future.* Palo Alto, CA: B.P. Beckwith.

Behnke, John A. and Sissela Bok (eds.). 1975. *The Dilemmas of Euthanasia* 2nd Edition. New York: Anchor Press/Doubleday.

Bell, Daniel. (1967) 1968. *Toward the Year 2000: Work in Progress.* Boston: Houghton Mifflin. First published as a special issue of *Daedalus* 96 (Summer, 1967).

———. (1973) 1976. *The Coming of Post-Industrial Society: A Venture in Social Forecasting.* New York: Basic Books.

Bell, Wendell. 1954. "A probability model for the measurement of ecological segregation." *Social Forces* 32 (May): 357–364.

———. 1964. *Jamaican Leaders: Political Attitudes in a New Nation.* Berkeley and Los Angeles: University of California Press.

———. (ed.). 1967. *The Democratic Revolution in the West Indies: Studies in Nationalism, Leadership, and the Belief in Progress.* Cambridge, MA: Schenkman.

———. 1971. "Epilogue." Pp. 324–338 in W. Bell and J. A. Mau (eds.), *The Sociology of the Future.* New York: Russell Sage Foundation.

———. 1974. "A conceptual analysis of equality and equity in evolutionary perspective." *American Behavioral Scientist* 18, No. 1 (September/October): 8–35.

———. 1977. "Inequality in independent Jamaica: A preliminary appraisal of elite performance." *Revista/Review Interamericana* 7, No. 2 (Summer): 294–308.

———. 1980. "The futurist as social scientist: From positivism to critical realism." *Futurics* 4, Nos. 3/4: 303–312.

———. 1983. "An introduction to futuristics: Assumptions, theories, methods, and research topics." *Social and Economic Studies* 32, No. 2: 1–64.

———. 1986. "The invasion of Grenada: A note on false prophecy." *The Yale Review* 75, No. 4 (October): 564–586.

———. 1987. "Is the futures field an art form or can it become a science?" *Futures Research Quarterly* 3, No. 1 (Spring): 27–44.

———. 1988. "What is a preferable future? How do we know?" Pp. 293–306 in J. Dator and M. G. Roulstone (eds.), *Who Cares? And How? Futures of Caring Societies.* Honolulu, HI: World Futures Studies Federation, University of Hawaii (Manoa).

———. 1991. "Values and the future in Marx and Marxism." *Futures* 23, No. 2 (March): 146–162.

———. 1993 "Bringing the good back in: Values, objectivity and the future." *International Social Science Journal* 137 (August): 333–347.

Bell, Wendell and Juan J. Baldrich. 1983. "Elites, economic ideologies, and democracy in Jamaica." Pp. 150–187 in M. M. Czudnowski (ed.), *Political Elites and Social Change*, International Yearbook for Studies of Leaders and Leadership, Vol. II. De Kalb, IL: Northern Illinois University Press.

Bell, Wendell and Walter E. Freeman (eds.). 1974. *Ethnicity and Nation-Building.* Beverly Hills, CA: Sage.

Bell, Wendell and James A. Mau. 1971. "Images of the future: Theory and research strategies." Pp. 6–44 in W. Bell and J. A. Mau (eds.), *The Sociology of the Future.* New York: Russell Sage Foundation.

Bell, Wendell and Jeffrey K. Olick. 1989. "An epistemology for the futures field: Problems and possibilities of prediction." *Futures* 21, No. 2 (April): 115–135.

Bell, Wendell and Ivar Oxaal. 1964. *Decisions of Nationhood: Political and Social Development in the British Caribbean.* Denver, CO: Social Science Foundation, University of Denver.

Bellah, Robert N., Richard Madsen, William M. Sullivan, Ann Swidler, and Steven M. Tipton. 1985. *Habits of the Heart: Individualism and Commitment in American Life*. Berkeley: University of California Press.

————. 1991. *The Good Society*. New York: Alfred A. Knopf.

Bennett, Jonathan. 1978. "On maximizing happiness." Pp. 61–73 in R. I. Sikora and B. Barry (eds.), *Obligations to Future Generations*. Philadelphia, PA: Temple University Press.

Bennett, Neil G. 1992. "Demographic methods." Pp. 434–445 in E. F. Borgatta and M. L. Borgatta (eds.), *Encyclopedia of Sociology*. New York: Macmillan.

Berger, Peter L. 1989. "Salvation through sociology." *The New York Times Book Review* (October 22): 34.

Bergmann, Werner. (1983) 1992. "The problem of time in sociology: An overview of the literature on the state of theory and research on the 'sociology of time', 1900–82." *Time and Society* 1, No. 1: 81–134.

Berk, Richard A. and Thomas F. Cooley. 1987. "Errors in forecasting social phenomena." Pp. 247–265 in K. C. Land and S. H. Schneider (eds.), *Forecasting in the Social and Natural Sciences*. Boston: D. Reidel.

Berkman, Lisa F. and Leonard S. Syme. 1979. "Social networks, host resistance, and mortality: A nine-year follow-up study of Alameda County residents." *American Journal of Epidemiology* 109: 186–204.

Berlin, Brent and Paul Kay. 1969. *Basic Color Terms: Their Universality and Evolution*. Berkeley and Los Angeles: University of California Press.

Bernard, Philippe J. (1963) 1966. *Planning in the Soviet Union*. Trans. by I. Nove. Oxford: Pergamon.

Bettelheim, Bruno. 1986. "Their Specialty Was Murder." *The New York Time Book Review* (October 5): 1, 61.

Bhaskar, Roy. 1978. *A Realist Theory of Science*. Sussex, England: Harvester Press.

Bickel, Alexander. 1962. *The Least Dangerous Branch: The Supreme Court at the Bar of Politics*. Indianapolis, IN: Bobbs-Merrill.

Black, Donald. 1976. *The Behavior of Law*. New York: Academic Press.

Blasco, Pedro Gonzales. 1974. "Modern nationalism in old nations as a consequence of earlier state-building: The case of Basque-Spain." Pp. 341–373 in W. Bell and W. E. Freeman (eds.), *Ethnicity and Nation-Building*. Beverly Hills, CA: Sage.

Bloch, Ernst. 1954–1959. *Collected Works*. Frankfurt-am-Main: Suhrkamp.

Bloch, Maurice. 1977. "The past and the present in the present." *Man* 12: 278–292.

Blum, Alan F. 1970. "The corpus of knowledge as a normative order." Pp. 319–336 in J. C. McKinney and E. A. Tiryakian (eds.), *Theoretical Sociology*. New York: Appleton-Century-Crofts.

Boldt, Menno. 1980. "Canadian native Indian leadership: Context and comparison." *Canadian Ethnic Studies* 12, No. 1: 15–33.

————. 1981a. "Enlightenment values, romanticism, and attitudes toward political status: A study of native leaders in Canada." *Canadian Review of Sociology and Anthropology* 18, No. 4: 545–565.

————. 1981b. "Philosophy, politics and extralegal action: Native Indian leaders in Canada." *Ethnic and Racial Studies* 4, No. 2 (April): 205–221.

————. 1982. "Intellectual orientations and nationalism among leaders in an internal colony: A theoretical and comparative perspective." *The British Journal of Sociology* 33, No. 4 (December): 484–510.

————. 1993. *Surviving as Indians*. Toronto: University of Toronto Press.

Boldt, Menno and J. Anthony Long in association with Leroy Little Bear (eds.). 1985. *The Quest for Justice*. Toronto: University of Toronto Press.

Boorman, S. A. and P. R. Leavitt. 1973. "A frequency-dependent natural selection model for the evolution of social cooperation networks." *Proceedings of the National Academy of Science* 70: 187–189.

Botkin, James W., Mahdi Elmadjra and Mircea Malitza. 1979. *No Limits to Learning: Bridging the Human Gap*. Oxford: Pergamon.

Boucher, Wayne I. 1977. "Introduction." Pp 3–13 in W. J. Boucher (ed.), *The Study of the Future: An Agenda for Research*. Washington, DC: U.S. Government Printing Office.

————. 1986. Comments on Early Warning Systems: Current Methods and Future Directions. Conference of the World Future Society, New York (July 14–17).

Boucher, Wayne I. and John V. Helb. 1977. "Appendix: Results from the Survey of Current Forecasting Efforts." Pp. 275–282 in W. I. Boucher (ed.), *The Study of the Future: An Agenda for Research*. Washington, DC: U.S. Government Printing Office.

Boucher, Wayne I. and Katherine H. Willson. 1977. "Monitoring the future." Pp. 210–232 in W. I. Boucher (ed.), *The Study of the Future: An Agenda for Research*. Washington, DC: U.S. Government Printing Office.

Boulding, Elise. 1978. "Futuristics and the imaging capacity of the west." Pp. 7–31 in M. Maruyama and A. M. Harkins (eds.), *Cultures of the Future*. The Hague: Mouton.

Boulding, Kenneth E. 1964. *The Meaning of the Twentieth Century: The Great Transition*. New York: Harper and Row.

————. 1985. *Human Betterment*. Beverly Hills, CA: Sage.

Box, G. E. P. and G. M. Jenkins. 1970. *Time Series Analysis: Forecasting and Control*. San Francisco, CA: Holden Day.

Bracher, Karl Dietrich. (1969) 1971. *The German Dictatorship*. Trans. by J. Steinberg. London: Weidenfeld and Nicolson.

Brand, Myles. 1979. "Causality." Pp. 252–290 in P. D. Asquith and H. E. Kyburg, Jr. (eds.), *Current Research in Philosophy of Science*. East Lansing, MI: Philosophy of Science Association.

Braybrooke, David. 1987. *Meeting Needs*. Princeton, NJ: Princeton University Press.

Brewer, Garry D. 1974. "The policy sciences emerge: To nurture and structure a discipline." RAND Paper Series P-5206 (April). Santa Monica, CA: The RAND Corporation.

Brewer, Garry D. and Peter deLeon. 1983. *The Foundations of Policy Analysis*. Homewood, IL: The Dorsey Press.

Brewer, Garry D. and Martin Shubik. 1979. *The War Game: A Critique of Military Problem Solving*. Cambridge, MA: Harvard University Press.

Brewer, Marilyn B. and Barry E. Collins (eds.). 1981. *Scientific Inquiry and the Social Sciences*. San Francisco, CA: Jossey-Bass.

Bright, James R. and Milton E. F. Schoeman (eds.), *A Guide to Practical Technological Forecasting*. Englewood Cliffs, NJ: Prentice-Hall.

Broad, William J. 1988. "Back into space." *The New York Times Magazine* (July 3): 10 et passim.

Broad, William and Nicholas Wade. 1982. *Betrayers of the Truth*. New York: Simon and Schuster.

Broszat, Martin. (1960) 1966. *German National Socialism, 1919–1945*. Trans. by K. Rosenbaum and I.P. Boehm. Santa Barbara, CA: Clio.

Brown, Donald E. 1991. *Human Universals*. Philadelphia, PA: Temple University Press.

Brown, Harrison. 1954. *The Challenge of Man's Future*. New York: Viking.

Brown, Lester R. et al. 1992. *State of the World 1992*. New York: W. W. Norton.

Brown, Lester R., Hal Hane, Ed Ayres et al. 1993. *Vital Signs 1993*. New York: W. W. Norton.

Brown, Robert. 1963. *Explanation in Social Science*. London: Routledge & Kegan Paul.

Brumbaugh, Robert S. 1966. "Applied metaphysics: Truth and passing time." *Review of Metaphysics* 19 (June): 647–666.

Bruner, Jerome and Carol Fleisher Feldman. 1986. "Under construction." *The New York Review of Books* 33 (March 27): 46–49.

Brutzkus, Boris. 1935. *Economic Planning in Soviet Russia*. Trans. by G. Gardiner. London: George Routledge & Sons.

Buber, Martin. 1957. *Pointing the Way*. Manchester, NH: Ayer.

Bulmer, Martin. 1983. "The British tradition of social administration: Moral concerns at the expense of scientific rigor." Pp. 161–185 in D. Callahan and B. Jennings (eds.), *Ethics, the Social Sciences, and Policy Analysis*. New York: Plenum.

Burchfield, R.W. 1972. "Futurism." P. 1182 in *A Supplement to the Oxford English Dictionary*. London: Oxford University Press.

Burk, James. 1995. "Collective violence and world peace: The social control of armed force." Paper read at the annual meetings of the American Sociological Association, Washington DC, August 19–23.

Caillois, Roger. (1958) 1961. *Man, Play, and Games*. Trans. by M. Barash. New York: The Free Press.

Calder, Nigel. 1969. "Goals, foresight, and politics." Pp. 251–255 in R. Jungk and J. Galtung (eds.), *Mankind 2000*. Oslo: Universitetsforlaget and London: Allen & Unwin.

———. 1983. *Timescale: An Atlas of the Fourth Dimension*. New York: Viking.

Callinicos, Alex. 1982. *Is There a Future for Marxism?* London: The Macmillan Press.

Campbell, Angus, Philip E. Converse, and Willard L. Rodgers. 1976. *The Quality of American Life: Perceptions, Evaluations, and Satisfactions*. New York: Russell Sage Foundation.

Campbell, Donald T. 1965. "Variation and selective retention in socio-cultural evolution." Pp. 19–49 in H. R. Barringer, G. I. Blanksten, and R. W. Mack (eds.), *Social Change in Developing Areas*. Cambridge, MA: Schenkman.

———. 1973. "Ostensive instances and entitavity in language learning." Pp. 1043–1057 in W. Gray and N.D. Rizzo (eds.), *Unity Through Diversity: A Festschrift for Ludwig von Bertalanffy*. New York: Gordon & Breach.

———. 1975. "On the conflicts between biological and social evolution and between psychology and moral tradition." *American Psychologist* 30: 1103–1126.

———. 1977. "Descriptive epistemology: psychological, sociological, and evolutionary." William James Lectures, Harvard University. Excerpts reprinted in M. B. Brewer and B. E. Collins (eds.), *Scientific Inquiry and the Social Sciences*. San Francisco, CA: Jossey-Bass, 1981: 11–17.

———. 1984a. "Can an open society be an experimenting society?" Preliminary draft of a paper read at the International Symposium on the Philosophy of Karl Popper. Madrid, November 6–9.

―――. 1984b. "Can we be scientific in applied social science?" Pp. 26–48 in R. F. Conner, D. G. Altman, and C. Jackson (eds.). *Evaluation Studies: Review Annual* Vol. 9. Beverly Hills, CA: Sage.

―――. 1986. "Science's social system of validity-enhancing collective belief change and the problems of the social sciences." Pp. 108–155 in D. W. Fiske and R. A. Schweder (eds.), *Metatheory in Social Sciences: Pluralisms and Subjectivities.* Chicago: University of Chicago Press.

Campbell, Joseph. (1949) 1968. *The Hero with a Thousand Faces.* Second Edition. Princeton, NJ: Princeton University Press.

Cantril, Hadley. 1963. "A study of aspirations." *Scientific American* 208 (February): 41–45.

―――. 1965. *The Pattern of Human Concerns.* New Brunswick, NJ: Rutgers University Press.

Cantril, Hadley and Lloyd Free. 1962. "Hopes and fears for self and country." Supplement to *The American Behavioral Scientist* 6 (October).

Carneiro, Robert L. 1978. "Political expansion as an expression of the principle of competitive exclusion." Pp. 205–223 in R. Cohen and E. R. Service (eds.), *Origins of the State.* Philadelphia, PA: Institute for the Study of Human Issues.

Caro, Francis G. 1983. "Program evaluation." Pp. 77–93 in H. E. Freeman, R. R. Dynes, P. H. Rossi, and W. F. Whyte (eds.), *Applied Sociology.* San Francisco, CA: Jossey-Bass.

Carroll, John B. (ed.). 1956. *Language, Thought, and Reality: Selected Writings of Benjamin Lee Whorf.* Boston: Technology Press of MIT.

Carter, Robert E. 1984. *Dimensions of Moral Education.* Toronto: University of Toronto Press.

Cassidy, Frederic G. 1961. *Jamaica Talk: Three Hundred Years of the English Language in Jamaica.* London: Macmillan.

Cecil, Andrew R. 1983. *The Foundations of a Free Society.* Austin: The University of Texas at Dallas.

Chandler, David P. 1991. *The Tragedy of Cambodian History.* New Haven, CT: Yale University Press.

Chaplin, George and Glenn D. Paige. 1973. *Hawaii 2000: Continuing Experiment in Anticipatory Democracy.* Honolulu: The University Press of Hawaii.

Charnov, Bruce H. 1987. "The academician as good citizen." Pp. 3–20 in S. L. Payne and B. H. Charnov (eds.), *Ethical Dilemmas for Academic Professionals.* Springfield, IL: Charles C. Thomas.

Chernoff, Herman. 1968. "Decision theory." Pp. 62–66 in D. L. Sills (ed.), *International Encyclopedia of the Social Sciences,* Vol. 4. New York: Macmillan & The Free Press.

Chomsky, Noam. 1972. *Language and Mind.* Enlarged edition. New York: Harcourt, Brace, Jovanovich.

Churchman, C. West. 1971. *The Design of Inquiring Systems.* New York: Basic Books.

―――. 1977. "A philosophy for complexity." Pp. 82–90 in H. A. Linstone and W.H. Clive Simmonds (eds.), *Futures Research: New Directions.* Reading, MA: Addison-Wesley.

Clark, Eve V. and Herbert H. Clark. 1978. "Universals, relativity, and language processing." Pp. 225–277 in J. H. Greenberg, C. A. Ferguson, & E. A. Moravcsik (eds.), *Universals of Human Language.* Stanford, CA: Stanford University Press.

Clarke, I.F. 1984. "Journeys through space and time—from the *Santa Maria* to the 'last Columbus.'" *Futures* 16 (August): 425–434.

Clausen, John A. 1986. "Early adult choices and the life course." *Zeitschrift für Sozialisationsforschuung und Erziehungssoziologie* 6 (September): 313–320.

Clayton, Audrey. 1988. "WFS professional members' forum: Winter 1988." *Futures Research Quarterly* 4, No. 4 (Winter): 87–92.

Cleveland, Harlan. 1994. "Foreword." Pp. xi–xiv in R. Kidder, *Shared Values for a Troubled World*. San Francisco, CA: Jossey-Bass Publishers.

———. 1995. "Foreword." P. v in M. Marien (ed.), *World Futures and the United Nations*. Bethesda, MD: World Future Society.

Cliff, Tony. 1974. *State Capitalism in Russia*. London: Pluto.

Clinard, Marshall B. 1990. *Corporate Corruption: The Abuse of Power*. New York: Praeger.

Coates, Joseph F. 1978. "Technology assessment." Pp. 397–421 in J. Fowles (ed.), *Handbook of Futures Research*. Westport, CT: Greenwood Press.

———. 1985. "Scenarios part two: Alternative futures." Pp. 21–46 in J. S. Mendell (ed.), *Nonextrapolative Methods in Business Forecasting*. Westport, CT: Quorum Books.

———. 1987. "Twenty years in the future." Pp. 129–136 in M. Marien and L. Jennings (eds.). *What I Have Learned*. New York: Greenwood Press.

Coates, Joseph F., Vary T. Coates, Jennifer Jarratt, and Lisa Heinz. 1986. *Issues Management*. Mt. Airy, MD: Lomond.

Coates, Joseph F. and Jennifer Jarratt. 1989. *What Futurists Believe*. Mt. Airy, MD: Lomond.

Coddington, Alan. 1975. "Creaking semaphore and beyond: A consideration of Shackle's 'epistemics and economics.'" *The British Journal for the Philosophy of Science* 26 (June): 151–163.

Coe, Michael D. 1994. "The language within us." *The New York Times Book Review* (February 27): 7–8.

Cohen, G. A. 1978. *Karl Marx's Theory of History: A Defence*. Princeton, NJ: Princeton University Press.

Cohen, Joel E. 1982. "How is the past related to the future?" Annual Report, Center for Advanced Study in the Behavioral Sciences. Stanford, CA.

Colby, Anne and Lawrence Kohlberg. 1984. "Invariant sequence and internal consistency in moral judgment stages." Pp. 41–51 in W. M. Kurtines and J. L Gewirtz (eds.), *Morality, Moral Behavior, and Moral Development*. New York: John Wiley & Sons.

Cole, H. S. D., C. Freeman, M. Jahoda, and K. L. R. Pavitt (eds.). 1975. *Models of Doom: A Critique of the Limits to Growth*. New York: Universe Books.

Cole, Sam. 1983. "Models, metaphors and the state of knowledge." Pp. 407–421 in M. Batty and B. Hutchinson (eds.), *Systems Analysis in Urban Policy-Making and Planning*. New York: Plenum Press.

———. 1993. "Learning to love *Limits*." *Futures* 25, No. 7 (September): 814–818.

Coleman, James S. 1977. "Social action systems." Pp. 11–50 in *Problems of Formalization in the Social Sciences*. UNESCO: Division for International Development of Social Sciences and the Polish Academy of Sciences.

———. 1990. *Foundations of Social Theory*. Cambridge, MA: The Belknap Press of Harvard University Press.

Coleman, J.S., E.Q. Campbell, C.J. Hobson, J. McPartland, A. Mood, F.D. Winfeld, and R.L. York. 1966. *Equality of Educational Opportunity*. Washington, DC: U.S. Government Printing Office.

Collard, David. 1978. *Altruism and Economy*. New York: Oxford University Press.

Collins, H.M. 1985. *Changing Order: Representation, and Induction in Scientific Practice*. Beverly Hills, CA: Sage.

Conant, James B. 1951. *On Understanding Science*. New York: Mentor.

Condorcet, Antoine-Nicolas de. (1795) 1955. *Sketch for a Historical Picture of the Progress of the Human Mind*. Trans. by J. Barraclough. London: Weidenfeld and Nicolson.

Cook, Lauren. 1990. "State government foresight in the US." *Futures Research Quarterly* 6, No. 4 (Winter): 27–40.

Cook, Thomas D. and Donald T. Campbell. 1979. *Quasi-Experimentation: Design & Analysis Issues for Field Settings*. Chicago: Rand McNally.

Cornish, Edward S. 1980. Personal communication to W. Bell (July 28).

Cornish, Edward, with the members and staff of the World Future Society. 1977. *The Study of the Future*. Washington, DC: World Future Society.

Cotterrell, Roger. 1984. *The Sociology of Law: An Introduction*. London: Butterworths.

Cowen, Tyler and Derek Parfit. 1992. "Against the social discount rate." Pp. 144–161 in P. Laslett and J. S. Fishkin (eds.), *Justice Between Age Groups and Generations*. New Haven, CT: Yale University Press.

Cox, Harvey. 1985. "Challenges to faith and religion in the age of high technology." The Tenth Sir Winston Scott Memorial Lecture. Bridgetown, Barbados: Central Bank of Barbados.

Creativity: The Human Resource. 1980. Creativity exhibit, New York (August).

Cressey, Donald R. 1953. *Other People's Money*. Glencoe, IL: Free Press.

Crews, Frederick. 1986. "In the big house of theory." *The New York Review of Books* 33 (May 29): 36–42.

Crick, Francis. 1988. *What Mad Pursuit*. New York: Basic.

Cronbach, Lee J., Sueann Robinson Ambron, Sanford M. Dornbusch, Robert D. Hess, Robert C. Hornik, D.C. Phillips, Decker F. Walker, and Stephen S. Weiner. (1980) 1981. *Toward Reform of Program Evaluation*. San Francisco, CA: Jossey-Bass.

Crowley, J. Donald. 1972. "Introduction." Pp. xii–xxi in D. Defoe, *The Life and Strange Surprizing Adventures of Robinson Crusoe, of York, Mariner*. London: Oxford University Press.

Cumper, Gloria. 1972. *Survey of Social Legislation in Jamaica*. Mona, Jamaica: Institute of Social and Economic Research, University of the West Indies.

Cunningham, F. 1973. *Objectivity in Social Science*. Toronto: University of Toronto Press.

Dahle, Kjell. 1991. *On Alternative Ways of Studying the Future: International Institutions, an Annotated Bibliography and a Norwegian Case*. Trans. by Alison Coulthard. Olso: The Alternative Future Project.

———. 1992. "Participatory futures studies: Concepts and realities." *Futures Research Quarterly* 8, No. 4 (Winter): 83–92.

Darnton, Robert. 1984. "Working class Casanova." *The New York Review of Books* 31 (June 28, 1984): 33.

Dator, Jim. 1983. "The 1982 Honolulu electronic town meeting." Pp. 211–220 in W. Page (ed.), *The Future of Politics*. London: Frances Pinter in association with the World Futures Studies Federation.

———. 1984a. "Quantum theory and political design." Pp. 53–65 in R. Homann, E. Masini, and A. Sicinski (eds.), *Changing Lifestyles as Indicators of New and Cultural Values*. Zurich: the Gottlieb Duttweiler Institute.

———. 1984b. Personal communication (July 27).

———. 1993. "President's Report to the General Assembly of the World Futures Studies Federation." Turku, Finland (August 25).

————. 1994a. "Women in futures studies and women's visions of the futures—one man's tentative view." *The Manoa Journal of Fried and Half-Fried Ideas*, Occasional paper 2 (January): 40–57.

————. 1994b. "What is (and what is not) futures studies." *Papers de Prospectiva* (May): 24–47.

Dator, James A., Christopher B. Jones, and Barbara G. Moir. 1986. *A Study of Preferred Futures for Telecommunications in Six Pacific Island Societies*. Honolulu, HI: Pacific International Center for High Technology Research and Social Science Research Institute.

Dator, James A. and Sharon J. Rodgers. 1991. *Alternative Futures for the State Courts of 2020*. Chicago: State Justice Institute and the American Judicature Society.

Davies, Merryl Wyn, Ashis Nandy, and Ziauddin Sardar. 1993. *Barbaric Others*. London: Pluto Press.

Davies, P.C.W. 1977. *Space and Time in the Modern Universe*. Cambridge: Cambridge University Press.

————. 1993. "The holy grail of physics." *The New York Times Book Review* (April 7): 11–12.

Dawes, R. M. 1986. "Forecasting one's own preference." *International Journal of Forecasting* 2: 5–14.

Defoe, Daniel. (1719) 1972. *The Life and Strange Surprizing Adventures of Robinson Crusoe, of York Mariner*. London: Oxford University Press.

deLeon, Peter. 1984. "Futures studies and the policy sciences." *Futures* 16, No. 6 (December): 586–593.

Denton, David E. 1986. "Images, plausibility and truth." *Futures Research Quarterly* 2, No. 2 (Summer): 53–62.

Derathe, Robert. 1968. "Rousseau, Jean Jacques." Pp. 563–571 in D. L. Sills (ed.), *International Encyclopedia of the Social Sciences*, Vol. 13. New York: Macmillan & the Free Press.

Deutsch, K. W. 1963. "Nation-building and national development: Some issues for political research." Pp. 1–16 in K. W. Deutsch and W. J. Foltz (eds.), *Nation-Building*. New York: Atherton Press.

Deutsch, Morton. 1986. "Cooperation, conflict, and justice." Pp. 3–18 in H. W. Bierhoff, R. L. Cohen, and J. Greenberg (eds.), *Justice in Social Relations*. New York: Plenum Press.

De Vos, George and Lola Romanucci-Ross. 1975. "Ethnicity: Vessel of meaning and emblem of contrast." Pp. 363–390 in G. De Vos and L. Romanucci-Ross (eds.), *Ethnic Identity*. Palo Alto, CA: Mayfield.

Dewey, John. 1959. *Moral Principle in Education*. New York: Philosophical Library.

Dewhurst, J.F. and Associates. 1947 and 1955. *America's Needs and Resources*. New York: The Twentieth Century Fund.

Diamond, Jared. 1992. *The Third Chimpanzee: The Evolution and Future of the Human Animal*. New York: HarperCollins.

Dickson, Paul. (1971) 1972. *Think Tanks*. New York: Atheneum (second printing).

————. 1977. *The Future File*. New York: Avon.

Dickson, Lovat. 1969. *H. G. Wells: His Turbulent Life and Times*. New York: Atheneum.

Didsbury, H. F., Jr. (ed.). 1991. *Prep 21 Bulletin* No. 2 (Spring).

Diesing, P. 1971. *Patterns of Discovery in the Social Sciences*. Chicago: Aldine-Atherton.

Dillon, Michele. 1993. *Debating Divorce: Moral Conflict in Ireland*. Lexington: The University Press of Kentucky.

DiMaggio, Paul. 1989. Personal communication (April 21).

Dolbeare, Kenneth M. and Patricia Dolbeare. 1976. *American Ideologies: The Competing Political Beliefs of the 1970s*. Third Edition. Boston: Houghton Mifflin.

Doob, Leonard W. 1988. *Inevitability: Determinism, Fatalism, and Destiny*. New York: Greenwood Press.

Doyal, Len and Ian Gough. 1991. *A Theory of Human Need*. London: Macmillan.

Dror, Yehezkel. 1971. *Ventures in Policy Sciences: Concepts and Applications*. New York: Elsevier.

———. 1975. "Some fundamental philosophical, psychological and intellectual assumptions of futures studies." Pp. 145–165 in *The Future as an Academic Discipline*. Ciba Foundation Symposium 36. Amsterdam: Elsevier.

Drucker, Malka and Gary Block. 1992. *Rescuers: Portraits in Moral Courage in the Holocaust*. New York: Holmes & Meier.

Dublin, Louis I., Alfred J. Lotka, and Mortimer Spiegelman. 1949. *Length of Life: A Study of the Life Table*, rev. ed.: New York: Ronald.

Dunne, J.W. (1927) no date. *An Experiment with Time*. Third Edition. London: Faber and Faber (paper).

Durand, John D. 1960. "Mortality estimates from Roman tombstone inscriptions." *American Journal of Sociology* 65, No. 4 (January): 365–374.

Dworkin, Ronald. 1981. "What is equality? Part I: Equality of welfare." *Philosophy and Public Affairs* 10: 185–246.

———. 1994. "Mr. Liberty." *The New York Review of Books* XLI, No. 14 (August 11): 17–22.

Dye, Thomas R. 1978. *Understanding Public Policy*. Third Edition. Englewood Cliffs, NJ: Prentice-Hall.

Dyson, Freeman. 1995. "The scientist as rebel." *The New York Review of Books* XLII, No. 9 (May 25): 31–33.

Eaton, Ralph. 1931. *General Logic: An Introductory Survey*. New York: C. Scribner's Sons.

Ebenstein, William. 1968. "National socialism." Pp. 45–50 in D. L. Sills (ed.), *International Encyclopedia of the Social Sciences*, Vol. 11. New York: Macmillan & The Free Press.

Edel, Abraham. (1955) 1994. *Ethical Judgment: The Use of Science in Ethics*. New Brunswick, NJ: Transaction.

Edel, Abraham, Elizabeth Flower, and Finbarr W. O'Connor. 1994. *Critique of Applied Ethics*. Philadelphia, PA: Temple University Press.

Edgerton, Robert B. 1992. *Sick Societies: Challenging the Myth of Primitive Harmony*. New York: The Free Press.

Edwards, Ward. 1968. "Decision making: Psychological aspects." Pp. 34–42 in D. L. Sills (ed.), *International Encyclopedia of the Social Sciences*, Vol. 4. New York: Macmillan & The Free Press.

Ehrenberg, Victor. 1951. *The People of Aristophanes: A Sociology of Old Attic Comedy*. Second Edition. Oxford: Basil Blackwell.

Ehrlich, Anne. 1985. "Critical masses." *The Humanist* 45 (July/August): 18–22 et passim.

Ehrlich, Paul R. and Anne H. Ehrlich. 1991. *The Population Explosion*. New York: Touchstone (Simon & Schuster).

Einaudi, Mario. 1968. "Fascism." Pp. 334–341 in D. L. Sills (ed.), *International Encyclopedia of the Social Sciences*, Vol. 5. New York: Macmillan & the Free Press.

Eisenberg, Nancy. 1986. *Altruistic Emotion, Cognition, and Behavior.* Hillsdale, NJ: Lawrence Erlbaum Associates.

Ekman, Paul. 1980. *The Face of Man.* New York: Garland STPM.

———. 1982. *Emotion in the Human Face.* New York: Cambridge University Press.

Elster, Jon. 1978. *Logic and Society: Contradictions and Possible Worlds.* New York: John Wiley.

———. 1985. *Making Sense of Marx.* Cambridge: Cambridge University Press.

Encel, Solomon, Pauline K. Marstrand, and William Page (eds.). 1975. *The Art of Anticipation.* London: Martin Robertson.

English-Lueck, J. A. 1990. "China 2020: Looking forward." *Futures Research Quarterly* 6, No. 3 (Fall): 5–12.

Etzioni, Amitai. 1968. *The Active Society.* New York: Free Press.

———. 1988. *The Moral Dimension.* New York: Free Press.

———. 1992. "How to fix the pharmaceuticals." *The New York Times* (February 23): F13.

Eulau, Heinz. 1958. "H. D. Lasswell's developmental analysis." *The Western Political Quarterly* XI (June): 229–242.

Falk, R. A. 1975. *A Study of Future Worlds.* New York: Free Press.

———. 1977. "Contending approaches to world order." *Journal of International Affairs* 31: 171–198.

———. 1983. *The End of World Order.* New York: Holmes and Meier.

Fanon, Frantz. 1966. *The Wretched of the Earth.* New York: Grove (First Evergreen Edition).

———. 1967. *Black Skin, White Masks.* New York: Grove.

Farrell, Warren. 1993. *The Myth of Male Power.* New York: Simon & Schuster.

Ferguson, Charles A. 1978. "Talking to children: A search for universals." Pp. 203–224 in J. H. Greenberg, C. A. Ferguson, & E. A. Moravscik (eds.), *Universals of Human Language.* Stanford, CA: Stanford University Press.

Ferkiss, Victor. 1974. *The Future of Technological Civilization.* New York: George Braziller.

———. 1977. "Futurology: Promise, performance, prospects." *The Washington Papers* V, No. 50. Beverly Hills, CA: Sage.

Ferrarotti, Franco. 1986. *Five Scenarios for the Year 2000.* New York: Greenwood.

Feyerabend, Paul. 1975. *Against Method: Outline of an Anarchistic Theory of Knowledge.* London: NLB.

Fink, Arlene and Jacqueline Kosecoff. 1985. *How to Conduct Surveys.* Beverly Hills, CA: Sage.

Flechtheim, Ossip K. 1966. *History and Futurology.* Meisenheim-am-Glan, Germany: Verlag Anton Hain.

———. (1969) 1971. "Is futurology the answer to the challenge of the future?" Pp. 264–269 in R. Jungk and J. Galtung (eds.), *Mankind 2000.* Oslo: Universitetsforlaget and London: Allen & Unwin.

Foerster, Heinz von. 1977. "The curious behavior of complex systems: Lessons from biology." Pp. 104–113 in Harold A. Linstone and W.H. Clive Simmonds (eds.), *Futures Research: New Directions.* Reading, MA: Addison-Wesley.

Fogel, R.W. 1964. *Railroads and American Economic Growth.* Baltimore: Johns Hopkins Press.

Folger, Robert. 1986. "Rethinking equity theory: A referent cognition model." Pp. 145–162 in H. W. Bierhoff, R. L. Cohen, and J. Greenberg (eds.), *Justice in Social Relations.* New York: Plenum Press.

Forrester, Jay W. 1971. *World Dynamics*. Cambridge, MA: Wright-Allen Press.

Foss, Dennis C. 1977. *The Value Controversy in Sociology*. San Francisco, CA: Jossey-Bass.

Fowles, Jib. 1978. "Preface." Pp. ix–xi in J. Fowles (ed.), *Handbook of Futures Research*. Westport, CT: Greenwood.

Fraisse, Paul. 1968. "Time: Psychological aspects." Pp. 25–30 in D. L. Sills (ed.), *International Encyclopedia of the Social Sciences*, Vol. 16. New York: Macmillan & the Free Press.

Fraser, J. T. 1982. *The Genesis and Evolution of Time*. Amherst: The University of Massachusetts Press.

Freeman, Christopher. 1975. "Malthus with a computer." Pp. 5–13 in H. S. D. Cole, C. Freeman, M. Jahoda, and K. L. R. Pavitt (eds.), *Models of Doom: A Critique of the Limits to Growth*. New York: Universe Books.

Freeman, Derek. 1983. *Margaret Mead and Samoa: The Making and Unmaking of an Anthropological Myth*. Cambridge, MA: Harvard University Press.

Frey, James H. 1989. *Survey Research by Telephone*. 2nd Printing. Newbury Park, CA: Sage.

Friedman, Lawrence M. 1987. Review of "The Court and the Constitution." *The New York Times Book Review*. September 20: 3.

Friedrichs, Robert W. 1970. *A Sociology of Sociology*. New York: Free Press.

Furbank, P. N. 1993. "Leave it to chance." *The New York Review of Books* XL, No. 19 (November 18): 48–50.

Gabor, Dennis. 1964. *Inventing the Future*. New York: Alfred A. Knopf.

Gabor, Thomas. 1986. *The Prediction of Criminal Behavior*. Toronto: University of Toronto Press.

Galtung, Johan. 1980. *The True Worlds*. New York: Free Press.

Galtung, Johan and Robert Jungk. (1969) 1971. "Postscript: A warning and a hope." P. 368 in R. Jungk and J. Galtung (eds.), *Mankind 2000*. Oslo: Universitets forlaget and London: Allen & Unwin.

Gappert, Gary. 1979. *Post Affluent America*. New York: Franklin Watts.

———. 1982. "Future urban America: Post-affluent or advanced industrial society?" Pp. 9–34 in G. Gappert and R. V. Knight (eds.), *Cities in the 21st Century*. Beverly Hills, CA: Sage.

Garcia, John and Robert A. Koelling. 1966. "Relation of cue to consequence in avoidance learning." *Psychonomic Science* 4: 123–124.

Gardet, Louis. 1976. "Moslem views of time and history: An essay in cultural typology." Pp. 197–227 in *Cultures and Time*. Paris: The Unesco Press.

Gaston, Jerry. (1970) 1973. *Originality and Competition in Science*. Chicago: The University of Chicago Press.

Geertz, Clifford. 1968. "Religion: Anthropological study." Pp. 398–406 in D. L. Sills (ed.), *International Encyclopedia of the Social Sciences*, Vol. 13. New York: Macmillan & The Free Press.

———. 1983. *Local Knowledge*. New York: Basic.

Gell, Alfred. 1992. *The Anthropology of Time*. Providence, RI: Berg.

Gellner, Ernest. 1981. "General introduction: Relativism and universals." Pp. 1–20 in B. Lloyd and J. Gay (eds.), *Universals of Human Thought: Some African Evidence*. Cambridge: Cambridge University Press.

———. 1985. *Relativism and the Social Sciences*. Cambridge: Cambridge University Press.

Geras, Norman. 1989. "The controversy about Marx and justice." Pp. 211–267 in A. Callinicos (ed.), *Marxist Theory*. Oxford: Oxford University Press.

Gereffi, Gary. 1983. *The Pharmaceutical Industry and Dependency in the Third World*. Princeton, NJ: Princeton University Press.

Gert, Bernard. 1988. *Morality: A New Justification of the Moral Rules*. New York: Oxford University Press.

Gewirth, Alan. 1978. *Reason and Morality*. Chicago: University of Chicago Press.

Gibbs, Jack P. 1989. *Control: Sociology's Central Notion*. Urbana and Chicago: University of Illinois Press.

Gibson, James William. 1986. *The Perfect War*. Boston: The Atlantic Monthly Press.

Giddens, Anthony. 1973. *The Class Structure of the Advanced Societies*. New York: Barnes & Noble.

————. (ed.). 1974. *Positivism and Sociology*. London: Heinemann.

Gifford, James C. 1978. "The prehistory of *Homo sapiens*: Touchstone for the future." Pp. 71–100 in M. Maruyama and A. M. Harkins (eds.), *Cultures of the Future*. The Hague: Mouton.

GilFillan, S. Colum. 1920. "Successful Social Prophecy in the Past." Unpublished M. A. Thesis. New York: Columbia University (Faculty of Political Science, Department of Sociology).

————. 1935. *The Sociology of Invention*. Chicago: Follet.

Gilligan, Carol. 1982. *In a Different Voice*. Cambridge, MA: Harvard University Press.

Gilmore, David D. 1990. *Manhood in the Making*. New Haven, CT: Yale University Press.

Glaser, Barney G. 1965. "The constant comparative method of qualitative analysis." *Social Problems* 12 (Spring): 436–445.

Glaser, Barney G. and Anselm L. Strauss. 1967. *The Discovery of Grounded Theory*. Chicago: Aldine.

Glassman, James K. 1995 "A program gone bonkers." *The Washington Post Weekly Edition* (October 16–22): 27.

Glazer, Myron Peretz and Penina Migdal Glazer. 1989. *Whistleblowers*. New York: Basic Books.

Glock, Charles Y. (1951) 1955. "Some applications of the panel method to the study of change." Pp. 242–250 in P. F. Lazarsfeld and M. Rosenberg (eds.), *The Language of Social Research*. Glencoe, IL: Free Press.

Goldschmidt, Walter. 1990. *The Human Career*. Cambridge, MA: Basil Blackwell.

Goldthorpe, John H. 1971. "Theories of industrial society: Reflections on recrudescence of historicism and the future of futurology." *Archives Européene de Sociologie* 12, No. 2: 263–288.

Goody, Jack. 1968. "Time: Social organization." Pp. 30–42 in D. L. Sills (ed.), *International Encyclopedia of the Social Sciences*, Vol. 16. New York: Macmillan & the Free Press.

Goodenough, Ward H. 1970. *Description and Comparison in Cultural Anthropology*. Chicago: Aldine.

Gordon, T. J. 1968. "New approaches to Delphi." In J. R. Bright (ed.), *Technological Forecasting for Industry and Government*. Englewood Cliffs, NJ: Prentice Hall.

————. 1990. Personal Communication.

————. 1992. "The methods of futures research." *The Annals of the American Academy of Political and Social Science* 522 (July): 25–35.

Gordon, Theodore J. and David Greenspan. 1988. "Chaos and fractals: New tools for technological and social forecasting." *Technological Forecasting and Social Change* 34: 1–25.

Gordon, Theodore J., Herbert Gerjuoy, and Mark Anderson (eds.). 1979. *Life Extending Technologies*. New York: Pergamon.

Gordon, Ted, Herbert Gerjuoy and Robert Jungk. 1987. "The business of forecasting: A discussion of ethical and practical considerations." *Futures Research Quarterly* 3 (Summer): 21–36.

Gordon, T. J. and J. Hayward. 1968. "Initial experiments with the cross-impact matrix method of forecasting." *Futures* 1, No. 2: 100–116.

Gordon, Theodore and Olaf Helmer. 1964. *Report on a Long-Range Forecasting Study*. Santa Monica, CA: RAND paper P-2982.

———. (1964) 1966. "Report on a long-range forecasting study." Pp. 44–96 in O. Helmer (ed), *Social Technology*. New York: Basic Books.

Gorney, Roderic. (1968) 1979. *The Human Agenda*. Los Angeles: Guild for Tutors Press.

Gottheil, Fred M. 1966. *Marx's Economic Predictions*. Evanston, IL: Northwestern University Press.

Gouldner, Alvin W. 1970. *The Coming Crisis of Western Sociology*. New York: Basic Books.

———. 1985. *Against Fragmentation: The Origins of Marxism and the Sociology of Intellectuals*. New York: Oxford University Press.

Goveia, Elsa V. 1956. *A Study on the Historiography of the British West Indies to the End of the Nineteenth Century*. Mexico: Instituto Panamericano de Geografia e Historia.

Granger, C. W. J. 1980. *Forecasting in Business and Economics*. New York: Academic.

Granger, Gilles-Gaston. 1968. "Condorcet." Pp. 213–215 in D. L. Sills (ed.), *International Encyclopedia of the Social Sciences*, Vol. 3. New York: Macmillan & the Free Press.

Greeley, Andrew M. 1989. *Religious Change in America*. Cambridge, MA: Harvard University Press.

Green, Ronald M. (1977) 1981. "Intergenerational distributive justice and environmental responsibility." Pp. 91–101 in E. Partridge (ed.), *Responsibilities to Future Generations*. Buffalo, NY: Prometheus Books.

Griffin, James. 1986. *Well-Being: Its Meaning, Measurement, and Moral Importance*. Oxford: Clarendon Press.

Grisez, Germain and Russell Shaw. 1988. *Beyond the New Morality*. Third Edition. Notre Dame, IN: University of Notre Dame Press.

Grunberger, Richard. 1971. *A Social History of the Third Reich*. London: Weidenfeld and Nicolson.

Guetzkow, H., C. F. Alger, R. Brody, R. D. Noël, and R. C. Snyder. 1963. *Simulation in International Relations: Developments for Research and Teaching*. Englewood Cliffs, NJ: Prentice-Hall.

Gurevich, A.J. 1976. "Time as a problem of cultural history." Pp. 229–245 in *Cultures and Time*. Paris: The Unesco Press.

Haan, Norma. 1983. "An interactional morality of everyday life." Pp. 218–250 in N. Haan, R. N. Bellah, P. Rabinow, and W. M. Sullivan (eds.), *Social Science as Moral Inquiry*. New York: Columbia University Press.

Habermas, Jürgen. 1970a. "On systematically distorted communication." *Inquiry* 13 (Autumn): 205–218.

———. 1970b. "Towards a theory of communicative competence." *Inquiry* 13 (Winter): 360–375.

————. 1973. *Theory and Practice*. Trans. by J. Viertel. Boston: Beacon Press.

————. (1981) 1984. *The Theory of Communicative Action*. Part I. Trans. by T. McCarth. Boston: Beacon.

Hacking, Ian. 1981. "Introduction." Pp. 1–5 in I. Hacking (ed.), *Scientific Revolutions*. Oxford: Oxford University Press.

————. 1986. "Science turned upside down." *The New York Review of Books* 33 (February 27): 21–26.

Hadley, Arthur T. (1971) 1986. *The Straw Giant*. New York: Random House.

Hahn, Walter A. 1985. "Futures in politics and the politics of futures." *Futures Research Quarterly* 1, No. 4 (Winter): 35–56.

Halfpenny, Peter. 1982. *Positivism and Sociology*. London: George Allen & Unwin.

Hall, Robert T. 1987. *Emile Durkheim: Ethics and the Sociology of Morals*. New York: Greenwood Press.

Halley, Edmund. 1693. "An estimate of the degrees of mortality of mankind." *Philosophical Transactions of the Royal Society of London* 17: 596–610.

Hallo, William W. 1993. "Digging up the future." Unpublished paper, New Haven, CT: Yale University.

Hampshire, Stuart. 1955. "Introduction." Pp. vii–xii in Condorcet, *Sketch for a Historical Picture of the Progress of the Human Mind*. Trans. by J. Barraclough. London: Weidenfeld and Nicolson.

Hanson, N.R. 1958. *Patterns of Discovery*. Cambridge: Cambridge University Press.

Hardin, Garrett. 1993. *Living within Limits*. Oxford: Oxford University Press.

Hare, R. M. 1952. *The Language of Morals*. Oxford: The Clarendon Press.

Harman, Gilbert. 1977. *The Nature of Morality*. New York: Oxford University Press.

Harman, Willis W. and Peter Schwartz. 1978. "Changes and challenges for futures research." Pp. 791–801 in J. Fowles (ed.), *Handbook of Futures Research*. Westport, CT: Greenwood Press.

Harner, L. 1975. "*Yesterday* and *tomorrow*: Development of early understanding of the terms." *Developmental Psychology* 11: 864–865.

Harris, Marvin. 1977. *Cannibals and Kings*. New York: Random House.

————. 1989. *Our Kind*. New York: Harper & Row.

Haste, Helen and Jane Baddeley. 1991. "Moral theory and culture: The case of gender." Pp. 223–249 in W. M. Kurtines and J. L. Gewirtz (eds.), *Handbook of Moral Behavior and Development*, Vol 1 "Theory." Hillsdale, NJ: Lawrence Erlbaum Associates.

Hawken, Paul, James Ogilvy, Peter Schwartz. 1982. *Seven Tomorrows*. New York: Bantam.

Hayashi, Yujiro. 1978. "Futures research in Japan." Pp. 31–38 in J. Fowles (ed.), *Handbook of Futures Research*. Westport, CT: Greenwood.

Heilbroner, Robert. 1993. *21st Century Capitalism*. New York: W. W. Norton.

————. 1995. *Visions of the Future*. New York: Oxford University Press.

Heineman, Kenneth J. 1993. *Campus Wars*. New York: New York University Press.

Helmer, Olaf. 1970. *Report on the Future of the Future-State-of-the-Union Reports* R-14. Middletown, CT: Institute for the Future.

————. 1983. *Looking Forward: A Guide to Futures Research*. Beverly Hills, CA: Sage.

Helmer, O. and N. Rescher. 1960. "On the Epistemology of the Inexact Sciences" R-353. Santa Monica, CA: The Rand Corporation.

Hemming, James. 1974. *Probe: 2. The Values of Survival*. Sydney, Australia: Angus & Robertson.

Hempel, Carl G. 1965. *Aspects of Scientific Explanation*. New York: Free Press.

Henshel, Richard L. 1976. *On the Future of Social Prediction*. Indianapolis, IN: Bobbs: Merrill.

———. 1978. "Self-altering predictions." Pp. 99–123 in J. Fowles (ed.), *Handbook of Futures Research*. Westport, CT: Greenwood Press.

———. 1981. "Evolution of controversial fields: Lessons from the past for futures." *Futures* 13 (October): 401–412.

———. 1982. "Sociology and social forecasting." Pp. 57–79 in R. H. Turner and J. F. Short, Jr. (eds.), *Annual Review of Sociology*, Vol. 8. Palo Alto, CA: Annual Reviews.

———. 1987. "Credibility and confidence: Feedback loops in social prediction." A paper read at the VII International Congress of Cybernetics and Systems, University of London (September).

———. 1990. *Thinking about Social Problems*. San Diego, CA: Harcourt Brace Jovanovich.

———. 1993. "Do self-fulfilling prophecies improve or degrade predictive accuracy? How sociology and economics can disagree and both be right." *The Journal of Socio-Economics* 22, No. 2: 85–104.

Henshel, Richard L. and William Johnston. 1987. "The emergence of bandwagon effects: A theory." *The Sociological Quarterly* 28, No. 4 (December): 493–511.

Hermkens, Piet and David van Kreveld. 1991. "Social justice, income distribution, and social stratification in the Netherlands: A review." Pp. 119–138 in H. Steensma and Riël Vermunt (eds.), *Social Justice in Human Relations*, Vol. 2, "Societal and Psychological Consequences of Justice and Injustice." New York: Plenum Press.

Hick, John. 1989. *An Interpretation of Religion*. New Haven, CT: Yale University Press.

Hill, K. Q. and J. Fowles. 1975. "The methodological worth of the Delphi forecasting technique." *Technological Forecasting and Social Change* 7: 179–192.

Hirschi, Travis and Michael Gottfredson (eds.). 1994. *The Generality of Deviance*. New Brunswick, NJ: Transaction.

Hirschi, Travis and Hanan C. Selvin. 1967. *Delinquency Research: An Appraisal of Analytic Methods*. New York: Free Press.

Hirschman, Albert O. 1970. *Exit, Voice, and Loyalty: Responses to Decline in Firms, Organizations, and States*. Cambridge, MA: Harvard University Press.

Hobsbawm, Eric. 1994. *The Age of Extremes*. New York: Pantheon.

Hogben, Lancelot. (1955) 1968. *The Wonderful World of Mathematics*. Garden City, NY: Doubleday.

Holden, K., D. A. Peel, and J. L. Thompson. 1990. *Economic Forecasting: An Introduction*. Cambridge: Cambridge University Press.

Holsti, Ole. 1969. *Content Analysis for the Social Sciences and Humanities*. Reading, MA: Addison-Wesley.

Hopkins, Terence K. and Immanuel Wallerstein. 1967. "The comparative study of national societies." *Social Science Information sur les Sciences Sociales*, VI, No. 5 (October): 25–58.

Horowitz, Irving Louis. 1993. *The Decomposition of Sociology*. New York: Oxford University Press.

———. 1994. "One day in the life of contemporary sociology." *Partisan Review*, LXI, No. 3: 501–510.

House, James S. 1986. "Social support and the quality and quantity of life." Pp. 253–269 in F. M. Andrews (ed.), *Research on the Quality of Life*. Ann Arbor: The University of Michigan.

Howells, W. W. 1960. "Estimating population numbers through archaeological and skeletal remains." Pp. 158–185 in R. F. Heizer and S. F. Cook (eds.), *The Application of Quantitative Methods in Archaeology*. Viking Fund Publications in Anthropology, No. 28. New York: Wenner-Gren Foundation for Anthropological Research, Inc.

Hughes, H. Stuart. 1958. *Consciousness and Society*. New York: Vintage Books (Random House).

Huber, Bettina J. 1973. "Images of the Future Among the White South African Elite." Unpublished Ph.D. dissertation, New Haven, CT: Yale University.

———. 1974. "Images of the future." Pp. 151–169 in H. W. van der Merwe, M. J. Ashley, N. C. J. Charton, and B. J. Huber, *White South African Elites*. Cape Town: Juta.

Huizinga, J.H. 1976. *Rousseau: The Self-made Saint*. New York: Grossman (Viking).

Huntington, Samuel P. 1993. "The clash of civilizations?" *Foreign Affairs* 72, No. 3 (Summer): 22–49.

Husserl, E. (1887) 1966. *The Phenomenology of Internal Time Consciousness*. Bloomington, IN: Midland Books.

Iacocca, Lee with William Novak. 1984. *Iacocca: An Autobiography*. New York: Bantam.

Inayatullah, Sohail. 1993. "From 'who am I?' to 'when am I?'" *Futures* 25, No. 3 (April): 235–253.

Inglehart, Ronald. 1990. *Culture Shift in Advanced Industrial Society*. Princeton, NJ: Princeton University Press.

Innes, Judith Eleanor. (1975) 1990. *Knowledge and Public Policy*. Second Expanded Edition. New Brunswick, NJ: Transaction.

Israeli, Nathan. 1932a. "The social psychology of time." *Journal of Abnormal and Social Psychology* 27 (July): 209–213.

———. 1932b. "The psychopathology of time." *Psychological Review* 39 (September): 486–491.

———. 1932c. "Wishes concerning improbable future events: Reactions to the future." *Journal of Applied Psychology* 16 (October): 584–588.

———. 1933a. "Attitudes to the Decline of the West." *Journal of Social Psychology* 4 (February): 92–101.

———. 1933b. "Group estimates of the divorce rate for the years 1935–1975." *Journal of Social Psychology* 4 (February): 102–115.

———. 1933c. "Group predictions of future events." *Journal of Social Psychology* 4 (May): 201–222.

———. 1933d. "Measurement of attitudes and reactions to the future." *Journal of Abnormal and Social Psychology* 28 (July): 181–193.

Jackson, Walter A. 1990. *Gunnar Myrdal and America's Conscience*. Chapel Hill: University of North Carolina Press.

Jacob, François. 1988. *The Statue Within: An Autobiography*, as quoted in *The New York Times Book Review* 10 (April).

Jacobs, Robert C. and Donald T. Campbell. 1961. "The perpetuation of an arbitrary tradition through several generations of a laboratory microculture." *Journal of Abnormal and Social Psychology* 62, No. 3: 649–658.

Jaffe, A. J. 1968. "Ogburn, William Fielding." Pp. 277–281 in D. L. Sills (ed.), *International Encyclopedia of the Social Sciences*, Vol. 11. New York: Macmillan & the Free Press.

Jahoda, Marie. 1988. "Time: A social psychological perspective." Pp. 53–94 in M. Young and T. Schuller (eds.), *The Rhythms of Society*. London: Routledge.

Jantsch, Erich. 1967. *Technological Forecasting in Perspective*. Paris: Organisation for Economic Cooperation and Development.

Jennings, Lane (ed.). 1993. *The Futures Research Directory: Organizations and Periodicals 1993–94*. Bethesda, MD: World Future Society.

Johnson, George. 1988. "Taking life three seconds at a time." *The New York Times Book Review* (March 27): 41.

Jonas, Hans. (1972) 1981. "Technology and responsibility: The ethics of an endangered future." Pp. 23–36 in E. Partridge (ed.), *Responsibilities to Future Generations*. Buffalo, NY: Prometheus Books.

Jones, Christopher B. 1992. "The *Manoa School* of futures studies." *Futures Research Quarterly* 8, No. 4 (Winter): 19–25.

Jones, Peter M.S. 1977. "One organization's experience." Pp. 194–209 in H. A. Linstone and W.H.C. Simmonds (eds.), *Futures Research: New Directions*. Reading, MA: Addison-Wesley.

Jones, Thomas E. 1979. "The futurist movement: A brief history." *World Future Society Bulletin* (July-August): 13–25.

———. 1980. *Options for the Future*. New York: Praeger.

Joseph, Earl C. 1985. "Editorial." *Future Trends* 16, No. 6 (September): 1.

———. 1987. "Editorial." *Future Trends* 18, No. 4 (April): 1–4.

Jouvenel, Bertrand de. 1963. "Introduction." Pp. ix–xi in B. Jouvenel (ed.), *Futuribles* I. Geneva: Droz.

———. (1964) 1967. *The Art of Conjecture*. New York: Basic Books.

Judd, Charles M., Eliot R. Smith, and Louise H. Kidder. 1991. *Research Methods in Social Relations*. Sixth Edition. Fort Worth, TX: Holt, Rinehart & Winston.

Jungk, Robert. (1969) 1971. "Preface." Pp. 9–10 in R. Jungk and J. Galtung (eds.), *Mankind 2000*. Oslo: Universitetsforlaget and London: Allen & Unwin.

———. (1973) 1976. *The Everyman Project*. New York: Liveright.

———. 1987. "Introduction to the UK edition." Pp. 5–6 in R. Jungk and N. Müllert, *Future Workshops*. London: Institute for Social Inventions.

Jungk, Robert and Norbert Müllert. 1987. *Future Workshops*. London: Institute for Social Inventions.

Kagame, Alexis. 1976. "The empirical apperception of time and the conception of history in Bantu thought." Pp. 89–116 in *Cultures and Time*. Paris: The Unesco Press.

Kahn, Herman. 1960. *On Thermonuclear War*. Princeton, NJ: Princeton University Press.

———. 1962. *Thinking about the Unthinkable*. London: Weidenfeld and Nicolson.

———. 1975. "On studying the future." Pp. 405–442 in F. I. Greenstein and N. W. Polsby (eds.), *Handbook of Political Science*, Vol. 7, "Strategies of Inquiry." Reading, MA: Addison-Wesley.

Kahn, Herman and Anthony J. Wiener. 1967. *The Year 2000: A Framework for Speculation on the Next Thirty-Three Years*. New York: Macmillan.

Kamenka, Eugene. (1962) 1972. *The Ethical Foundations of Marxism*. London: Routledge & Kegan Paul.

———. 1986. "Why was the Bolshevik terror wrong?" *The New York Times Book Review* (February 2): 20.

Kamm, Henry. 1992. "Sowing the killing fields." *The New York Times Book Review* (January 12): 7.

Kant, Immanuel. 1958. *Groundwork of the Metaphysics of Morals*. Trans. by H. J. Paton. New York: Harper & Row.

Kavka, Gregory. (1978) 1981. "The futurity problem." Pp. 109–122 in E. Partridge (ed.), *Responsibilities to Future Generations*. Buffalo, NY: Prometheus Books.

Kelley, J. and M.D.R. Evans. 1990. "Legitimate inequality: Norms on occupational earnings in eight nations." A paper read at the meetings of the International Social Survey Programme, Graz, Austria (May).

Kelly, Janice R. and Joseph E. McGrath. 1988. *On Time and Method*. Newbury Park, CA: Sage.

Kemp, Martin. 1988. *The Science of Art*. New Haven, CT: Yale University Press.

Kennedy, Paul M. 1993. *Preparing for the Twenty-First Century*. New York: Random House.

Kershaw, David N. 1972. "Issues in income maintenance experimentation." Pp. 221–245 in P.H. Rossi and W. Williams (eds.), *Evaluating Social Programs*. New York and London: Seminar Press.

———. (1972) 1980. "A negative-income tax experiment." Pp. 27–41 in D. Nachmias (ed.), *The Practice of Policy Evaluation*. New York: St. Martin's Press.

Keyfitz, Nathan. 1986. "The social and political context of population forecasting." Pp. 235–258 in W. Alonso and P. Starr (eds.), *The Politics of Numbers*. New York: Russell Sage Foundation.

Kidder, Louise H. and Susan Muller. 1991. "What is 'fair' in Japan?" Pp. 139–154 in H. Steensma and R. Vermunt (eds.), *Social Justice in Human Relations*, Vol. 2 "Societal and Psychological Consequences of Justice and Injustice." New York: Plenum Press.

Kidder, Rushworth M. 1993. "A.H. Halsey: Dialects of a common language." *Insights on Global Ethics* 3, No. 8 (August): 1 et passim.

———. 1994. *Shared Values for a Troubled World*. San Francisco, CA: Jossey-Bass Publishers.

———. 1995. *How Good People Make Tough Choices*. New York: William Morrow.

Kim, Tae-Chang. 1994. "Toward a new theory of value for the global age." Pp. 116–141 in *Why Future Generations Now?* Umeda, Kitaku, Osaka: Future Generations Alliance Foundation.

Kimmel, Allan J. 1988. *Ethics and Values in Applied Social Research*. Newbury Park, CA: Sage.

King, Alexander and Bertrand Schneider. 1991. *The First Global Revolution*. London: Simon & Shuster.

King, Martin Luther, Jr. 1964. *Why We Can't Wait*. New York: Harper and Row.

Kiser, Edgar and Kriss A. Drass. 1987. "Changes in the core of the world-system and the production of utopian literature in Great Britain and the United States, 1883–1975." *American Sociological Review* 52, No. 2 (April): 286–293.

Kizlos, Peter J. 1989. "Faces of mid-life." *Yale Alumni Magazine* LII, No. 8 (Summer): 46–49.

Kluckhohn, Clyde. 1953. "Universal categories of culture." Pp. 507–523 in A. L. Kroeber (ed.), *Anthropology Today*. Chicago: University of Chicago Press.

Kohlberg, Lawrence. (1971) 1981. "From is to ought: How to commit the naturalistic fallacy and get away with it in the study of moral development." Pp. 101–189 in L. Kohlberg (ed.), *The Philosophy of Moral Development*. New York: Harper & Row.

———. 1984. *The Psychology of Moral Development*. San Francisco, CA: Harper & Row.

Kolakowski, Leszek. 1978. *Main Currents of Marxism*, Vol. III "The Breakdown." Trans. by P. S. Falla. Oxford: Clarendon Press.

Kolata, Gina. 1992. "Scientists fluff the answer to a billion-dollar question." *The New York Times* (November 1): E2.

Kondo, Tetsuo. 1990. "Some notes on rational behavior, normative behavior, moral behavior, and cooperation." *The Journal of Conflict Resolution* 34, No. 3 (September): 495–530.

Konner, Melvin. 1990. "Mutilated in the name of tradition." *The New York Times Book Review* (April 15): 5–6.

Kothari, R. 1974. *Footsteps into the Future*. New York: Free Press.

Kott, Jan. 1984. *The Theater of Essence*. Evanston, IL: Northwestern University Press.

Kuhn, Thomas S. 1962. *The Structure of Scientific Revolutions*. Chicago: University of Chicago Press.

———. (1969) 1977a. "Second thoughts on paradigms." Pp. 459–517 in F. Suppe (ed.), *The Structure of Scientific Theories*, Second Edition. Urbana: University of Illinois Press.

———. 1977b. *The Essential Tension*. Chicago: The University of Chicago Press.

———. (1970) 1978. "Reflections on my critics." Pp. 231–278 in I. Lakatos and A. Musgrave (eds.), *Criticism and the Growth of Knowledge*. Cambridge: Cambridge University Press.

Küng, Hans. 1991. *Global Responsibility: In Search of a New World Ethic*. New York: Crossroad.

Kurian, George Thomas and Graham T. T. Molitor (eds.). 1996. *Encyclopedia of the Future*, Vols. 1 and 2. New York: Simon & Schuster Macmillan.

Lakatos, Imre. 1968. *The Problem of Inductive Logic*. Amsterdam: North Holland.

Land, Kenneth C. 1986. "Methods for national population forecasts: A review." *Journal of the American Statistical Association* 81., No. 396 (December): 888–901.

Land, Kenneth C. and Stephen H. Schneider (eds.). 1987a. *Forecasting in the Social and Natural Sciences*. Dordrecht, Holland: D. Reidel.

———. 1987b. "Forecasting in the social and natural sciences: An overview and analysis of isomorphisms." Pp. 7–31 in K.C. Land and S.H. Schneider (eds.), *Forecasting in the Social and Natural Sciences*. Dordrecht, Holland: D. Reidel.

Landes, David S. 1983. *Revolution in Time*. Cambridge, MA: Belknap Press of Harvard University Press.

Lane, Robert E. 1962. *Political Ideology*. New York: The Free Press.

———. 1986. "Market justice, political justice." *American Political Science Review* 80, No. 2 (June): 383–402.

———. 1991. *The Market Experience*. Cambridge: Cambridge University Press.

Langer, Susanne K. 1937. *An Introduction to Symbolic Logic*. Boston: Houghton Mifflin.

Lapham, Lewis H. 1986. "America's armchair generals." *The Wall Street Journal* (October 2): 28.

Larmore, Charles. 1987. "Review of *After Philosophy*." *The New York Times Book Review* (March): 21.

Larre, Claude. 1976. "The empirical apperception of time and the conception of history in Chinese thought." Pp. 35–62 in *Cultures and Time*. Paris: The Unesco Press.

Laslett, Peter. 1992. "Is there a generational contract?" Pp. 24–47 in P. Laslett and J. S. Fishkin (eds.), *Justice Between Age Groups and Generations*. New Haven, CT: Yale University Press.

Laslett, Peter and James S. Fishkin. 1992. "Introduction." Pp. 1–23 in P. Laslett and J. S. Fishkin (eds.), *Justice Between Age Groups and Generations*. New Haven, CT: Yale University Press.

Lasswell, H. D. 1935. *World Politics and Personal Insecurity*. New York: McGraw-Hill.

——. 1937. "Sino-Japanese crisis: The garrison state versus the civilian state." *China Quarterly* XI: 643–649.

——. 1941. "The garrison state." *The American Journal of Sociology* XLVI (January): 455–468.

——. 1948. *The Analysis of Political Behavior: An Empirical Approach*. London: Routledge & Kegan Paul.

——. 1951a. "The policy orientation." Pp. 3–15 in D. Lerner and H.D. Lasswell et al. (eds.), *The Policy Sciences*. Stanford, CA: Stanford University Press.

——. (1946) 1951b. "World organization and society." Pp. 102–117 in D. Lerner and H.D. Lasswell et al. (eds.), *The Policy Sciences*. Stanford, CA: Stanford University Press.

——. 1965. "The world revolution of our time: A framework for basic policy research." Pp. 29–96 in H.D. Lasswell and D. Lerner (eds.), *World Revolutionary Elites*. Cambridge, MA: MIT Press.

——. 1971. *A Pre-View of Policy Sciences*. New York: Elsevier.

——. (1975) 1977. "The scope of the conference: Postconference objectives." Pp. 41–57 in B. Pregel, H.D. Lasswell, and J. McHale (eds.), *World Priorities*. New Brunswick, NJ: Transaction.

Lasswell, Harold D. and J. Z. Namenwirth. 1968. *The Lasswell Value Dictionary* (3 volumes). New Haven, CT: Yale University, mimeo.

Laszlo, Ervin. 1994. *Vision 2020*. Yverdon, Switzerland: Gordon and Breach.

Latour, Bruno and Steve Woolgar. 1979. *Laboratory Life*. Beverly Hills, CA: Sage.

Laudan, Larry. 1981. "A problem-solving approach to scientific progress." Pp. 144–155 in I. Hacking (ed.), *Scientific Revolutions*. Oxford: Oxford University Press.

Lee, Keekok. 1985. *A New Basis for Moral Philosophy*. London: Routledge & Kegan Paul.

——. 1989. *Social Philosophy and Ecological Scarcity*. London: Routledge.

Lemert, Charles C. and Garth Gillan. 1982. *Michel Foucault: Social Theory and Transgression*. New York: Columbia University Press.

Lerner, Daniel and Harold D. Lasswell et al. (eds.). 1951. *The Policy Sciences*. Stanford, CA: Stanford University Press.

Lerner, Melvin J. 1980. *The Belief in a Just World*. New York: Plenum Press.

Leslie, Stuart W. 1993. *The Cold War and American Science*. New York: Columbia University Press.

Lewis, J. David and Andrew J. Weigart. (1981) 1990. "The structures and meanings of social-time." Pp. 77–101 in J. Hassard (ed.), *The Sociology of Time*. London: Macmillan.

Lewis, Paul. 1994. "Rise of the Blue Helmets." *The New York Times Book Review* (November 6): 14–15.

Lewis, W. Arthur. 1968. "Planning, economic: III development planning." Pp. 118–125 in D. L. Sills (ed.), *International Encyclopedia of the Social Sciences*, Vol. 12. New York: Macmillan & the Free Press.

Lieberson, Stanley. 1985. *Making It Count*. Berkeley and Los Angeles: University of California Press.

Lincoln, Yvonna S. and Egon G. Guba. 1985. *Naturalistic Inquiry*. Beverly Hills, CA: Sage.

Linn, Ruth. 1989. *Not Shooting and Not Crying: Psychological Inquiry into Moral Disobedience*. New York: Greenwood Press.

Linstone, Harold A. 1975. "Eight basic pitfalls: A checklist." Pp. 573–586 in H. A. Linstone and M. Turoff (eds.), *The Delphi Method: Techniques and Applications.* Reading, MA: Addison-Wesley.

———. 1977. "Confessions of a forecaster." Pp. 3–12 in H.A. Linstone and W.H.C. Simmonds (eds.), *Futures Research: New Directions.* Reading, MA: Addison-Wesley.

Lipset, Seymour Martin. 1963. *The First New Nation.* New York: Basic Books.

Livermore, W. R. 1898. *The American Kriegspiel.* Second Edition. Boston: W. B. Clarke.

Lloyd, G.E.R. 1976. "Views on time in Greek thought." Pp. 117–148 in *Cultures and Time.* Paris: The Unesco Press.

Lombardi, Louis G. 1988. *Moral Analysis: Foundations, Guides, and Applications.* Albany: State University of New York Press.

Long, John F. and David Byron McMillen. 1987. "A survey of Census Bureau population projection methods." Pp. 141–177 in K. C. Land and S. H. Schneider (eds.), *Forecasting in the Social and Natural Sciences.* Dordrecht, Holland: D. Reidel.

Lonner, Walter J. 1980. "The search for psychological universals." Pp. 143–204 in H. C. Triandis and W. W. Lambert (eds.), *Handbook of Cross-Cultural Psychology,* Vol. 1 "Perspectives." Boston: Allyn and Bacon.

Luker, Kristin. 1984. *Abortion and the Politics of Motherhood.* Berkeley and Los Angeles: University of California Press.

Lukes, Steven. 1985. *Marxism and Morality.* New York: Clarendon Press, Oxford University Press.

Lutz, Wolfgang. 1994a. "World population trends: Global and regional interactions between population and environment." Pp. 41–65 in L. M. Arizpe, M. P. Stone, and D. C. Major (eds.), *Population & Environment.* Boulder, CO: Westview Press.

———. 1994b. "The future of world population." *Population Bulletin* 49, 1 (June). Washington, DC: Population Reference Bureau.

Lynch, Michael. 1985. *Art and Artifact in Laboratory Science.* Boston: Routledge & Kegan Paul.

Lyons, Oren. 1985. "Traditional native philosophies relating to aboriginal rights." Pp. 19–23 in M. Boldt and J.A. Long in association with L. Little Bear (eds.), *The Quest for Justice.* Toronto: University of Toronto Press.

McFalls, Jr., Joseph A. 1991. "Population: A lively introduction." *Population Bulletin* 46, No. 2 (October): 2–41.

McHale, John. 1969. *The Future of the Future.* New York: George Braziller.

———. 1971–72. "A Continuation of the Typological Survey of Futures Research, U.S." Division of Special Mental Health Programs, Center for Studies of Metropolitan Problems, National Institute of Mental Health (mimeographed).

———. 1978. "The emergence of futures research." Pp. 5–15 in J. Fowles (ed.), *Handbook of Futures Research.* Westport, CT: Greenwood.

McHale, John and Magda Cordell McHale. n.d. *Futures Studies: An International Survey.* New York: United Nations Institute for Training and Research.

———. 1977. *The Futures Directory: An International Listing and Description of Organizations and Individuals Active in Future Studies and Long-Range Planning.* Guildford, England: IPC Science and Technology Press and Boulder, CO: Westview.

McNamara, Robert S. with Brian VanDeMark. 1995. *In Retrospect: The Tragedy and Lessons of Vietnam.* New York: Times Books/Random House.

McHugh, Francis J. 1966. *Fundamentals of War Gaming*. Third Edition. Newport, RI: The United States Naval War College.

McKeown, C. Timothy. 1990. "The futures of science: The human context of scientific expectations." *Futures* 22, No. 1 (January/February): 46–56.

MacIntyre, Alisdair. 1977. "Epistemological crises, dramatic narrative and the philosophy of science." *The Monist* 60: 453–472.

————. 1984. *After Virtue*. Notre Dame, IN: University of Notre Dame Press.

Macquarrie, John. 1985. "Clearing the mists from Olympus." *The New York Times Book Review* (September 22): 30.

Madge, Charles. 1968. "Planning, social. Introduction." Pp. 125–129 in D. L. Sills (ed.), *International Encyclopedia of the Social Sciences*, Vol. 12. New York: Macmillan & The Free Press.

Maier, Charles S. 1984. "August 1914: The whys of war." *The New York Times Book Review*. (July 29): 1, 22–23.

Maines, David R., Noreen M. Sugrue, and Michael A. Katovich. 1983. "The sociological import of G.H. Mead's theory of the past." *American Sociological Review* 48 (April): 161–173.

Malaska, Pentti. 1995. "The futures field of research." *Futures Research Quarterly* 11, No. 1 (Spring): 79–90.

Malcolm X. (1964) 1968. *The Autobiography of Malcolm X*, with the assistance of Alex Haley. Harmondsworth, England: Penquin.

Malinowski, Bronislaw. (1927) 1961. *Sex and Repression in Savage Society*. Cleveland, OH: World.

Malotki, Ekkehart. 1983. *Hopi Time*. Berlin: Mouton.

Mannermaa, Mika. 1986. "Futures research and social decision making." *Futures* 18, No. 5 (October): 658–670.

Manuel, Frank E. and Fritzie P. Manuel. 1979. *Utopian Thought in the Western World*. Cambridge, MA: Belknap Press of Harvard University Press.

Marano, Louis A. 1973. "A macrohistoric trend toward world government." *Behavior Science Notes* 8: 35–40.

Marcuse, Herbert. (1964) 1970. *One-Dimensional Man*. London: Sphere Books.

Marien, Michael. 1985 "Toward a new futures research: Insights from twelve types of futurists." *Futures Research Quarterly* 1, No. 1 (Spring 1985): 13–35.

————. 1987. "What *is* the nature of our embryonic enterprise? An open letter to Wendell Bell." *Futures Research Quarterly* 3, No. 4 (Winter): 71–79.

————. 1992. "The scope of policy studies: Reclaiming Lasswell's lost vision." Pp. 449–493 in W. N. Dunn and R. M. Kelly (eds.), *Advances in Policy Studies Since 1950*. New Brunswick, NJ: Transaction.

————. 1991. "Scanning: An imperfect activity in an era of fragmentation and uncertainty." *Futures Research Quarterly* 7, No. 3 (Fall): 82–90.

Marien, Michael with Lane Jennings (eds.). 1979 yearly through 1995. *Future Survey Annual: 1979 [through 1995]* Vols. 1 through 15. Bethesda, MD: World Future Society.

Markley, O.W. 1983. "Preparing for the professional futures field: Observations from the UHCLC futures program." *Futures* 16 (February): 47–64.

Marschak, Jacob. 1968. "Decision-making: Economic aspects." Pp. 42–55 in D. L. Sills (ed.), *International Encyclopedia of the Social Sciences*, Vol. 4. New York: Macmillan & The Free Press.

Marshack, Alexander. 1972. *The Roots of Civilization*. New York: McGraw-Hill.

Martino, J. P. 1983. *Technological Forecasting for Decision Making*. Second Edition. New York: North-Holland.

———. 1987. "The Gods of the copybook headings: A caution to forecasters." Pp. 143–152 in M. Marien and L. Jennings (eds.), *What I Have Learned*. New York: Greenwood.

———. 1993. "Technological forecasting: An introduction." *The Futurist* 27, No. 4 (July-August): 13–16.

Maruyama, Magoroh. 1978a. "Introduction." Pp. xvii–xxii in M. Maruyama and A. M. Harkins (eds.), *Cultures of the Future*. The Hague: Mouton.

———. 1978b. "Toward human futuristics." Pp. 33–59 in M. Maruyama and A. M. Harkins (eds.), *Cultures of the Future*. The Hague: Mouton.

Marx, Karl. (1875) 1962. "Critique of the Gotha Program." Pp. 45–65 in *The Communist Blueprint for the Future*. New York: E.P. Dutton.

Marx, Karl and Friedrich Engels. (1848) 1962. "Manifesto of the Communist Party." Pp. 9–44 in *The Communist Blueprint for the Future*. New York: E.P. Dutton.

Masini, Eleonora Barbieri. 1978. "The global diffusion of futures research." Pp. 17–29 in J. Fowles (ed.), *Handbook of Futures Research*. Westport, CT: Greenwood.

———. 1981. "Philosophical and ethical foundations of future studies: A discussion." *World Futures* 17: 1–14.

———. 1982. "Reconceptualizing futures: A need and a hope." *World Future Society Bulletin* (November/December): 1–8.

———. 1988. "Future technology and its social implications." *World Futures Studies Federation Newsletter* 14, No. 1 (March): 17.

———. 1993. *Why Futures Studies?* London: Grey Seal.

Maslow, Abraham H. 1968. *Toward a Psychology of Being*. Rev. ed. Princeton, NJ: Van Nostrand.

Masterman, Margaret. (1970) 1978. "The nature of a paradigm." Pp. 59–89 in I. Lakatos and A. Musgrave (eds.), *Criticism and the Growth of Knowledge*. Cambridge: Cambridge University Press.

Mau, James A. 1967. "Images of Jamaica's future." Pp. 197–223 in W. Bell (ed.), *The Democratic Revolution in the West Indies*. Cambridge, MA: Schenkman.

———. 1968. *Social Change and Images of the Future*. Cambridge, MA: Schenkman.

Mead, George H. 1934. *Mind, Self & Society*. Chicago: The University of Chicago Press.

Mead, Margaret. 1928. *Coming of Age in Samoa*. New York: Morrow.

Meadows, Donella H., Dennis L. Meadows, Jorgen Randers, and William W. Behrens III. 1972. *The Limits to Growth*: New York: Universe.

———. 1975. "A response to Sussex." Pp. 217–240 in H. S. D. Cole, C. Freeman, M. Jahoda, and K. L. R. Pavitt (eds.), *Models of Doom*. New York: Universe Books.

Meadows, Donella H., Dennis L. Meadows, and Jorgen Randers. 1992. *Beyond the Limits*. Post Mills, VT: Chelsea Green Publishing Company.

Meadows, D. H. and J. M. Robinson. 1985. *The Electronic Oracle: Computer Models and Social Decisions*. New York: John Wiley & Sons.

Meadows, D. L. and D. H. Meadows (eds.). 1973. *Toward Global Equilibrium*. Cambridge, MA: Wright-Allen Press.

Meadows, Dennis L., William W. Behrens III, Donella H. Meadows, Roger F. Naill, Jorgen Randers, and Erich K. O. Zahn. 1974. *The Dynamics of Growth in a Finite World*. Cambridge, MA: Wright-Allen Press.

Medawar, Peter. 1984. *Pluto's Republic*. Oxford: Oxford University Press.

Meeker, Heidi. 1993. "Hands-on futurism: How to run a scanning project." *The Futurist* 27, No. 3 (May-June): 22–26.

Meeks, Wayne A. 1989. Personal communication.

————. 1993. *The Origins of Christian Morality*. New Haven, CT: Yale University Press.

Merkl, Peter. (1960) 1966. "Introduction." Pp. 1–8 in M. Broszat, *German National Socialism, 1919–1945*. Trans. by K. Rosenbaum and I.P. Boem. Santa Barbara, CA: Clio.

Merton, Robert K. (1938) 1973. *The Sociology of Science*. Chicago and London: The University of Chicago Press.

Mettler, Peter H. (ed.). 1995. *Science and Technology for Eight Billion People*. London: New European Publications in association with Adamantine Press.

Michael, Donald. 1963. *The New Generation*. New York: Random House, Vintage Books.

————. 1985. "With both feet planted firmly in mid-air: Reflections on thinking about the future." *Futures* 17 (April): 94–103.

————. (1985) 1987. "The futurist tells stories." Pp. 75–86 in M. Marien and L. Jennings (eds.), *What I Have Learned*. New York: Greenwood Press.

Michalos, Alex C. 1979. "Philosophy of social science." Pp. 463–502 in P.D. Asquith and H.E. Kyburg, Jr. (eds.), *Current Research in Philosophy of Science*. East Lansing, MI: Philosophy of Science Association.

Midgley, Mary. (1991) 1993. *Can't We Make Moral Judgements?* New York: St. Martin's Press.

Miles, Ian. 1975. *The Poverty of Prediction*. Westmead, Farnborough, England: Saxon House, D.C. Heath.

————. 1978. "The ideologies of futurists." Pp. 67–97 in J. Fowles (ed.), *Handbook of Futures Research*. Westport, CT: Greenwood Press.

————. 1985. *Social Indicators for Human Development*. London: Frances Pinter.

Miller, James. 1984. *Rousseau: Dreamer of Democracy*. New Haven, CT: Yale University Press.

Millett, Stephen M. and Edward J. Honton. 1991. *A Manager's Guide to Technology Forecasting and Strategy Analysis Methods*. Columbus, OH: Battelle Press.

Mills, Charles W. 1989. Personal communication (April 9).

Mitchell, Robert Cameron and Richard T. Carson. 1989. *Using Surveys to Value Public Goods*. Washington, DC: Resources for the Future.

Mitroff, Ian. 1974. *The Subjective Side of Science*. New York: Elsevier.

Mitroff, Ian I. and Murray Turoff. 1975. "Philosophical and methodological foundations of Delphi." Pp. 17–36 in H.A. Linstone and M. Turoff (eds.), *The Delphi Method: Techniques and Applications*. Reading, MA: Addison-Wesley.

Mitroff, Ian I. and Ralph H. Kilmann. 1978. *Methodological Approaches to Social Science*. San Francisco, CA: Jossey-Bass.

Moghadam, Valentine M. 1994. "Women in societies." *International Social Science Journal* 139 (February): 95–115.

Moll, Peter. 1991. *From Scarcity to Sustainability*. Frankfurt am Main: Peter Lang.

————. 1993. "The discreet charm of the Club of Rome." *Futures* 25, No. 7 (September): 801–805.

Monro, D. H. 1967. *Empiricism and Ethics*. Cambridge: Cambridge University Press.

Montias, John Michael. 1968. "Planning, economic. Eastern Europe." Pp. 110–118 in D. L. Sills (ed.), *International Encyclopedia of the Social Sciences*, Vol. 12. New York: Macmillan & The Free Press.

Moore, Sally Falk. 1986. "Legal systems of the world." Pp. 11–62 in L. Lipson and S. Wheeler (eds.), *Law and the Social Sciences*. New York: Russell Sage Foundation.

Moore, Wilbert E. 1963. *Social Change*. Englewood Cliffs, NJ: Prentice-Hall.

More, Sir Thomas. No date (1516). "Utopia." Pp. 127–232 in *Famous Utopias*. New York: Tudor.

Morowitz, Harold J. and James S. Tefil. 1992. *The Facts of Life: Science and the Abortion Controversy*. New York: Oxford University Press.

Morris, Richard. 1984. *Time's Arrows*. New York: Simon and Schuster.

Morrison, Roy. 1991. *We Build the Road as We Travel*. Philadelphia, PA: New Society Publishers.

Moskos, Charles C., Jr. 1967. *The Sociology of Political Independence*. Cambridge, MA: Schenkman.

Moynihan, Daniel Patrick. 1990. *On the Law of Nations*. Cambridge, MA: Harvard University Press.

Mukherjee, Ramkrishna. 1989. *The Quality of Life*. New Delhi: Sage.

Mumford, Lewis. 1922. *The Story of Utopias*. New York: Boni and Liveright.

Munting, Roger. 1982. *The Economic Development of the USSR*. London & Canberra: Croom Helm.

Murdock, George P. 1945. "The common denominator of cultures." Pp. 123–142 in R. Linton (ed.), *The Science of Man in the World Crisis*. New York: Columbia University Press.

Murphy, Brian. 1992. "Linking present decisions to long-range ethical visions in organizations using stakeholder audits." Pp. 321–329 in M. Mannermaa (ed.), *Linking Present Decisions to Long-Range Visions*, Vol. II. Budapest, Hungary: World Futures Studies Federation.

Musgrave, Alan. 1993. *Common Sense, Science and Scepticism*. Cambridge: Cambridge University Press.

Myrdal, Gunnar with the assistance of Richard Sterner and Arnold Rose. 1944. *An American Dilemma*. New York: Harper & Brothers.

Naisbitt, John. (1982) 1984. *Megatrends: The New Directions Transforming Our Lives*. New York: Warner Books.

Naisbitt, John and Patricia Aburdene. 1990. *Megatrends 2000*. New York: William Morrow and Co.

Namenwirth, J. Zvi and Harold D. Lasswell. 1970. "The changing language of American values." *Sage Professional Papers in Comparative Politics*. Beverly Hills, CA: Sage.

Namenwirth, J. Zvi and Robert Philip Weber. 1987. *Dynamics of Culture*. Boston: Allen & Unwin.

Nanus, Burt. 1984. "Futures research—stage three." *Futures* 16 (August): 405–407.

Naroll, Raoul. 1967. "Imperial cycles and world order." *Peace Research Society Papers* 7: 83–101.

———. 1983. *The Moral Order*. Beverly Hills, CA: Sage.

National Center for Health Statistics. 1993, 1994, and 1995. "Vital statistics of the United States, 1989 (1990 and 1991)" Section 6. Washington, DC: Public Health Service.

Neher, André. 1976. "The view of time and history in Jewish culture." Pp. 148–167 in *Cultures and Time*. Paris: The Unesco Press.

Neisser, Ulric. 1976. *Cognition and Reality*. San Francisco, CA: W. H. Freeman.

Neurath, Otto. (1931/2) 1959. "Sociology and physicalism." Pp. 282–317 in A.J. Ayer (ed.), *Logical Positivism*. Glencoe, IL: The Free Press.

Neustadt, Richard E. and Ernest R. May. 1986. *Thinking in Time: The Uses of History for Decision-Makers*. New York: Free Press.

New Scientist. 1984. No. 1435/1436 (December 20/27): 8.

Newton-Smith, W.H. 1981. *The Rationality of Science*. Boston: Routledge & Kegan Paul.

Nisbet, Robert A. 1966. *The Sociological Tradition*. New York: Basic Books.

Noelle-Neumann, Elisabeth. 1989. "The public as prophet: Findings from continuous survey research and their importance for early diagnosis of economic growth." *International Journal of Public Opinion Research* 1, No. 2 (Summer): 136–150.

———. 1994. "Aussichten für 1995." Allensbach am Bodensee, Germany: Institut für Demoskopie Allensbach (Dezember), originalmanuskript.

Nonet, Philippe and Philip Selznick. 1978. *Law and Society in Transition*. New York: Farrar, Straus and Giroux.

Novak, Maximillian E. 1969. "The economic meaning of *Robinson Crusoe*." Pp. 97–102 in F. H. Ellis (ed.), *Twentieth Century Interpretations of Robinson Crusoe*. Englewood Cliffs, NJ: Prentice-Hall.

Nove, Alec. 1969. *An Economic History of the U.S.S.R.* London: Allen Lane, The Penquin Press.

———. 1977. *The Soviet Economic System*. London: George Allen & Unwin.

Nussbaum, Martha. 1986. "Review of Jane Roland Martin's Reclaiming a Conversation: The Ideal of the Educated Woman." *The New York Review of Books* 33 (January 30): 7–12.

NYT. *The New York Times* (date given in text).

NYTBR. *The New York Times Book Review* (date given in text).

OECD (Organization for Economic Cooperation and Development). 1973. "List of social concerns common to most OECD countries." Paris: OECD Social Indicator Development Programme.

Ogilvy, James. 1992. "Futures studies and the human sciences: The case for normative scenarios." *Futures Research Quarterly* 8, No. 2 (Summer): 5–65.

Oldfield, F. 1975. "Discussion." Pp. 154–165 in *The Future as an Academic Discipline*. Ciba Foundation Symposium 36. Amsterdam: Elsevier.

Olshansky, S. Jay, Bruce A. Carnes, Christine Cassel. 1990. "In search of Methuselah: Estimating the upper limits to human longevity." *Science* 250 (2 November): 634–640.

O'Neill, Molly. 1991. "Am I the diner or am I the dish?" *The New York Times Book Review*. (July 28): 7.

Ono, Ryota and Dan J. Wedemeyer. 1994. "Assessing the validity of the Delphi technique." *Futures* 26, No. 3 (April): 289–304.

Ornauer, H., H. Wiberg, A. Sicinski, and J. Galtung (eds). 1976. *Images of the World in the Year 2000: A Comparative Ten Nation Study*. Atlantic Highlands, NJ: Humanities Press.

Orwell, George. 1949. *Nineteen Eighty-Four*. New York: Harcourt, Brace & World.

Osgood, Charles E., William H. May, and Murray S. Miron. 1975. *Cross-Cultural Universals of Affective Meaning*. Urbana: University of Illinois Press.

Pagels, Heinz R. 1982. *The Cosmic Code*. New York: Simon and Schuster.

Palmore, James A. and Robert W. Gardner. (1983) 1991. *Measuring Mortality, Fertility, and Natural Increase*. Honolulu, HI: The East-West Center.

Papineau, David. 1993. "How to think about science." *The New York Times Book Review* (July 25): 14–15.

Partridge, Ernest. 1991. "On the rights of future generations." Pp. 1–21 in D. Scherer (ed.), *Upstream/Downstream: Issues in Environmental Ethics*. Philadelphia, PA: Temple University Press.

———. 1981a. "Introduction." Pp. 1–16 in E. Partridge (ed.), *Responsibilities to Future Generations*. Buffalo, NY: Prometheus Books.

———. (1980) 1981b. "Why care about the future?" Pp. 203–220 in E. Partridge (ed.), *Responsibilities to Future Generations*. Buffalo, NY: Prometheus Books.

Passant, E.J. 1966. *A Short History of Germany 1815–1945*. Cambridge: University Press.

Passmore, John. (1974) 1981. "Conservation." Pp. 45–59 in E. Partridge (ed.), *Responsibilities to Future Generations*. Buffalo, NY: Prometheus Books.

———. 1985. "An end to science?" *The Times Higher Education Supplement* (April 19).

Pàttaro, Germano. 1976. "The Christian conception of time." Pp. 169–195 in *Cultures and Time*. Paris: The Unesco Press.

Patterson, Edwin W. 1953. *Jurisprudence*. Brooklyn, NY: Foundation Press.

Payne, Stephen L. and Robert A. Desman. 1987. "The academician as a consultant." Pp. 95–115 in S.L. Payne and B.H. Charnov (eds.), *Ethical Dilemmas for Academic Professionals*. Springfield, IL: Charles C. Thomas.

Pearson, K. 1901–1902. "On the change in expectation of life in man during a period of circa 2000 years." *Biometrika* I: 261–264.

Pelikan, Jaroslav. 1992. *The Idea of the University—A Reexamination*. New Haven, CT: Yale University Press.

Perkins, H. Wesley and James L. Spates. 1986. "Mirror images? Three analyses of values in England and the United States." *International Journal of Comparative Sociology* 27, Nos. 1–2: 31–52.

Perry, Ralph Barton. (1954) 1978. "A definition of morality." Pp. 12–22 in P. W. Taylor (ed.), *Problems of Moral Philosophy*. Third Edition. Belmont, CA: Wadsworth.

Perun, Pamela and Denise Del Veuto Bielby. 1979. "Midlife: A discussion of competing models." *Research on Aging* 1: 275–300.

Petersen, William. (1961) 1975. *Population*, Third Edition. New York: Macmillan.

Pettit, Philip. (n.d.). "The philosophies of social science." In R.J. Anderson and W.W. Sharrock (eds.), *Teaching Papers in Sociology*. York, England: Longman.

Phillips, Andrew P. 1964. "The Development of a Modern Labor Force in Antigua." Unpublished Ph.D. dissertation, Los Angeles: University of California, Los Angeles.

———. 1967. "Management and workers face an independent Antigua." Pp. 165–196 in W. Bell (ed.), *The Democratic Revolution in the West Indies*. Cambridge, MA: Schenkman.

Phillips, Derek L. 1973. *Abandoning Method*. San Francisco, CA: Jossey-Bass.

———. 1986. *Toward a Just Social Order*. Princeton, N.J.: Princeton University Press.

Phillips, Dretha M. 1983. *A Bibliography Toward Sociological Futures Research and Instruction*. Public Administration Series: Bibliography. Monticello, IL: Vance Bibliographies.

Piaget, Jean. 1965. *The Moral Judgment of the Child*. Trans. by M. Gabain. New York: John Wiley & Sons.

Pickett, Neil. 1992. *A History of Hudson Institute*. Indianapolis, IN: Hudson Institute.

Pieper, Josef. 1966. *The Four Cardinal Virtues: Prudence, Justice, Fortitude, Temperance* (Trans. by R. Winston, C. Winston et al.). Notre Dame, IN: University of Notre Dame Press.

Plato. no date. *The Republic*. Trans. by B. Jowett. New York: The Modern Library, Random House.

Platt, John Rader. 1966. *The Step to Man*. New York: John Wiley & Sons.

———. 1975. "Discussion." Pp. 154–165 in *The Future as an Academic Discipline*. Ciba Foundation Symposium 36. Amsterdam: Elsevier.

Polak, Frederik L. (1955) 1961. *The Image of the Future: Enlightening the Past, Orientating the Present, Forecasting the Future*, Vols. I and II. New York: Oceana.

Polgar, Steven. 1978. "The possible and the desirable: Population and environmental problems." Pp. 63–70 in M. Maruyama and A.M. Harkins (eds.), *Cultures of the Future*. The Hague: Mouton.

Popper, K.R. (1945) 1952. *The Open Society and Its Enemies*. Second Edition. London: Routledge.

———. 1957. *The Poverty of Historicism*. London: Routledge and Kegan Paul.

———. 1959. *The Logic of Scientific Discovery*. New York: Basic Books.

———. 1965. *Conjectures and Refutations: The Growth of Scientific Knowledge*. Second Edition. New York: Basic Books.

Porter, John. 1965. *The Vertical Mosaic: An Analysis of Social Class and Power in Canada*. Toronto: University of Toronto Press.

Preble, J. F. 1983. "Public sector use of the Delphi technique." *Technological Forecasting and Social Change* 23: 75–88.

President's Research Committee on Social Trends. 1933. *Recent Social Trends in the United States*. Two vols. New York: McGraw-Hill.

Priestley, J.B. 1968. *Man and Time*. New York: Dell, a Laurel edition.

Prigogine, Ilya and Isabelle Stengers. 1984. *Order Out of Chaos*. New York: Bantam.

Public Opinion. 1978. Vol. 1 (July/August): 40.

Pugh, George Edgin. 1977. *The Biological Origin of Human Values*. New York: Basic Books.

Punch, Maurice. 1986. *The Politics and Ethics of Fieldwork*. Beverly Hills, CA: Sage.

Putnam, Hilary (1974) 1981. "The 'corroboration' of theories." Pp. 60–79 in I. Hacking (ed.), *Scientific Revolutions*. Oxford: Oxford University Press.

Quine, W.V. 1951. "Two dogmas of empiricism." *Philosphical Review* 60 (January): 20–43.

Rabinow, Paul. 1983. "Humanism as nihilism: The bracketing of truth and seriousness in American cultural anthropology." Pp. 52–75 in N. Haan, R. N. Bellah, P. Rabinow, and W. M. Sullivan (eds.), *Social Science as Moral Inquiry*. New York: Columbia University Press.

Rappaport, Roy A. 1986. "The construction of time and eternity in ritual." The David Skomp Distinguished Lectures in Anthropology. Bloomington: Indiana University.

Ratner, Steven R. 1995. *The New UN Peacekeeping*. New York: St. Martin's Press.

Rawls, John. 1971. *A Theory of Justice*. Cambridge, MA: Belknap Press of Harvard University Press.

Raz, J. 1977. "Promises and obligations." Pp. 210–228 in P.M.S. Hacker and J. Raz (eds.), *Law, Morality, and Society*. Oxford: Clarendon Press.

Razak, Victoria and Sam Cole (eds.). 1995. "Anthropological Perspectives on the Future of Culture and Society." Special issue of *Futures* 27, No. 4 (May).

Rees, Albert. (1974) 1980. "An overview of the labor-supply results." Pp. 41–63 in D. Nachmias (ed.), *The Practice of Policy Evaluation*. New York: St. Martin's Press.

Reich, Walter. 1993. "Erasing the Holocaust." *The New York Times Book Review* (July 11): 1 et passim.

Reichenbach, Hans. 1951. *The Rise of Scientific Philosophy*. Berkeley and Los Angeles: University of California Press.

Reiman, Jeffrey. 1990. *Justice and Modern Moral Philosophy*. New Haven, CT: Yale University Press.

Reinharz, Shulamit. 1979. *On Becoming a Social Scientist*. San Francisco, CA: Jossey-Bass.

Rest, James R. et al. 1986. *Moral Development*. New York: Praeger.

Riasanovsky, Nicholas V. 1969. *The Teaching of Charles Fourier*. Berkeley and Los Angeles: University of California Press.

Richardson, John M. 1984. "The state of futures research." *Futures* 16 (August): 382–395.

Riner, Reed D. 1987. "Doing futures research—anthropologically." *Futures* 19, No. 3 (June): 311–328.

———. 1991a. "From description to design: Ethnographic futures research methods applied in small town revitalization and economic development." *Futures Research Quarterly* 7, No. 1 (Spring): 17–30.

———. 1991b. "Anthropology about the future: Limits and potentials." *Human Organization* 50, No. 3 (Fall): 297–311.

Robinson, James A. 1968. "Decision making: Political aspects." Pp. 55–62 in D. L. Sills (ed.), *International Encyclopedia of the Social Sciences*, Vol. 4. New York: Macmillan & The Free Press.

Robinson, Robert V. and Wendell Bell. 1978. "Equality, success, and social justice in England and the United States." *American Sociological Review* 43, No. 2 (April): 125–143.

Robinson, William S. 1949. *Class Notes for the Logic of Social Inquiry*. Los Angeles: University of California, unpublished.

Roddenberry, Gene. 1984. "The literary image of the future," a talk given at the Fifth General Assembly and Exposition of the World Future Society, Washington, DC, June 10–14.

Rohner, Ronald P. 1986. *The Warmth Dimension*. Beverly Hills, CA: Sage.

Rohrbaugh, J. 1979. "Improving the quality of group judgment: Social judgment analysis and the Delphi technique." *Organizational Behavior and Human Performance* 24: 79–92.

Rojas, Billy and H. Wentworth Eldredge. 1974. "Appendix. Status Report: Sample Syllabi and Directory of Futures Studies." Pp. 345–399 in A. Toffler (ed.), *Learning for Tomorrow*. New York: Random House.

Rokeach, Milton. 1968. *Beliefs, Attitudes, and Values*. San Francisco, CA: Jossey-Bass.

Rolston, Holmes III. 1981. "The river of life: Past, present, and future." Pp. 123–137 in E. Partridge (ed.), *Responsibilities to Future Generations*. Buffalo, NY: Prometheus Books.

Rorty, Richard. 1979. *Philosophy and the Mirror of Nature*. Princeton, NJ: Princeton University Press.

Rosenau, Pauline Marie. 1992. *Post-Modernism and the Social Sciences*. Princeton, NJ: Princeton University Press.

Rosenbaum, David E. 1994. "Down at the statehouse, legislators have more fun." *The New York Times* (March 20): 3E.

Rossi, Peter. 1987. "Unemployment insurance payments and recidivism among released prisoners." Pp. 107–124 in B. Barber (ed.), *Effective Social Science*. New York: Russell Sage Foundation.

Rossi, Peter H. and Howard E. Freeman with the collaboration of Sonia Rosenbaum. 1982. *Evaluation: A Systematic Approach*. Second Edition. Beverly Hills, CA: Sage.

Rossi, Peter H. and William Foote Whyte. 1983. "The applied side of sociology." Pp. 5–31 in H.E. Freeman, R.R. Dynes, P.H. Rossi, and W. F Whyte (eds.), *Applied Sociology*. San Francisco, CA: Jossey-Bass.

Rossi, Peter H., James D. Wright, and Andy B. Anderson (eds.). 1983. *Handbook of Survey Research*. New York: Academic Press.

Rudel, Thomas K. with Bruce Horowitz. 1993. *Tropical Deforestation*. New York: Columbia University Press.

Rudner, Richard S. 1966. *Philosophy of Social Science*. Englewood Cliffs, NJ: Prentice-Hall.

Ryan, Alan. 1995. "The women in the cowshed." *The New York Review of Books* XLII, 8 (May 11): 24–26.

Sackman, H. 1975. *Delphi Critique*. Lexington, MA: D. C. Heath.

Sagan, Leonard A. 1989. *The Health of Nations*. New York: Basic Books.

Saltman, Juliet. 1975. "Implementing open housing laws through social action." *The Journal of Applied Behavioral Science* 11, No. 1: 39–61.

Sartre, Jean-Paul. (1965) 1978. "The humanism of existentialism." Pp. 646–661 in P. W. Taylor (ed.), *Problems of Moral Philosophy*. Third Ed. Belmont, CA: Wadsworth.

Schaefer, Richard T. and Robert P. Lamm. 1992. *Sociology*. Fourth Edition. New York: McGraw-Hill.

Schattschneider, Doris. 1992. "The universal mind at work." *The New York Times Book Review* (April 19): 15.

Scheele, D. S. 1975. "Reality construction as a product of Delphi interaction." Pp. 37–71 in H.A. Linstone and M. Turoff (eds.), *The Delphi Method: Techniques and Applications*. Reading, MA: Addison-Wesley.

Scheer, Lore. 1980. "Experience with quality of life comparisons." Pp. 145–155 in A. Szalai and F.M. Andrews (eds.), *The Quality of Life*. Beverly Hills, CA: Sage.

Scheffler, Israel. 1967. *Science and Subjectivity*. Indianapolis, IN: Bobbs-Merrill.

Schluchter, Wolfgang. (1980) 1989. *Rationalism, Religion, and Domination*. Trans. by N. Solomon. Berkeley: University of California Press.

Schnaiberg, Allan. 1995. "How I learned to reject recycling, Part 2. paradoxes and contraditions: A contextual framework." *Blazing Tattles* 4, No. 1 (January): 1 et passim.

Schoedinger, Andrew B. (ed.). 1992. *The Problem of Universals*. Atlantic Highlands, NJ: Humanities Press International.

Schuessler, Karl F. 1968. "Prediction." Pp. 418–425 in D. L. Sills (ed.), *International Encyclopedia of the Social Sciences*, Vol. 12. New York: Macmillan & The Free Press.

Schuessler, Karl. 1971. "Continuities in social prediction." Pp. 302–329 in H.L. Costner (ed.), *Sociological Methodology*. San Francisco, CA: Jossey-Bass.

Schwartz, Richard D. 1986. "Law and normative order." Pp. 63–107 in L. Lipson and S. Wheeler (eds.), *Law and the Social Sciences*. New York: Russell Sage Foundation.

Schwarz, Brita, Uno Svedin, and Björn Wittrock. 1982. *Methods in Futures Studies*. Boulder, CO: Westview Press.

Sen, Amartya. 1981. *Poverty and Famines*. New York: Oxford University Press.

Sheldon, Eleanor Bernert and Wilbert E. Moore (eds.). 1968. *Indicators of Social Change: Concepts and Measurements*. New York: Russell Sage Foundation.

Shepher, Joseph. 1983. *Incest: A Biosocial View*. New York: Academic Press.

Sher, George. 1992. "Ancient wrongs and modern rights." Pp. 48–61 in P. Laslett and J. S. Fishkin (eds.), *Justice between Age Groups and Generations*. New Haven, CT: Yale University Press.

Shils, Edward. 1963. "On the comparative study of the new states." Pp. 1–26 in C. Geertz (ed.), *Old Societies and New States*. New York: The Free Press of Glencoe.

———. 1981. *Tradition*. Chicago: The University of Chicago Press.

Shrady, Nicholas. 1992. "Glorious in its very stories." *New York Times Book Review* (March 15): 1, 24–25.

Shubik, Martin. 1975. *The Uses and Methods of Gaming*. New York: Elsevier.

———. 1982. *Game Theory in the Social Sciences*. Cambridge, MA: The MIT Press.

Sikora, R. I. 1978. "Is it wrong to prevent the existence of future generations?" Pp. 112–166 in R.I. Sikora and B. Barry (eds.), *Obligations to Future Generations*. Philadelphia, PA: Temple University Press.

Simmonds, W.H. Clive. 1977. "The nature of futures problems." Pp. 13–26 in H. A. Linstone and W.H.C. Simmonds (eds.), *Futures Research: New Directions*. Reading, MA: Addison-Wesley.

Simon, Julian L. 1981. *The Ultimate Resource*. Princeton, NJ: Princeton University Press.

———. 1995. "Why do we hear prophecies of doom from every side?" *The Futurist* 29, No. 1 (January-February): 19–23.

Simon, Julian. L. and Herman Kahn (eds.). 1984. *The Resourceful Earth: A Response to Global 2000*. Oxford: Basil Blackwell.

Singer, Max and Aaron Wildavsky. 1993. *The Real World Order: Zones of Peace/ Zones of Turmoil*. Chatham, NJ: Chatham.

Sinha, Durganand. 1984. "Community as target: A new perspective to research on prosocial behavior." Pp. 445–455 in E. Staub, D. Bar-Tal, J. Karylowski, and J. Reykowski (eds.), *Development and Maintenance of Prosocial Behavior*. New York: Plenum Press.

Sippanondha, Ketudat with Robert B. Textor et al. 1990. *The Middle Path for the Future of Thailand*. Honolulu, HI: East-West Center.

Skagestad, Peter. 1981. "Hypothetical realism." Pp. 77–97 in M.B. Brewer and B.E. Collins (eds.), *Scientific Inquiry and the Social Sciences*. San Francisco, CA: Jossey-Bass.

Slaughter, Richard A. (ed.). 1993a. "Special issue: The knowledge base of futures studies." *Futures* 25, No. 3 (April).

———. 1993b. "The substantive knowledge base of futures studies." *Futures* 25, No. 3 (April): 227–233.

———. 1993c. "Futures concepts." *Futures* 25, No. 3 (April): 289–314.

———. 1993d. "Looking for the real 'megatrends.'" *Futures* 25, No. 8 (October): 827–849.

———. 1996. *The Knowledge Base of Futures Studies*, Vols. 1–3. Hawthorn, Victoria, Australia: DDM Media.

Slottje, Daniel J., Gerald W. Scully, Joseph G. Hirschberg, and Kathy J. Hayes. 1991. *Measuring the Quality of Life Across Countries*. Boulder, CO: Westview Press.

Smart, J. J. C. 1984. *Ethics, Persuasion and Truth*. London: Routledge & Kegan Paul.

Smith, D. Kimball. 1983. "Putting the wings on man and overcoming limited views." *Yale Alumni Magazine and Journal* XLVI (June): 38–42.

Smith, Herbert L. 1984. "The social forecasting industry." Paper prepared for the Social Science Research Council's Conference on Forecasting in the Social and Natural Sciences. Boulder, CO, June 10–13.

———. 1987. "The social forecasting industry." Pp. 35–60 in K.C. Land and S.H. Schneider (eds.), *Forecasting in the Social and Natural Sciences*. Dordrecht, Holland: D. Reidel.

Smith, Steven B. 1987. "Functional analysis and Marxian ideology." *Review of Politics* 49: 287–290.

Snarey, John. 1993. *How Fathers Care for the Next Generation*. Cambridge, MA: Harvard University Press.

Snell, George D. 1988. *Search for a Rational Ethic*. New York: Springer-Verlag.

Snyder, Richard C., Charles F. Hermann, and Harold D. Lasswell. 1976. "A global monitoring system: Appraising the effects of government on human dignity." *International Studies Quarterly* 20, No. 2 (June): 221–260.

Snyder, Richard C., H.W. Bruck, and Burton Sapin. (1954) 1962. "Decison-making as an approach to the study of international politics." Pp. 14–185 in R.C. Snyder, H.W. Bruck, and B. Sapin (eds.), *Foreign Policy Decision-Making*. New York: The Free Press.

Sorokin, Pitirim and Robert Merton. (1937) 1990. "Social-time: A methodological and functional analysis." Pp. 56–66 in J. Hassard (ed.), *The Sociology of Time*. London: Macmillan.

Speer, Albert. (1969) 1970. *Inside the Third Reich*. Trans. by Richard and Clara Winston. New York: Macmillan.

Spence, Jonathan. 1992. "From the stone age to Tiananmen Square." *The New York Times Book Review* (May 24): 2.

Sperber, Dan. 1974. *Rethinking Symbolism*. Cambridge: Cambridge University Press.

Spiro, Melford. 1958. *Children of the Kibbutz*. Cambridge, MA: Harvard University Press.

———. 1982. *Oedipus in the Trobriands*. Chicago: University of Chicago Press.

———. 1992. *Anthropological Other or Burmese Brother?* New Brunswick, NJ: Transaction Publishers.

Sprigge, T. L. S. 1988. *The Rational Foundations of Ethics*. London and New York: Routledge & Kegan Paul.

Staal, Frits. 1988. *Universals: Studies in Indian Logic and Linguistics*. Chicago: University of Chicago Press.

Stafford, Frank P. 1988. "A model of Harmony." *ISR Newsletter* 16, No. 1: 10–11.

Stanford Research Institute. 1962. *International Industrial Development Center Study*. Stanford, CA.

Stark, Rodney and William Sims Bainbridge. 1985. *The Future of Religion*. Berkeley and Los Angeles: University of California Press.

Stehr, Nico. 1978. "The ethos of science revisited: Social and cognitive norms." Pp. 172–196 in J. Gaston (ed.), *Sociology of Science*. San Francisco, CA: Jossey-Bass.

Stephens, Evelyne Huber and John D. Stephens. 1986. *Democratic Socialism in Jamaica*. Princeton, NJ: Princeton University Press.

Stevenson, Charles L. 1963. *Facts and Values*. New Haven, CT: Yale University Press.

Steward, Thomas R. 1987. "The Delphi technique and judgmental forecasting." Pp. 97–113 in K. C. Land and S. H. Schneider (eds.), *Forecasting in the Social and Natural Sciences*. Dordrecht, Holland: D. Reidel.

Stinchcombe, Arthur L. 1982a. "On softheadedness on the future." *Ethics* 93 (October): 114–128.

————. 1982b. "The deep structure of moral categories: Eighteenth-century French stratification, and the revolution." Pp. 66–95 in I. Rossi (ed.), *Structural Sociology*. New York: Columbia University Press.

Stone, Philip J., Dexter C. Dunphy, Marshall S. Smith, Daniel M. Ogilvie and associates. 1966. *The General Inquirer: A Computer Approach to Content Analysis*. Cambridge, MA: The M.I.T. Press.

Sudman, Seymour and Norman M. Bradburn. 1982. *Asking Questions*. San Francisco, CA: Jossey-Bass.

Sullivan, Michael J., III. 1991. *Measuring Global Values*. New York: Greenwood Press.

Sumner, L. W. 1987. *The Moral Foundation of Rights*. Oxford: Clarendon Press.

Sumner, W. G. (1906) 1960. *Folkways*. New York: New American Library.

Suppe, Frederick (ed.), 1977. *The Structure of Scientific Theories*. Second Edition. Urbana: University of Illinois Press.

Sylvan, David and Barry Glassner. 1985. *A Rationalist Methodology for the Social Sciences*. Oxford: Basil Blackwell.

Szalai, Alexander (ed.). 1972. *The Use of Time*. The Hague: Mouton.

————. 1980. "The meaning of comparative research on the quality of life." Pp. 7–21 in A. Szalai and F.M. Andrews (eds.), *The Quality of Life*. Beverly Hills, CA: Sage.

Szalai, Alexander and Frank M. Andrews (eds.). 1980. *The Quality of Life*. Beverly Hills, CA: Sage.

Sztompka, Piotr. 1979. *Sociological Dilemmas*. New York: Academic.

Taeuber, Karl E. and Alma F. Taeuber. 1965. *Negroes in Cities*. Chicago: Aldine.

Talbot, Michael. 1986. *Beyond the Quantum*. New York: Macmillan.

Taylor, Paul W. 1981. "The ethics of respect for nature." *Environmental Ethics* 3 (Fall): 197–218.

Taylor, Shelley E. 1989. *Positive Illusions*. New York: Basic Books.

Textor, Robert B. 1979. "The natural partnership between ethnographic futures research and futures education." *Journal of Cultural and Educational Futures* 1 (April): 13–18.

————. 1980. *A Handbook on Ethnographic Futures Research*. Third Edition: Version A. Stanford University (mimeographed).

————. 1990. "Introduction" and "Methodological appendix." Pp. xxiii–xlvii and 135–152 in K. Sippanondha with R. B. Textor et al., *The Middle Path for the Future of Thailand*. Honolulu, HI: East-West Center.

————. 1995. "The ethnographic futures research method: An application to Thailand." *Futures* 27, No. 4 (May): 461–471.

————. Forthcoming. *Anticipatory Anthropology and Ethnographic Futures Research*.

Textor, Robert B. et al. 1983. *Austria 2005*. Vienna: Orac Pietsch.

Textor, Robert B. et al. 1984. *Anticipatory Anthropology and the Telemicroelectronic Revolution: A Preliminary Report from Silicon Valley*. Unpublished manuscript.

Textor, Robert B., M.L. Bhansoon, Ladavalya, and Sidthinat Prabudhanitisarn. 1984. *Alternative Sociocultural Futures for Thailand*. Chiang Mai, Thailand: Chiang Mai University.

Thom, W. Taylor, Jr. 1961. "Science and engineering—and the future of man." In H. Boyko (ed.), *Science and the Future of Mankind*. World Academy of Art and Science 1. Den Haag: Vitgeverij Dr. W. Junk.

Thomlinson, Ralph. 1965 (and 1976). *Population Dynamics*. (and Second Edition). New York: Random House.

Thorsrud, Einar. 1977. "Democracy at work: Norwegian experience with non-bureaucratic forms of organization." *Applied Behavioral Science* 13: 410–421.

Thrift, Nigel. 1988. "Vivos voco. Ringing the changes in historical geography of time consciousness." Pp. 53–94 in M. Young and T. Schuller (eds.), *The Rhythms of Society*. London: Routledge.

Tiger, Lionel and Robin Fox. 1971. *The Imperial Animal*. New York: Holt, Rinehart & Winston.

Tinbergen, J. 1968. "Planning, economic." Pp. 102–110 in D. L. Sills (ed.), *International Encyclopedia of the Social Sciences*, Vol. 12. New York: MacMillan & The Free Press.

Toch, Hans H. 1958. "The perception of future events: Case studies in social prediction." *Public Opinion Quarterly* 22 (Spring): 57–66.

Toffler, Alvin. 1970. *Future Shock*. New York: Random House.

———. 1978. "Foreword." Pp. ix–xi in M. Maruyama and A.M. Harkins (eds.), *Cultures of the Future*. The Hague: Mouton.

———. 1981. *The Third Wave*. New York: Bantam.

———. 1984. "Foreword. Science and change." Pp. xi–xxvi in I. Prigogine and I. Stengers, *Order Out of Chaos*. New York: Bantam.

Tong, Rosemarie. 1986. *Ethics in Policy Analysis*. Englewood Cliffs, NJ: Prentice-Hall

Tonn, Bruce E. 1991. "The court of generations: A proposed amendment to the US Constitution." *Futures* 23, No. 5 (June): 482–98.

Tough, Allen. 1991a. "Intellectual leaders in futures studies: A survey." *Futures* 23, No. 4 (May): 436–437.

———. 1991b. *Crucial Questions about the Future*. Lanham, MD: University Press of America.

———. 1993a. "Making a pledge to future generations." *Futures* 25, No. 1 (January/ February): 90–92.

———. 1993b. "What future generations need from us." *Futures* 25, No. 10 (December): 1041–1050.

Toulmin, Stephen. 1953. *The Philosophy of Science: An Introduction*. London: Hutchinson.

———. 1972. *Human Understanding,* Vol. 1, Part 1. *The Collective Use and Evolution of Concepts*. Princeton, NJ: Princeton University Press.

———. 1981. "Evolution, adaptation, and human understanding." Pp. 18–36 in M.B. Brewer and B.E. Collins (eds.), *Scientific Inquiry and the Social Sciences*. San Francisco, CA: Jossey-Bass.

Turner, Charles F. and Elizabeth Martin (eds.). 1984. *Surveying Subjective Phenomena,* Vols. 1 and 2. New York: Russell Sage Foundation.

Turner, Victor W. 1968. "Religious specialists: Anthropological study." Pp. 437–444 in D. L. Sills (ed.), *International Encyclopedia of the Social Sciences*, Vol. 9. New York: Macmillan & The Free Press.

Tyler, Tom R. 1990. *Why People Obey the Law*. New Haven, CT: Yale University Press.

U.S. Executive Office of the President, Office of Management and Budget. 1973. *Social Indicators 1973*. Washington, DC: U.S. Government Printing Office.

U.S. National Resources Committee, Science Committee. 1937. *Technological Trends and National Policy, Including the Social Implications of New Inventions*. Washington, DC: Government Printing Office.

Unger, Roberto Mangabeira. 1976. *Law in Modern Society*. New York: Free Press.

United Nations. 1990. *1988 Demographic Yearbook*. New York: Department of International Economic and Social Affairs, Statistical Office.

United Nations. 1991. *The World's Women 1970–1990*. New York: Social Statistics and Indicators, Series K, No. 8.

United Nations. 1994. *1992 Demographic Yearbook*. New York: Department for Economic and Social Information and Policy Analysis.

Van Steenbergen, Bart. 1983. "The sociologist as social architect: A new task for macro-sociology?" *Futures* 15, No. 5 (October): 376–386.

———. 1990. "Potential influence of the holistic paradigm on the social sciences." *Futures* 22, No. 10 (December): 1071–1083.

Varenne, Hervé. 1977. *Americans Together*. New York: Teachers College Press.

Vermunt, Riël and Herman Steensma. 1991. "Introduction." Pp. 1–9 in R. Vermunt and H. Steensma (eds.), *Social Justice in Human Relations*. Vol. 1 "Societal and Psychological Origins of Justice." New York: Plenum Press.

Vickers, Geoffrey. 1977. "The future of culture." Pp. 37–44 in H.A. Linstone and W.H.C. Simmonds (eds.), *Futures Research: New Directions*. Reading, MA: Addison-Wesley.

Vitz, Paul C. and Arnold B. Glimcher. 1984. *Modern Art and Modern Science*. New York: Praeger.

Vught, F. A. van. 1987. "Pitfalls of forecasting: Fundamental problems for the methodology of forecasting from the philosophy of science." *Futures* 19 (April): 184–196.

Wachs, Martin. 1987. "Ethical dilemmas in forecasting for public policy." *Futures Research Quarterly* 3, No. 1 (Spring): 45–57.

Waddington, C.H. 1975. "Discussion." Pp. 154–165 in *The Future as an Academic Discipline*. Ciba Foundation Symposium 36. Amsterdam: Elsevier.

Wagar, W. Warren. 1991. *The Next Three Futures*. New York: Praeger.

Wagschall, Peter H. 1983. "Judgmental forecasting techniques and institutional planning: An example." Pp. 39–49 in J. L. Morrison, W. L. Renfro, and W. I. Boucher (eds.), *Applying Methods and Techniques of Futures Research*. San Francisco, CA: Jossey-Bass.

Wallace, Walter L. 1988. "Toward a disciplinary matrix in sociology." Pp. 23–76 in N. J. Smelser (ed.), *Handbook of Sociology*. Newbury Park, CA: Sage.

Walster, Elaine, G. William Walster, and Ellen Berscheid in collaboration with William Austin, Jane Traupmann, and Mary K. Utne. 1978. *Equity: Theory and Research*. Boston: Allyn and Bacon.

Watt, Ian. 1969. "Robinson Crusoe, individualism and the novel." Pp. 39–54 in F.H. Ellis (ed.), *Twentieth Century Interpretations of Robinson Crusoe*. Englewood Cliffs, NJ: Prentice-Hall.

Weber, Max. (1904, 1905, 1917) 1949. *The Methdology of the Social Sciences*, E.A. Shils and H.A. Finch (trans., eds.). Glencoe, IL: Free Press.

———. (1919) 1958a. "Science as a vocation." Pp. 129–156 in H. H. Gerth and C.W. Mills (trans., eds.), *From Max Weber: Essays in Sociology*. New York: Oxford University Press, a Galaxy Book.

———. (1919) 1958b. "Politics as a vocation." Pp. 77–128 in Gerth and Mills, *ibid.*

Weightman, John. 1993. "The human comedy of the divine Marquis." *The New York Review of Books* (September 23): 6–10.

Weil, Andrew. 1972. *The Natural Mind*. Boston: Houghton Mifflin.

Weimer, Walter B. 1979. *Notes on the Methodology of Scientific Research*. Hillsdale, NJ: Lawrence Erlbaum Associates.

Weiss, Edith Brown. (1988) 1992. *In Fairness to Future Generations*. Tokyo: The United Nations University.

Wells, H. G. (1932) 1987. "Wanted—professors of foresight!" *Futures Research Quarterly* 3, No. 1 (Spring): 89–91.

Wendt, Alexander. 1994. "Collective identity formation and the international state." *American Political Science Review* 88, No. 2 (June): 384–396.

Wescott, Roger W. 1970. "Of guilt and gratitude: Further reflections on human uniqueness." *The Dialogist*. 2, No. 3: 69–85.

———. 1978. "The anthropology of the future as an academic discipline." Pp. 509–528 in M. Maruyama and A.M. Harkins (eds.), *Cultures of the Future*. The Hague: Mouton.

———. 1978. "Traditional Greek conceptions of the future." Pp. 281–291 in M. Maruyama and A.M. Harkins (eds.), *Cultures of the Future*. The Hague: Mouton.

Wesson, Robert (ed.). 1987. *Democracy: World Survey 1987*. New York: Praeger.

WFSF (World Futures Studies Federation) Newsletter. 1985. Vol 11 (March/April).

Whyte, William Foote. 1989. "Advancing scientific knowledge through participatory action research." *Sociological Forum* 4, No. 3 (September): 367–385.

———. 1991. *Social Theory for Action*. Newbury Park, CA: Sage.

Whyte, William F. and Kathleen King Whyte. 1988. *Making Mondragón: The Growth and Dynamics of the Worker Cooperative Complex*. Ithaca, NY: ILR Press.

Whitney, Thomas P. 1962. "Introduction." Pp. vii–xiv in *The Communist Blueprint for the Future*. New York: E.P. Dutton (paper).

Wilcox, L.D., R.M. Brooks, G.M. Beal and G.E. Klonglan. 1972. *Social Indicators and Societal Monitoring: An Annotated Bibliography*. San Francisco, CA: Jossey-Bass.

Wilkening, Eugene A. 1974. "Futurology and quality of life in sociological research." Paper read at the annual meeting of the Rural Sociological Society, Montreal (August).

Williams, Bernard. 1985. *Ethics and the Limits of Philosophy*. Cambridge, MA: Harvard University Press.

Williams, Rhys H. and N. J. Demerath III. 1991. "Religion and political process in an American city." *American Sociological Review* 56, No. 4 (August): 417–431.

Williams, Robin M., Jr. 1970. *American Society*. Third Edition. New York: Alfred A. Knopf.

Wockler, R. 1978. "Perfectible apes in decadent cultures: Rousseau's anthropology revisited." *Daedalus* 107, No. 3 (Summer): 107–134.

Wood, Gordon S. 1984. "History lessons: A review of Barbara W. Tuchman, The March of Folly: From Troy to Vietnam." *The New York Review of Books* 31 (March 29): 8–10.

Woolf, Virginia. 1969. "Robinson Crusoe." Pp. 19–24 in F.H. Ellis (ed.), *Twentieth Century Interpretations of Robinson Crusoe*. Englewood Cliffs, NJ: Prentice-Hall.

Worchel, Stephen. 1984. "The darker side of helping: The social dynamics of helping and cooperation." Pp. 379–395 in E. Staub, D. Bar-Tal, J. Karylowski, and J. Reykowski (eds.), *Development and Maintenance of Prosocial Behavior*. New York: Plenum Press.

World Future Society. 1979. *The Future: A Guide to Information Sources*. Washington, DC: World Future Society.

Wright, James D. 1991. "Review of Culture Shift in Advanced Industrial Society." *Contemporary Sociology* 20, No. 6 (November): 892–894.

Wright, Robert. 1990. "Our animals, our selves." *The New York Times Book Review* (July 29): 27

Wuthnow, Robert. 1993. *Christianity in the Twenty-First Century*. New York: Oxford University Press.

Yalman, Nur. 1968. "Magic." Pp. 521–528 in D. L. Sills (ed.), *International Encyclopedia of the Social Sciences*, Vol. 9. New York: Macmillan & The Free Press.

Yaukey, David. 1985. *Demography*. New York: St. Martin's Press.

Yeager, Peter Cleary. 1991. *The Limits of Law*. Cambridge: Cambridge University Press.

Young, Michael and Tom Schuller. 1988. "Introduction: Towards chronosociology." Pp. 1–16 in M. Young and T. Schuller (eds.), *The Rhythms of Society*. London: Routledge.

Zarnowitz, Victor. 1968. "Prediction and forecasting, economic." Pp. 425–439 in D. L. Sills (ed.), *International Encyclopedia of the Social Sciences*, Vol. 12. New York: Macmillan & The Free Press.

Zavalloni, Marisa. 1980. "Values." Pp. 73–120 in H.C. Triandis and R.W. Brislin (eds.), *Handbook of Cross-Cultural Psychology*, Vol. 5 "Social Psychology." Boston: Allyn and Bacon.

Zerubavel, Eviatar. 1981. *Hidden Rhythms: Schedules and Calendars in Social Life*. Chicago: The University of Chicago Press.

———. 1985. *The Seven Day Circle: The History and Meaning of the Week*. New York: Free Press.

Index

About the Author

Wendell Bell, although born in Chicago, was raised from the age of four in Fresno, California. During World War II, he served as a Naval aviator and did a tour of duty in the Philippine theatre. After the war, he earned his living for a time as a commerical pilot while continuing to fly in the Naval Reserve. He started college under provisions of the G.I. Bill, got married, and contributed to the baby boom. He received his B.A. degree in social science from Fresno State University in California, and his M.A. and Ph.D. degrees in sociology from the University of California, Los Angeles.

He held faculty positions at Stanford University, 1952–54, where he directed the Stanford Survey Research Facility; Northwestern University, 1954–57; and back at UCLA, 1957–63, where he directed the West Indies Study Program. He became a professor at Yale University in 1963 where he remained until his retirement in 1995. At Yale, he served at various times as chairman of the Department of Sociology, director of Undergraduate Studies, director of Graduate Studies, and director of the Comparative Sociology Training Program.

Bell's early work dealt with urban sociology, particularly social area analysis and suburbanization, followed by about two decades of research on political and social change in the former colonies and now politically independent states of the Caribbean, especially in Jamaica. He has been a futurist since about 1960, introducing futures studies courses at Yale beginning in 1967 and co-authoring a book, *The Sociology of the Future*, in 1971. He has served as president of the Caribbean Studies Association, a gubernatorial appointee to the Commission on Connecticut's Future, a fellow of the Center for Advanced Study in the Behavioral Sciences at Stanford, California and of the Institute of Advanced Studies, the Australian National University, Canberra, Australia. He is a member of the World Future Society and the World Futures Studies Federation, and he now works as a consulting futurist.

Other books and monographs authored or co-authored by Bell include *Social Area Analysis*; *Public Leadership*; *Jamaican Leaders: Political Attitudes in a New Nation*; *Decisions of Nationhood: Political and Social Development in the British Caribbean*; *The Democratic Revolution in the West Indies*; and *Ethnicity and Nation-Building*.